SELECTED

Poetry and Prose

OF

William Blake

EDITED BY

Northrop Frye

VICTORIA COLLEGE, UNIVERSITY OF TORONTO

THE MODERN LIBRARY · NEW YORK

DISTRIBUTED BY McGRAW-HILL, INC.

THE MODERN LIBRARY

is published by RANDOM HOUSE, INC.

Manufactured in the United States of America

CONTENTS

PART ONE

LYRICAL POEMS

PART TWO

MINOR PROPHECIES

PART THREE

MAJOR PROPHECIES

PART FOUR

LATER WORKS

PART FIVE

PROSE

CONTENTS   xi

INTRODUCTION

WILLIAM BLAKE was born in 1757, the second of five children in the family of a London shopkeeper, a retail hosier. In the days before photography, illustrations to books had to be engraved by hand, and it was possible for an artist without influence or income to make a fairly steady living as an engraver. When Blake showed a talent for drawing, therefore, he was promptly apprenticed to that trade, as the shortest way of making him self-supporting. He was thus committed in his early teens to a life of constant association with books and the pictorial arts. His master was James Basire, from whom he absorbed the love for "Gothic" that was then in fashion, and who held some curious views about the antiquity and traditions of Druids which probably left their mark on Blake's symbolism.

After serving his apprenticeship, Blake spent the remainder of his life as a London engraver, dependent on publishers' commissions, and, when they failed, on private patrons. He could manage his financial affairs well enough, but he had no aptitude for the fierce competition in his crowded trade, and he complained of living in a "City of Assassinations." He had little sense either of the pictorial clichés and conventions that the public were used to, and when he tried to follow them, he unconsciously caricatured them. Without two or three patrons—Thomas Butts, who bought his work steadily for over twenty years, William Hayley, John Linnell—it is difficult to see how he could have survived, much less produced so much work of his own.

The poem "How sweet I roam'd" is said on good contemporary authority to have been written at about the age of fourteen, and all the early poems in *Poetical Sketches* were completed by his twenty-first year. *Poetical Sketches* was printed in 1783, through the good offices of a clergyman named Henry Mathew, who was the center of a group to which Blake was attached for a time, and which included two women writers of some fame, Anna

xiii

Letitia Barbauld (a possible influence on Blake's lyrics) and
Hannah More. Mathew contributed a preface to *Poetical Sketches*
stating that Blake had not bothered to revise the poems because he
was abandoning poetry for his profession—*i.e.*, engraving. It was
the first and last book of Blake's to appear in a conventional form
during his life. Five years later Blake had worked out a method
of engraving which would enable him to print words and design
illustrations at the same time. It is clear from the references to
this process in *An Island in the Moon* that Blake expected it to
be far less expensive and cumbersome than it proved to be. He
must at one time, in fact, have hoped that it would make him
independent of publishers, and enable him to become his own
publisher on a uniquely lavish scale. His disappointment, if there
was one, did not prevent him from sticking to the process for at
least twenty years, and employing it for all his poetry except what
he left in manuscript.

The years between 1788 and 1795, when Blake was living at
Lambeth in South London, are a period of extraordinary creative
energy. Besides a wonderful series of what he called "colour
printed drawings," "The Elohim Creating Adam," "Satan Exulting over Eve," "Elijah in the Chariot of Fire," and others equally
famous, he produced nearly all his shorter poems. Two volumes,
Songs of Innocence and *Songs of Experience,* contained the lyrics;
the other poems were in a new genre which has generally been
called "Prophecies," the name that Blake himself gave to two of
them (*America* and *Europe*) and which is as appropriate as any
other. All were engraved except *The French Revolution*, which
he evidently tried to publish in the regular way—the one surviving
copy appears to be a proof—and *Tiriel* (not given here) which he
left in manuscript. A set of illustrations for *Tiriel* exists, indicating
that Blake at first thought of illustrated rather than illuminated
books, keeping text and design separate. But very shortly he had
launched into his wonderful new art-form, a sequence of plates
with a free interpenetration of text and design, so that a plate
may be a picture, or all text, or a text marginally decorated, or
a design with a few lines of text in the center, or any other proportion of words and pictures. The engraved poems of Blake are
one of the few successful combinations of two arts by one master
in the world, and one of the most startlingly and radically original
productions of modern culture.

After 1795 Blake became preoccupied with the task of con-
solidating his essential ideas, both poetic and pictorial, into some

kind of vast synthesis, with the Bible as its model. Some years later he wrote that he had at this time "recollected all my scatter'd thoughts on Art & resumed my primitive & original ways of Execution in both painting & engraving." Similarly, his next poetic efforts were directed toward an epic or "major" prophecy that would follow the pattern of the Bible and present a visionary narrative of the life of man between creation and apocalypse. First of all, he plunged into an extravagant but superb scheme of illustrating Young's *Night Thoughts,* for which he made over five hundred designs. Blake, like Housman's God, creates a world his poet never made, and as we see Young's meditative verse placidly ambling, like a middle-aged Alice, through a wonderland of Oriental splendors and demonic terrors, it becomes very clear that what Blake is really illustrating is the Bible. His greatest pictures almost always illustrate Biblical allusions in Young's text. The next step for Blake was to write a Biblical poem of his own for which illustration on this level would be more appropriate. For an undetermined time—perhaps seven years—he worked at his epic, a poem which, like Young's, was a "dream of nine nights" ending in a Last Judgement, and which bore the titles *Vala* and *The Four Zoas.* Several recensions of it failed to satisfy him, and he left it in manuscript—a manuscript full of sketches showing that he worked on text and design simultaneously, and thought from the beginning in terms of a sequence of plates.

His work during this period was interrupted by a three-year sojourn (1800–3) at Felpham in Sussex, where he came under the patronage of the poet William Hayley and attempted, unsuccessfully, to execute the sort of commissions he got through Hayley. At Felpham he went through two crucial experiences, one intellectual and artistic, the other physical and social, in the course of which his vision of life took final shape, and by doing so consolidated the form of everything opposed to that vision.

The first experience was the temptation presented by Hayley and the kind of Augustan culture he stood for. This culture had its own standards of beauty and good taste, which were backed by the whole classical tradition and had been dominant in France and England for over a century. In addition, it had the moral virtues that belonged to it, including tact and generosity. Blake had nothing to meet this with but the ungracious defiance of his own tradition, the line of prophets crying in the wilderness. This experience forms the basis of the poem *Milton,* in which Blake presents himself as a battlefield over which the prophetic tradition, headed by Milton, defeats the powers of Satan, the spirit of compromise, prudence and hypocrisy. Satan is formidable only when he is disguised—transformed into an angel of light, as the Bible says—as a reasonable and cultivated man who is a sincere personal friend. Blake is not interested in the moral problem of what he did or should have done: he is interested in tracing out the ramifications of the prophetic and worldly attitudes until they reach their apocalyptic limits. These limits are represented by the story of Michael and Satan fighting over the body of Moses— *i.e.,* man in this world.

Blake's second experience was his trial for treason as a result of a quarrel with the soldier Schofield. Blake found Schofield trespassing in his garden and threw him out, whereupon Schofield went to a magistrate and swore that Blake had damned the king and said that he hoped and expected to see Napoleon win the war. Schofield had, fortunately for Blake, overestimated the extent of judicial hysteria in wartime. But Blake had glimpsed for a moment the lethal malignity in human nature which makes the Crucifixion the central event of history. This experience forms the autobiographical core of *Jerusalem*, which, like *Milton*, expands from an event in Blake's life to the apocalyptic form of the same event, the salvation of the world by God contrasted with what Blake calls "Druidism," or the attempt of man by searching to find out God, with the object of torturing and killing him. *Milton* and *Jerusalem* consist of fifty and one hundred plates respectively. It is probable that, besides *The Four Zoas*, there were earlier and much longer versions of these poems, though the story of a great holocaust of Blake's writings after his death is not now generally accepted.

Blake was, in literature, more of an amateur than any other English poet of his rank; and with *Jerusalem*, which has the date 1804 on its title page, and was probably complete by 1808 except for minor revisions, he considered that he had said all he had to say as a poet. Until his death in 1827, he contented himself with re-engraving his old poems and writing a few occasional verses, notably *The Everlasting Gospel*. In 1808 he writes that his time "in future must alone be devoted to Designing & Painting." By 1809 he was full of a new project: to decorate public buildings with paintings in a new kind of fresco, which would be applied, not directly to the plaster on the wall, but to canvas stretched over the plaster, so that they could be taken off and changed at pleasure. The only exhibition of his life, in 1809, was designed to advertise, not his paintings, but a practicable method of producing "portable frescoes," and it was for this exhibition that he wrote his *Descriptive Catalogue*. Only one reviewer noticed the exhibition, Robert Hunt of the *Examiner*, brother of Leigh Hunt, who had already made one attack on Blake which has left its traces in *Jerusalem*. Hunt said this time that Blake was a harmless lunatic who would have to be shut up if he insisted on making a nuisance of himself by publicly exhibiting his pictures. Hunt's review in itself was merely typical of the nineteenth-century conception of criticism as a moral steam roller, and, except for laboring the charge of insanity, is not very different in tone from the *Quarterly* on Keats or Ruskin on Whistler. But it does help to explain why the next few years of Blake's life were quiet ones. No longer particularly interested in writing poetry, and with no encouragement to continue with frescoes, he turned for his last period to the illustrating of other poets, beginning with Bunyan and Milton.

Basire had taught Blake a great respect for clear outline, and for making figure drawing and landscape depend on pictorial and not on representative considerations. To Blake a painting was a colored drawing, and he even regarded oil painting as an illegitimate art, because, unlike water color and fresco, it seemed to emphasize color at the expense of outline. To "firm, determinate outline," as he went on, he attached enormous importance. The Roman (or Florentine) school of Raphael and Michelangelo (whom Blake knew chiefly by prints), and the German school of Dürer were, Blake felt, of his mind in this matter. The Venetians, especially Titian and Correggio, the Dutch, especially Rembrandt and Rubens, and of course Reynolds were against him. He was accustomed to hearing his type of art described as hard, stiff, angular and awkward, but, as with Hayley, opposition merely consolidated his own views. For some years before his exhibition, Blake's isolation had been embittered by a series of disappointments and misunderstandings, and Stothard's rival illustration of Chaucer, which Blake ridicules in his catalogue, had been painted as a result of some sharp practice, not far removed from swindling, by a printseller named Cromek. The *Descriptive Catalogue* is in part an appeal to the public over the heads of what Blake considered a conspiratorial monopoly of bad artists. The only contemporary painter with whom Blake felt anything in common was Fuseli, who shared some of his reputation for eccentricity.

A somewhat quixotic admiration for the painter James Barry, from whom he may have derived his idea of "portable frescoes," was the only other exception Blake made to his condemnation of contemporary art.

His meeting with John Linnell in 1818 was one of the great events of Blake's life. Linnell brought friends, money, sympathy and recognition to Blake, who, at the age of sixty, found himself at last talking to other artists who did not think of him as someone to be cheated or ridiculed. Disciples gathered around him—Linnell himself, Samuel Palmer, Edward Calvert, George Richmond—and the extent to which Blake mellowed, both as a painter and as a man, shows how forced and unnatural his sectarian pose had been for him all along. One of the group, John Varley, had occult interests, and for him Blake turned a painfully acquired skill in drawing from direct visualization, without models, into a social asset. The result was the series of "Visionary Heads," drawings of Solomon, Saul, Richard III, the man who built the pyramids, the ghost of a flea—anything his friends asked for or might be interested in. More important results were the two astounding series of illustrations to Dante and to the Book of Job, which were the work of his last years, and with which he was still occupied when he died in 1827.

His life, then, was on the whole a lonely one; but it was very far from being miserable. There was his wife Catherine, who signed her marriage register with a cross, but learned to read, write and help in the preparing and coloring of prints. Blake's life, even without children, seems almost excessively domesticated. The pictures of his "sweet shadow of delight" show an unexpectedly strong face, with a twist to the mouth full of a tough and resilient humor—the face of a woman well designed by nature to live with William Blake. One of the few anecdotes about Blake that I believe tells how she annihilated a visitor who wondered where the soap was with: "Mr. Blake's skin don't dirt!" And there was London. Whatever his ancestry—Yeats's struggles to add Blake to the roster of great Irishmen are not very convincing—Blake was as rooted in London as the dome of St. Paul's. He would not often have agreed with Samuel Johnson, but Johnson's remark that the full tide of human existence was to be found at Charing Cross expresses a feeling that was deep in Blake as well.

> The fields from Islington to Marybone,
> To Primrose Hill and Saint John's Wood,

> Were builded over with pillars of gold,
> And there Jerusalem's pillars stood.

He loved London, and he never left it, except for his three dismal years on the Sussex coast, a good fifty miles from the full tide of human existence. It was partly, of course, war and poverty that kept him so confined: a pathetic letter, written at the time of the six-months' peace of Amiens with Napoleon, says: "Now I hope to see the Great Works of Art, as they are so near to Felpham." But still he is temperamentally the complete opposite of the poets of savage pilgrimage, like Byron or D. H. Lawrence, who use a variety of scenes and places to intensify a subjective attitude. Blake is one of the wise typified by Wordsworth's skylark, who soar but never roam. That is, he had a markedly introverted temperament, but he did not identify introversion with profundity; and by staying where he was, he intensified the reality, for himself, of everything he meant by "Albion": the cities, countries, people and buildings that make up the structure of human society.

Blake was systematically taught only in the trade of engraving, if we except a few rebellious months at the Royal Academy in 1779–80. In all other fields he was essentially self-educated. He read, or at least looked through, the books he had to illustrate or engrave illustrations for, and we have to allow for a large amount of desultory and miscellaneous reading in his background that we cannot now recapture. Otherwise he read what he liked—or what he disliked: the vitriolic wit of his marginalia had more scope with books that he found only just short of being beneath contempt. He was not an industrious reader, or even a persistent one. Some of the books surviving from his library are uncut; his marginalia, even the exhaustive annotations to Reynolds, often fail to follow a book through to the end; and he read in the light, or darkness, of some violent prejudices. He divided the world of culture into an Armageddon between the imaginative and the malignant, and, once he had decided that Plato or Virgil or Titian or Locke belonged on the wrong side, he never slackened in the intensity with which he misunderstood them.

Much of his intolerance was merely the result of his isolation, but one would not have had him different: anyone can be "fair" to Francis Bacon, but only Blake could have said "King James was Bacon's primum mobile." And one should not underestimate Blake's grasp even of what he disliked. Among classical poets,

his friend and biographer Tatham tells us that "he was very fond
of Ovid, especially the *Fasti*"—though I think this must be a slip
for the *Metamorphoses*. He knew the Platonist Thomas Taylor,
and not only read but used Taylor's translations from Plato and
the Neoplatonists. He knew Aristotle's *Poetics;* he had read Voltaire and Rousseau, probably in French, and he tells us that he
had read and annotated Locke's *Essay on the Human Understanding,* Burke's *Treatise on the Sublime and Beautiful,* and Bacon's
Advancement of Learning—all books he loathed. He learned
enough Greek and Hebrew to read his Bible in the original, but
does not seem otherwise to have been greatly interested in other
languages.

Even more than Bunyan, Blake was a poet of the Bible. The
Bible accounts for, I should guess, at least nine-tenths of the
literary echoes and allusions in his work. The number of these
echoes cannot be estimated by casual reading. Such a line as this
from *The Four Zoas:*

Man began
To wake upon the Couch of Death; he sneezed seven times;

does not look like an explicit reference to a miracle of Elisha, but
it is; and the striking image:

That line of blood that stretch'd across the windows of the
morning,

from the same poem, does not immediately impress one as being
connected with the story of Rahab in Joshua, though the connection is clear enough if one knows what Rahab means in Blake's
symbolism. Even so apparently spontaneous a line as "O Earth,
O Earth, return!", in the Introduction to the *Songs of Experience,*
is quoted from Jeremiah, perhaps by way of the conclusion of
Milton's *Ready and Easy Way.* Blake seems in general to have
admired other literature in proportion as it resembled the Bible.
This is the chief reason why he knew Hesiod and Ovid, with their
creation myths and theogonies, so much better than Homer and
Virgil; and why the Icelandic Eddas, especially the Prose Edda,
which, like the Bible, is a narrative stretching from creation to
apocalypse, are so important an influence on his work. Again,
Milton had a far greater hold on his imagination than any other
English poet, but for Shakespeare he seems not to have had

much deep affection. We should perhaps not have guessed that Chaucer was a favorite of his without the *Descriptive Catalogue,* but his affinity to Spenser and Bunyan is clear enough.

Blake regarded the "Augustan" period of English literature between Dryden and Johnson as an unqualified disaster, but still he was very much a poet of his own age. Literary critics, however, have remained obstinately confused about what that age was. Blake's formative period was the period of Gray, Cowper, Collins, Smart, Chatterton, Ossian, the Wartons and Percy's *Reliques*—roughly the English equivalent of *Sturm und Drang.* Admiration for the Gothic, for Druids and ancient bards, for Spenser and Milton as opposed to Dryden and Pope, for enthusiasm, fancy, imagination and political liberty, for the primitive, the sublime and the apocalyptic: every one of these values becomes an influence on Blake. In prose, Blake's period is the age of "sensibility," of the influence of Richardson, whom Blake apparently liked, and of Sterne, whom he seems to imitate to some extent in *An Island in the Moon.* We open *The Vicar of Wakefield* and find "the tame correct paintings of the Flemish school" contrasted with "the erroneous, but sublime animations of the Roman pencil," a contrast which, though Blake would not have accepted "correct" or "erroneous," clearly belongs in his cultural milieu. The age of Blake is not the Augustan age, not a mere reaction against it, not the Romantic age, and above all not "pre-Romantic." It is a perfectly definable cultural entity, and much of our difficulty in understanding Blake begins with our difficulty in understanding Ossian, Chatterton, and Smart's *Jubilate Agno.*

The *Lyrical Ballads,* with its manifesto of Romanticism, appeared when Blake was forty, had written half his own poetry and formed all his attitudes. Later, he came into personal contact with some of the Romantics. He appears in Crabb Robinson's useful diary as an artist who met with some appreciation along with much misunderstanding. He met Southey and Wordsworth, who dismissed him as mad; Lamb was deeply impressed by "The Tyger" and by his Chaucer criticism, and Coleridge made some kindly if rather episcopal comments on his lyrics. He kept in touch with Romantic poetry; he read Wordsworth with great but not uncritical admiration, and his late *Ghost of Abel* is partly an answer to Byron's *Cain.* But there is a dogged loyalty to his own age in the marginal note on Wordsworth written at the very end of his life: "I own myself an admirer of Ossian equally with any other Poet whatever, Rowley & Chatterton also."

His intellectual interests are also of his age. The great religious force in Blake's day was Swedenborg, and Blake appears to have joined the Swedenborgian Church of the New Jerusalem in London for a time (the statement that Blake's *father* was Swedenborgian is very dubious). The apocalyptic tone of Swedenborg, his emphasis on open vision, his doctrine of "correspondence" between physical and spiritual worlds which underlies much of Blake's technique of symbolism, his conception of a Christianity based on the unity of God and Man in Christ instead of on the duality of a divine and a human nature, were some of his teachings that interested Blake. The attacks on Swedenborg in *The Marriage of Heaven and Hell* imply a strong sense of his importance. In the rather schematic quality of Swedenborg's thinking there is much to remind us that Swedenborg was a converted scientist. This comes out again in his tendency to treat his own visions of the spiritual world not imaginatively, as Blake does, but existentially, as experiences to be described in the same way that a scientist describes what he sees in nature. Consequently orthodox Swedenborgians could regard their master's religious teachings as fulfilling rather than contradicting his earlier scientific work.

Blake's view of science was very different. Just as he distinguished between art and the art of Pope and Reynolds, so he at least tried to distinguish between science and Newtonian science, which latter he thought was superstitious nonsense. On this point it was very difficult for him to make himself understood, as there was nothing in the science, philosophy or even religion of his own time to appeal to. It was one thing for Blake to explain in his poetry, by means of a complicated theory of vortices, that the earth is really "one infinite plane": it was quite another to find himself asserting to a good-humored Crabb Robinson that the earth was flat. "But when I urgec̕ ᵗhe circumnavigation," said Robinson, "dinner was announced.'' Blake could make no sense out of a scientific world-view which regarded matter as a congealed mass of solid particles, which regarded space as containing matter in the same way that a bag of beans contains beans, which regarded time as having no real connection with space, and which nevertheless thought of both time and space as endless extension. But there were as yet no objections

to these views from any reputable quarter, and all Blake could say
was that he would rather be mad with Cowper than sane with
Newton and Locke.

He reached a similar deadlock in his political thinking. After
dropping out of the Mathew circle, he became acquainted with
the publisher Joseph Johnson, who was the medium for a good
deal of liberal and radical opinion. The people Blake met or may
have met in Johnson's company included Godwin, with his wife
Mary Wollstonecraft, Thomas Paine, Joseph Priestley (who may
be "Inflammable Gass the Wind-finder" in *An Island in the
Moon*), Thomas Holcroft, and the clergyman Richard Price, who
had defended the American and French revolutions—quite a
representative group of contemporary radicals. Blake's own sympathy with the two revolutions is clear enough from his poetry,
and his contempt for all forms of worldly greatness, whether
military or civilian, is written all over his work. On the outbreak
of war with France, a censorship was clamped down in England.
Paine escaped to France, as a result, it is said, of a warning by
Blake. It is pleasant to think of so materialistic a thinker owing
his life to someone's second sight, but Paine was jailed and
nearly guillotined in France, so apparently even second sight
cannot see everything. Paine's publisher, however (not Johnson,
though Johnson was fined and imprisoned some years later), was
imprisoned for blasphemy.

Blake retired into obscurity, muttering and growling. "To
defend the Bible in this year 1798 would cost a man his life,"
he wrote on the margin of Bishop Watson's complacent attack on
Paine's *Age of Reason*. His later prophecies are full of allusions
to political events—to an extent that students of these works
are only just beginning to realize. But if he remained quiescent,
it was not wholly from prudence, a virtue which he defined as
"a rich, ugly old maid courted by Incapacity." It was partly
through a profound disbelief in the intellectual basis of the revolutionary creed, which he called "Deism." First Louis XIV
and his successors, then Voltaire (who, as Blake points out, was
not a radical but the flatterer of Frederick the Great), then a
Reason-worshipping Robespierre, then Napoleon. There was for
Blake no progress in liberty there, so he confined his attention
to the poetry and art in which he could believe.

Much of Blake's poetry is for the common reader, and will not
mislead him. The lyrics speak for themselves: they may contain
great riches of meaning, but still what the attentive and sympa-

thetic reader thinks they mean is basically what they do mean. It is otherwise with the "Prophecies," where commentaries can save one a good deal of time. The statements originally made about these poems, that they are a hopeless jumble of private associations and the like, have been thoroughly disproved years ago, and no critic now makes them who has any notion of what he is talking about. The Prophecies are based on a rigorously consistent body of ideas; they have been most carefully constructed and revised, and they are difficult because it was impossible to make them simpler. The few genuine obscurities arising from unfinished revision or from veiled references to Blake's life or political events do not affect the main arguments. Without making any promises to supply a "key" to Blake's thought, a few suggestions about the leading ideas of the Prophecies may be useful.

The central conception in Blake's thought might be expressed somewhat as follows: the imagination turns nature inside out. "Where man is not, nature is barren," said Blake, and by "nature" he meant the world as, say, it would have appeared to a single intelligence at the beginning of human life. Such an intelligence would be a tiny center of a universe stretching away from him in all directions, a universe with plenty of resources for killing him, and full of force and will to survive, but with nothing in it to respond to his intelligence. The "natural man" stares helplessly at nature, minimizing his own intelligence and fascinated by its mysterious remoteness and stupid power. He builds his own societies on the analogy of nature, giving the primary place to force and cunning, so that the "natural society" which was so widely discussed in Blake's day is, for Blake, identical with tyranny, class distinctions and economic injustice. The natural man builds his religions on the assumption that some "god" must lurk behind nature, combining its mystery with something analogous to intelligence. Religion of this kind—natural religion as Blake calls it—begins by personifying the forces of nature, then goes on to erect, on the analogy of human society, a ruling class of Olympian aristocrats, and finally arrives at its masterpiece, a whiskery old man up in the sky, with an uncertain temper and reactionary political views, whom Blake calls Nobodaddy, and, in the Prophecies, Urizen or Satan. Whatever the name of God may be, whether Jehovah or Jesus, there are always some who will think of him in terms of this Nobodaddy.

Or, varying the psychological symbols, we may say that an

isolated intelligence wholly surrounded by nature is, in a sense, unborn. The body of Mother Nature surrounds us like an embryo. Hence our sexual desires, as long as they are directed toward something outside us, are really desires for a mother, and in the final analysis are desires for a death which is complete identification with Mother Nature. Blake's lyrics are full of symbols, crystal cabinets, golden chapels and nets, cups of gold, and others, which represent both Nature and the womb. We note that Nobodaddy's habitation in the Old Testament, first in the ark of the covenant and then in the Temple, had a feminine touch—curtains. Natural religion, then, leads to a mother as well as to a father. Blake calls this mother, as Queen of Heaven, Enitharmon or space; as vegetable nature, Vala; as the maternal principle, Tirzah; as the harlot, not the harlot of commercial exploitation but the symbol of the mocking, coy, elusive and remote outside world, Rahab.

Can human beings do any better than this? They can, and they do whenever they are engaged in real work, *i.e.*, not making war or feeding parasites. When they are working, men are building cities and planting gardens, that is, making nature into the form of human life. Work is man's response to his own desire, and this desire can only be called a desire to see the world in a human form. Such desire is not need, for an animal may need food without planting a garden to get it, nor is it want, or desire *for* something in particular. Cities and gardens reverse the "natural" perspective: here man is surrounding nature. Works of art are, if we like, "imitated" from nature: but their function is not to reproduce nature at second hand, but to give nature the form of civilized human intelligence.

We think of the child as more "natural" than the adult, but the precise opposite is true. The child is born civilized: he assumes that the world he is born into has a human shape and meaning, and was probably made for his own benefit. This is known as the "state of innocence": only after years of exposure to nature is he resigned to accepting the vast, mysterious, unconscious world of "experience," with all the human cruelties and stupidities that result from the view that man is a helpless captive of nature. The child's innocence, however, is not extinguished: it is only driven underground into his subconscious, where it becomes a world of suppressed and smoldering desire, joined by other outlawed desires of largely sexual origin. Creative artists can release this power, but in most people it remains stifled, emerging spasmodically in wars and revolutions. The buried power of human desire, symbolized in mythology by stories of Titans imprisoned under volcanoes, is called Orc in Blake's symbolism; the power which liberates it by creating the world of civilization and art ("Golgonooza") is called Los. The world of experience that sits grimly on top of Orc is the domain of Urizen. This word is of Greek origin, and is from the same root as "horizon"—the sense of a bound or limit to human effort.

"The marriage of heaven and hell" means that some day man's "hell," or buried furnace of desire, will explode and burn up "heaven," or the remote and mocking sky. It has been said that *The Marriage of Heaven and Hell* contains all Freud, but this is true only of its psychological aspect: on its social and political side it could be said in the same sense to contain all Marx. (Assuming, that is, that "all" means essential: Blake would have regarded both Freud and Marx as heathen idolaters and high priests of Nobodaddy.) Ordinarily, however, a revolutionary upheaval settles into the form of what had preceded it, just as the child grows into an adult like his father. This cycle of the growth of Orc into Urizen and the rebirth of Orc is traced in "The Mental Traveller," where the symbolism has both psychological and social aspects.

As long as human life is an antithesis of desire and reason, it will be full of chaos and anarchy. Reason tries to control or suppress desire, in the name of order, and desire periodically retaliates by smashing the order. Man in a state of mere desire or mere reason is called by Blake a "Spectre." Intellectually, the Spectre works with abstractions, trying to understand nature by patterns and diagrams. These have no power to order life, but the Spectre cannot realize that, and keeps trying to fit human life to nature by imitating nature's regularity, or law. The result of this is morality, the futile attempt to make the reasonable desirable. Emotionally and sexually, the Spectre is a "ravening devouring lust," looking outside himself for gratification, instead of understanding that everything he can love is his "Emanation," loved by virtue of his capacity to love. Only creative work, which never attempts either to destroy or to suppress, can resolve the deadlock. Creation releases desire, and so provides the real form of desire, which is desire for freedom, equality, love and innocence. Creation puts reason to work, and so provides the real form of reason, the constructive and unified shape of human intelligence, for true reason is "the bound or outward circumference of Energy."

There are thus four levels of human existence. There is the savage and lonely world of unworked nature, Blake's Ulro or hell, where life is, in Hobbes's phrase, nasty, brutish and short. This world of "single vision and Newton's sleep" has retreated to the stars, but is still watching us, and waiting its chance to return. Above this is ordinary life trying to struggle out of savagery, which Blake calls Generation or experience. Above this again is the life of expanded and released desire which we all have some glimpses of in inspired moments, but which is most commonly the world of children and lovers. Blake calls this state Beulah or innocence. Finally, there is the "fourfold vision" of a life in which creation dominates reason, the life of "Wisdom, Art and Science" which Blake calls Eden.

We cannot, by ourselves, get outside nature. However splendid our natural cities and gardens, they will only be little hollowings on the surface of the earth. But suppose we could think away the external or nonhuman world: what would the shape of things be like then? Clearly the whole universe would then have the shape of a single infinite human body. Everything that we call "real" in nature would then be inside the body and mind of this human being, just as in the dream the world of suppressed desire is all inside the mind of the dreamer. There would no longer be any difference, except one of perspective, between the group and the individual, as all individuals would be members of one human body. Everything in the world, including the sun, moon and stars, would be part of this human body, and everything would be identical with everything else. This does not mean that all things would be separate and similar, like peas in a pod or "identical" twins: it means identical in the sense in which a grown man feels identical with himself at the age of seven, though he is identifying himself with another human being, quite different in time, space, matter, form and personality.

For Blake, Christianity is the religion which teaches that this is in fact the real shape of things, and that the only God is universal and perfect Man, the risen Jesus. It is man, not of course natural man, but man as a creator, struggling to achieve his real human form, that God is interested in. The Bible speaks of an apocalypse or revelation of a world transformed into an infinite city, garden and human body, as the state from which man fell, and to which he has again to be restored. The Bible calls this redeemed man Adam or Israel; Blake, being an Englishman, calls him Albion. What Albion is looking for is Jerusalem, "a City, yet a Woman," the human form that is at once his bride and his own home. The world of the apocalypse is not a future ideal, for ideals are, like the natural stars, always out of reach. It is a real presence, the authentic form of what exists here and now, and is not something to be promised to the dead, but something to be manifested to the living.

Everything that Blake means by "art" is the attempt of the trained and disciplined human mind to present this concrete, simple, and outrageously anthropomorphic view of reality. "Jesus & his Apostles & Disciples were all Artists," Blake says. Such a statement will seem nonsense as long as we think of art in conventional terms, according to which Reynolds and Blake are both eighteenth-century English painters. Blake means that the reason alone, no matter in how rarefied a way it may be conceived, cannot comprehend the human shape of reality, for reason sooner or later will come to terms with the persisting appearance of a subhuman nature, and start suppressing desire. The desire which rebels against reason cannot comprehend it either, as, whether it takes the form of a lusting individual or of a revolutionary society, it is looking for something in the external world to gratify it. Only the effort of a mind in which intelligence and love are equally awake, a mind in the creative state that Blake calls imagination, can know what it means to

>Hold Infinity in the palm of your hand
>And Eternity in an hour.

NORTHROP FRYE

BIBLIOGRAPHICAL NOTE

(Only a few books of general interest are included)

BIOGRAPHY. The primary sources are conveniently assembled in the back of Arthur Symons, *William Blake* (1907). The first important biography, Alexander Gilchrist's *Life of William Blake* (1863, 2nd ed. 1880) has been reprinted in Everyman's Library with an introduction by Ruthven Todd. The standard biography is Mona Wilson's *Life of William Blake* (1927, reissued with additions, 1948), though Thomas Wright's two-volume *Life of William Blake* (1929) contains much material not easily available elsewhere. *Blake Studies,* by Geoffrey Keynes (1949) are mainly biographical, and a useful supplement to the Wilson biography.

COMMENTARY AND CRITICISM. Good general introductions to Blake are offered by H. M. Margoliouth, *William Blake* (1951), and Max Plowman, *An Introduction to the Study of Blake* (1927). Longer and more elaborate ones include Middleton Murry, *William Blake* (1933) and Bernard Blackstone, *English Blake* (1949). Much detail on Blake's iconography can be obtained from two books by J. H. Wicksteed, *Blake's Vision of the Book of Job* (revised ed., 1924) and *Blake's Innocence and Experience* (1928), especially the former. Of commentaries on the symbolism, the standard one is *William Blake: His Philosophy and Symbols,* by Foster Damon (1924, reissued 1949). M. O. Percival, *The Circle of Destiny* (1938) and Northrop Frye, *Fearful Symmetry* (1947), follow its lead. Jacob Bronowski, *A Man Without a Mask* (1943) and Mark Schorer, *William Blake: the Politics of Vision* (1946), place the chief emphasis on historical and social background. An important study of this aspect of Blake's thought by David Erdman is in course of publication. For Blake's intellectual background, see Denis Saurat,

Blake and Modern Thought (1929) and the essay in Ruthven Todd, *Tracks in the Snow* (1946). In briefer compass, *English Institute Essays 1950* (1951) contain essays on the linguistic, archetypal and historical approaches to Blake by Josephine Miles, Northrop Frye and David Erdman respectively.

TEXTS. The definitive edition is that of Geoffrey Keynes, *The Writings of William Blake* (3 vols., 1925), reprinted in one volume as *The Poetry and Prose of William Blake* (4th ed., 1948). The present text, with some rearrangement, reproduces Keynes's text. The Oxford edition of the shorter poems is by John Sampson (1st ed. 1905); the Prophetic Books are in a separate two-volume edition by Sloss and Wallis (1926)—textual criticism very able; interpretations of less value.

DESIGNS. Most of the above books are illustrated. *The Paintings of William Blake*, by Darrell Figgis (1925) and *The Engraved Designs of William Blake*, by Laurence Binyon (1926) contain well reproduced collections. The third volume of *The Works of William Blake, Poetic, Symbolic and Critical*, ed. by Ellis and Yeats (1893), contains a practically complete set of reproductions of the prophetic books. The reproductions are in black and white lithograph and very bad, but for many of the prophecies they are the only ones available. Several colored editions of the shorter prophecies, of varying merit, exist: a gorgeous reproduction of the only surviving colored copy of *Jerusalem* was privately printed in England last year. See also *Pencil Drawings*, ed. Geoffrey Keynes (1927) and *William Blake's Engravings* (1950) also by Keynes. Blake's engraving process, a mystery for over a century, has been plausibly reconstructed by Ruthven Todd in an article in *Print*, Vol. VI (1948), No. 1.

N. F.

PART ONE

LYRICAL POEMS

To Spring

O THOU with dewy locks, who lookest down
Thro' the clear windows of the morning, turn
Thine angel eyes upon our western isle,
Which in full choir hails thy approach, O Spring!

The hills tell each other, and the list'ning
Vallies hear; all our longing eyes are turned
Up to thy bright pavillions: issue forth,
And let thy holy feet visit our clime.

Come o'er the eastern hills, and let our winds
Kiss thy perfumed garments; let us taste
Thy morn and evening breath; scatter thy pearls
Upon our love-sick land that mourns for thee.

O deck her forth with thy fair fingers; pour
Thy soft kisses on her bosom; and put
Thy golden crown upon her languish'd head,
Whose modest tresses were bound up for thee!

To Summer

O THOU, who passest thro' our vallies in
Thy strength, curb thy fierce steeds, allay the heat
That flames from their large nostrils! thou, O Summer,
Oft pitched'st here thy golden tent, and oft
Beneath our oaks hast slept, while we beheld
With joy thy ruddy limbs and flourishing hair.

Beneath our thickest shades we oft have heard
Thy voice, when noon upon his fervid car
Rode o'er the deep of heaven; beside our springs
Sit down, and in our mossy vallies, on
Some bank beside a river clear, throw thy
Silk draperies off, and rush into the stream:
Our vallies love the Summer in his pride.

Our bards are fam'd who strike the silver wire:
Our youth are bolder than the southern swains:
Our maidens fairer in the sprightly dance:
We lack not songs, nor instruments of joy,
Nor echoes sweet, nor waters clear as heaven,
Nor laurel wreaths against the sultry heat.

To Autumn

O AUTUMN, laden with fruit, and stained
With the blood of the grape, pass not, but sit
Beneath my shady roof; there thou may'st rest,
And tune thy jolly voice to my fresh pipe;
And all the daughters of the year shall dance!
Sing now the lusty song of fruits and flowers.

"The narrow bud opens her beauties to
The sun, and love runs in her thrilling veins;
Blossoms hang round the brows of morning, and
Flourish down the bright cheek of modest eve,
Till clust'ring Summer breaks forth into singing,
And feather'd clouds strew flowers round her head.

"The spirits of the air live on the smells
Of fruit; and joy, with pinions light, roves round
The gardens, or sits singing in the trees."
Thus sang the jolly Autumn as he sat;
Then rose, girded himself, and o'er the bleak
Hills fled from our sight; but left his golden load.

To Winter

O WINTER! bar thine adamantine doors:
The north is thine; there hast thou built thy dark
Deep-founded habitation. Shake not thy roofs,
Nor bend thy pillars with thine iron car.

He hears me not, but o'er the yawning deep
Rides heavy; his storms are unchain'd, sheathed
In ribbed steel; I dare not lift mine eyes,
For he hath rear'd his sceptre o'er the world.

Lo! now the direful monster, whose skin clings
To his strong bones, strides o'er the groaning rocks:
He withers all in silence, and his hand
Unclothes the earth, and freezes up frail life.

He takes his seat upon the cliffs; the mariner
Cries in vain. Poor little wretch! that deal'st
With storms, till heaven smiles, and the monster
Is driv'n yelling to his caves beneath mount Hecla.

To the Evening Star

THOU fair-hair'd angel of the evening,
Now, whilst the sun rests on the mountains, light
Thy bright torch of love; thy radiant crown
Put on, and smile upon our evening bed!
Smile on our loves, and, while thou drawest the
Blue curtains of the sky, scatter thy silver dew
On every flower that shuts its sweet eyes
In timely sleep. Let thy west wind sleep on
The lake; speak silence with thy glimmering eyes,
And wash the dusk with silver. Soon, full soon,
Dost thou withdraw; then the wolf rages wide,
And the lion glares thro' the dun forest:
The fleeces of our flocks are cover'd with
Thy sacred dew: protect them with thine influence.

To Morning

O HOLY virgin! clad in purest white,
Unlock heav'n's golden gates, and issue forth;
Awake the dawn that sleeps in heaven; let light
Rise from the chambers of the east, and bring
The honied dew that cometh on waking day.
O radiant morning, salute the sun,
Rouz'd like a huntsman to the chace, and, with
Thy buskin'd feet, appear upon our hills.

Fair Elenor

THE bell struck one, and shook the silent tower;
The graves give up their dead: fair Elenor
Walk'd by the castle gate, and looked in.
A hollow groan ran thro' the dreary vaults.

She shriek'd aloud, and sunk upon the steps
On the cold stone her pale cheeks. Sickly smells
Of death issue as from a sepulchre,
And all is silent but the sighing vaults.

Chill death withdraws his hand, and she revives;
Amaz'd, she finds herself upon her feet,
And, like a ghost, thro' narrow passages
Walking, feeling the cold walls with her hands.

Fancy returns, and now she thinks of bones,
And grinning skulls, and corruptible death,
Wrap'd in his shroud; and now fancies she hears
Deep sighs, and sees pale sickly ghosts gliding.

At length, no fancy, but reality
Distracts her. A rushing sound, and the feet
Of one that fled, approaches—Ellen stood,
Like a dumb statue, froze to stone with fear.

The wretch approaches, crying, "The deed is done;
Take this, and send it by whom thou wilt send;
It is my life—send it to Elenor:—
He's dead, and howling after me for blood!

"Take this," he cry'd; and thrust into her arms
A wet napkin, wrap'd about; then rush'd
Past, howling: she receiv'd into her arms
Pale death, and follow'd on the wings of fear.

They pass'd swift thro' the outer gate; the wretch,
Howling, leap'd o'er the wall into the moat,
Stifling in mud. Fair Ellen pass'd the bridge,
And heard a gloomy voice cry, "Is it done?"

As the deer wounded, Ellen flew over
The pathless plain; as the arrows that fly
By night, destruction flies, and strikes in darkness.
She fled from fear, till at her house arriv'd.

Her maids await her; on her bed she falls,
That bed of joy, where erst her lord hath press'd:
"Ah, woman's-fear!" she cry'd; "Ah, cursed duke!
Ah, my dear lord! ah, wretched Elenor!

"My lord was like a flower upon the brows
Of lusty May! Ah, life as frail as flower!
O ghastly death! withdraw thy cruel hand,
Seek'st thou that flow'r to deck thy horrid temples?

"My lord was like a star, in highest heav'n
Drawn down to earth by spells and wickedness;
My lord was like the opening eyes of day,
When western winds creep softly o'er the flowers:

"But he is darken'd; like the summer's noon,
Clouded; fall'n like the stately tree, cut down;
The breath of heaven dwelt among his leaves.
O Elenor, weak woman, fill'd with woe!"

Thus having spoke, she raised up her head,
And saw the bloody napkin by her side,

Which in her arms she brought; and now, tenfold
More terrified, saw it unfold itself.

Her eyes were fix'd; the bloody cloth unfolds,
Disclosing to her sight the murder'd head
Of her dear lord, all ghastly pale, clotted
With gory blood; it groan'd, and thus it spake:

"O Elenor, I am thy husband's head,
Who, sleeping on the stones of yonder tower,
Was 'reft of life by the accursed duke!
A hired villain turn'd my sleep to death!

"O Elenor, beware the cursed duke;
O give not him thy hand now I am dead;
He seeks thy love, who, coward, in the night,
Hired a villain to bereave my life."

She sat with dead cold limbs, stiffen'd to stone;
She took the gory head up in her arms;
She kiss'd the pale lips; she had no tears to shed;
She hugg'd it to her breast, and groan'd her last.

Song

HOW sweet I roam'd from field to field,
    And tasted all the summer's pride,
'Til I the prince of love beheld,
    Who in the sunny beams did glide!

He shew'd me lilies for my hair,
    And blushing roses for my brow;
He led me through his gardens fair,
    Where all his golden pleasures grow.

With sweet May dews my wings were wet,
    And Phœbus fir'd my vocal rage;
He caught me in his silken net,
    And shut me in his golden cage.

He loves to sit and hear me sing,
　　Then, laughing, sports and plays with me;
Then stretches out my golden wing,
　　And mocks my loss of liberty.

Song

MY silks and fine array,
　　My smiles and languish'd air,
By love are driv'n away;
　　And mournful lean Despair
Brings me yew to deck my grave:
Such end true lovers have.

His face is fair as heav'n,
　　When springing buds unfold;
O why to him was't giv'n,
　　Whose heart is wintry cold?
His breast is love's all worship'd tomb,
Where all love's pilgrims come.

Bring me an axe and spade,
　　Bring me a winding sheet;
When I my grave have made,
　　Let winds and tempests beat:
Then down I'll lie, as cold as clay.
True love doth pass away!

Song

LOVE and harmony combine,
And around our souls intwine,
While thy branches mix with mine,
And our roots together join.

Joys upon our branches sit,
Chirping loud, and singing sweet;
Like gentle streams beneath our feet
Innocence and virtue meet.

Thou the golden fruit dost bear,
I am clad in flowers fair;
Thy sweet boughs perfume the air,
And the turtle buildeth there.

There she sits and feeds her young,
Sweet I hear her mournful song;
And thy lovely leaves among,
There is love: I hear his tongue.

There his charming nest doth lay,
There he sleeps the night away;
There he sports along the day,
And doth among our branches play.

Song

I LOVE the jocund dance,
  The softly-breathing song,
Where innocent eyes do glance,
  And where lisps the maiden's tongue.

I love the laughing vale,
  I love the echoing hill,
Where mirth does never fail,
  And the jolly swain laughs his fill.

I love the pleasant cot,
  I love the innocent bow'r,
Where white and brown is our lot,
  Or fruit in the mid-day hour.

I love the oaken seat,
  Beneath the oaken tree,
Where all the old villagers meet,
  And laugh our sports to see.

I love our neighbours all,
  But, Kitty, I better love thee;
And love them I ever shall;
  But thou art all to me.

Song

MEMORY, hither come,
    And tune your merry notes;
And, while upon the wind
    Your music floats,
I'll pore upon the stream,
Where sighing lovers dream,
And fish for fancies as they pass
Within the watery glass.

I'll drink of the clear stream,
    And hear the linnet's song;
And there I'll lie and dream
    The day along:
And, when night comes, I'll go
    To places fit for woe,
Walking along the darken'd valley
    With silent Melancholy.

Mad Song

THE wild winds weep,
    And the night is a-cold;
Come hither, Sleep,
    And my griefs unfold:
But lo! the morning peeps
    Over the eastern steeps,
And the rustling birds of dawn
The earth do scorn.

Lo! to the vault
    Of paved heaven,
With sorrow fraught
    My notes are driven:
They strike the ear of night,
    Make weep the eyes of day;
They make mad the roaring winds,
    And with tempests play.

Like a fiend in a cloud,
    With howling woe,
After night I do croud,
    And with night will go;
I turn my back to the east,
From whence comforts have increas'd;
For light doth seize my brain
With frantic pain.

Song

FRESH from the dewy hill, the merry year
Smiles on my head, and mounts his flaming car;
Round my young brows the laurel wreathes a shade,
And rising glories beam around my head.

My feet are wing'd, while o'er the dewy lawn
I meet my maiden, risen like the morn:
Oh bless those holy feet, like angels' feet;
Oh bless those limbs, beaming with heav'nly light!

Like as an angel glitt'ring in the sky
In times of innocence and holy joy;
The joyful shepherd stops his grateful song
To hear the music of an angel's tongue.

So when she speaks, the voice of Heaven I hear:
So when we walk, nothing impure comes near;
Each field seems Eden, and each calm retreat;
Each village seems the haunt of holy feet.

But that sweet village, where my black-ey'd maid
Closes her eyes in sleep beneath night's shade,
Whene'er I enter, more than mortal fire
Burns in my soul, and does my song inspire.

Song

WHEN early morn walks forth in sober grey,
Then to my black ey'd maid I haste away;
When evening sits beneath her dusky bow'r,
And gently sighs away the silent hour,
The village bell alarms, away I go,
And the vale darkens at my pensive woe.

To that sweet village, where my black ey'd maid
Doth drop a tear beneath the silent shade,
I turn my eyes; and, pensive as I go,
Curse my black stars, and bless my pleasing woe.

Oft when the summer sleeps among the trees,
Whisp'ring faint murmurs to the scanty breeze,
I walk the village round; if at her side
A youth doth walk in stolen joy and pride,
I curse my stars in bitter grief and woe,
That made my love so high, and me so low.

O should she e'er prove false, his limbs I'd tear,
And throw all pity on the burning air;
I'd curse bright fortune for my mixed lot,
And then I'd die in peace, and be forgot.

To the Muses

WHETHER on Ida's shady brow,
   Or in the chambers of the East,
The chambers of the sun, that now
   From antient melody have ceas'd;

Whether in Heav'n ye wander fair,
   Or the green corners of the earth,
Or the blue regions of the air,
   Where the melodious winds have birth;

Whether on chrystal rocks ye rove,
   Beneath the bosom of the sea
Wand'ring in many a coral grove,
   Fair Nine, forsaking Poetry!

How have you left the antient love
   That bards of old enjoy'd in you!
The languid strings do scarcely move!
   The sound is forc'd, the notes are few!

Gwin, King of Norway

COME, Kings, and listen to my song:
   When Gwin, the son of Nore,
Over the nations of the North
   His cruel sceptre bore,

The Nobles of the land did feed
   Upon the hungry Poor;
They tear the poor man's lamb, and drive
   The needy from their door!

"The land is desolate; our wives
   And children cry for bread;
Arise, and pull the tyrant down!
   Let Gwin be humbled!"

Gordred the giant rous'd himself
   From sleeping in his cave;
He shook the hills, and in the clouds
   The troubl'd banners wave.

Beneath them roll'd, like tempests black,
   The num'rous sons of blood;
Like lions' whelps, roaring abroad,
   Seeking their nightly food.

Down Bleron's hills they dreadful rush,
   Their cry ascends the clouds;
The trampling horse, and clanging arms
   Like rushing mighty floods!

Their wives and children, weeping loud,
   Follow in wild array,
Howling like ghosts, furious as wolves
   In the bleak wintry day.

"Pull down the tyrant to the dust,
   Let Gwin be humbled,"
They cry, "and let ten thousand lives
   Pay for the tyrant's head."

From tow'r to tow'r the watchmen cry:
   "O Gwin, the son of Nore,
Arouse thyself! the nations, black
   Like clouds, come rolling o'er!"

Gwin rear'd his shield, his palace shakes,
   His chiefs come rushing round;
Each, like an awful thunder cloud,
   With voice of solemn sound:

Like reared stones around a grave
   They stand around the King;
Then suddenly each seiz'd his spear,
   And clashing steel does ring.

The husbandman does leave his plow,
   To wade thro' fields of gore;
The merchant binds his brows in steel,
   And leaves the trading shore;

The shepherd leaves his mellow pipe,
   And sounds the trumpet shrill;
The workman throws his hammer down
   To heave the bloody bill.

Like the tall ghost of Barraton,
   Who sports in stormy sky,
Gwin leads his host, as black as night,
   When pestilence does fly,

With horses and with chariots—
   And all his spearmen bold

March to the sound of mournful song,
  Like clouds around him roll'd.

Gwin lifts his hand—the nations halt;
  "Prepare for war," he cries——
"Gordred appears!—his frowning brow
  Troubles our northern skies."

The armies stand, like balances
  Held in th' Almighty's hand:
"Gwin, thou hast fill'd thy measure up,
  Thou'rt swept from out the land."

And now the raging armies rush'd,
  Like warring mighty seas;
The Heav'ns are shook with roaring war,
  The dust ascends the skies!

Earth smokes with blood, and groans, and shakes
  To drink her children's gore,
A sea of blood; nor can the eye
  See to the trembling shore!

And on the verge of this wild sea
  Famine and death doth cry;
The cries of women and of babes
  Over the field doth fly.

The King is seen raging afar,
  With all his men of might,
Like blazing comets, scattering death
  Thro' the red fev'rous night.

Beneath his arm like sheep they die,
  And groan upon the plain;
The battle faints, and bloody men
  Fight upon hills of slain.

Now death is sick, and riven men
  Labour and toil for life;
Steed rolls on steed, and shield on shield,
  Sunk in the sea of strife!

The god of war is drunk with blood;
 The earth doth faint and fail;
The stench of blood makes sick the heav'ns;
 Ghosts glut the throat of hell!

O what have Kings to answer for,
 Before that awful throne!
When thousand deaths for vengeance cry,
 And ghosts accusing groan!

Like blazing comets in the sky,
 That shake the stars of light,
Which drop like fruit unto the earth
 Thro' the fierce burning night;

Like these did Gwin and Gordred meet,
 And the first blow decides;
Down from the brow unto the breast
 Gordred his head divides!

Gwin fell; the Sons of Norway fled,
 All that remain'd alive;
The rest did fill the vale of death,
 For them the eagles strive.

The river Dorman roll'd their blood
 Into the northern sea,
Who mourn'd his sons, and overwhelm'd
 The pleasant south country.

FROM *King Edward the Third*

SCENE, *in the Camp. Several of the Warriors met at the King's Tent with a* MINSTREL, *who sings the following song:*

O SONS of Trojan Brutus, cloath'd in war,
Whose voices are the thunder of the field,
Rolling dark clouds o'er France, muffling the sun
In sickly darkness like a dim eclipse,
Threatening as the red brow of storms, as fire
Burning up nations in your wrath and fury!

Your ancestors came from the fires of Troy,
(Like lions rouz'd by light'ning from their dens,
Whose eyes do glare against the stormy fires)
Heated with war, fill'd with the blood of Greeks,
With helmets hewn, and shields covered with gore,
In navies black, broken with wind and tide!

They landed in firm array upon the rocks
Of Albion; they kiss'd the rocky shore;
"Be thou our mother, and our nurse," they said;
"Our children's mother, and thou shalt be our grave;
The sepulchre of ancient Troy, from whence
Shall rise cities, and thrones, and arms, and awful pow'rs."

Our fathers swarm from the ships. Giant voices
Are heard from the hills, the enormous sons
Of Ocean run from rocks and caves: wild men,
Naked and roaring like lions, hurling rocks,
And wielding knotty clubs, like oaks entangled
Thick as a forest, ready for the axe.

Our fathers move in firm array to battle;
The savage monsters rush like roaring fire;
Like as a forest roars, with crackling flames,
When the red lightning, borne by furious storms,
Lights on some woody shore; the parched heavens
Rain fire into the molten raging sea!

The smoaking trees are strewn upon the shore,
Spoil'd of their verdure! O how oft have they
Defy'd the storm that howled o'er their heads!
Our fathers, sweating, lean on their spears, and view
The mighty dead: giant bodies streaming blood,
Dread visages frowning in silent death!

Then Brutus spoke, inspir'd; our fathers sit
Attentive on the melancholy shore:——
Hear ye the voice of Brutus—"The flowing waves
Of time come rolling o'er my breast," he said;

"And my heart labours with futurity:
Our sons shall rule the empire of the sea.

"Their mighty wings shall stretch from east to west,
Their nest is in the sea; but they shall roam
Like eagles for the prey; nor shall the young
Crave or be heard; for plenty shall bring forth,
Cities shall sing, and vales in rich array
Shall laugh, whose fruitful laps bend down with fulness.

"Our sons shall rise from thrones in joy,
Each one buckling on his armour; Morning
Shall be prevented by their swords gleaming,
And Evening hear their song of victory!
Their towers shall be built upon the rocks,
Their daughters shall sing, surrounded with shining spears!

"Liberty shall stand upon the cliffs of Albion,
Casting her blue eyes over the green ocean;
Or, tow'ring, stand upon the roaring waves,
Stretching her mighty spear o'er distant lands;
While, with her eagle wings, she covereth
Fair Albion's shore, and all her families."

PROLOGUE,

INTENDED FOR A DRAMATIC PIECE OF

King Edward the Fourth

O FOR a voice like thunder, and a tongue
To drown the throat of war!—When the senses
Are shaken, and the soul is driven to madness,
Who can stand? When the souls of the oppressed
Fight in the troubled air that rages, who can stand?
When the whirlwind of fury comes from the
Throne of God, when the frowns of his countenance
Drive the nations together, who can stand?
When Sin claps his broad wings over the battle,
And sails rejoicing in the flood of Death;

When souls are torn to everlasting fire,
And fiends of Hell rejoice upon the slain,
O who can stand? O who hath caused this?
O who can answer at the throne of God?
The Kings and Nobles of the Land have done it!
Hear it not, Heaven, thy Ministers have done it!

POEMS WRITTEN IN A COPY OF *Poetical Sketches*

SONG 1ST BY A SHEPHERD

WELCOME, stranger, to this place,
Where joy doth sit on every bough,
Paleness flies from every face;
We reap not what we do not sow.

Innocence doth like a rose
Bloom on every maiden's cheek;
Honour twines around her brows,
The jewel health adorns her neck.

SONG 2ND BY A YOUNG SHEPHERD

WHEN the trees do laugh with our merry wit,
And the green hill laughs with the noise of it,
When the meadows laugh with lively green
And the grasshopper laughs in the merry scene,

When the greenwood laughs with the voice of joy,
And the dimpling stream runs laughing by,
When Edessa, and Lyca, and Emilie,
With their sweet round mouths sing ha, ha, he,

When the painted Birds laugh in the shade,
Where our table with cherries and nuts is spread;
Come live and be merry and join with me
To sing the sweet chorus of ha, ha, he.

SONG BY AN OLD SHEPHERD

WHEN silver snow decks Sylvio's clothes
And jewel hangs at shepherd's nose,
We can abide life's pelting storm
That makes our limbs quake, if our hearts be warm.

Whilst Virtue is our walking-staff
And Truth a lantern to our path,
We can abide life's pelting storm
That makes our limbs quake, if our hearts be warm.

Blow, boisterous wind, stern winter frown,
Innocence is a winter's gown;
So clad, we'll abide life's pelting storm
That makes our limbs quake, if our hearts be warm.

Songs of Innocence
and of
Experience

**SHEWING THE TWO CONTRARY
STATES OF THE HUMAN SOUL**

SONGS OF INNOCENCE

Introduction

PIPING down the valleys wild,
Piping songs of pleasant glee,
On a cloud I saw a child,
And he laughing said to me:

"Pipe a song about a Lamb!"
So I piped with merry chear.
"Piper, pipe that song again;"
So I piped: he wept to hear.

"Drop thy pipe, thy happy pipe;
Sing thy songs of happy chear:"
So I sung the same again,
While he wept with joy to hear.

"Piper, sit thee down and write
In a book, that all may read."
So he vanish'd from my sight,
And I pluck'd a hollow reed,

And I made a rural pen,
And I stain'd the water clear,

22

And I wrote my happy songs
Every child may joy to hear.

The Shepherd

HOW sweet is the Shepherd's sweet lot!
From the morn to the evening he strays;
He shall follow his sheep all the day,
And his tongue shall be filled with praise.

For he hears the lamb's innocent call,
And he hears the ewe's tender reply;
He is watchful while they are in peace,
For they know when their Shepherd is nigh.

The Ecchoing Green

THE Sun does arise,
And make happy the skies;
The merry bells ring
To welcome the Spring;
The skylark and thrush,
The birds of the bush,
Sing louder around
To the bells' chearful sound,
While our sports shall be seen
On the Ecchoing Green.

Old John, with white hair,
Does laugh away care,
Sitting under the oak,
Among the old folk.
They laugh at our play,
And soon they all say:
"Such, such were the joys
When we all, girls & boys,
In our youth time were seen
On the Ecchoing Green."

Till the little ones, weary,
No more can be merry;
The sun does descend,
And our sports have an end.
Round the laps of their mothers
Many sisters and brothers,
Like birds in their nest,
Are ready for rest,
And sport no more seen
On the darkening Green.

The Lamb

LITTLE Lamb, who made thee?
    Dost thou know who made thee?
Gave thee life, & bid thee feed
By the stream & o'er the mead;
Gave thee clothing of delight,
Softest clothing, wooly, bright;
Gave thee such a tender voice,
Making all the vales rejoice?
    Little Lamb, who made thee?
    Dost thou know who made thee?

    Little Lamb, I'll tell thee,
    Little Lamb, I'll tell thee:
He is called by thy name,
For he calls himself a Lamb.
He is meek, & he is mild;
He became a little child.
I a child, & thou a lamb,
We are called by his name.
    Little Lamb, God bless thee!
    Little Lamb, God bless thee!

The Little Black Boy

MY mother bore me in the southern wild,
And I am black, but O! my soul is white;
White as an angel is the English child,
But I am black, as if bereav'd of light.

My mother taught me underneath a tree,
And sitting down before the heat of day,
She took me on her lap and kissed me,
And pointing to the east, began to say:

"Look on the rising sun: there God does live,
And gives his light, and gives his heat away;
And flowers and trees and beasts and men receive
Comfort in morning, joy in the noonday.

"And we are put on earth a little space,
That we may learn to bear the beams of love;
And these black bodies and this sunburnt face
Is but a cloud, and like a shady grove.

"For when our souls have learn'd the heat to bear,
The cloud will vanish; we shall hear his voice,
Saying: 'Come out from the grove, my love & care,
And round my golden tent like lambs rejoice.' "

Thus did my mother say, and kissed me;
And thus I say to little English boy:
When I from black and he from white cloud free,
And round the tent of God like lambs we joy,

I'll shade him from the heat, till he can bear
To lean in joy upon our father's knee;
And then I'll stand and stroke his silver hair,
And be like him, and he will then love me.

The Blossom

MERRY, Merry Sparrow!
Under leaves so green
A happy Blossom
Sees you swift as arrow
Seek your cradle narrow
Near my Bosom.

Pretty, Pretty Robin!
Under leaves so green
A happy Blossom
Hears you sobbing, sobbing,
Pretty, Pretty Robin,
Near my Bosom.

The Chimney Sweeper

WHEN my mother died I was very young,
And my father sold me while yet my tongue
Could scarcely cry " 'weep! 'weep! 'weep! 'weep!"
So your chimneys I sweep, & in soot I sleep.

There's little Tom Dacre, who cried when his head,
That curl'd like a lamb's back, was shav'd: so I said
"Hush, Tom! never mind it, for when your head's bare
You know that the soot cannot spoil your white hair."

And so he was quiet, & that very night,
As Tom was a-sleeping, he had such a sight!
That thousands of sweepers, Dick, Joe, Ned, & Jack,
Were all of them lock'd up in coffins of black.

And by came an Angel who had a bright key,
And he open'd the coffins & set them all free;
Then down a green plain leaping, laughing, they run,
And wash in a river, and shine in the Sun.

Then naked & white, all their bags left behind,
They rise upon clouds and sport in the wind;
And the Angel told Tom, if he'd be a good boy,
He'd have God for his father, & never want joy.

And so Tom awoke; and we rose in the dark,
And got with our bags & our brushes to work.
Tho' the morning was cold, Tom was happy & warm;
So if all do their duty they need not fear harm.

The Little Boy Lost

"FATHER! father! where are you going?
O do not walk so fast.
Speak, father, speak to your little boy,
Or else I shall be lost."

The night was dark, no father was there;
The child was wet with dew;
The mire was deep, & the child did weep,
And away the vapour flew.

The Little Boy Found

THE little boy lost in the lonely fen,
Led by the wand'ring light,
Began to cry; but God, ever nigh,
Appear'd like his father in white.

He kissed the child & by the hand led
And to his mother brought,
Who in sorrow pale, thro' the lonely dale,
Her little boy weeping sought.

Laughing Song

WHEN the green woods laugh with the voice of joy,
And the dimpling stream runs laughing by;

When the air does laugh with our merry wit,
And the green hill laughs with the noise of it;

When the meadows laugh with lively green,
And the grasshopper laughs in the merry scene,
When Mary and Susan and Emily
With their sweet round mouths sing "Ha, Ha, He!"

When the painted birds laugh in the shade,
Where our table with cherries and nuts is spread,
Come live & be merry, and join with me,
To sing the sweet chorus of "Ha, Ha, He!"

A Cradle Song

SWEET dreams, form a shade
O'er my lovely infant's head;
Sweet dreams of pleasant streams
By happy, silent, moony beams.

Sweet sleep, with soft down
Weave thy brows an infant crown.
Sweet sleep, Angel mild,
Hover o'er my happy child.

Sweet smiles, in the night
Hover over my delight;
Sweet smiles, Mother's smiles,
All the livelong night beguiles.

Sweet moans, dovelike sighs,
Chase not slumber from thy eyes.
Sweet moans, sweeter smiles,
All the dovelike moans beguiles.

Sleep, sleep, happy child,
All creation slept and smil'd;
Sleep, sleep, happy sleep,
While o'er thee thy mother weep.

Sweet babe, in thy face
Holy image I can trace.
Sweet babe, once like thee,
Thy maker lay and wept for me,

Wept for me, for thee, for all,
When he was an infant small.
Thou his image ever see,
Heavenly face that smiles on thee,

Smiles on thee, on me, on all;
Who became an infant small.
Infant smiles are his own smiles;
Heaven & earth to peace beguiles.

The Divine Image

TO Mercy, Pity, Peace, and Love
All pray in their distress;
And to these virtues of delight
Return their thankfulness.

For Mercy, Pity, Peace, and Love
Is God, our father dear,
And Mercy, Pity, Peace, and Love
Is Man, his child and care.

For Mercy has a human heart,
Pity a human face,
And Love, the human form divine,
And Peace, the human dress.

Then every man, of every clime,
That prays in his distress,
Prays to the human form divine,
Love, Mercy, Pity, Peace.

And all must love the human form,
In heathen, turk, or jew;
Where Mercy, Love, & Pity dwell
There God is dwelling too.

Holy Thursday

'TWAS on a Holy Thursday, their innocent faces clean,
The children walking two & two, in red & blue & green,
Grey-headed beadles walk'd before, with wands as white as
    snow,
Till into the high dome of Paul's they like Thames' waters flow.

O what a multitude they seem'd, these flowers of London town!
Seated in companies they sit with radiance all their own.
The hum of multitudes was there, but multitudes of lambs,
Thousands of little boys & girls raising their innocent hands.

Now like a mighty wind they raise to heaven the voice of song,
Or like harmonious thunderings the seats of Heaven among.
Beneath them sit the aged men, wise guardians of the poor;
Then cherish pity, lest you drive an angel from your door.

Night

THE sun descending in the west,
The evening star does shine;
The birds are silent in their nest,
And I must seek for mine.
The moon like a flower
In heaven's high bower,
With silent delight
Sits and smiles on the night.

Farewell, green fields and happy groves,
Where flocks have took delight.
Where lambs have nibbled, silent moves
The feet of angels bright;
Unseen they pour blessing
And joy without ceasing,
On each bud and blossom,
And each sleeping bosom.

They look in every thoughtless nest,
Where birds are cover'd warm;

They visit caves of every beast,
To keep them all from harm.
If they see any weeping
That should have been sleeping,
They pour sleep on their head,
And sit down by their bed.

When wolves and tygers howl for prey,
They pitying stand and weep;
Seeking to drive their thirst away,
And keep them from the sheep;
But if they rush dreadful,
The angels, most heedful,
Receive each mild spirit,
New worlds to inherit.

And there the lion's ruddy eyes
Shall flow with tears of gold,
And pitying the tender cries,
And walking round the fold,
Saying "Wrath, by his meekness,
And by his health, sickness
Is driven away
From our immortal day.

"And now beside thee, bleating lamb,
I can lie down and sleep;
Or think on him who bore thy name,
Graze after thee and weep.
For, wash'd in life's river,
My bright mane for ever
Shall shine like the gold
As I guard o'er the fold."

Spring

SOUND the Flute!
Now it's mute.
Birds delight
Day and Night;

Nightingale
In the dale,
Lark in Sky,
Merrily,
Merrily, Merrily, to welcome in the Year.

Little Boy,
Full of joy;
Little Girl,
Sweet and small;
Cock does crow,
So do you;
Merry voice,
Infant noise,
Merrily, Merrily, to welcome in the Year.

Little Lamb,
Here I am;
Come and lick
My white neck;
Let me pull
Your soft Wool;
Let me kiss
Your soft face:
Merrily, Merrily, we welcome in the Year.

Nurse's Song

WHEN the voices of children are heard on the green
And laughing is heard on the hill,
My heart is at rest within my breast
    And everything else is still.

"Then come home, my children, the sun is gone down
And the dews of night arise;
Come, come, leave off play, and let us away
Till the morning appears in the skies."

"No, no, let us play, for it is yet day
And we cannot go to sleep;

Besides, in the sky the little birds fly
And the hills are all cover'd with sheep."

"Well, well, go & play till the light fades away
And then go home to bed."
The little ones leaped & shouted & laugh'd
    And all the hills ecchoed.

Infant Joy

"I HAVE no name:
I am but two days old."
What shall I call thee?
"I happy am,
Joy is my name."
Sweet joy befall thee!

Pretty joy!
Sweet joy but two days old,
Sweet joy I call thee:
Thou dost smile,
I sing the while,
Sweet joy befall thee!

A Dream

ONCE a dream did weave a shade
O'er my Angel-guarded bed,
That an Emmet lost its way
Where on grass methought I lay.

Troubled, 'wilder'd, and forlorn,
Dark, benighted, travel-worn,
Over many a tangled spray,
All heart-broke I heard her say:

"O, my children! do they cry?
Do they hear their father sigh?

Now they look abroad to see:
Now return and weep for me."

Pitying, I drop'd a tear;
But I saw a glow-worm near,
Who replied: "What wailing wight
Calls the watchman of the night?

"I am set to light the ground,
While the beetle goes his round:
Follow now the beetle's hum;
Little wanderer, hie thee home."

On Another's Sorrow

CAN I see another's woe,
And not be in sorrow too?
Can I see another's grief,
And not seek for kind relief?

Can I see a falling tear,
And not feel my sorrow's share?
Can a father see his child
Weep, nor be with sorrow fill'd?

Can a mother sit and hear
An infant groan an infant fear?
No, no! never can it be!
Never, never can it be!

And can he who smiles on all
Hear the wren with sorrows small,
Hear the small bird's grief & care,
Hear the woes that infants bear,

And not sit beside the nest,
Pouring pity in their breast;
And not sit the cradle near,
Weeping tear on infant's tear;

And not sit both night & day,
Wiping all our tears away?
O, no! never can it be!
Never, never can it be!

He doth give his joy to all;
He becomes an infant small;
He becomes a man of woe;
He doth feel the sorrow too.

Think not thou canst sigh a sigh
And thy maker is not by;
Think not thou canst weep a tear
And thy maker is not near.

O! he gives to us his joy
That our grief he may destroy;
Till our grief is fled & gone
He doth sit by us and moan.

SONGS OF EXPERIENCE

Introduction

HEAR the voice of the Bard!
Who Present, Past, & Future, sees;
Whose ears have heard
The Holy Word
That walk'd among the ancient trees,

Calling the lapsed Soul,
And weeping in the evening dew;
That might controll
The starry pole,
And fallen, fallen light renew!

"O Earth, O Earth, return!
Arise from out the dewy grass;
Night is worn,
And the morn
Rises from the slumberous mass.

"Turn away no more;
Why wilt thou turn away?
The starry floor,
The wat'ry shore,
Is giv'n thee till the break of day."

Earth's Answer

EARTH rais'd up her head
From the darkness dread & drear.
Her light fled,
Stony dread!
And her locks cover'd with grey despair.

"Prison'd on wat'ry shore,
Starry Jealousy does keep my den:
Cold and hoar,
Weeping o'er,
I hear the father of the ancient men.

"Selfish father of men!
Cruel, jealous, selfish fear!
Can delight,
Chain'd in night,
The virgins of youth and morning bear?

"Does spring hide its joy
When buds and blossoms grow?
Does the sower
Sow by night,
Or the plowman in darkness plow?

"Break this heavy chain
That does freeze my bones around.
Selfish! vain!
Eternal bane!
That free Love with bondage bound."

The Clod and the Pebble

"LOVE seeketh not Itself to please,
Nor for itself hath any care,
But for another gives its ease,
And builds a Heaven in Hell's despair."

So sung a little Clod of Clay
Trodden with the cattle's feet,
But a Pebble of the brook
Warbled out these metres meet:

"Love seeketh only Self to please,
To bind another to Its delight,
Joys in another's loss of ease,
And builds a Hell in Heaven's despite."

Holy Thursday

IS this a holy thing to see
In a rich and fruitful land,
Babes reduc'd to misery,
Fed with cold and usurous hand?

Is that trembling cry a song?
Can it be a song of joy?
And so many children poor?
It is a land of poverty!

And their sun does never shine,
And their fields are bleak & bare,
And their ways are fill'd with thorns:
It is eternal winter there.

For where-e'er the sun does shine,
And where-e'er the rain does fall,
Babe can never hunger there,
Nor poverty the mind appall.

The Little Girl Lost

IN futurity
I prophetic see
That the earth from sleep
(Grave the sentence deep)

Shall arise and seek
For her maker meek;
And the desart wild
Become a garden mild.

*   *   *

In the southern clime,
Where the summer's prime
Never fades away,
. Lovely Lyca lay.

Seven summers old
Lovely Lyca told;
She had wander'd long
Hearing wild birds' song.

"Sweet sleep, come to me
Underneath this tree.
Do father, mother weep,
Where can Lyca sleep?

"Lost in desart wild
Is your little child.
How can Lyca sleep
If her mother weep? ·

"If her heart does ake
Then let Lyca wake;
If my mother sleep,
Lyca shall not weep.

"Frowning, frowning night,
O'er this desart bright

Let thy moon arise
While I close my eyes."

Sleeping Lyca lay
While the beasts of prey,
Come from caverns deep,
View'd the maid asleep.

The kingly lion stood
And the virgin view'd,
Then he gamboll'd round
O'er the hallow'd ground.

Leopards, tygers, play
Round her as she lay,
While the lion old
Bow'd his mane of gold

And her bosom lick,
And upon her neck
From his eyes of flame
Ruby tears there came;

While the lioness
Loos'd her slender dress,
And naked they convey'd
To caves the sleeping maid.

The Little Girl Found

ALL the night in woe
Lyca's parents go
Over vallies deep,
While the desarts weep.

Tired and woe-begone,
Hoarse with making moan,
Arm in arm seven days
They trac'd the desart ways.

Seven nights they sleep
Among shadows deep,
And dream they see their child
Starv'd in desart wild.

Pale, thro' pathless ways
The fancied image strays
Famish'd, weeping, weak,
With hollow piteous shriek.

Rising from unrest,
The trembling woman prest
With feet of weary woe:
She could no further go.

In his arms he bore
Her, arm'd with sorrow sore;
Till before their way
A couching lion lay.

Turning back was vain:
Soon his heavy mane
Bore them to the ground.
Then he stalk'd around,

Smelling to his prey;
But their fears allay
When he licks their hands,
And silent by them stands.

They look upon his eyes
Fill'd with deep surprise,
And wondering behold
A spirit arm'd in gold.

On his head a crown,
On his shoulders down
Flow'd his golden hair.
Gone was all their care.

"Follow me," he said;
"Weep not for the maid;
In my palace deep
Lyca lies asleep."

Then they followed
Where the vision led,
And saw their sleeping child
Among tygers wild.

To this day they dwell
In a lonely dell;
Nor fear the wolvish howl
Nor the lions' growl.

The Chimney Sweeper

A LITTLE black thing among the snow,
Crying ' 'weep! 'weep!' in notes of woe!
"Where are thy father & mother? say?"
"They are both gone up to the church to pray.

"Because I was happy upon the heath,
And smil'd among the winter's snow,
They clothed me in the clothes of death,
And taught me to sing the notes of woe.

"And because I am happy & dance & sing,
They think they have done me no injury,
And are gone to praise God & his Priest & King,
Who make up a heaven of our misery."

Nurse's Song

WHEN the voices of children are heard on the green
And whisp'rings are in the dale,
The days of my youth rise fresh in my mind,
My face turns green and pale.

Then come home, my children, the sun is gone down,
And the dews of night arise;
Your spring & your day are wasted in play,
And your winter and night in disguise.

The Sick Rose

O ROSE, thou art sick!
The invisible worm
That flies in the night,
In the howling storm,

Has found out thy bed
Of crimson joy,
And his dark secret love
Does thy life destroy.

The Fly

LITTLE Fly,
Thy summer's play
My thoughtless hand
Has brush'd away.

Am not I
A fly like thee?
Or art not thou
A man like me?

For I dance,
And drink, & sing,
Till some blind hand
Shall brush my wing.

If thought is life
And strength & breath,
And the want
Of thought is death;

Then am I
A happy fly,
If I live
Or if I die.

The Angel

I DREAMT a Dream! what can it mean?
And that I was a maiden Queen,
Guarded by an Angel mild:
Witless woe was ne'er beguil'd!

And I wept both night and day,
And he wip'd my tears away,
And I wept both day and night,
And hid from him my heart's delight.

So he took his wings and fled;
Then the morn blush'd rosy red;
I dried my tears, & arm'd my fears
With ten thousand shields and spears.

Soon my Angel came again:
I was arm'd, he came in vain;
For the time of youth was fled,
And grey hairs were on my head.

The Tyger

TYGER! Tyger! burning bright
In the forests of the night,
What inmortal hand or eye
Could frame thy fearful symmetry?

In what distant deeps or skies
Burnt the fire of thine eyes?
On what wings dare he aspire?
What the hand dare sieze the fire?

And what shoulder, & what art,
Could twist the sinews of thy heart?
And when thy heart began to beat,
What dread hand? & what dread feet?

What the hammer? what the chain?
In what furnace was thy brain?
What the anvil? what dread grasp
Dare its deadly terrors clasp?

When the stars threw down their spears,
And water'd heaven with their tears,
Did he smile his work to see?
Did he who made the Lamb make thee?

Tyger! Tyger! burning bright
In the forests of the night,
What immortal hand or eye,
Dare frame thy fearful symmetry?

My Pretty Rose-tree

A FLOWER was offer'd to me,
Such a flower as May never bore;
But I said "I've a Pretty Rose-tree,"
And I passed the sweet flower o'er.

Then I went to my Pretty Rose-tree,
To tend her by day and by night;
But my Rose turn'd away with jealousy,
And her thorns were my only delight.

Ah! Sun-flower

AH, Sun-flower! weary of time,
Who countest the steps of the Sun,
Seeking after that sweet golden clime
Where the traveller's journey is done:

Where the Youth pined away with desire,
And the pale Virgin shrouded in snow
Arise from their graves, and aspire
Where my Sun-flower wishes to go.

The Lilly

THE modest Rose puts forth a thorn,
The humble Sheep a threat'ning horn;
While the Lilly white shall in Love delight,
Nor a thorn, nor a threat, stain her beauty bright.

The Garden of Love

I WENT to the Garden of Love,
And saw what I never had seen:
A Chapel was built in the midst,
Where I used to play on the green.

And the gates of this Chapel were shut,
And "Thou shalt not" writ over the door;
So I turn'd to the Garden of Love
That so many sweet flowers bore;

And I saw it was filled with graves,
And tomb-stones where flowers should be;
And Priests in black gowns were walking their rounds,
And binding with briars my joys & desires.

The Little Vagabond

DEAR Mother, dear Mother, the Church is cold,
But the Ale-house is healthy & pleasant & warm;
Besides I can tell where I am used well,
Such usage in Heaven will never do well.
But if at the Church they would give us some Ale,
And a pleasant fire our souls to regale,
We'd sing and we'd pray all the live-long day,
Nor ever once wish from the Church to stray.

Then the Parson might preach, & drink, & sing,
And we'd be as happy as birds in the spring;

And modest Dame Lurch, who is always at Church,
Would not have bandy children, nor fasting, nor birch.
And God, like a father rejoicing to see
His children as pleasant and happy as he,
Would have no more quarrel with the Devil or the Barrel,
But kiss him, & give him both drink and apparel.

London

I WANDER thro' each charter'd street,
Near where the charter'd Thames does flow,
And mark in every face I meet
Marks of weakness, marks of woe.

In every cry of every Man,
In every Infant's cry of fear,
In every voice, in every ban,
The mind-forg'd manacles I hear.

How the Chimney-sweeper's cry
Every black'ning Church appalls;
And the hapless Soldier's sigh
Runs in blood down Palace walls.

But most thro' midnight streets I hear
How the youthful Harlot's curse
Blasts the new born Infant's tear,
And blights with plagues the Marriage hearse.

The Human Abstract

PITY would be no more
If we did not make somebody Poor;
And Mercy no more could be
If all were as happy as we.

And mutual fear brings peace,
Till the selfish loves increase:

Then Cruelty knits a snare,
And spreads his baits with care.

He sits down with holy fears,
And waters the ground with tears;
Then Humility takes its root
Underneath his foot.

Soon spreads the dismal shade
Of Mystery over his head;
And the Catterpiller and Fly
Feed on the Mystery.

And it bears the fruit of Deceit,
Ruddy and sweet to eat;
And the Raven his nest has made
In its thickest shade.

The Gods of the earth and sea
Sought thro' Nature to find this Tree;
But their search was all in vain:
There grows one in the Human Brain.

Infant Sorrow

MY mother groan'd! my father wept.
Into the dangerous world I leapt:
Helpless, naked, piping loud:
Like a fiend hid in a cloud.

Struggling in my father's hands,
Striving against my swadling bands,
Bound and weary I thought best
To sulk upon my mother's breast.

A Poison Tree

I WAS angry with my friend:
I told my wrath, my wrath did end.
I was angry with my foe:
I told it not, my wrath did grow.

And I water'd it in fears,
Night & morning with my tears;
And I sunned it with smiles,
And with soft deceitful wiles.

And it grew both day and night,
Till it bore an apple bright;
And my foe beheld it shine,
And he knew that it was mine,

And into my garden stole
When the night had veil'd the pole:
In the morning glad I see
My foe outstretch'd beneath the tree.

A Little Boy Lost

"NOUGHT loves another as itself,
Nor venerates another so,
Nor is it possible to Thought
A greater than itself to know:

"And Father, how can I love you
Or any of my brothers more?
I love you like the little bird
That picks up crumbs around the door."

The Priest sat by and heard the child,
In trembling zeal he siez'd his hair:
He led him by his little coat,
And all admir'd the Priestly care.

And standing on the altar high,
"Lo! what a fiend is here!" said he,
"One who sets reason up for judge
Of our most holy Mystery."

The weeping child could not be heard,
The weeping parents wept in vain;
They strip'd him to his little shirt,
And bound him in an iron chain;

And burn'd him in a holy place,
Where many had been burn'd before:
The weeping parents wept in vain.
Are such things done on Albion's shore?

A Little Girl Lost

Children of the future Age
Reading this indignant page,
Know that in a former time
Love! sweet Love! was thought a crime.

IN the Age of Gold,
Free from winter's cold,
Youth and maiden bright
To the holy light,
Naked in the sunny beams delight.

Once a youthful pair,
Fill'd with softest care,
Met in garden bright
Where the holy light
Had just remov'd the curtains of the night.

There, in rising day,
On the grass they play;
Parents were afar,
Strangers came not near,
And the maiden soon forgot her fear.

Tired with kisses sweet,
They agree to meet
When the silent sleep
Waves o'er heaven's deep,
And the weary tired wanderers weep.

To her father white
Came the maiden bright;
But his loving look,
Like the holy book,
All her tender limbs with terror shook.

"Ona! pale and weak!
To thy father speak:
O, the trembling fear!
O, the dismal care!
That shakes the blossoms of my hoary hair."

To Tirzah

WHATE'ER is Born of Mortal Birth
Must be consumed with the Earth
To rise from Generation free:
Then what have I to do with thee?

The Sexes sprung from Shame & Pride,
Blow'd in the morn; in evening died;
But Mercy chang'd Death into Sleep;
The Sexes rose to work & weep.

Thou, Mother of my Mortal part,
With cruelty didst mould my Heart,
And with false self-decieving tears
Didst bind my Nostrils, Eyes, & Ears:

Didst close my Tongue in senseless clay,
And me to Mortal Life betray.
The Death of Jesus set me free:
Then what have I to do with thee?

The Schoolboy

I LOVE to rise in a summer morn
When the birds sing on every tree;
The distant huntsman winds his horn,
And the sky-lark sings with me.
O! what sweet company.

But to go to school in a summer morn,
O! it drives all joy away;
Under a cruel eye outworn,
The little ones spend the day
In sighing and dismay.

Ah! then at times I drooping sit,
And spend many an anxious hour,
Nor in my book can I take delight,
Nor sit in learning's bower,
Worn thro' with the dreary shower.

How can the bird that is born for joy
Sit in a cage and sing?
How can a child, when fears annoy,
But droop his tender wing,
And forget his youthful spring?

O! father & mother, if buds are nip'd
And blossoms blown away,
And if the tender plants are strip'd
Of their joy in the springing day,
By sorrow and care's dismay,

How shall the summer arise in joy,
Or the summer fruits appear?
Or how shall we gather what griefs destroy,
Or bless the mellowing year,
When the blasts of winter appear?

The Voice of the Ancient Bard

YOUTH of delight, come hither,
And see the opening morn,
Image of truth new born.
Doubt is fled, & clouds of reason,
Dark disputes & artful teazing.
Folly is an endless maze,
Tangled roots perplex her ways.
How many have fallen there!
They stumble all night over bones of the dead,
And feel they know not what but care,
And wish to lead others, when they should be led.

A Divine Image

CRUELTY has a Human Heart,
And Jealousy a Human Face;
Terror the Human Form Divine,
And Secrecy the Human Dress.

The Human Dress is forged Iron,
The Human Form a fiery Forge,
The Human Face a Furnace seal'd,
The Human Heart its hungry Gorge.

⌗

NEVER seek to tell thy love
Love that never told can be;
For the gentle wind does move
Silently, invisibly.

I told my love, I told my love,
I told her all my heart,
Trembling, cold, in ghastly fears—
Ah, she doth depart.

Soon as she was gone from me
A traveller came by
Silently, invisibly—
O, was no deny.

⌗

I LAID me down upon a bank
Where love lay sleeping.
I heard among the rushes dank
Weeping, Weeping.

Then I went to the heath & the wild
To the thistles & thorns of the waste
And they told me how they were beguil'd,
Driven out, & compel'd to be chaste.

⌗

I SAW a chapel all of gold
That none did dare to enter in,

53

And many weeping stood without,
Weeping, mourning, worshipping.

I saw a serpent rise between
The white pillars of the door,
And he forc'd & forc'd & forc'd,
Down the golden hinges tore.

And along the pavement sweet,
Set with pearls & rubies bright,
All his slimy length he drew,
Till upon the altar white

Vomiting his poison out
On the bread & on the wine.
So I turn'd into a sty
And laid me down among the swine.

✳

I ASKED a thief to steal me a peach:
He turned up his eyes.
I ask'd a lithe lady to lie her down:
Holy & meek she cries.

As soon as I went an angel came:
He wink'd at the thief
And smil'd at the dame,
And without one word spoke
Had a peach from the tree,
And 'twixt earnest & joke
Enjoy'd the Lady.

✳

I HEARD an Angel singing
When the day was springing,
"Mercy, Pity, Peace
Is the world's release."

Thus he sung all day
Over the new mown hay,
Till the sun went down
And haycocks looked brown.

I heard a Devil curse
Over the heath & the furze,
"Mercy could be no more,
If there was nobody poor,

"And pity no more could be,
If all were as happy as we."
At his curse the sun went down,
And the heavens gave a frown.

Down pour'd the heavy rain
Over the new reap'd grain,
And Miseries' increase
Is Mercy, Pity, Peace.

A Cradle Song

SLEEP, Sleep, beauty bright
Dreaming o'er the joys of night.
Sleep, Sleep: in thy sleep
Little sorrows sit & weep.

Sweet Babe, in thy face
Soft desires I can trace
Secret joys & secret smiles
Little pretty infant wiles.

As thy softest limbs I feel
Smiles as of the morning steal
O'er thy cheek & o'er thy breast
Where thy little heart does rest.

O, the cunning wiles that creep
In thy little heart asleep.
When thy little heart does wake,
Then the dreadful lightnings break.

From thy cheek & from thy eye
O'er the youthful harvests nigh
Infant wiles & infant smiles
Heaven & Earth of peace beguiles.

※

I FEAR'D the fury of my wind
Would blight all blossoms fair & true;
And my sun it shin'd & shin'd
And my wind it never blew.

But a blossom fair or true
Was not found on any tree;
For all blossoms grew & grew
Fruitless, false, tho' fair to see.

※

WHY should I care for the men of thames,
Or the cheating waves of charter'd streams,
Or shrink at the little blasts of fear
That the hireling blows into my ear?

Tho' born on the cheating banks of Thames,
Tho' his waters bathed my infant limbs,
The Ohio shall wash his stains from me:
I was born a slave, but I go to be free.

Infant Sorrow

MY mother groan'd, my father wept;
Into the dangerous world I leapt,
Helpless, naked, piping loud,
Like a fiend hid in a cloud.

Struggling in my father's hands
Striving against my swaddling bands,

Bound & weary, I thought best
To sulk upon my mother's breast.

When I saw that rage was vain,
And to sulk would nothing gain,
Turning many a trick & wile,
I began to soothe & smile.

And I sooth'd day after day
Till upon the ground I stray;
And I smil'd night after night,
Seeking only for delight.

And I saw before me shine
Clusters of the wand'ring vine,
And many a lovely flower & tree
Stretch'd their blossoms out to me.

My father then with holy look,
In his hands a holy book,
Pronounc'd curses on my head
And bound me in a mirtle shade.

In a Mirtle Shade

WHY should I be bound to thee,
O my lovely mirtle tree?
Love, free love, cannot be bound
To any tree that grows on ground.

O, how sick & weary I
Underneath my mirtle lie,
Like to dung upon the ground
Underneath my mirtle bound.

Oft my mirtle sigh'd in vain
To behold my heavy chain;
Oft my father saw us sigh,
And laugh'd at our simplicity.

So I smote him & his gore
Stain'd the roots my mirtle bore.
But the time of youth is fled,
And grey hairs are on my head.

✳

SILENT, Silent Night
Quench the holy light
Of thy torches bright.

For possess'd of Day
Thousand spirits stray
That sweet joys betray

Why should joys be sweet
Used with deceit
Nor with sorrows meet?

But an honest joy
Does itself destroy
For a harlot coy.

✳

O LAPWING, thou fliest around the heath,
Nor seest the net that is spread beneath.
Why dost thou not fly among the corn fields?
They cannot spread nets where a harvest yields.

✳

THOU hast a lap full of seed,
And this is a fine country.
Why dost thou not cast thy seed
And live in it merrily?

Shall I cast it on the sand
And turn it into fruitful land?

For on no other ground
Can I sow my seed
Without tearing up
Some stinking weed.

To Nobodaddy

WHY art thou silent & invisible,
Father of Jealousy?
Why dost thou hide thy self in clouds
From every searching Eye?

Why darkness & obscurity
In all thy words & laws,
That none dare eat the fruit but from
The wily serpent's jaws?
Or is it because Secresy gains females' loud applause?

⚥

ARE not the joys of morning sweeter
Than the joys of night?
And are the vig'rous joys of youth
Ashamed of the light?

Let age & sickness silent rob
The vineyards in the night;
But those who burn with vig'rous youth
Pluck fruits before the light.

⚥

LOVE to faults is always blind,
Always is to joy inclin'd,
Lawless, wing'd, & unconfin'd,
And breaks all chains from every mind.

Deceit to secresy confin'd,
Lawful, cautious, & refin'd;
To every thing but interest blind,
And forges fetters for the mind.

The Wild Flower's Song

AS I wander'd the forest,
The green leaves among,
I heard a wild flower
Singing a song:

"I slept in the dark
In the silent night,
I murmur'd my fears
And I felt delight.

"In the morning I went
As rosy as morn
To seek for new Joy,
But I met with scorn."

Soft Snow

I WALKED abroad in a snowy day:
I ask'd the soft snow with me to play:
She play'd & she melted in all her prime,
And the winter call'd it a dreadful crime.

An Ancient Proverb

REMOVE away that black'ning church:
Remove away that marriage hearse:
Remove away that place of blood:
You'll quite remove the ancient curse.

To My Mirtle

TO a lovely mirtle bound,
Blossoms show'ring all around,
Oh, how sick & weary I
Underneath my mirtle lie.
Why should I be bound to thee,
O, my lovely mirtle tree?

Merlin's Prophecy

THE harvest shall flourish in wintry weather
When two virginities meet together:

The King & the Priest must be tied in a tether
Before two virgins can meet together.

Day

THE Sun arises in the East,
Cloth'd in robes of blood & gold;
Swords & spears & wrath increast
All around his bosom roll'd,
Crown'd with warlike fires & raging desires.

The Marriage Ring

"COME hither my sparrows,
My little arrows.
If a tear or a smile
Will a man beguile,
If an amorous delay
Clouds a sunshiny day,
If the step of a foot

Smites the heart to its root,
'Tis the marriage ring
Makes each fairy a king."

So a fairy sung.
From the leaves I sprung.
He leap'd from the spray
To flee away.
But in my hat caught
He soon shall be taught.
Let him laugh, let him cry,
He's my butterfly;
For I've pull'd out the sting
Of the marriage ring.

⚥

THE sword sung on the barren heath,
The sickle in the fruitful field:
The sword he sung a song of death,
But could not make the sickle yield.

⚥

ABSTINENCE sows sand all over
The ruddy limbs & flaming hair,
But Desire Gratified
Plants fruits of life & beauty there.

⚥

IN a wife I would desire
What in whores is always found—
The lineaments of Gratified desire.

⚥

IF you trap the moment before it's ripe,
The tears of repentance you'll certainly wipe;

But if once you let the ripe moment go
You can never wipe off the tears of woe.

Eternity

HE who binds to himself a joy
Does the winged life destroy;
But he who kisses the joy as it flies
Lives in eternity's sun rise.

The Question Answer'd

WHAT is it men in women do require?
The lineaments of Gratified Desire.
What is it women do in men require?
The lineaments of Gratified Desire.

Lacedemonian Instruction

"COME hither, my boy, tell me what thou seest there."
"A fool tangled in a religious snare."

Riches

THE countless gold of a merry heart,
The rubies & pearls of a loving eye,
The indolent never can bring to the mart,
Nor the secret hoard up in his treasury.

An Answer to the Parson

"WHY of the sheep do you not learn peace?"
"Because I don't want you to shear my fleece."

❉

THE look of love alarms
Because 'tis fill'd with fire;
But the look of soft deceit
Shall win the lover's hire.

❉

WHICH are beauties sweetest dress?
Soft deceit & idleness,
These are beauties sweetest dress.

Motto to the Songs of Innocence & of Experience

THE Good are attracted by Men's perceptions,
And think not for themselves;
Till Experience teaches them to catch
And to cage the Fairies & Elves.

And then the Knave begins to snarl
And the Hypocrite to howl;
And all his good Friends shew their private ends,
And the Eagle is known from the Owl.

❉

HER whole Life is an Epigram, smart, smooth, & neatly
    pen'd,
Platted quite neat to catch applause with a sliding noose at
    the end.

❉

AN old maid early—e'er I knew
Ought but the love that on me grew·

And now I'm cover'd o'er & o'er
And wish that I had been a whore.

O, I cannot, cannot find
The undaunted courage of a Virgin Mind,
For Early I in love was crost,
Before my flower of love was lost.

✠

"LET the Brothels of Paris be opened
With many an alluring dance
To awake the Pestilence thro' the city,"
Said the beautiful Queen of France.

The King awoke on his couch of gold,
As soon as he heard these tidings told:
"Arise & come, both fife & drum,
And the Famine shall eat both crust & crumb."

Then he swore a great & solemn Oath:
"To kill the people I am loth,
But If they rebel, they must go to hell:
They shall have a Priest & a passing bell."

Then old Nobodaddy aloft
Farted & belch'd & cough'd,
And said, "I love hanging & drawing & quartering
Every bit as well as war & slaughtering.
Damn praying & singing,
Unless they will bring in
The blood of ten thousand by fighting or swinging."

The Queen of France just touched this Globe,
And the Pestilence darted from her robe;
But our good Queen quite grows to the ground,
And a great many suckers grow all around.

Fayette beside King Lewis stood;
He saw him sign his hand;
And soon he saw the famine rage
About the fruitful land.

Fayette beheld the Queen to smile
And wink her lovely eye;
And soon he saw the pestilence
From street to street to fly.

Fayette beheld the King & Queen
In tears & iron bound;
But mute Fayette wept tear for tear,
And guarded them around.

Fayette, Fayette, thou'rt bought & sold,
And sold is thy happy morrow;
Thou gavest the tears of Pity away
In exchange for the tears of sorrow.

Who will exchange his own fire side
For the steps of another's door?
Who will exchange his wheaten loaf
For the links of a dungeon floor?

O, who would smile on the wintry seas,
& Pity the stormy roar?
Or who will exchange his new born child
For the dog at the wintry door?

                          ¤

WHEN Klopstock England defied,
Uprose William Blake in his pride;
For old Nobodaddy aloft
Farted & Belch'd & cough'd;
Then swore a great oath that made heaven quake,
And call'd aloud to English Blake.
Blake was giving his body ease
At Lambeth beneath the poplar trees.
From his seat then started he,
And turned him round three times three.
The Moon at that sight blush'd scarlet red,
The stars threw down their cups & fled,
And all the devils that were in hell
Answered with a ninefold yell.

Klopstock felt the intripled turn,
And all his bowels began to churn,
And his bowels turned round three times three,
And lock'd in his soul with a ninefold key,
That from his body it ne'er could be parted
Till to the last trumpet it was farted.
Then again old Nobodaddy swore
He ne'er had seen such a thing before,
Since Noah was shut in the ark,
Since Eve first chose her hellfire spark,
Since 'twas the fashion to go naked,
Since the old anything was created,
And so feeling, he beg'd me to turn again
And ease poor Klopstock's ninefold pain.
If Blake could do this when he rose up from a shite,
What might he not do if he sat down to write?

❧

A FAIRY leapt upon my knee
Singing & dancing merrily;
I said, "Thou thing of patches, rings,
Pins, Necklaces, & such like things,
Disguiser of the Female Form,
Thou paltry, gilded, poisonous worm!"
Weeping, he fell upon my thigh,
And thus in tears did soft reply:
"Knowest thou not, O Fairies' Lord!
How much by us Contemn'd, Abhorr'd,
Whatever hides the Female form
That cannot bear the Mental storm?
Therefore in Pity still we give
Our lives to make the Female live;
And what would turn into disease
We turn to what will joy & please."

❧

MY Spectre around me night & day
Like a Wild beast guards my way.

My Emanation far within
Weeps incessantly for my Sin.

A Fathomless & boundless deep,
There we wander, there we weep;
On the hungry craving wind
My Spectre follows thee behind.

He scents thy footsteps in the snow,
Wheresoever thou dost go
Thro' the wintry hail & rain.
When wilt thou return again?

Dost thou not in Pride & scorn
Fill with tempests all my morn,
And with jealousies & fears
Fill my pleasant nights with tears?

Seven of my sweet loves thy knife
Has bereaved of their life.
Their marble tombs I built with tears
And with cold &.shuddering fears.

Seven more loves weep night & day
Round the tombs where my loves lay,
And seven more loves attend each night
Around my couch with torches bright.

And seven more Loves in my bed
Crown with wine my mournful head,
Pitying & forgiving all
Thy transgressions, great & small.

When wilt thou return & view
My loves, & them to life renew?
When wilt thou return & live?
When wilt thou pity as I forgive?

"Never, Never, I return:
Still for Victory I burn.
Living, thee alone I'll have
And when dead I'll be thy Grave.

"Thro' the Heaven & Earth & Hell
Thou shalt never never quell:
I will fly & thou pursue,
Night & Morn the flight renew."

Till I turn from Female Love,
And root up the Infernal Grove,
I shall never worthy be
To Step into Eternity.

And, to end thy cruel mocks,
Annihilate thee on the rocks,
And another form create
To be subservient to my Fate.

Let us agree to give up Love,
And root up the infernal grove;
Then shall we return & see
The worlds of happy Eternity.

& Throughout all Eternity
I forgive you, you forgive me.
As our dear Redeemer said:
"This the Wine & this the Bread."

[Additional Stanzas]

O'er my Sins thou sit & moan:
Hast thou no sins of thy own?
O'er my Sins thou sit & weep,
And lull thy own Sins fast asleep.

What Transgressions I commit
Are for thy Transgressions fit.
They thy Harlots, thou their slave,
And my Bed becomes their Grave.

Poor pale pitiable form
That I follow in a Storm,
Iron tears & groans of lead
Bind around my aking head.

H

WHEN a Man has Married a Wife, he finds out whether
Her knees & elbows are only glewed together.

H

MOCK on, Mock on Voltaire, Rousseau:
Mock on, Mock on: 'tis all in vain!
You throw the sand against the wind,
And the wind blows it back again.

And every sand becomes a Gem
Reflected in the beams divine;
Blown back they blind the mocking Eye,
But still in Israel's paths they shine.

The Atoms of Democritus
And Newton's Particles of light
Are sands upon the Red sea shore,
Where Israel's tents do shine so bright.

Morning

TO find the Western path
Right thro' the Gates of Wrath
I urge my way;
Sweet Mercy leads me on:
With soft repentant moan
I see the break of day.

The war of swords & spears
Melted by dewy tears
Exhales on high;
The Sun is freed from fears
And with soft grateful tears
Ascends the sky.

ℋ

EACH Man is in his Spectre's power
Untill the arrival of that hour,
When his Humanity awake
And cast his own Spectre into the Lake.

The Birds

HE. WHERE thou dwellest, in what Grove,
Tell me, Fair one, tell me, love;
Where thou thy charming Nest dost build,
O thou pride of every field!

SHE. Yonder stands a lonely tree,
There I live & mourn for thee.
Morning drinks my silent tear,
And evening winds my sorrows bear.

HE. O thou Summer's harmony,
I have liv'd & mourn'd for thee.
Each day I mourn along the wood,
And night hath heard my sorrows loud.

SHE. Dost thou truly long for me?
And am I thus sweet to thee?
Sorrow now is at an End,
O my Lover & my Friend!

HE. Come, on wings of joy we'll fly
To where my Bower hangs on high!
Come, & make thy calm retreat
Among green leaves & blossoms sweet!

To the Queen

THE Door of Death is made of Gold,
That Mortal Eyes cannot behold;

But, when the Mortal Eyes are clos'd,
And cold and pale the Limbs repos'd,
The Soul awakes; and, wond'ring, sees
In her mild Hand the golden Keys:
The Grave is Heaven's golden Gate,
And rich and poor around it wait;
O Shepherdess of England's Fold,
Behold this Gate of Pearl and Gold!

To dedicate to England's Queen
The Visions that my Soul has seen,
And, by Her kind permission, bring
What I have borne on solemn Wing
From the vast regions of the Grave,
Before Her Throne my Wings I wave;
Bowing before my Sov'reign's Feet,
"The Grave produc'd these Blossoms sweet
In mild repose from Earthly strife;
The Blossoms of Eternal Life!"

X

THE Angel that presided o'er my birth
Said, "Little creature, form'd of Joy & Mirth,
Go love without the help of any Thing on Earth."

X

GROWN old in Love from Seven till Seven times Seven,
I oft have wish'd for Hell for Ease from Heaven.

X

WHY was Cupid a Boy
And why a boy was he?
He should have been a Girl
For ought that I can see.

For he shoots with his bow,
And the Girl shoots with her Eye,

And they both are merry & glad
And laugh when we do cry.

And to make Cupid a Boy
Was the Cupid Girl's mocking plan;
For a boy can't interpret the thing
Till he is become a man.

And then he's so pierc'd with cares
And wounded with arrowy smarts,
That the whole business of his life
Is to pick out the heads of the darts.

'Twas the Greeks' love of war
Turn'd Love into a Boy,
And Woman into a Statue of Stone—
And away flew every Joy.

§

SINCE all the Riches of this World
May be gifts from the Devil & Earthly Kings,
I should suspect that I worship'd the Devil
If I thank'd my God for Worldly things.

§

NAIL his neck to the Cross: nail it with a nail.
Nail his neck to the Cross: ye all have power over his tail.

§

THE Caverns of the Grave I've seen,
And these I shew'd to England's Queen.
But now the Caves of Hell I view:
Who shall I dare to shew them to?
What mighty Soul in Beauty's form
Shall dauntless View the Infernal Storm?
Egremont's Countess can controll

The flames of Hell that round me roll.
If she refuse, I still go on
Till the Heavens & Earth are gone,
Still admir'd by Noble minds,
Follow'd by Envy on the winds,
Re-engrav'd Time after Time,
Ever in their youthful prime,
My designs unchang'd remain.
Time may rage but rage in vain.
Far above Time's troubled Fountains
On the Great Atlantic Mountains,
In my Golden House on high,
There they Shine Eternally.

H

I ROSE up at the dawn of day—
Get thee away! get thee away!
Pray'st thou for Riches? away! away!
This is the Throne of Mammon grey.

Said I, "this sure is very odd.
I took it to be the Throne of God.
For every Thing besides I have:
It is only for Riches that I can crave.

"I have Mental Joy & Mental Health
And Mental Friends & Mental wealth;
I've a Wife I love & that loves me;
I've all but Riches Bodily.

"I am in God's presence night & day,
And he never turns his face away.
The accuser of sins by my side does stand
And he holds my money bag in his hand.

"For my worldly things God makes him pay,
And he'd pay more if to him I would pray;
And so you may do the worst you can do:
Be assur'd Mr. devil I won't pray to you.

"Then If for Riches I must not Pray,
God knows I little of Prayers need say.
So as a Church is known by its Steeple,
If I pray it must be for other People.

"He says, if I do not worship him for a God,
I shall eat coarser food & go worse shod;
So as I don't value such things as these,
You must do, Mr. devil, just as God please."

Miscellaneous Epigrams and Fragments

✠

YOU don't believe—I won't attempt to make ye:
You are asleep—I won't attempt to wake ye.
Sleep on, Sleep on! while in your pleasant dreams
Of Reason you may drink of Life's clear streams.
Reason and Newton, they are quite two things;
For so the Swallow & the Sparrow sings.
Reason says "Miracle": Newton says "Doubt".
Aye! that's the way to make all Nature out.
"Doubt, Doubt, & don't believe without experiment":
That is the very thing that Jesus meant,
When he said, "Only Believe! Believe & try!
Try, Try, and never mind the Reason why."

✠

ANGER & Wrath my bosom rends:
I thought them the Errors of friends.
But all my limbs with warmth glow:
I find them the Errors of the foe.

✠

"MADMAN" I have been call'd: "Fool" they call thee:
I wonder which they Envy, Thee or Me?

To F[laxman]

I MOCK thee not, tho' I by thee am Mocked.
Thou call'st me Madman, but I call thee Blockhead.

✷

S[TOTHARD] in Childhood on the Nursery floor
Was extreme Old & most extremely poor.
He is grown old & rich & what he will:
He is extreme old & extreme poor still.

To Nancy F[laxman]

HOW can I help thy Husband's copying Me?
Should that make difference 'twixt me & Thee?

✷

OF H[ayley]'s birth this was the happy lot,
His Mother on his Father him begot.

✷

HE's a Blockhead who wants a proof of what he can't Percieve,
And he's a Fool who tries to make such a Blockhead believe.

✷

CR[OMEK] loves artists as he loves his Meat.
He loves the Art, but 'tis the Art to Cheat.

�֍

A PETTY Sneaking Knave I knew——
O Mr. Cr[omek], how do ye do?

To S[tothar]d

YOU all your Youth observ'd the Golden Rule
Till you're at last become the golden fool.
I sport with Fortune, Merry, Blithe & Gay,
Like to the Lion Sporting with his Prey.
Take you the hide & horns which you may wear:
Mine is the flesh—the bones may be your Share.

�֍

I AM no Homer's Hero, you all know,
I profess not Generosity to a Foe.
My Generosity is to my Friends,
That for their Friendship I may make amends.
The Generous to Enemies promotes their Ends
And becomes the Enemy & Betrayer of his Friends.

✖

TO forgive Enemies H[ayley] does pretend,
Who never in his Life forgave a friend.

On H[ayley]'s Friendship

WHEN H[ayley] finds out what you cannot do,
That is the very thing he'll set you to.
If you break not your Neck, 'tis not his fault,
But pecks of poison are not pecks of salt.
And when he could not act upon my wife
Hired a Villain to bereave my Life.

Imitation of Pope: a Compliment to the Ladies

WONDROUS the Gods, more wondrous are the Men,
More Wondrous Wondrous still the Cock & Hen,
More Wondrous still the Table, Stool & Chair;
But Ah! More wondrous still the Charming Fair.

To H[ayley]

THY Friendship oft has made my heart to ake:
Do be my Enemy for Friendship's sake.

※

HERE lies John Trot, the Friend of all mankind:
He has not left one Enemy behind.
Friends were quite hard to find, old authors say;
But now they stand in every bodies way.

※

MY title as a Genius thus is prov'd:
Not Prais'd by Hayley nor by Flaxman lov'd.

※

I, RUBENS, am a Statesman & a Saint.
Deceptions? And so I'll learn to Paint.

On H[ayley] the Pick Thank

I WRITE the Rascal Thanks till he & I
With Thanks & Compliments are quite drawn dry.

Cromek Speaks

I ALWAYS take my judgment from a Fool
Because his judgment is so very Cool,
Not prejudic'd by feelings great or small.
Amiable state! he cannot feel at all.

❌

YOU say their Pictures well Painted be,
And yet they are Blockheads you all agree.
Thank God, I never was sent to school
To be Flog'd into following the Style of a Fool.

The Errors of a Wise Man make your Rule
Rather than the Perfections of a Fool.

❌

GREAT things are done when Men & Mountains meet;
This is not done by Jostling in the Street.

❌

IF you play a Game of Chance, know, before you begin,
If you are benevolent you will never win.

❌

THE only Man that e'er I knew
Who did not make me almost spew
Was Fuseli: he was both Turk & Jew—
And so, dear Christian Friends, how do you do?

To God

IF you have form'd a Circle to go into,
Go into it yourself & see how you would do.

❈

"NOW Art has lost its mental Charms
France shall subdue the World in Arms."
So spoke an Angel at my birth,
Then said, "Descend thou upon Earth.
Renew the Arts on Britain's Shore,
And France shall fall down & adore.
With works of Art their Armies meet,
And War shall sink beneath thy feet.
But if thy Nation Arts refuse,
And if they scorn the immortal Muse,
France shall the arts of Peace restore,
And save thee from the Ungrateful shore."

The Smile

THERE is a Smile of Love,
And there is a Smile of Deceit,
And there is a Smile of Smiles
In which these two Smiles meet.

And there is a Frown of Hate,
And there is a Frown of Disdain,
And there is a Frown of Frowns
Which you strive to forget in vain,

For it sticks in the Heart's deep Core
And it sticks in the deep Back bone;
And no Smile that ever was smil'd,
But only one Smile alone,

That betwixt the Cradle & Grave
It only once Smil'd can be;
But, when it once is Smil'd,
There's an end to all Misery.

The Golden Net

THREE Virgins at the break of day:
"Whither, young Man, whither away?
Alas for woe! alas for woe!"
They cry, & tears for ever flow.
The one was Cloth'd in flames of fire,
The other Cloth'd in iron wire,
The other Cloth'd in tears & sighs

Dazling bright before my Eyes.
They bore a Net of golden twine
To hang upon the branches fine.
Pitying I wept to see the woe
That Love & Beauty undergo,
To be consum'd in burning Fires
And in ungratified desires,
And in tears cloth'd Night & day
Melted all my Soul away.
When they saw my Tears, a Smile
That did Heaven itself beguile,
Bore the Golden Net aloft
As on downy Pinions soft
Over the Morning of my day.
Underneath the Net I stray,
Now intreating Burning Fire,
Now intreating Iron Wire,
Now intreating Tears & Sighs.
O when will the morning rise?

The Mental Traveller

I TRAVEL'D thro' a Land of Men,
A Land of Men & Women too,
And heard & saw such dreadful things
As cold Earth wanderers never knew.

For there the Babe is born in joy
That was begotten in dire woe;
Just as we Reap in joy the fruit
Which we in bitter tears did sow.

And if the Babe is born a Boy
He's given to a Woman Old,
Who nails him down upon a rock,
Catches his shrieks in cups of gold.

She binds iron thorns around his head,
She pierces both his hands & feet,

She cuts his heart out at his side
To make it feel both cold & heat.

Her fingers number every Nerve,
Just as a Miser counts his gold;
She lives upon his shrieks & cries,
And she grows young as he grows old.

Till he becomes a bleeding youth,
And she becomes a Virgin bright;
Then he rends up his Manacles
And binds her down for his delight.

He plants himself in all her Nerves,
Just as a Husbandman his mould;
And she becomes his dwelling place
And Garden fruitful seventy fold.

An aged Shadow, soon he fades,
Wand'ring round an Earthly Cot,
Full filled all with gems & gold
Which he by industry had got.

And these are the gems of the Human Soul,
The rubies & pearls of a lovesick eye,
The countless gold of the akeing heart,
The martyr's groan & the lover's sigh.

They are his meat, they are his drink;
He feeds the Beggar & the Poor
And the wayfaring Traveller:
For ever open is his door.

His grief is their eternal joy;
They make the roofs & walls to ring;
Till from the fire on the hearth
A little Female Babe does spring.

And she is all of solid fire
And gems & gold, that none his hand
Dares stretch to touch her Baby form,
Or wrap her in his swaddling-band.

But She comes to the Man she loves,
If young or old, or rich or poor;
They soon drive out the aged Host,
A Beggar at another's door.

He wanders weeping far away,
Untill some other take him in;
Oft blind & age-bent, sore distrest,
Untill he can a Maiden win.

And to allay his freezing Age
The Poor Man takes her in his arms;
The Cottage fades before his sight,
The Garden & its lovely Charms.

The Guests are scatter'd thro' the land,
For the Eye altering alters all;
The Senses roll themselves in fear,
And the flat Earth becomes a Ball;

The stars, sun, Moon, all shrink away,
A desart vast without a bound,
And nothing left to eat or drink,
And a dark desart all around.

The honey of her Infant lips,
The bread & wine of her sweet smile,
The wild game of her roving Eye,
Does him to Infancy beguile;

For as he eats & drinks he grows
Younger & younger every day;
And on the desart wild they both
Wander in terror & dismay.

Like the wild Stag she flees away,
Her fear plants many a thicket wild;
While he pursues her night & day,
By various arts of Love beguil'd,

By various arts of Love & Hate,
Till the wide desart planted o'er

With Labyrinths of wayward Love,
Where roam the Lion, Wolf & Boar,

Till he becomes a wayward Babe,
And she a weeping Woman Old.
Then many a Lover wanders here;
The Sun & Stars are nearer roll'd.

The trees bring forth sweet Extacy
To all who in the desert roam;
Till many a City there is Built,
And many a pleasant Shepherd's home.

But when they find the frowning Babe,
Terror strikes thro' the region wide:
They cry "The Babe! the Babe is Born!"
And flee away on Every side.

For who dare touch the frowning form,
His arm is wither'd to its root;
Lions, Boars, Wolves, all howling flee,
And every Tree does shed its fruit.

And none can touch that frowning form,
Except it be a Woman Old;
She nails him down upon the Rock,
And all is done as I have told.

The Land of Dreams

AWAKE, awake, my little Boy!
Thou wast thy Mother's only joy;
Why dost thou weep in thy gentle sleep?
Awake! thy Father does thee keep.

"O, what Land is the Land of Dreams?
What are its Mountains & what are its Streams?
O Father, I saw my Mother there,
Among the Lillies by waters fair.

"Among the Lambs, clothed in white,
She walk'd with her Thomas in sweet delight.
I wept for joy, like a dove I mourn;
O! when shall I again return?"

Dear Child, I also by pleasant Streams
Have wander'd all Night in the Land of Dreams;
But tho' calm & warm the waters wide,
I could not get to the other side.

"Father, O Father! what do we here
In this Land of unbelief & fear?
The Land of Dreams is better far,
Above the light of the Morning Star."

Mary

SWEET Mary, the first time she ever was there,
Came into the Ball room among the Fair;
The young Men & Maidens around her throng,
And these are the words upon every tongue:

"An Angel is here from the heavenly climes,
Or again does return the golden times;
Her eyes outshine every brilliant ray,
She opens her lips—'tis the Month of May."

Mary moves in soft beauty & conscious delight
To augment with sweet smiles all the joys of the Night,
Nor once blushes to own to the rest of the Fair
That sweet Love & Beauty are worthy our care.

In the Morning the Villagers rose with delight
And repeated with pleasure the joys of the night,
And Mary arose among Friends to be free,
But no Friend from henceforward thou, Mary, shalt see.

Some said she was proud, some call'd her a whore,
And some, when she passed by, shut to the door;

A damp cold came o'er her, her blushes all fled;
Her lillies & roses are blighted & shed.

"O, why was I born with a different Face?
Why was I not born like this Envious Race?
Why did Heaven adorn me with bountiful hand,
And then set me down in an envious Land?

"To be weak as a Lamb & smooth as a dove,
And not to raise Envy, is call'd Christian Love;
But if you raise Envy your Merit's to blame
For planting such spite in the weak & the tame.

"I will humble my Beauty, I will not dress fine,
I will keep from the Ball, & my Eyes shall not shine;
And if any Girl's Lover forsakes her for me,
I'll refuse him my hand & from Envy be free."

She went out in Morning attir'd plain & neat;
"Proud Mary's gone Mad," said the Child in the Street;
She went out in Morning in plain neat attire,
And came home in Evening bespatter'd with mire.

She trembled & wept, sitting on the Bed side;
She forgot it was Night, & she trembled & cried;
She forgot it was Night, she forgot it was Morn,
Her soft Memory imprinted with Faces of Scorn,

With Faces of Scorn & with Eyes of disdain
Like foul Fiends inhabiting Mary's mild Brain;
She remembers no Face like the Human Divine.
All Faces have Envy, sweet Mary, but thine;

And thine is a Face of sweet Love in despair,
And thine is a Face of mild sorrow & care,
And thine is a Face of wild terror & fear
That shall never be quiet till laid on its bier.

The Crystal Cabinet

THE Maiden caught me in the Wild,
Where I was dancing merrily;
She put me into her Cabinet
And Lock'd me up with a golden Key.

This Cabinet is form'd of Gold
And Pearl & Crystal shining bright,
And within it opens into a World
And a little lovely Moony Night.

Another England there I saw,
Another London with its Tower,
Another Thames & other Hills,
And another pleasant Surrey Bower,

Another Maiden like herself,
Translucent, lovely, shining clear,
Threefold each in the other clos'd—
O, what a pleasant trembling fear!

O, what a smile! a threefold Smile
Fill'd me, that like a flame I burn'd;
I bent to Kiss the lovely Maid,
And found a Threefold Kiss return'd.

I strove to sieze the inmost Form
With ardor fierce & hands of flame,
But burst the Crystal Cabinet,
And like a Weeping Babe became—

A weeping Babe upon the wild,
And Weeping Woman pale reclin'd,
And in the outward air again
I fill'd with woes the passing Wind.

The Grey Monk

"I DIE, I DIE!" the Mother said,
"My Children die for lack of Bread.
What more has the merciless Tyrant said?"
The Monk sat down on the Stony Bed.

The blood red ran from the Grey Monk's side,
His hands & feet were wounded wide,
His Body bent, his arms & knees
Like to the roots of ancient trees.

His eye was dry; no tear could flow:
A hollow groan first spoke his woe.
He trembled & shudder'd upon the Bed;
At length with a feeble cry he said:

"When God commanded this hand to write
In the studious hours of deep midnight,
He told me the writing I wrote should prove
The Bane of all that on Earth I lov'd.

"My Brother starv'd between two Walls,
His Children's Cry my Soul appalls;
I mock'd at the wrack & griding chain,
My bent body mocks their torturing pain.

"Thy Father drew his sword in the North,
With his thousands strong he marched forth;
Thy Brother has arm'd himself in Steel
To avenge the wrongs thy Children feel.

"But vain the Sword & vain the Bow,
They never can work War's overthrow.
The Hermit's Prayer & the Widow's tear
Alone can free the World from fear.

"For a Tear is an Intellectual Thing,
And a Sigh is the Sword of an Angel King,

And the bitter groan of the Martyr's woe
Is an Arrow from the Almightie's Bow.

"The hand of Vengeance found the Bed
To which the Purple Tyrant fled;
The iron hand crush'd the Tyrant's head
And became a Tyrant in his stead."

Auguries of Innocence

TO see a World in a Grain of Sand
And a Heaven in a Wild Flower,
Hold Infinity in the palm of your hand
And Eternity in an hour.

A Robin Red breast in a Cage
Puts all Heaven in a Rage.
A dove house fill'd with doves & Pigeons
Shudders Hell thro' all its regions.
A dog starv'd at his Master's Gate
Predicts the ruin of the State.
A Horse misus'd upon the Road
Calls to Heaven for Human blood.
Each outcry of the hunted Hare
A fibre from the Brain does tear.
A Skylark wounded in the wing,
A Cherubim does cease to sing.
The Game Cock clip'd & arm'd for fight
Does the Rising Sun affright.
Every Wolf's & Lion's howl
Raises from Hell a Human Soul.
The wild deer, wand'ring here & there,
Keeps the Human Soul from Care.
The Lamb misus'd breeds Public strife
And yet forgives the Butcher's Knife.
The Bat that flits at close of Eve
Has left the Brain that won't Believe.
The Owl that calls upon the Night
Speaks the Unbeliever's fright.
He who shall hurt the little Wren

Shall never be belov'd by Men.
He who the Ox to wrath has mov'd
Shall never be by Woman lov'd.
The wanton Boy that kills the Fly
Shall feel the Spider's enmity.
He who torments the Chafer's sprite
Weaves a Bower in endless Night.
The Catterpiller on the Leaf
Repeats to thee thy Mother's grief.
Kill not the Moth nor Butterfly,
For the Last Judgment draweth nigh.
He who shall train the Horse to War
Shall never pass the Polar Bar.
The Beggar's Dog & Widow's Cat,
Feed them & thou wilt grow fat.
The Gnat that sings his Summer's song
Poison gets from Slander's tongue.
The poison of the Snake & Newt
Is the sweat of Envy's Foot.
The Poison of the Honey Bee
Is the Artist's Jealousy.
The Prince's Robes & Beggar's Rags
Are Toadstools on the Miser's Bags.
A truth that's told with bad intent
Beats all the Lies you can invent.
It is right it should be so;
Man was made for Joy & Woe;
And when this we rightly know
Thro' the World we safely go.
Joy & Woe are woven fine,
A Clothing for the Soul divine;
Under every grief & pine
Runs a joy with silken twine.
The Babe is more than swadling Bands;
Throughout all these Human Lands
Tools were made, & Born were hands,
Every Farmer Understands.
Every Tear from Every Eye
Becomes a Babe in Eternity;
This is caught by Females bright
And return'd to its own delight.
The Bleat, the Bark, Bellow & Roar

Are Waves that Beat on Heaven's Shore.
The Babe that weeps the Rod beneath
Writes Revenge in realms of death.
The Beggar's Rags, fluttering in Air,
Does to Rags the Heavens tear.
The Soldier, arm'd with Sword & Gun,
Palsied strikes the Summer's Sun.
The poor Man's Farthing is worth more
Than all the Gold on Afric's Shore.
One Mite wrung from the Labrer's hands
Shall buy & sell the Miser's Lands:
Or, if protected from on high,
Does that whole Nation sell & buy.
He who mocks the Infant's Faith
Shall be mock'd in Age & Death.
He who shall teach the Child to Doubt
The rotting Grave shall ne'er get out.
He who respects the Infant's faith
Triumphs over Hell & Death.
The Child's Toys & the Old Man's Reasons
Are the Fruits of the Two seasons.
The Questioner, who sits so sly,
Shall never know how to Reply.
He who replies to words of Doubt
Doth put the Light of Knowledge out.
The Strongest Poison ever known
Came from Caesar's Laurel Crown.
Nought can deform the Human Race
Like to the Armour's iron brace.
When Gold & Gems adorn the Plow
To peaceful Arts shall Envy Bow.
A Riddle or the Cricket's Cry
Is to Doubt a fit Reply.
The Emmet's Inch & Eagle's Mile
Make Lame Philosophy to smile.
He who Doubts from what he sees
Will ne'er Believe, do what you Please.
If the Sun & Moon should doubt,
They'd immediately Go out.
To be in a Passion you Good may do,
But no Good if a Passion is in you.
The Whore & Gambler, by the State

Licenc'd, build that Nation's Fate.
The Harlot's cry from Street to Street
Shall weave Old England's winding Sheet.
The Winner's Shout, the Loser's Curse,
Dance before dead England's Hearse.
Every Night & every Morn
Some to Misery are Born.
Every Morn & every Night
Some are Born to sweet delight.
Some are Born to sweet delight,
Some are Born to Endless Night.
We are led to Believe a Lie
When we see not Thro' the Eye
Which was Born in a Night to perish in a Night
When the Soul Slept in Beams of Light.
God Appears & God is Light
To those poor Souls who dwell in Night,
But does a Human Form Display
To those who Dwell in Realms of day.

Long John Brown & Little Mary Bell

LITTLE Mary Bell had a Fairy in a Nut,
Long John Brown had the Devil in his Gut;
Long John Brown lov'd Little Mary Bell,
And the Fairy drew the Devil into the Nut-shell.

Her Fairy Skip'd out & her Fairy Skip'd in;
He laugh'd at the Devil saying 'Love is a Sin.'
The Devil he raged & the Devil he was wroth,
And the Devil enter'd into the Young Man's broth.

He was soon in the Gut of the loving Young Swain,
For John eat & drank to drive away Love's pain;
But all he could do he grew thinner & thinner,
Tho' he eat & drank as much as ten Men for his dinner.

Some said he had a Wolf in his stomach day & night,
Some said he had the Devil & they guess'd right;

The Fairy skip'd about in his Glory, Joy & Pride,
And he laugh'd at the Devil till poor John Brown died.

Then the Fairy skip'd out of the old Nut shell,
And woe & alack for Pretty Mary Bell!
For the Devil crept in when the Fairy skip'd out,
And there goes Miss Bell with her fusty old Nut.

William Bond

I WONDER whether the Girls are mad,
And I wonder whether they mean to kill,
And I wonder if William Bond will die,
For assuredly he is very ill.

He went to Church in a May morning
Attended by Fairies, one, two & three;
But the Angels of Providence drove them away,
And he return'd home in Misery.

He went not out to the Field nor Fold,
He went not out to the Village nor Town,
But he came home in a black, black cloud,
And took to his Bed & there lay down.

And an Angel of Providence at his Feet,
And an Angel of Providence at his Head,
And in the midst a Black, Black Cloud,
And in the midst the Sick Man on his Bed.

And on his Right hand was Mary Green,
And on his Left hand was his Sister Jane,
And their tears fell thro' the black, black Cloud
To drive away the sick man's pain.

"O William, if thou dost another Love,
"Dost another Love better than poor Mary,
"Go & take that other to be thy Wife,
"And Mary Green shall her servant be."

"Yes, Mary, I do another Love,
"Another I Love far better than thee,
"And Another I will have for my Wife;
"Then what have I to do with thee?

"For thou art Melancholy Pale,
"And on thy Head is the cold Moon's shine,
"But she is ruddy & bright as day,
"And the sun beams dazzle from her eyne."

Mary trembled & Mary chill'd
And Mary fell down on the right hand floor,
That William Bond & his Sister Jane
Scarce could recover Mary more.

When Mary awoke & found her Laid
On the Right hand of her William dear,
On the Right hand of his loved Bed,
And saw her William Bond so near,

The Fairies that fled from William Bond
Danced around her Shining Head;
They danced over the Pillow white,
And the Angels of Providence left the Bed.

I thought Love liv'd in the hot sun shine,
But O, he lives in the Moony light!
I thought to find Love in the heat of day,
But sweet Love is the Comforter of Night.

Seek Love in the Pity of others' Woe,
In the gentle relief of another's care,
In the darkness of night & the winter's snow,
In the naked & outcast, Seek Love there!"

PART TWO

MINOR PROPHECIES

MINOR PROPHECIES

There Is No Natural Religion

[a]

THE *Argument.* Man has no notion of moral fitness but from Education. Naturally he is only a natural organ subject to Sense.

I. Man cannot naturally Percieve but through his natural or bodily organs.

II. Man by his reasoning power can only compare & judge of what he has already perciev'd.

III. From a perception of only 3 senses or 3 elements none could deduce a fourth or fifth.

· IV. None could have other than natural or organic thoughts if he had none but organic perceptions.

V. Man's desires are limited by his perceptions, none can desire what he has not perciev'd.

VI. The desires & perceptions of man, untaught by any thing but organs of sense, must be limited to objects of sense.

Conclusion. If it were not for the Poetic or Prophetic character the Philosophic & Experimental would soon be at the ratio of all things, & stand still, unable to do other than repeat the same dull round over again.

There Is No Natural Religion

[b]

I. Man's perceptions are not bounded by organs of perception; he percieves more than sense (tho' ever so acute) can discover.

II. Reason, or the ratio of all we have already known, is not the same that it shall be when we know more.

III. [*Lost*]

IV. The bounded is loathed by its possessor. The same dull round, even of a universe, would soon become a mill with complicated wheels.

V. If the many become the same as the few when possess'd, More! More! is the cry of a mistaken soul; less than All cannot satisfy Man.

VI. If any could desire what he is incapable of possessing, despair must be his eternal lot.

VII. The desire of Man being Infinite, the possession is Infinite & himself Infinite.

Application. He who sees the Infinite in all things, sees God. He who sees the Ratio only, sees himself only.

Therefore God becomes as we are, that we may be as he is.

All Religions Are One

The Voice of one crying in the Wilderness

THE *Argument.* As the true method of knowledge is experiment, the true faculty of knowing must be the faculty which experiences. This faculty I treat of.

PRINCIPLE 1st. That the Poetic Genius is the true Man, and that the body or outward form of Man is derived from the Poetic Genius. Likewise that the forms of all things are derived from their Genius, which by the Ancients was call'd an Angel & Spirit & Demon.

PRINCIPLE 2d. As all men are alike in outward form, So (and with the same infinite variety) all are alike in the Poetic Genius.

PRINCIPLE 3d. No man can think, write, or speak from his heart, but he must intend truth. Thus all sects of Philosophy are from the Poetic Genius adapted to the weaknesses of every individual.

PRINCIPLE 4th. As none by traveling over known lands can find out the unknown, So from already acquired knowledge Man could not acquire more: therefore an universal Poetic Genius exists.

PRINCIPLE 5th. The Religions of all Nations are derived from each Nation's different reception of the Poetic Genius, which is every where call'd the Spirit of Prophecy.

PRINCIPLE 6th. The Jewish & Christian Testaments are An original derivation from the Poetic Genius; this is necessary from the confined nature of bodily sensation.

PRINCIPLE 7th. As all men are alike (tho' infinitely various), So all Religions &, as all similars, have one source.

The true Man is the source, he being the Poetic Genius.

The Book of Thel

THEL'S MOTTO

Does the Eagle know what is in the pit?
Or wilt thou go ask the Mole?
Can Wisdom be put in a silver rod?
Or Love in a golden bowl?

I

THE daughters of the Seraphim led round their sunny flocks,
All but the youngest: she in paleness sought the secret air,
To fade away like morning beauty from her mortal day:
Down by the river of Adona her soft voice is heard,
And thus her gentle lamentation falls like morning dew:

"O life of this our spring! why fades the lotus of the water,
Why fade these children of the spring, born but to smile & fall?

Ah! Thel is like a wat'ry bow, and like a parting cloud;
Like a reflection in a glass; like shadows in the water;
Like dreams of infants, like a smile upon an infant's face;
Like the dove's voice; like transient day; like music in the air.
Ah! gentle may I lay me down, and gentle rest my head,
And gentle sleep the sleep of death, and gentle hear the voice
Of him that walketh in the garden in the evening time."

The Lilly of the valley, breathing in the humble grass,
Answer'd the lovely maid and said: "I am a wat'ry weed,
And I am very small and love to dwell in lowly vales;
So weak, the gilded butterfly scarce perches on my head.
Yet I am visited from heaven, and he that smiles on all
Walks in the valley and each morn over me spreads his hand,
Saying, 'Rejoice, thou humble grass, thou new-born lilly flower,
Thou gentle maid of silent valleys and of modest brooks;
For thou shalt be clothed in light, and fed with morning
    manna,
Till summer's heat melts thee beside the fountains and the
    springs
To flourish in eternal vales.' Then why should Thel complain?
Why should the mistress of the vales of Har utter a sigh?"

She ceas'd & smil'd in tears, then sat down in her silver shrine.

Thel answer'd: "O thou little virgin of the peaceful valley,
Giving to those that cannot crave, the voiceless, the o'ertired;
Thy breath doth nourish the innocent lamb, he smells thy milky
    garments,
He crops thy flowers while thou sittest smiling in his face,
Wiping his mild and meekin mouth from all contagious taints.
Thy wine doth purify the golden honey; thy perfume,
Which thou dost scatter on every little blade of grass that
    springs,
Revives the milked cow, & tames the fire-breathing steed.
But Thel is like a faint cloud kindled at the rising sun:
I vanish from my pearly throne, and who shall find my place?"

"Queen of the vales," the Lilly answer'd, "ask the tender cloud,
And it shall tell thee why it glitters in the morning sky,
And why it scatters its bright beauty thro' the humid air.
Descend, O little Cloud, & hover before the eyes of Thel."

The Cloud descended, and the Lilly bow'd her modest head
And went to mind her numerous charge among the verdant
grass.

II

"O little Cloud," the virgin said, "I charge thee tell to me
Why thou complainest not when in one hour thou fade away:
Then we shall seek thee, but not find. Ah! Thel is like to thee:
I pass away: yet I complain, and no one hears my voice."

The Cloud then shew'd his golden head & his bright form
emerg'd,
Hovering and glittering on the air before the face of Thel.

"O virgin, know'st thou not our steeds drink of the golden
springs
Where Luvah doth renew his horses? Look'st thou on my
youth,
And fearest thou, because I vanish and am seen no more,
Nothing remains? O maid, I tell thee, when I pass away
It is to tenfold life, to love, to peace and raptures holy:
Unseen descending, weigh my light wings upon balmy flowers,
And court the fair-eyed dew to take me to her shining tent:
The weeping virgin, trembling kneels before the risen sun,
Till we arise link'd in a golden band and never part,
But walk united, bearing food to all our tender flowers."

"Dost thou, O little Cloud? I fear that I am not like thee,
For I walk thro' the vales of Har, and smell the sweetest
flowers,
But I feed not the little flowers; I hear the warbling birds,
But I feed not the warbling birds; they fly and seek their food:
But Thel delights in these no more, because I fade away;
And all shall say, 'Without a use this shining woman liv'd,
Or did she only live to be at death the food of worms?' "

The Cloud reclin'd upon his airy throne and answer'd thus:

"Then if thou art the food of worms, O virgin of the skies,
How great thy use, how great thy blessing! Every thing that
lives
Lives not alone nor for itself. Fear not, and I will call

The weak worm from its lowly bed, and thou shalt hear its
  voice.
Come forth, worm of the silent valley, to thy pensive queen."

The helpless worm arose, and sat upon the Lilly's leaf,
And the bright Cloud sail'd on, to find his partner in the vale.

III

Then Thel astonish'd view'd the Worm upon its dewy bed.

"Art thou a Worm? Image of weakness, art thou but a Worm?
I see thee like an infant wrapped in the Lilly's leaf.
Ah! weep not, little voice, thou canst not speak, but thou canst
  weep.
Is this a Worm? I see thee lay helpless & naked, weeping,
And none to answer, none to cherish thee with mother's
  smiles."

The Clod of Clay heard the Worm's voice & rais'd her pitying
  head:
She bow'd over the weeping infant, and her life exhal'd
In milky fondness: then on Thel she fix'd her humble eyes.

"O beauty of the vales of Har! we live not for ourselves.
Thou seest me the meanest thing, and so I am indeed.
My bosom of itself is cold, and of itself is dark;
But he, that loves the lowly, pours his oil upon my head,
And kisses me, and binds his nuptial bands around my breast,
And says: 'Thou mother of my children, I have loved thee
And I have given thee a crown that none can take away.'
But how this is, sweet maid, I know not, and I cannot know;
I ponder, and I cannot ponder; yet I live and love."

The daughter of beauty wip'd her pitying tears with her white
  veil,
And said: "Alas! I knew not this, and therefore did I weep.
That God would love a Worm I knew, and punish the evil foot
That wilful bruis'd its helpless form; but that he cherish'd it
With milk and oil I never knew, and therefore did I weep;
And I complain'd in the mild air, because I fade away,
And lay me down in thy cold bed, and leave my shining lot."

"Queen of the vales," the matron Clay answer'd, "I heard thy
    sighs,
And all thy moans flew o'er my roof, but I have call'd them down.
Wilt thou, O Queen, enter my house? 'Tis given thee to enter
And to return: fear nothing, enter with thy virgin feet."

IV

The eternal gates' terrific porter lifted the northern bar:
Thel enter'd in & saw the secrets of the land unknown.
She saw the couches of the dead, & where the fibrous roots
Of every heart on earth infixes deep its restless twists:
A land of sorrows & of tears where never smile was seen.

She wander'd in the land of clouds thro' valleys dark, list'ning
Dolours & lamentations; waiting oft beside a dewy grave
She stood in silence, list'ning to the voices of the ground,
Till to her own grave plot she came, & there she sat down,
And heard this voice of sorrow breathed from the hollow pit.

"Why cannot the Ear be closed to its own destruction?
Or the glist'ning Eye to the poison of a smile?
Why are Eyelids stor'd with arrows ready drawn,
Where a thousand fighting men in ambush lie?
Or an Eye of gifts & graces show'ring fruits & coined gold?
Why a Tongue impress'd with honey from every wind?
Why an Ear, a whirlpool fierce to draw creations in?
Why a Nostril wide inhaling terror, trembling, & affright?
Why a tender curb upon the youthful burning boy?
Why a little curtain of flesh on the bed of our desire?"

The Virgin started from her seat, & with a shriek
Fled back unhinder'd till she came into the vales of Har.

THE END

The French Revolution

A POEM IN SEVEN BOOKS

BOOK THE FIRST

THE dead brood over Europe, the cloud and vision descends over chearful France;

O cloud well appointed! Sick, sick, the Prince on his couch, wreath'd in dim

And appalling mist, his strong hand outstretch'd, from his shoulder down the bone

Runs aching cold into the scepter, too heavy for mortal grasp, no more

To be swayed by visible hand, nor in cruelty bruise the mild flourishing mountains.

Sick the mountains, and all their vineyards weep, in the eyes of the kingly mourner;

Pale is the morning cloud in his visage. Rise, Necker! the ancient dawn calls us

To awake from slumbers of five thousand years. I awake, but my soul is in dreams;

From my window I see the old mountains of France, like aged men, fading away.

Troubled, leaning on Necker, descends the King to his chamber of council; shady mountains

In fear utter voices of thunder; the woods of France embosom the sound;

Clouds of wisdom prophetic reply, and roll over the palace roof heavy.

Forty men, each conversing with woes in the infinite shadows of his soul,

Like our ancient fathers in regions of twilight, walk, gathering round the King;

Again the loud voice of France cries to the morning; the morning prophecies to its clouds.

For the Commons convene in the Hall of the Nation. France
shakes! And the heavens of France
Perplex'd vibrate round each careful countenance! Darkness of
old times around them
Utters loud despair, shadowing Paris; her grey towers groan,
and the Bastile trembles.
In its terrible towers the Governor stood, in dark fogs list'ning
the horror;
A thousand his soldiers, old veterans of France, breathing red
clouds of power and dominion.
Sudden seiz'd with howlings, despair, and black night, he stalk'd
like a lion from tower
To tower; his howlings were heard in the Louvre; from court
to court restless he dragg'd
His strong limbs; from court to court curs'd the fierce torment
unquell'd,
Howling and giving the dark command; in his soul stood the
purple plague,
Tugging his iron manacles, and piercing through the seven
towers dark and sickly,
Panting over the prisoners like a wolf gorg'd; and the den
nam'd Horror held a man
Chain'd hand and foot, round his neck an iron band, bound to
the impregnable wall.
In his soul was the serpent coil'd round in his heart, hid from
the light, as in a cleft rock:
And the man was confin'd for a writing prophetic: in the tower
nam'd Darkness was a man
Pinion'd down to the stone floor, his strong bones scarce
cover'd with sinews; the iron rings
Were forg'd smaller as the flesh decay'd, a mask of iron on his
face hid the lineaments
Of ancient Kings, and the frown of the eternal lion was hid
from the oppressed earth.
In the tower nam'd Bloody, a skeleton yellow remained in its
chains on its couch
Of stone, once a man who refus'd to sign papers of abhorrence;
the eternal worm

Crept in the skeleton. In the den nam'd Religion, a loathsome
    sick woman bound down
To a bed of straw; the seven diseases of earth, like birds of
    prey, stood on the couch
And fed on the body. She refus'd to be whore to the Minister,
    and with a knife smote him.
In the tower nam'd Order, an old man, whose white beard
    cover'd the stone floor like weeds
On margin of the sea, shrivel'd up by heat of day and cold of
    night; his den was short
And narrow as a grave dug for a child, with spider's webs wove,
    and with slime
Of ancient horrors cover'd, for snakes and scorpions are his
    companions; harmless they breathe
His sorrowful breath: he, by conscience urg'd, in the city of
    Paris rais'd a pulpit,
And taught wonders to darken'd souls. In the den nam'd Des-
    tiny a strong man sat,
His feet and hands cut off, and his eyes blinded; round his mid-
    dle a chain and a band
Fasten'd into the wall; fancy gave him to see an image of
    despair in his den,
Eternally rushing round, like a man on his hands and knees,
    day and night without rest:
He was friend to the favourite. In the seventh tower, nam'd the
    tower of God, was a man
Mad, with chains loose, which he dragg'd up and down; fed
    with hopes year by year, he pined
For liberty; vain hopes! his reason decay'd, and the world of
    attraction in his bosom
Center'd, and the rushing of chaos overwhelm'd his dark soul.
    He was confin'd
For a letter of advice to a King, and his ravings in winds are
    heard over Versailles.

But the dens shook and trembled: the prisoners look up and
    assay to shout; they listen,
Then laugh in the dismal den, then are silent, and a light walks
    round the dark towers:
For the Commons convene in the Hall of the Nation, like
    spirits of fire in the beautiful

Porches of the Sun, to plant beauty in the desart craving abyss,
    they gleam
On the anxious city; all children new-born first behold them;
    tears are fled,
And they nestle in earth-breathing bosoms. So the city of Paris,
    their wives and children,
Look up to the morning Senate, and visions of sorrow leave
    pensive streets.

But heavy brow'd jealousies lower o'er the Louvre, and terrors
    of ancient Kings
Descend from the gloom and wander thro' the palace, and
    weep round the King and his Nobles.
While loud thunders roll, troubling the dead, Kings are sick
    throughout all the earth.
The voice ceas'd: the Nation sat: And the triple forg'd fetters
    of times were unloos'd.
The voice ceas'd: the Nation sat: but ancient darkness and
    trembling wander thro' the palace.

As in day of havock and routed battle, among thick shades of
    discontent,
On the soul-skirting mountains of sorrow, cold waving the
    Nobles fold round the King;
Each stern visage lock'd up as with strong bands of iron, each
    strong limb bound down as with marble,
In flames of red wrath burning, bound in astonishment a quar-
    ter of an hour.

Then the King glow'd: his Nobles fold round, like the sun of
    old time quench'd in clouds;
In their darkness the King stood; his heart flam'd, and utter'd
    a with'ring heat, and these words burst forth:

"The nerves of five thousand years' ancestry tremble, shaking
    the heavens of France;
Throbs of anguish beat on brazen war foreheads, they descend
    and look into their graves.
I see thro' darkness, thro' clouds rolling round me, the spirits of
    ancient Kings
Shivering over their bleached bones; round them their counsel-
    lors look up from the dust,

Crying: 'Hide from the living! Our bonds and our prisoners
   shout in the open field,
Hide in the nether earth! Hide in the bones! Sit obscured in
   the hollow scull!
Our flesh is corrupted, and we wear away. We are not numbered among the living. Let us hide
In stones, among roots of trees. The prisoners have burst their
   dens.
Let us hide; let us hide in the dust; and plague and wrath and
   tempest shall cease.' "

He ceas'd, silent pond'ring; his brows folded heavy, his forehead
   was in affliction.
Like the central fire. from the window he saw his vast armies
   spread over the hills,
Breathing red fires from man to man, and from horse to horse:
   then his bosom
Expanded like starry heaven; he sat down: his Nobles took
   their ancient seats.

Then the ancientest Peer, Duke of Burgundy, rose from the
   Monarch's right hand, red as wines
From his mountains; an odor of war, like a ripe vineyard, rose
   from his garments,
And the chamber became as a clouded sky; o'er the council he
   stretch'd his red limbs,
Cloth'd in flames of crimson; as a ripe vineyard stretches over
   sheaves of corn,
The fierce Duke hung over the council; around him croud,
   weeping in his burning robe,
A bright cloud of infant souls; his words fall like purple autumn
   on the sheaves:

"Shall this marble built heaven become a clay cottage, this
   earth an oak stool, and these mowers
From the Atlantic mountains mow down all this great starry
   harvest of six thousand years?
And shall Necker, the hind of Geneva, stretch out his crook'd
   sickle o'er fertile France
Till our purple and crimson is faded to russet, and the kingdoms
   of earth bound in sheaves,

And the ancient forests of chivalry hewn, and the joys of the
　　combat burnt for fuel;
Till the power and dominion is rent from the pole, sword and
　　scepter from sun and moon,
The law and gospel from fire and air, and eternal reason and
　　science
From the deep and the solid, and man lay his faded head down
　　on the rock
Of eternity, where the eternal lion and eagle remain to devour?
This to prevent—urg'd by cries in day, and prophetic dreams
　　hovering in night,
To enrich the lean earth that craves, furrow'd with plows,
　　whose seed is departing from her—
Thy Nobles have gather'd thy starry hosts round this rebellious
　　city,
To rouze up the ancient forests of Europe, with clarions of
　　cloud breathing war,
To hear the horse neigh to the drum and trumpet, and the
　　trumpet and war shout reply.
Stretch the hand that beckons the eagles of heaven; they cry
　　over Paris, and wait
Till Fayette point his finger to Versailles; the eagles of heaven
　　must have their prey!"

He ceas'd and burn'd silent; red clouds roll round Necker; a
　　weeping is heard o'er the palace.
Like a dark cloud Necker paus'd, and like thunder on the just
　　man's burial day he paus'd;
Silent sit the winds, silent the meadows, while the husbandman
　　and woman of weakness
And bright children look after him into the grave, and water his
　　clay with love,
Then turn towards pensive fields; so Necker paus'd, and his vis-
　　age was cover'd with clouds.

The King lean'd on his mountains, then lifted his head and
　　look'd on his armies, that shone
Through heaven, tinging morning with beams of blood; then
　　turning to Burgundy, troubled:
"Burgundy, thou wast born a lion! My soul is o'ergrown with
　　distress

For the Nobles of France, and dark mists roll round me and
    blot the writing of God
Written in my bosom. Necker rise! leave the kingdom, thy life
    is surrounded with snares.
We have call'd an Assembly, but not to destroy; we have given
    gifts, not to the weak;
I hear rushing of muskets, and bright'ning of swords, and vis-
    ages redd'ning with war,
Frowning and looking up from brooding villages and every
    dark'ning city.
Ancient wonders frown over the kingdom, and cries of women
    and babes are heard,
And tempests of doubt roll around me, and fierce sorrows,
    because of the Nobles of France.
Depart! answer not! for the tempest must fall, as in years that
    are passed away."

Dropping a tear the old man his place left, and when he was
    gone out
He set his face toward Geneva to flee; and the women and chil-
    dren of the city
Kneel'd round him and kissed his garments and wept: he stood
    a short space in the street,
Then fled; and the whole city knew he was fled to Geneva, and
    the Senate heard it.

But the Nobles burn'd wrathful at Necker's departure, and
    wreath'd their clouds and waters
In dismal volumes, as, risen from beneath, the Archbishop of
    Paris arose
In the rushing of scales and hissing of flames and rolling of sul-
    phurous smoke:

"Hearken Monarch of France, to the terrors of heaven, and
    let thy soul drink of my counsel!
Sleeping at midnight in my golden tower, the repose of the
    labours of men
Wav'd its solemn cloud over my head. I awoke; a cold hand
    passed over my limbs, and behold
An aged form, white as snow, hov'ring in mist, weeping in the
    uncertain light.

Dim the form almost faded, tears fell down the shady cheeks;
at his feet, many cloth'd

In white robes; strewn in air, censers and harps; silent they lay
prostrated;

Beneath, in the awful void, myriads descending and weeping
thro' dismal winds;

Endless the shady train shiv'ring descended from the gloom
where the aged form wept.

At length, trembling, the vision, sighing in a low voice like the
voice of the grasshopper, whisper'd:

'My groaning is heard in the abbeys, and God, so long wor-
shipp'd, departs as a lamp

Without oil; for a curse is heard hoarse thro' the land from a
godless race

Descending to beasts; they look downward and labour and
forget my holy law;

The sound of prayer fails from lips of flesh. and the holy hymn
from thicken'd tongues;

For the bars of Chaos are burst; her millions prepare their fiery
way

Thro' the orbed abode of the holy dead, to root up and pull
down and remove,

And Nobles and Clergy shall fail from before me, and my
cloud and vision be no more;

The mitre become black, the crown vanish, and the scepter and
ivory staff

Of the ruler wither among bones of death; they shall consume
from the thistly field,

And the sound of the bell, and voice of the sabbath, and singing
of the holy choir

Is turn'd into songs of the harlot in day, and cries of the virgin
in night.

They shall drop at the plow and faint at the harrow, unre-
deem'd, unconfess'd, unpardon'd;

The priest rot in his surplice by the lawless lover, the holy beside the accursed,

The King, frowning in purple, beside the grey plowman, and
their worms embrace together.'

The voice ceas'd: a groan shook my chamber; I slept, for the
cloud of repose returned,

But morning dawn'd heavy upon me. I rose to bring my Prince
heaven utter'd counsel.

Hear my counsel, O King, and send forth thy Generals, the
    command of Heaven is upon thee!
Then do thou command, O King, to shut up this Assembly in
    their final home;
Let thy soldiers possess this city of rebels, that threaten to
    bathe their feet
In the blood of Nobility, trampling the heart and the head; let
    the Bastile devour
These rebellious seditious; seal them up, O Anointed, in ever-
    lasting chains."
He sat down: a damp cold pervaded the Nobles, and monsters
    of worlds unknown
Swam round them, watching to be delivered; When Aumont,
    whose chaos-born soul
Eternally wand'ring a Comet and swift-falling fire, pale enter'd
    the chamber.
Before the red Council he stood, like a man that returns from
    hollow graves:

"Awe-surrounded, alone thro' the army, a fear and a with'ring
    blight blown by the north,
The Abbé de Sieyes from the Nation's Assembly, O Princes and
    Generals of France,
Unquestioned, unhindered! awe-struck are the soldiers; a dark
    shadowy man in the form
Of King Henry the Fourth walks before him in fires; the cap-
    tains like men bound in chains
Stood still as he pass'd: he is come to the Louvre, O King, with
    a message to thee!
The strong soldiers tremble, the horses their manes bow, and
    the guards of thy palace are fled!"

Up rose awful in his majestic beams Bourbon's strong Duke;
    his proud sword from his thigh
Drawn, he threw on the Earth! the Duke of Bretagne and the
    Earl of Bourgogne
Rose inflam'd, to and fro in the chamber, like thunderclouds
    ready to burst.
"What! damp all our fires, O spectre of Henry?" said Bourbon,
    "and rend the flames
From the head of our King? Rise, Monarch of France! com-
    mand me, and I will lead

This army of superstition at large, that the ardor of noble souls, quenchless,

May yet burn in France, nor our shoulders be plow'd with the furrows of poverty."

Then Orleans, generous as mountains, arose and unfolded his robe, and put forth

His benevolent hand, looking on the Archbishop who, changed as pale as lead,

Would have risen but could not: his voice issued harsh grating; instead of words harsh hissings

Shook the chamber; he ceas'd abash'd. Then Orleans spoke; all was silent.

He breath'd on them, and said: "O princes of fire, whose flames are for growth, not consuming,

Fear not dreams, fear not visions, nor be you dismay'd with sorrows which flee at the morning!

Can the fires of Nobility ever be quench'd, or the stars by a stormy night?

Is the body diseas'd when the members are healthful? can the man be bound in sorrow

Whose ev'ry function is fill'd with its fiery desire? can the soul whose brain and heart

Cast their rivers in equal tides thro' the great Paradise, languish because the feet,

Hands, head, bosom, and parts of love follow their high breathing joy?

And can Nobles be bound when the people are free, or God weep when his children are happy?

Have you never seen Fayette's forehead, or Mirabeau's eyes, or the shoulders of Target,

Or Bailly the strong foot of France, or Clermont the terrible voice? and your robes

Still retain their own crimson: mine never yet faded, for fire delights in its form.

But go! merciless man! enter into the infinite labyrinth of another's brain

Ere thou measure the circle that he shall run. Go, thou cold recluse, into the fires

Of another's high flaming rich bosom, and return unconsum'd, and write laws.

If thou canst not do this, doubt thy theories; learn to consider
    all men as thy equals,
Thy brethren, and not as thy foot or thy hand, unless thou first
    fearest to hurt them."

The Monarch stood up; the strong Duke his sword to its golden
    scabbard return'd;
The Nobles sat round like clouds on the mountains, when the
    storm is passing away:
"Let the Nation's Ambassador come among Nobles, like incense
    of the valley!"

Aumont went out and stood in the hollow porch, his ivory
    wand in his hand;
A cold orb of disdain revolv'd round him, and covered his soul
    with snows eternal.
Great Henry's soul shuddered, a whirlwind and fire tore furious
    from his angry bosom;
He indignant departed on horses of heav'n. Then the Abbé de
    Sieyes rais'd his feet
On the steps of the Louvre; like a voice of God following a
    storm, the Abbé follow'd
The pale fires of Aumont into the chamber; as a father that
    bows to his son,
Whose rich fields inheriting spread their old glory, so the voice
    of the people bowed
Before the ancient seat of the kingdom and mountains to be
    renewed.

"Hear, O Heavens of France, the voice of the people arising
    from valley and hill,
O'erclouded with power. Hear the voice of vallies, the voice of
    meek cities,
Mourning oppressed on village and field, till the village and field
    is a waste.
For the husbandman weeps at blights of the fife, and blasting
    of trumpets consume
The souls of mild France; the pale mother nourishes her child
    to the deadly slaughter.
When the heavens were seal'd with a stone, and the terrible
    sun clos'd in an orb, and the moon

Rent from the nations, and each star appointed for watchers of night,

The millions of spirits immortal were bound in the ruins of sulphur, heaven

To wander enslav'd; black, deprest in dark ignorance, kept in awe with the whip

To worship terrors, bred from the blood of revenge and breath of desire

In beastial forms, or more terrible men; till the dawn of our peaceful morning,

Till dawn, till morning, till the breaking of clouds, and swelling of winds, and the universal voice;

Till man raise his darken'd limbs out of the caves of night: his eyes and his heart

Expand: where is Space? where, O Sun, is thy dwelling? where thy tent, O faint slumb'rous Moon?

Then the valleys of France shall cry to the soldier: 'Throw down thy sword and musket,

And run and embrace the meek peasant.' Her Nobles shall hear and shall weep, and put off

The red robe of terror, the crown of oppression, the shoes of contempt, and unbuckle

The girdle of war from the desolate earth; then the Priest in his thund'rous cloud

Shall weep, bending to earth, embracing the valleys, and putting his hand to the plow,

Shall say: 'No more I curse thee; but now I will bless thee: No more in deadly black

Devour thy labour; nor lift up a cloud in thy heavens, O laborious plow,

That the wild raging millions, that wander in forests, and howl in law blasted wastes,

Strength madden'd with slavery, honesty bound in the dens of superstition,

May sing in the village, and shout in the harvest, and woo in pleasant gardens

Their once savage loves, now beaming with knowledge, with gentle awe adorned;

And the saw, and the hammer, the chisel, the pencil, the pen, and the instruments

Of heavenly song sound in the wilds once forbidden, to teach the laborious plowman

And shepherd, deliver'd from clouds of war, from pestilence,
    from night-fear, from murder,
From falling, from stifling, from hunger, from cold, from slan-
    der, discontent and sloth,
That walk in beasts and birds of night, driven back by the sandy
    desart,
Like pestilent fogs round cities of men; and the happy earth
    sing in its course,
The mild peaceable nations be opened to heav'n, and men walk
    with their fathers in bliss.'
Then hear the first voice of the morning: 'Depart, O clouds of
    night, and no more
Return; be withdrawn cloudy war, troops of warriors depart,
    nor around our peaceable city
Breathe fires; but ten miles from Paris let all be peace, nor a
    soldier be seen!' "

He ended: the wind of contention arose, and the clouds cast
    their shadows; the Princes,
Like the mountains of France, whose aged trees utter an awful
    voice, and their branches
Are shatter'd, till gradual a murmur is heard descending into
    the valley,
Like a voice in the vineyards of Burgundy when grapes are
    shaken on grass,
Like the low voice of the labouring man, instead of the shout of
    joy;
And the palace appear'd like a cloud driven abroad; blood ran
    down the ancient pillars.
Thro' the cloud a deep thunder, the Duke of Burgundy, delivers
    the King's command:

"Seest thou yonder dark castle, that moated around, keeps this
    city of Paris in awe?
Go command yonder tower, saying: 'Bastile, depart! and take
    thy shadowy course;
Overstep the dark river, thou terrible tower, and get thee up
    into the country ten miles.
And thou black southern prison, move along the dusky road to
    Versailles; there
Frown on the gardens'; and if it obey and depart, then the King
    will disband

This war-breathing army; but if it refuse, let the Nation's
  Assembly thence learn
That this army of terrors, that prison of horrors, are the bands
  of the murmuring kingdom."

Like the morning star arising above the black waves, when a
  shipwreck'd soul sighs for morning,
Thro' the ranks, silent, walk'd the Ambassador back to the
  Nation's Assembly, and told
The unwelcome message; silent they heard; then a thunder
  roll'd round loud and louder;
Like pillars of ancient halls and ruins of times remote, they sat.
Like a voice from the dim pillars Mirabeau rose; the thun-
  ders subsided away;
A rushing of wings around him was heard as he brighten'd,
  and cried out aloud:
"Where is the General of the Nation?" The walls re-echo'd:
  "Where is the General of the Nation?"

Sudden as the bullet wrapp'd in his fire, when brazen cannons
  rage in the field,
Fayette sprung from his seat saying "Ready!" Then bowing like
  clouds, man toward man, the Assembly
Like a council of ardors seated in clouds, bending over the cities
  of men,
And over the armies of strife, where their children are marshall'd together to battle,
They murmuring divide; while the wind sleeps beneath, and
  the numbers are counted in silence,
While they vote the removal of War, and the pestilence weighs
  his red wings in the sky.

So Fayette stood silent among the Assembly, and the votes were
  given, and the numbers numb'red;
And the vote was that Fayette should order the army to remove ten miles from Paris.

The aged sun rises appall'd from dark mountains, and gleams
  a dusky beam
On Fayette; but on the whole army a shadow, for a cloud on
  the eastern hills

Hover'd, and stretch'd across the city, and across the army,
and across the Louvre.
Like a flame of fire he stood before dark ranks, and before expecting captains:
On pestilent vapours around him flow frequent spectres of
religious men, weeping
In winds; driven out of the abbeys, their naked souls shiver in
keen open air;
Driven out by the fiery cloud of Voltaire, and thund'rous rocks
of Rousseau,
They dash like foam against the ridges of the army, uttering a
faint feeble cry.

Gleams of fire streak the heavens, and of sulphur the earth,
from Fayette as he lifted his hand;
But silent he stood, till all the officers rush round him like
waves
Round the shore of France, in day of the British flag, when
heavy cannons
Affright the coasts, and the peasant looks over the sea and
wipes a tear;
Over his head the soul of Voltaire shone fiery; and over the
army Rousseau his white cloud
Unfolded, on souls of war, living terrors, silent list'ning toward
Fayette.
His voice loud inspir'd by liberty, and by spirits of the dead,
thus thunder'd:

"The Nation's Assembly command that the Army remove ten
miles from Paris;
Nor a soldier be seen in road or in field, till the Nation command return."

Rushing along iron ranks glittering, the officers each to his
station
Depart, and the stern captain strokes his proud steed, and in
front of his solid ranks
Waits the sound of trumpet; captains of foot stand each by his
cloudy drum:
Then the drum beats, and the steely ranks move, and trumpets
rejoice in the sky.

Dark cavalry, like clouds fraught with thunder, ascend on the hills, and bright infantry, rank
Behind rank, to the soul shaking drum and shrill fife, along the roads glitter like fire.

The noise of trampling, the wind of trumpets, smote the palace walls with a blast,
Pale and cold sat the King in midst of his peers, and his noble heart sunk, and his pulses
Suspended their motion; a darkness crept over his eyelids, and chill cold sweat
Sat round his brows faded in faint death; his peers pale, like mountains of the dead
Cover'd with dews of night, groaning, shaking forests and floods. The cold newt,
And snake, and damp toad on the kingly foot crawl, or croak on the awful knee,
Shedding their slime; in folds of the robe the crown'd adder builds and hisses
From stony brows; shaken the forests of France, sick the kings of the nations,
And the bottoms of the world were open'd, and the graves of arch-angels unseal'd:
The enormous dead lift up their pale fires and look over the rocky cliffs.

A faint heat from their fires reviv'd the cold Louvre; the frozen blood reflow'd.
Awful up rose the king; him the peers follow'd; they saw the courts of the Palace
Forsaken, and Paris without a soldier, silent; for the noise was gone up
And follow'd the army, and the Senate in peace sat beneath morning's beam.

END OF THE FIRST BOOK

The Marriage of Heaven and Hell

THE ARGUMENT

RINTRAH roars & shakes his fires in the burden'd air;
Hungry clouds swag on the deep.

Once meek, and in a perilous path,
The just man kept his course along
The vale of death.
Roses are planted where thorns grow,
And on the barren heath
Sing the honey bees.

Then the perilous path was planted,
And a river and a spring
On every cliff and tomb,
And on the bleached bones
Red clay brought forth;

Till the villain left the paths of ease,
To walk in perilous paths, and drive
The just man into barren climes.

Now the sneaking serpent walks
In mild humility,
And the just man rages in the wilds
Where lions roam.

Rintrah roars & shakes his fires in the burden'd air;
Hungry clouds swag on the deep.

❌

AS a new heaven is begun, and it is now thirty-three years since its advent, the Eternal Hell revives. And lo! Swedenborg is the Angel sitting at the tomb: his writings are the linen clothes folded up. Now is the dominion of Edom, & the return of Adam into Paradise. See Isaiah xxxiv & xxxv Chap.

Without Contraries is no progression. Attraction and Repulsion, Reason and Energy, Love and Hate, are necessary to Human existence.

From these contraries spring what the religious call Good & Evil. Good is the passive that obeys Reason. Evil is the active springing from Energy.

Good is Heaven. Evil is Hell.

THE VOICE OF THE DEVIL

ALL Bibles or sacred codes have been the causes of the following Errors:

1. That Man has two real existing principles: Viz: a Body & a Soul.

2. That Energy, call'd Evil, is alone from the Body; & that Reason, call'd Good, is alone from the Soul.

3. That God will torment Man in Eternity for following his Energies.

But the following Contraries to these are True:

1. Man has no Body distinct from his Soul; for that call'd Body is a portion of Soul discern'd by the five Senses, the chief inlets of Soul in this age.

2. Energy is the only life, and is from the Body; and Reason is the bound or outward circumference of Energy.

3. Energy is Eternal Delight.

❌

THOSE who restrain desire, do so because theirs is weak enough to be restrained; and the restrainer or reason usurps its place & governs the unwilling.

And being restrain'd, it by degrees becomes passive, till it is only the shadow of desire.

The history of this is written in Paradise Lost, & the Governor or Reason is call'd Messiah.

And the original Archangel, or possessor of the command of the heavenly host, is call'd the Devil or Satan, and his children are call'd Sin & Death.

But in the Book of Job, Milton's Messiah is call'd Satan.

For this history has been adopted by both parties.

It indeed appear'd to Reason as if Desire was cast out; but the Devil's account is, that the Messiah fell, & formed a heaven of what he stole from the Abyss.

This is shewn in the Gospel, where he prays to the Father to send the comforter, or Desire, that Reason may have Ideas to build on; the Jehovah of the Bible being no other than he who dwells in flaming fire.

Know that after Christ's death, he became Jehovah.

But in Milton, the Father is Destiny, the Son a Ratio of the five senses, & the Holy-ghost Vacuum!

Note: The reason Milton wrote in fetters when he wrote of Angels & God, and at liberty when of Devils & Hell, is because he was a true Poet and of the Devil's party without knowing it.

A MEMORABLE FANCY

AS I was walking among the fires of hell, delighted with the enjoyments of Genius, which to Angels look like torment and insanity, I collected some of their Proverbs; thinking that as the sayings used in a nation mark its character, so the Proverbs of Hell show the nature of Infernal wisdom better than any description of buildings or garments.

When I came home: on the abyss of the five senses, where a flat sided steep frowns over the present world, I saw a mighty Devil folded in black clouds, hovering on the sides of the rock: with corroding fires he wrote the following sentence now percieved by the minds of men, & read by them on earth:

How do you know but ev'ry Bird that cuts the airy way,
Is an immense world of delight, clos'd by your senses five?

PROVERBS OF HELL

IN seed time learn, in harvest teach, in winter enjoy.

Drive your cart and your plow over the bones of the dead.

The road of excess leads to the palace of wisdom.

Prudence is a rich, ugly old maid courted by Incapacity.

He who desires but acts not, breeds pestilence.

The cut worm forgives the plow.

Dip him in the river who loves water.

A fool sees not the same tree that a wise man sees.

He whose face gives no light, shall never become a star.

Eternity is in love with the productions of time.

The busy bee has no time for sorrow.

The hours of folly are measur'd by the clock; but of wisdom, no clock can measure.

All wholesome food is caught without a net or a trap.

Bring out number, weight & measure in a year of dearth.

No bird soars too high, if he soars with his own wings.

A dead body revenges not injuries.

The most sublime act is to set another before you.

If the fool would persist in his folly he would become wise.

Folly is the cloke of knavery.

Shame is Pride's cloke.

Prisons are built with stones of Law, Brothels with bricks of Religion.

The pride of the peacock is the glory of God.

The lust of the goat is the bounty of God.

The wrath of the lion is the wisdom of God.

The nakedness of woman is the work of God.

Excess of sorrow laughs. Excess of joy weeps.

The roaring of lions, the howling of wolves, the raging of the stormy sea, and the destructive sword, are portions of eternity, too great for the eye of man.

The fox condemns the trap, not himself.

Joys impregnate. Sorrows bring forth.

Let man wear the fell of the lion, woman the fleece of the sheep.

The bird a nest, the spider a web, man friendship.

The selfish, smiling fool, & the sullen, frowning fool shall be both thought wise, that they may be a rod.

What is now proved was once only imagin'd.

The rat, the mouse, the fox, the rabbet watch the roots; the lion, the tyger, the horse, the elephant watch the fruits.

The cistern contains: the fountain overflows.

One thought fills immensity.

Always be ready to speak your mind, and a base man will avoid you.

Every thing possible to be believ'd is an image of truth.

The eagle never lost so much time as when he submitted to learn of the crow.

The fox provides for himself, but God provides for the lion.

Think in the morning. Act in the noon. Eat in the evening. Sleep in the night.

He who has suffer'd you to impose on him, knows you.

As the plow follows words, so God rewards prayers.

The tygers of wrath are wiser than the horses of instruction.

Expect poison from the standing water.

You never know what is enough unless you know what is more than enough.

Listen to the fool's reproach! it is a kingly title!

The eyes of fire, the nostrils of air, the mouth of water, the beard of earth.

The weak in courage is strong in cunning.

The apple tree never asks the beech how he shall grow; nor the lion, the horse, how he shall take his prey.

The thankful reciever bears a plentiful harvest.

If others had not been foolish, we should be so.

The soul of sweet delight can never be defil'd.

When thou seest an Eagle, thou seest a portion of Genius; lift up thy head!

As the caterpiller chooses the fairest leaves to lay her eggs on, so the priest lays his curse on the fairest joys.

To create a little flower is the labour of ages.

Damn braces. Bless relaxes.

The best wine is the oldest, the best water the newest.

Prayers plow not! Praises reap not!

Joys laugh not! Sorrows weep not!

The head Sublime, the heart Pathos, the genitals Beauty, the hands & feet Proportion.

As the air to a bird or the sea to a fish, so is contempt to the contemptible.

Songs of Innocence: "Infant Joy"

The First Book of Urizen: Title Page

The School Boy

I love to rise in a summer morn,
When the birds sing on every tree;
The distant huntsman winds his horn,
And the sky-lark sings with me.
O! what sweet company.

But to go to school in a summer morn
O! it drives all joy away;
Under a cruel eye outworn.
The little ones spend the day.
In sighing and dismay.

Ah! then at times I drooping sit,
And spend many an anxious hour,
Nor in my book can I take delight,
Nor sit in learnings bower
Worn thro' with the dreary shower.

How can the bird that is born for joy,
Sit in a cage and sing.
How can a child when fears annoy,
But droop his tender wing.
And forget his youthful spring.

O! father & mother, if buds are nip'd,
And blossoms blown away.
And if the tender plants are strip'd
Of their joy in the springing day,
By sorrow and cares dismay.

How shall the summer arise in joy,
Or the summer fruits appear.
Or how shall we gather what griefs destroy
Or bless the mellowing year.
When the blasts of winter appear.

Songs of Experience: "The School Boy"

...se, not from rules.

When he had so spoken: I beheld the Angel who stretched out his arms embracing the flame of fire & he was consumed and arose as Elijah.

Note. This Angel, who is now become a Devil, is my particular friend: we often read the Bible together in its infernal or diabolical sense which the world shall have if they behave well.

I have also: The Bible of Hell: which the world shall have whether they will or no.

One Law for the Lion & Ox is Oppression

The Marriage of Heaven and Hell: Plate 24

America: Plate 7

Jerusalem: Plate 25

But Los, who is the Vehicular Form of strong Urthona
Wept vehemently over Albion where Thames currents spring
From the rivers of Beulah; pleasant river! soft, mild, parent stream
And the roots of Albions Tree enterd the Soul of Los
As he sat before his Furnaces clothed in sackcloth of hair
In gnawing pain dividing him from his Emanation;
Inclosing all the Children of Los time after time.
Their lovely limbs condensing into Nations & Peoples & Tongues
Translucent the Furnaces of Beryll & Emerald immortal:
And Seven-fold each within other; incomprehensible
To the Vegetated Mortal Eye's perverted & single vision
The Bellows are the Animal Lungs: the Hammers the Animal Heart
The Furnaces, the Stomach for Digestion: terrible their fury
Like seven burning heavens range'd from South to North

Here on the banks of the Thames, Los builded Golgonooza,
Outside of the Gates of the Human Heart, beneath Beulah
In the midst of the rocks of the Altars of Albion. In fears
He builded it, in rage & in fury. It is the Spiritual Fourfold
London: continually building & continually decaying desolate:
In eternal labours: loud the Furnaces & loud the Anvils
Of Death thunder incessant around the flaming Couches of
The Twentyfour Friends of Albion, and round the awful Four
For the protection of the Twelve Emanations of Albions Sons
The Mystic Union of the Emanation in the Lord; Because
Man divided from his Emanation is a dark Spectre
His Emanation is an ever-weeping melancholy Shadow
But she is made receptive of Generation thro' mercy
In the Potters Furnace, among the Funeral Urns of Beulah
From Surrey hills, thro' Italy and Greece, to Hinnoms vale.

Jerusalem: Plate 53

Jerusalem: **Plate 70**

The crow wish'd every thing was black, the owl that every thing was white.

Exuberance is Beauty.

If the lion was advised by the fox, he would be cunning.

Improvement makes strait roads; but the crooked roads without Improvement are roads of Genius.

Sooner murder an infant in its cradle than nurse unacted desires.

Where man is not, nature is barren.

Truth can never be told so as to be understood, and not be believ'd.

Enough! or Too much.

⚒

THE ancient Poets animated all sensible objects with Gods or Geniuses, calling them by the names and adorning them with the properties of woods, rivers, mountains, lakes, cities, nations, and whatever their enlarged & numerous senses could percieve.

And particularly they studied the genius of each city & country, placing it under its mental deity;

Till a system was formed, which some took advantage of, & enslav'd the vulgar by attempting to realize or abstract the mental deities from their objects: thus began Priesthood;

Choosing forms of worship from poetic tales.

And at length they pronounc'd that the Gods had order'd such things.

Thus men forgot that All deities reside in the human breast.

A MEMORABLE FANCY

THE Prophets Isaiah and Ezekiel dined with me, and I asked them how they dared so roundly to assert that God spoke to them; and whether they did not think at the time that they would be misunderstood, & so be the cause of imposition.

Isaiah answer'd: "I saw no God, nor heard any, in a finite organical perception; but my senses discover'd the infinite in everything, and as I was then perswaded, & remain confirm'd, that the voice of honest indignation is the voice of God, I cared not for consequences, but wrote."

Then I asked: "does a firm perswasion that a thing is so, make it so?"

He replied: "All poets believe that it does, & in ages of imagination this firm perswasion removed mountains; but many are not capable of a firm perswasion of any thing."

Then Ezekiel said: "The philosophy of the east taught the first principles of human perception: some nations held one principle for the origin, and some another: we of Israel taught that the Poetic Genius (as you now call it) was the first principle and all the others merely derivative, which was the cause of our despising the Priests & Philosophers of other countries, and prophecying that all Gods would at last be proved to originate in ours & to be the tributaries of the Poetic Genius; it was this that our great poet, King David, desired so fervently & invokes so pathetic'ly, saying by this he conquers enemies & governs kingdoms; and we so loved our God, that we cursed in his name all the deities of surrounding nations, and asserted that they had rebelled: from these opinions the vulgar came to think that all nations would at last be subject to the jews."

"This," said he, "like all firm perswasions, is come to pass; for all nations believe the jews' code and worship the jews' god, and what greater subjection can be?"

I heard this with some wonder, & must confess my own conviction. After dinner I ask'd Isaiah to favour the world with his lost works; he said none of equal value was lost. Ezekiel said the same of his.

I also asked Isaiah what made him go naked and barefoot three years? he answer'd: "the same that made our friend Diogenes, the Grecian."

I then asked Ezekiel why he eat dung, & lay so long on his right & left side? he answer'd, "the desire of raising other men into a perception of the infinite: this the North American tribes practise, & is he honest who resists his genius or conscience only for the sake of present ease or gratification?"

※

THE ancient tradition that the world will be consumed in fire at the end of six thousand years is true, as I have heard from Hell.

For the cherub with his flaming sword is hereby commanded to leave his guard at tree of life; and when he does, the whole creation will be consumed and appear infinite and holy, whereas it now appears finite & corrupt.

This will come to pass by an improvement of sensual enjoyment.

But first the notion that man has a body distinct from his soul is to be expunged; this I shall do by printing in the infernal method, by corrosives, which in Hell are salutary and medicinal, melting apparent surfaces away, and displaying the infinite which was hid.

If the doors of perception were cleansed every thing would appear to man as it is, infinite.

For man has closed himself up, till he sees all things thro' narrow chinks of his cavern.

A MEMORABLE FANCY

I WAS in a Printing house in Hell, & saw the method in which knowledge is transmitted from generation to generation.

In the first chamber was a Dragon-Man, clearing away the rubbish from a cave's mouth; within, a number of Dragons were hollowing the cave.

In the second chamber was a Viper folding round the rock & the cave, and others adorning it with gold, silver and precious stones.

In the third chamber was an Eagle with wings and feathers of air: he caused the inside of the cave to be infinite; around were numbers of Eagle-like men who built palaces in the immense cliffs.

In the fourth chamber were Lions of flaming fire, raging around & melting the metals into living fluids.

In the fifth chamber were Unnam'd forms, which cast the metals into the expanse.

There they were reciev'd by Men who occupied the sixth chamber, and took the forms of books & were arranged in libraries.

※

THE Giants who formed this world into its sensual existence, and now seem to live in it in chains, are in truth the causes of its life & the sources of all activity; but the chains are the cunning of weak and tame minds which have power to resist energy; according to the proverb, the weak in courage is strong in cunning.

Thus one portion of being is the Prolific, the other the Devouring: to the Devourer it seems as if the producer was in his chains; but it is not so, he only takes portions of existence and fancies that the whole.

But the Prolific would cease to be Prolific unless the Devourer, as a sea, received the excess of his delights.

Some will say: "Is not God alone the Prolific?" I answer: "God only Acts & Is, in existing beings or Men."

These two classes of men are always upon earth, & they should be enemies: whoever tries to reconcile them seeks to destroy existence.

Religion is an endeavour to reconcile the two.

Note: Jesus Christ did not wish to unite, but to separate them, as in the Parable of sheep and goats! & he says: "I came not to send Peace, but a Sword."

Messiah or Satan or Tempter was formerly thought to be one of the Antediluvians who are our Energies.

A MEMORABLE FANCY

AN Angel came to me and said: "O pitiable foolish young man! O horrible! O dreadful state! consider the hot burning dungeon thou art preparing for thyself to all eternity, to which thou art going in such career."

I said: "Perhaps you will be willing to shew me my eternal lot, & we will contemplate together upon it, and see whether your lot or mine is most desirable."

So he took me thro' a stable & thro' a church & down into the church vault, at the end of which was a mill: thro' the mill we went, and came to a cave: down the winding cavern we groped our tedious way, till a void boundless as a nether sky appear'd beneath us, & we held by the roots of trees and hung over this immensity; but I said: "if you please, we will commit ourselves to this void, and see whether providence is here also: if you will not, I will:" but he answer'd: "do not presume, O young man, but as we here remain, behold thy lot which will soon appear when the darkness passes away."

So I remain'd with him, sitting in the twisted root of an oak; he was suspended in a fungus, which hung with the head downward into the deep.

By degrees we beheld the infinite Abyss, fiery as the smoke of a burning city; beneath us, at an immense distance, was the sun, black but shining; round it were fiery tracks on which revolv'd vast spiders, crawling after their prey, which flew, or rather swum, in the infinite deep, in the most terrific shapes of animals sprung from corruption; & the air was full of them, & seem'd composed of them: these are Devils, and are called Powers of the air. I now asked my companion which was my eternal lot? he said: "between the black & white spiders."

But now, from between the black & white spiders, a cloud and fire burst and rolled thro' the deep, black'ning all beneath, so that the nether deep grew black as a sea, & rolled with a terrible noise; beneath us was nothing now to be seen but a black tempest, till looking east between the clouds & the waves, we saw a cataract of blood mixed with fire, and not many stones' throw from us appear'd and sunk again the scaly fold of a monstrous serpent; at last, to the east, distant about three degrees, appear'd a fiery crest above the waves; slowly it reared like a ridge of golden rocks, till we discover'd two globes of crimson fire, from which the sea fled away in clouds of smoke; and now we saw it was the head of Leviathan; his forehead was divided into streaks of green & purple like those on a tyger's forehead: soon we saw his mouth & red gills hang just above the raging foam, tinging the black deep with beams of blood, advancing toward us with all the fury of a spiritual existence.

My friend the Angel climb'd up from his station into the mill: I remain'd alone; & then this appearance was no more, but I found myself sitting on a pleasant bank beside a river by moonlight, hearing a harper, who sung to the harp; & his theme was: "The man who never alters his opinion is like standing water, & breeds reptiles of the mind."

But I arose and sought for the mill, & there I found my Angel, who, surprised, asked me how I escaped?

I answer'd: "All that we saw was owing to your metaphysics; for when you ran away, I found myself on a bank by moonlight hearing a harper. But now we have seen my eternal lot, shall I shew you yours?" he laugh'd at my proposal; but I by force suddenly caught him in my arms, & flew westerly thro' the night, till we were elevated above the earth's shadow; then I flung myself with him directly into the body of the sun; here I clothed myself in white, & taking in my hand Swedenborg's volumes, sunk from the glorious clime, and passed all the planets till we came to saturn: here I stay'd to rest, & then leap'd into the void between saturn & the fixed stars.

"Here," said I, "is your lot, in this space—if space it may be call'd." Soon we saw the stable and the church, & I took him to the altar and open'd the Bible, and lo! it was a deep pit, into which I descended, driving the Angel before me; soon we saw seven houses of brick; one we enter'd; in it were a number of monkeys, baboons, & all of that species, chain'd by the middle, grinning and snatching at one another, but withheld by the shortness of their chains: however, I saw that they sometimes grew numerous, and then the weak were caught by the strong, and with a grinning aspect, first coupled with, & then devour'd, by plucking off first one limb and then another, till the body was left a helpless trunk; this, after grinning & kissing it with seeming fondness, they devour'd too; and here & there I saw one savourily picking the flesh off his own tail; as the stench terribly annoy'd us both, we went into the mill, & I in my hand brought the skeleton of a body, which in the mill was Aristotle's Analytics.

So the Angel said: "thy phantasy has imposed upon me, & thou oughtest to be ashamed."

I answer'd: "we impose on one another, & it is but lost time to converse with you whose works are only Analytics."

                                            ✠

OPPOSITION is true Friendship. [*Blake may have intended to obliterate this sentence in his manuscript.*]

                                            ✠

I HAVE always found that Angels have the vanity to speak of themselves as the only wise; this they do with a confident insolence sprouting from systematic reasoning.

Thus Swedenborg boasts that what he writes is new: tho' it is only the Contents or Index of already publish'd books.

A man carried a monkey about for a shew, & because he

was a little wiser than the monkey, grew vain, and conciev'd himself as much wiser than seven men. It is so with Swedenborg: he shews the folly of churches, & exposes hypocrites, till he imagines that all are religious, & himself the single one on earth that ever broke a net.

Now hear a plain fact: Swedenborg has not written one new truth. Now hear another: he has written all the old falsehoods.

And now hear the reason. He conversed with Angels who are all religious, & conversed not with Devils who all hate religion, for he was incapable thro' his conceited notions.

Thus Swedenborg's writings are a recapitulation of all superficial opinions, and an analysis of the more sublime—but no further.

Have now another plain fact. Any man of mechanical talents may, from the writings of Paracelsus or Jacob Behmen, produce ten thousand volumes of equal value with Swedenborg's, and from those of Dante or Shakespear an infinite number.

But when he has done this, let him not say that he knows better than his master, for he only holds a candle in sunshine.

A MEMORABLE FANCY

ONCE I saw a Devil in a flame of fire, who arose before an Angel that sat on a cloud, and the Devil utter'd these words:

"The worship of God is: Honouring his gifts in other men, each according to his genius, and loving the greatest men best: those who envy or calumniate great men hate God; for there is no other God."

The Angel hearing this became almost blue; but mastering himself he grew yellow, & at last white, pink, & smiling, and then replied:

"Thou Idolater! is not God One? & is not he visible in Jesus Christ? and has not Jesus Christ given his sanction to the law of ten commandments? and are not all other men fools, sinners, & nothings?"

The Devil answer'd: "bray a fool in a morter with wheat, yet shall not his folly be beaten out of him; if Jesus Christ is the greatest man, you ought to love him in the greatest degree; now hear how he has given his sanction to the law of ten commandments: did he not mock at the sabbath and so mock the sabbath's God? murder those who were murder'd because of him? turn away the law from the woman taken in adultery? steal the labor of others to support him? bear false witness when he omitted making a defence before Pilate? covet when he pray'd for his disciples, and when he bid them shake off the dust of their feet against such as refused to lodge them? I tell you, no virtue can exist without breaking these ten commandments. Jesus was all virtue, and acted from impulse, not from rules."

When he had so spoken, I beheld the Angel, who stretched out his arms, embracing the flame of fire, & he was consumed and arose as Elijah.

Note: This Angel, who is now become a Devil, is my particular friend; we often read the Bible together in its infernal or diabolical sense, which the world shall have if they behave well.

I have also The Bible of Hell, which the world shall have whether they will or no.

⛧

ONE Law for the Lion & Ox is Oppression.

A SONG OF LIBERTY

1

THE Eternal Female groan'd! it was heard over all the Earth.
2. Albion's coast is sick, silent; the American meadows faint!
3. Shadows of Prophecy shiver along by the lakes and the rivers, and mutter across the ocean: France, rend down thy dungeon!
4. Golden Spain, burst the barriers of old Rome!
5. Cast thy keys, O Rome, into the deep down falling, even to eternity down falling,
6. And weep.
7. In her trembling hand she took the new born terror, howling.
8. On those infinite mountains of light, now barr'd out by the atlantic sea, the new born fire stood before the starry king!
9. Flag'd with grey brow'd snows and thunderous visages, the jealous wings wav'd over the deep.

10. The speary hand burned aloft, unbuckled was the shield; forth went the hand of jealousy among the flaming hair, and hurl'd the new born wonder thro' the starry night.

11. The fire, the fire is falling!

12. Look up! look up! O citizen of London, enlarge thy countenance! O Jew, leave counting gold! return to thy oil and wine. O African! black African! (go, winged thought, widen his forehead.)

13. The fiery limbs, the flaming hair, shot like the sinking sun into the western sea.

14. Wak'd from his eternal sleep, the hoary element roaring fled away.

15. Down rush'd, beating his wings in vain, the jealous king; his grey brow'd councellors, thunderous warriors, curl'd veterans, among helms, and shields, and chariots, horses, elephants, banners, castles, slings, and rocks.

16. Falling, rushing, ruining! buried in the ruins, on Urthona's dens;

17. All night beneath the ruins; then, their sullen flames faded, emerge round the gloomy king.

18. With thunder and fire, leading his starry hosts thro' the waste wilderness, he promulgates his ten commands, glancing his beamy eyelids over the deep in dark dismay,

19. Where the son of fire in his eastern cloud, while the morning plumes her golden breast,

20. Spurning the clouds written with curses, stamps the stony law to dust, loosing the eternal horses from the dens of night, crying:

EMPIRE IS NO MORE! AND NOW THE LION
& WOLF SHALL CEASE.

CHORUS

Let the Priests of the Raven of dawn no longer, in deadly black, with hoarse note curse the sons of joy. Nor his accepted brethren—whom, tyrant, he calls free—lay the bound or build the roof. Nor pale religious letchery call that virginity that wishes but acts not!

For every thing that lives is Holy.

Visions of the Daughters of Albion

The Eye sees more than the Heart knows

THE ARGUMENT

I LOVED Theotormon,
And I was not ashamed;
I trembled in my virgin fears,
And I hid in Leutha's vale!

I plucked Leutha's flower,
And I rose up from the vale;
But the terrible thunders tore
My virgin mantle in twain.

VISIONS

ENSLAV'D, the Daughters of Albion weep; a trembling lamentation
Upon their mountains; in their valleys, sighs toward America.

For the soft soul of America, Oothoon, wander'd in woe,
Along the vales of Leutha seeking flowers to comfort her;
And thus she spoke to the bright Marygold of Leutha's vale:

"Art thou a flower? art thou a nymph? I see thee now a flower,
Now a nymph! I dare not pluck thee from thy dewy bed!"

The Golden nymph replied: "Pluck thou my flower, Oothoon the mild!
Another flower shall spring, because the soul of sweet delight
Can never pass away." She ceas'd, & clos'd her golden shrine.

Then Oothoon pluck'd the flower, saying: "I pluck thee from thy bed,
Sweet flower, and put thee here to glow between my breasts,
And thus I turn my face to where my whole soul seeks."

Over the waves she went in wing'd exulting swift delight,
And over Theotormon's reign took her impetuous course.

Bromion rent her with his thunders; on his stormy bed
Lay the faint maid, and soon her woes appall'd his thunders
 hoarse.

Bromion spoke: "Behold this harlot here on Bromion's bed,
And let the jealous dolphins sport around the lovely maid!
Thy soft American plains are mine, and mine thy north &
 south:
Stampt with my signet are the swarthy children of the sun;
They are obedient, they resist not, they obey the scourge;
Their daughters worship terrors and obey the violent.
Now thou maist marry Bromion's harlot, and protect the child
Of Bromion's rage, that Oothoon shall put forth in nine moons'
 time."

Then storms rent Theotormon's limbs: he roll'd his waves
 around
And folded his black jealous waters round the adulterate pair.
Bound back to back in Bromion's caves, terror & meekness
 dwell:

At entrance Theotormon sits, wearing the threshold hard
With secret tears; beneath him sound like waves on a desart
 shore
The voice of slaves beneath the sun, and children bought with
 money,
That shiver in religious caves beneath the burning fires
Of lust, that belch incessant from the summits of the earth.

Oothoon weeps not; she cannot weep! her tears are locked up;
But she can howl incessant writhing her soft snowy limbs
And calling Theotormon's Eagles to prey upon her flesh.

"I call with holy voice! Kings of the sounding air,
Rend away this defiled bosom that I may reflect
The image of Theotormon on my pure transparent breast."

The Eagles at her call descend & rend their bleeding prey:
Theotormon severely smiles; her soul reflects the smile,

As the clear spring, mudded with feet of beasts, grows pure &
    smiles.

The Daughters of Albion hear her woes, & eccho back her
    sighs.

"Why does my Theotormon sit weeping upon the threshold
And Oothoon hovers by his side, perswading him in vain?
I cry: arise, O Theotormon! for the village dog
Barks at the breaking day; the nightingale has done lamenting
The lark does rustle in the ripe corn, and the Eagle return
From nightly prey and lifts his golden beak to the pure east,
Shaking the dust from his immortal pinions to awake
The sun that sleeps too long. Arise, my Theotormon, I am pure
Because the night is gone that clos'd me in its deadly black.
They told me that the night & day were all that I could see:
They told me that I had five senses to inclose me up,
And they inclos'd my infinite brain into a narrow circle,
And sunk my heart into the Abyss, a red, round globe, hot
    burning,
Till all from life I was obliterated and erased.
Instead of morn arises a bright shadow, like an eye
In the eastern cloud; instead of night a sickly charnel house
That Theotormon hears me not! to him the night and morn
Are both alike; a night of sighs, a morning of fresh tears,
And none but Bromion can hear my lamentations.

"With what sense is it that the chicken shuns the ravenous
    hawk?
With what sense does the tame pigeon measure out the ex-
    panse?
With what sense does the bee form cells? have not the mouse
    & frog
Eyes and ears and sense of touch? yet are their habitation.
And their pursuits as different as their forms and as their joys
Ask the wild ass why he refuses burdens, and the meek camel
Why he loves man: is it because of eye, ear, mouth, or skin
Or breathing nostrils? No, for these the wolf and tyger have
Ask the blind worm the secrets of the grave, and why her spire
Love to curl round the bones of death; and ask the rav'nous
    snake

Where she gets poison, & the wing'd eagle why he loves the
    sun;
And then tell me the thoughts of man, that have been hid of
    old.

"Silent I hover all the night, and all day could be silent
If Theotormon once would turn his loved eyes upon me.
How can I be defil'd when I reflect thy image pure?
Sweetest the fruit that the worm feeds on, & the soul prey'd on
    by woe,
The new wash'd lamb ting'd with the village smoke, & the
    bright swan
By the red earth of our immortal river. I bathe my wings,
And I am white and pure to hover round Theotormon's breast."

Then Theotormon broke his silence, and he answered:—
"Tell me what is the night or day to one o'erflow'd with woe?
Tell me what is a thought, & of what substance is it made?
Tell me what is a joy, & in what gardens do joys grow?
And in what rivers swim the sorrows? and upon what moun-
    tains
Wave shadows of discontent? and in what houses dwell the
    wretched,
Drunken with woe forgotten, and shut up from cold despair?

"Tell me where dwell the thoughts forgotten till thou call them
    forth?
Tell me where dwell the joys of old? & where the ancient loves,
And when will they renew again, & the night of oblivion past,
That I might traverse times & spaces far remote, and bring
Comforts into a present sorrow and a night of pain?
Where goest thou, O thought? to what remote land is thy
    flight?
If thou returnest to the present moment of affliction
Wilt thou bring comforts on thy wings, and dews and honey
    and balm,
Or poison from the desert wilds, from the eyes of the envier?"

Then Bromion said, and shook the cavern with his lamenta-
    tion:

"Thou knowest that the ancient trees seen by thine eyes have
    fruit,
But knowest thou that trees and fruits flourish upon the earth
To gratify senses unknown? trees, beasts and birds unknown;
Unknown, not unperciev'd, spread in the infinite microscope,
In places yet unvisited by the voyager, and in worlds
Over another kind of seas, and in atmospheres unknown:
Ah! are there other wars beside the wars of sword and fire?
And are there other sorrows beside the sorrows of poverty?
And are there other joys beside the joys of riches and ease?
And is there not one law for both the lion and the ox?
And is there not eternal fire and eternal chains
To bind the phantoms of existence from eternal life?"

Then Oothoon waited silent all the day and all the night;
But when the morn arose, her lamentation renew'd.
The Daughters of Albion hear her woes, & eccho back her
    sighs.

"O Urizen! Creator of men! mistaken Demon of heaven!
Thy joys are tears, thy labour vain to form men to thine image.
How can one joy absorb another? are not different joys
Holy, eternal, infinite? and each joy is a Love.

"Does not the great mouth laugh at a gift, & the narrow eyelids
    mock
At the labour that is above payment? and wilt thou take the ape
For thy councellor, or the dog for a schoolmaster to thy chil-
    dren?
Does he who contemns poverty and he who turns with abhor-
    rence
From usury feel the same passion, or are they moved alike?
How can the giver of gifts experience the delights of the mer-
    chant?
How the industrious citizen the pains of the husbandman?
How different far the fat fed hireling with hollow drum,
Who buys whole corn fields into wastes, and sings upon the
    heath!
How different their eye and ear! how different the world to
    them!
With what sense does the parson claim the labour of the
    farmer?

What are his nets & gins & traps; & how does he surround him
With cold floods of abstraction, and with forests of solitude,
To build him castles and high spires, where kings & priests may
    dwell;
Till she who burns with youth, and knows no fixed lot, is
    bound
In spells of law to one she loaths? and must she drag the chain
Of life in weary lust? must chilling, murderous thoughts obscure
The clear heaven of her eternal spring; to bear the wintry rage
Of a harsh terror, driv'n to madness, bound to hold a rod
Over her shrinking shoulders all the day, & all the night
To turn the wheel of false desire, and longings that wake her
    womb
To the abhorred birth of cherubs in the human form,
That live a pestilence & die a meteor, & are no more;
Till the child dwell with one he hates, and do the deed he
    loaths,
And the impure scourge force his seed into its unripe birth
Ere yet his eyelids can behold the arrows of the day?

"Does the whale worship at thy footsteps as the hungry dog;
Or does he scent the mountain prey because his nostrils wide
Draw in the ocean? does his eye discern the flying cloud
As the raven's eye? or does he measure the expanse like the
    vulture?
Does the still spider view the cliffs where eagles hide their
    young;
Or does the fly rejoice because the harvest is brought in?
Does not the eagle scorn the earth & despise the treasures be-
    neath?
But the mole knoweth what is there, & the worm shall tell it
    thee.
Does not the worm erect a pillar in the mouldering church yard
And a palace of eternity in the jaws of the hungry grave?
Over his porch these words are written: 'Take thy bliss, O Man!
And sweet shall be thy taste, & sweet thy infant joys renew!'

"Infancy! fearless, lustful, happy, nestling for delight
In laps of pleasure: Innocence! honest, open, seeking
The vigorous joys of morning light; open to virgin bliss.
Who taught thee modesty, subtil modesty, child of night &
    sleep?

When thou awakest wilt thou dissemble all thy secret joys,
Or wert thou not awake when all this mystery was disclos'd?
Then com'st thou forth a modest virgin, knowing to dissemble,
With nets found under thy night pillow, to catch virgin joy
And brand it with the name of whore, & sell it in the night,
In silence, ev'n without a whisper, and in seeming sleep.
Religious dreams and holy vespers light thy smoky fires:
Once were thy fires lighted by the eyes of honest morn.
And does my Theotormon seek this hypocrite modesty,
This knowing, artful, secret, fearful, cautious, trembling hypo-
        crite?
Then is Oothoon a whore indeed! and all the virgin joys
Of life are harlots, and Theotormon is a sick man's dream;
And Oothoon is the crafty slave of selfish holiness.

"But Oothoon is not so: a virgin fill'd with virgin fancies,
Open to joy and to delight where ever beauty appears;
If in the morning sun I find it, there my eyes are fix'd
In happy copulation; if in evening mild, wearied with work,
Sit on a bank and draw the pleasures of this free born joy.

"The moment of desire! the moment of desire! The virgin
That pines for man shall awaken her womb to enormous joys
In the secret shadows of her chamber: the youth shut up from
The lustful joy shall forget to generate & create an amorous
        image
In the shadows of his curtains and in the folds of his silent pil-
        low.
Are not these the places of religion, the rewards of continence,
The self enjoyings of self denial? why dost thou seek religion?
Is it because acts are not lovely that thou seekest solitude
Where the horrible darkness is impressed with reflections of
        desire?

"Father of Jealousy, be thou accursed from the earth!
Why hast thou taught my Theotormon this accursed thing?
Till beauty fades from off my shoulders, darken'd and cast out,
A solitary shadow wailing on the margin of non-entity.

"I cry: Love! Love! Love! happy happy Love! free as the
        mountain wind!

Can that be Love that drinks another as a sponge drinks
    water,
That clouds with jealousy his nights, with weepings all the day,
To spin a web of age around him, grey and hoary, dark,
Till his eyes sicken at the fruit that hangs before his sight?
Such is self-love that envies all, a creeping skeleton
With lamplike eyes watching around the frozen marriage bed.

"But silken nets and traps of adamant will Oothoon spread,
And catch for thee girls of mild silver, or of furious gold.
I'll lie beside thee on a bank & view their wanton play
In lovely copulation, bliss on bliss, with Theotormon:
Red as the rosy morning, lustful as the first born beam,
Oothoon shall view his dear delight, nor e'er with jealous cloud
Come in the heaven of generous love, nor selfish blightings
    bring.

"Does the sun walk in glorious raiment on the secret floor
Where the cold miser spreads his gold; or does the bright cloud
    drop
On his stone threshold? does his eye behold the beam that
    brings
Expansion to the eye of pity? or will he bind himself
Beside the ox to thy hard furrow? does not that mild beam blot
The bat, the owl, the glowing tyger, and the king of night?
The sea fowl takes the wintry blast for a cov'ring to her limbs,
And the wild snake the pestilence to adorn him with gems &
    gold;
And trees & birds & beasts & men behold their eternal joy.
Arise, you little glancing wings, and sing your infant joy!
Arise, and drink your bliss, for every thing that lives is holy!"

Thus every morning wails Oothoon; but Theotormon sits
Upon the margin'd ocean conversing with shadows dire.

The Daughters of Albion hear her woes, & eccho back her
    sighs.

THE END

America: A Prophecy

PRELUDIUM

THE shadowy Daughter of Urthona stood before red Orc,
When fourteen suns had faintly journey'd o'er his dark abode:
His food she brought in iron baskets, his drink in cups of iron:
Crown'd with a helmet & dark hair the nameless female stood;
A quiver with its burning stores, a bow like that of night,
When pestilence is shot from heaven: no other arms she need!
Invulnerable tho' naked, save where clouds roll round her loins
Their awful folds in the dark air: silent she stood as night;
For never from her iron tongue could voice or sound arise,
But dumb till that dread day when Orc assay'd his fierce em-
  brace.

"Dark Virgin," said the hairy youth, "thy father stern, abhorr'd,
Rivets my tenfold chains while still on high my spirit soars;
Sometimes an eagle screaming in the sky, sometimes a lion
Stalking upon the mountains, & sometimes a whale, I lash
The raging fathomless abyss; anon a serpent folding
Around the pillars of Urthona, and round thy dark limbs
On the Canadian wilds I fold; feeble my spirit folds,
For chain'd beneath I rend these caverns: when thou bringest
  food
I howl my joy, and my red eyes seek to behold thy face—
In vain! these clouds roll to & fro, & hide thee from my sight."

Silent as despairing love, and strong as jealousy,
The hairy shoulders rend the links; free are the wrists of fire;
Round the terrific loins he siez'd the panting, struggling womb;
It joy'd: she put aside her clouds & smiled her first-born smile,
As when a black cloud shews its lightnings to the silent deep.

Soon as she saw the terrible boy, then burst the virgin cry:

"I know thee, I have found thee, & I will not let thee go:
Thou art the image of God who dwells in darkness of Africa,
And thou art fall'n to give me life in regions of dark death.
On my American plains I feel the struggling afflictions

Endur'd by roots that writhe their arms into the nether deep.
I see a Serpent in Canada who courts me to his love,
In Mexico an Eagle, and a Lion in Peru;
I see a Whale in the South-sea, drinking my soul away.
O what limb rending pains I feel! thy fire & my frost
Mingle in howling pains, in furrows by thy lightnings rent.
This is eternal death, and this the torment long foretold."

A PROPHECY

THE Guardian Prince of Albion burns in his nightly tent:
Sullen fires across the Atlantic glow to America's shore,
Piercing the souls of warlike men who rise in silent night.
Washington, Franklin, Paine & Warren, Gates, Hancock &
    Green
Meet on the coast glowing with blood from Albion's fiery
    Prince.

Washington spoke: "Friends of America! Look over the At-
    lantic sea;
A bended bow is lifted in heaven, & a heavy iron chain
Descends, link by link, from Albion's cliffs across the sea, to
    bind
Brothers & sons of America till our faces pale and yellow,
Heads deprest, voices weak, eyes downcast, hands work-
    bruis'd,
Feet bleeding on the sultry sands, and the furrows of the whip
Descend to generations that in future times forget."

The strong voice ceas'd, for a terrible blast swept over the heav-
    ing sea:
The eastern cloud rent: on his cliffs stood Albion's wrathful
    Prince,
A dragon form, clashing his scales: at midnight he arose,
And flam'd red meteors round the land of Albion beneath;
His voice, his locks, his awful shoulders, and his glowing eyes
Appear to the Americans upon the cloudy night.
Solemn heave the Atlantic waves between the gloomy nations,
Swelling, belching from its deeps red clouds & raging fires.
Albion is sick! America faints! enrag'd the Zenith grew.
As human blood shooting its veins all round the orbed heaven,

Red rose the clouds from the Atlantic in vast wheels of blood,
And in the red clouds rose a Wonder o'er the Atlantic sea,
Intense! naked! a Human fire, fierce glowing, as the wedge
Of iron heated in the furnace: his terrible limbs were fire
With myriads of cloudy terrors, banners dark & towers
Surrounded: heat but not light went thro' the murky atmosphere.

The King of England looking westward trembles at the vision.

Albion's Angel stood beside the Stone of night, and saw
The terror like a comet, or more like the planet red
That once enclos'd the terrible wandering comets in its sphere.
Then, Mars, thou wast our center, & the planets three flew round
Thy crimson disk: so e'er the Sun was rent from thy red sphere.
The Spectre glow'd his horrid length staining the temple long
With beams of blood; & thus a voice came forth, and shook the temple:

"The morning comes, the night decays, the watchmen leave their stations;
The grave is burst, the spices shed, the linen wrapped up;
The bones of death, the cov'ring clay, the sinews shrunk & dry'd
Reviving shake, inspiring move, breathing, awakening,
Spring like redeemed captives when their bonds & bars are burst.
Let the slave grinding at the mill run out into the field,
Let him look up into the heavens & laugh in the bright air;
Let the inchained soul, shut up in darkness and in sighing,
Whose face has never seen a smile in thirty weary years,
Rise and look out; his chains are loose, his dungeon doors are open;
And let his wife and children return from the oppressor's scourge.
They look behind at every step & believe it is a dream,
Singing: 'The Sun has left his blackness & has found a fresher morning,
And the fair Moon rejoices in the clear & cloudless night;
For Empire is no more, and now the Lion & Wolf shall cease.' "

In thunders ends the voice. Then Albion's Angel wrathful burnt
Beside the Stone of Night, and like the Eternal Lion's howl
In famine & war, reply'd: "Art thou not Orc, who serpent-
     form'd
Stands at the gate of Enitharmon to devour her children?
Blasphemous Demon, Antichrist, hater of Dignities,
Lover of wild rebellion, and transgressor of God's Law,
Why dost thou come to Angel's eyes in this terrific form?"

The Terror answer'd: "I am Orc, wreath'd round the accursed
     tree:
The times are ended; shadows pass, the morning 'gins to break;
The fiery joy, that Urizen perverted to ten commands,
What night he led the starry hosts thro' the wide wilderness,
That stony law I stamp to dust; and scatter religion abroad
To the four winds as a torn book, & none shall gather the
     leaves;
But they shall rot on desart sands, & consume in bottomless
     deeps,
To make the desarts blossom, & the deeps shrink to their foun-
     tains,
And to renew the fiery joy, and burst the stony roof;
That pale religious letchery, seeking Virginity,
May find it in a harlot, and in coarse-clad honesty
The undefil'd, tho' ravish'd in her cradle night and morn;
For everything that lives is holy, life delights in life;
Because the soul of sweet delight can never be defil'd.
Fires inwrap the earthly globe, yet man is not consum'd;
Amidst the lustful fires he walks; his feet become like brass,
His knees and thighs like silver, & his breast and head like
     gold."

"Sound! sound! my loud war-trumpets, & alarm my Thirteen
     Angels!
Loud howls the eternal Wolf! the eternal Lion lashes his tail!
America is darken'd; and my punishing Demons, terrified,
Crouch howling before their caverns deep, like skins dry'd in
     the wind.
They cannot smite the wheat, nor quench the fatness of the
     earth;
They cannot smite with sorrows, nor subdue the plow and
     spade;

They cannot wall the city, nor moat round the castle of princes;
They cannot bring the stubbed oak to overgrow the hills;
For terrible men stand on the shores, & in their robes I see
Children take shelter from the lightnings: there stands Wash-
    ington
And Paine and Warren with their foreheads rear'd toward the
    east. ·
But clouds obscure my aged sight. A vision from afar!
Sound! sound! my loud war-trumpets, & alarm my thirteen
    Angels!
Ah vision from afar! Ah rebel form that rent the ancient
Heavens! Eternal Viper, self-renew'd, rolling in clouds,
I see thee in thick clouds and darkness on America's shore,
Writhing in pangs of abhorred birth; red flames the crest
    rebellious
And eyes of death; the harlot womb, oft opened in vain,
Heaves in enormous circles: now the times are return'd upon
    thee,
Devourer of thy parent, now thy unutterable torment renews.
Sound! sound! my loud war-trumpets, & alarm my thirteen
    Angels!
Ah terrible birth! a young one bursting! where is the weeping
    mouth,
And where the mother's milk? instead, those ever-hissing jaws
And parched lips drop with fresh gore: now roll thou in the
    clouds;
Thy mother lays her length outstretch'd upon the shore be-
    neath.
Sound! sound! my loud war-trumpets, & alarm my thirteen
    Angels!
Loud howls the eternal Wolf! the eternal Lion lashes his tail!"

Thus wept the Angel voice, & as he wept, the terrible blasts
Of trumpets blew a loud alarm across the Atlantic deep.
No trumpets answer; no reply of clarions or of fifes:
Silent the Colonies remain and refuse the loud alarm.

On those vast shady hills between America & Albion's shore,
Now barr'd out by the Atlantic sea, call'd Atlantean hills,
Because from their bright summits you may pass to the Golden
    world,
An ancient palace, archetype of mighty Emperies,

Rears its immortal pinnacles, built in the forest of God
By Ariston, the king of beauty, for his stolen bride.

Here on their magic seats the thirteen Angels sat perturb'd,
For clouds from the Atlantic hover o'er the solemn roof.

Fiery the Angels rose, & as they rose deep thunder roll'd
Around their shores, indignant burning with the fires of Orc;
And Boston's angel cried aloud as they flew thro' the dark
    night.

He cried: "Why trembles honesty, and like a murderer
Why seeks he refuge from the frowns of his immortal station?
Must the generous tremble & leave his joy to the idle, to the
    pestilence,
That mock him? who commanded this? what God? what Angel?
To keep the gen'rous from experience till the ungenerous
Are unrestrain'd performers of the energies of nature;
Till pity is become a trade, and generosity a science
That men get rich by; & the sandy desert is giv'n to the strong?
What God is he writes laws of peace & clothes him in a
    tempest?
What pitying Angel lusts for tears and fans himself with sighs?
What crawling villain preaches abstinence & wraps himself
In fat of lambs? no more I follow, no more obedience pay!"

So cried he, rending off his robe & throwing down his
    scepter
In sight of Albion's Guardian; and all the thirteen Angels
Rent off their robes to the hungry wind, & threw their golden
    scepters
Down on the land of America; indignant they descended
Headlong from out their heav'nly heights, descending swift as
    fires
Over the land; naked & flaming are their lineaments seen
In the deep gloom; by Washington & Paine & Warren they
    stood;
And the flame folded, roaring fierce within the pitchy night
Before the Demon red, who burnt towards America,
In black smoke, thunders, and loud winds, rejoicing in its
    terror,

Breaking in smoky wreaths from the wild deep, & gath'ring
    thick
In flames as of a furnace on the land from North to South,
What time the thirteen Governors that England sent, convene
In Bernard's house; the flames cover'd the land, they rouze,
    they cry;
Shaking their mental chains, they rush in fury to the sea
To quench their anguish; at the feet of Washington down fall'n
They grovel on the sand and writhing lie, while all
The British soldiers thro' the thirteen states sent up a howl
Of anguish, threw their swords & muskets to the earth, & ran
From their encampments and dark castles, seeking where to
    hide
From the grim flames, and from the visions of Orc, in sight
Of Albion's Angel; who, enrag'd, his secret clouds open'd
From north to south and burnt outstretch'd on wings of wrath,
    cov'ring
The eastern sky, spreading his awful wings across the heavens.
Beneath him roll'd his num'rous hosts, all Albion's Angels
    camp'd
Darken'd the Atlantic mountains; & their trumpets shook the
    valleys,
Arm'd with diseases of the earth to cast upon the Abyss,
Their numbers forty millions, must'ring in the eastern sky.

In the flames stood & view'd the armies drawn out in the sky,
Washington, Franklin, Paine, & Warren, Allen, Gates, & Lee,
And heard the voice of Albion's Angel give the thunderous
    command;
His plagues, obedient to his voice, flew forth out of their clouds,
Falling upon America, as a storm to cut them off,
As a blight cuts the tender corn when it begins to appear.
Dark is the heaven above, & cold & hard the earth beneath:
And as a plague wind fill'd with insects cuts off man & beast,
And as a sea o'erwhelms a land in the day of an earthquake,
Fury! rage! madness! in a wind swept through America;
And the red flames of Orc, that folded roaring, fierce, around
The angry shores; and the fierce rushing of th' inhabitants to-
    gether!
The citizens of New York close their books & lock their chests;
The mariners of Boston drop their anchors and unlade;

The scribe of Pensylvania casts his pen upon the earth;
The builder of Virginia throws his hammer down in fear.

Then had America been lost, o'erwhelm'd by the Atlantic,
And Earth had lost another portion of the infinite,
But all rush together in the night in wrath and raging fire.
The red fires rag'd! the plagues recoil'd! then roll'd they back with fury
On Albion's Angels: then the Pestilence began in streaks of red
Across the limbs of Albion's Guardian; the spotted plague smote Bristol's
And the Leprosy London's Spirit, sickening all their bands:
The millions sent up a howl of anguish and threw off their hammer'd mail,
And cast their swords & spears to earth, & stood, a naked multitude:
Albion's Guardian writhed in torment on the eastern sky,
Pale, quiv'ring toward the brain his glimmering eyes, teeth chattering,
Howling & shuddering, his legs quivering, convuls'd each muscle & sinew:
Sick'ning lay London's Guardian, and the ancient miterd York,
Their heads on snowy hills, their ensigns sick'ning in the sky.
The plagues creep on the burning winds driven by flames of Orc,
And by the fierce Americans rushing together in the night,
Driven o'er the Guardians of Ireland, and Scotland and Wales.
They, spotted with plagues, forsook the frontiers; & their banners, sear'd
With fires of hell, deform their ancient heavens with shame & woe.
Hid in his caves the Bard of Albion felt the enormous plagues,
And a cowl of flesh grew o'er his head, & scales on his back & ribs;
And, rough with black scales, all his Angels fright their ancient heavens.
The doors of marriage are open, and the Priests in rustling scales
Rush into reptile coverts, hiding from the fires of Orc,
That play around the golden roofs in wreaths of fierce desire,
Leaving the females naked and glowing with the lusts of youth.

For the female spirits of the dead, pining in bonds of religion,
Run from their fetters reddening, & in long drawn arches sitting,
They feel the nerves of youth renew, and desires of ancient times
Over their pale limbs, as a vine when the tender grape appears.

Over the hills, the vales, the cities, rage the red flames fierce:
The Heavens melted from north to south; and Urizen, who sat
Above all heavens, in thunders wrap'd, emerg'd his leprous head
From out his holy shrine, his tears in deluge piteous
Falling into the deep sublime; flag'd with grey-brow'd snows
And thunderous visages, his jealous wings wav'd over the deep;
Weeping in dismal howling woe, he dark descended, howling
Around the smitten bands, clothed in tears & trembling, shudd'ring cold.
His stored snows he poured forth, and his icy magazines
He open'd on the deep, and on the Atlantic sea white shiv'ring
Leprous his limbs, all over white, and hoary was his visage,
Weeping in dismal howlings before the stern Americans,
Hiding the Demon red with clouds & cold mists from the earth;
Till Angels & weak men twelve years should govern o'er the strong;
And then their end should come, when France receiv'd the Demon's light.

Stiff shudderings shook the heav'nly thrones! France, Spain, & Italy
In terror view'd the bands of Albion, and the ancient Guardians,
Fainting upon the elements, smitten with their own plagues.
They slow advance to shut the five gates of their law-built heaven,
Filled with blasting fancies and with mildews of despair,
With fierce disease and lust, unable to stem the fires of Orc.
But the five gates were consum'd, & their bolts and hinges melted;
And the fierce flames burnt round the heavens & round the abodes of men.

FINIS

[CANCELLED PLATES]

THE Guardian Prince of Albion burns in his nightly tent:
Sullen fires across the Atlantic glow to America's shore,
Piercing the souls of warlike men who rise in silent night.
Washington, Hancock, Paine & Warren, Gates, Franklin &
    Green
Meet on the coast glowing with blood from Albion's fiery
    Prince.
Washington spoke: "Friends of America! look over the Atlantic
    sea;
A bended bow in heaven is lifted, & a heavy iron chain
Descends, link by link, from Albion's cliffs across the sea, to
    bind
Brothers & sons of America till our faces pale and yellow,
Heads deprest, voices weak, eyes downcast, hands work-bruised,
Feet bleeding on the sultry sands, & the furrows of the whip
Descend to generations that in future times forget."
The strong voice ceas'd, for a terrible blast swept over the heav-
    ing sea:
The eastern cloud rent: on his cliffs stood Albions fiery Prince,
A dragon form, clashing his scales: at midnight he arose,
And flam'd fierce meteors round the band of Albion beneath;
His voice, his locks, his awful shoulders, & his glowing eyes
Reveal the dragon thro' the human; coursing swift as fire
To the close hall of counsel, where his Angel form renews.
In a sweet vale shelter'd with cedars, that eternal stretch
Their unmov'd branches, stood the hall, built when the moon
    shot forth,
In that dread night when Urizen call'd the stars round his feet;
Then burst the center from its orb, and found a place beneath;
And Earth conglob'd, in narrow room, roll'd round its sulphur
    Sun.
To this deep valley situated by the flowing Thames,
Where George the third holds council & his Lords & Commons
    meet,
Shut out from mortal sight the Angel came; the vale was dark
With clouds of smoke from the Atlantic, that in volumes roll'd
Between the mountains; dismal visions mope around the house
On chairs of iron, canopied with mystic ornaments

Of life by magic power condens'd; infernal forms art-bound
The council sat; all rose before the aged apparition,
His snowy beard that streams like lambent flames down his
    wide breast
Wetting with tears, & his white garments cast a wintry light.
Then as arm'd clouds arise terrific round the northern drum,
The world is silent at the flapping of the folding banners.
So still terrors rent the house, as when the solemn globe
Launch'd to the unknown shore, while Sotha held the northern
    helm,
Till to that void it came & fell; so the dark house was rent.
The valley mov'd beneath; its shining pillars split in twain,
And its roofs crack across down falling on th' Angelic seats.

Then Albion's Angel rose resolv'd to the cove of armoury:
His shield that bound twelve demons & their cities in its orb
He took down from its trembling pillar; from its cavern deep,
His helm was brought by London's Guardian, & his thirsty
    spear
By the wise spirit of London's river; silent stood the King
    breathing damp mists,
And on his aged limbs they clasp'd the armour of terrible gold.
Infinite London's awful spires cast a dreadful cold
Even on rational things beneath and from the palace walls
Around Saint James's, chill & heavy, even to the city gate.
On the vast stone whose name is Truth he stood, his cloudy
    shield
Smote with his scepter, the scale bound orb loud howl'd; the
    pillar
Trembling sunk, an earthquake roll'd along the mossy pile.
In glitt'ring armour, swift as winds, intelligent as clouds
Four winged heralds mount the furious blasts & blow their
    trumps;
Gold, silver, brass & iron clangors clamoring rend the shores.
Like white clouds rising from the deeps his fifty-two armies
From the four cliffs of Albion rise, mustering around their
    Prince;
Angels of cities and of parishes and villages and families,
In armour as the nerves of wisdom, each his station holds.
In opposition dire, a warlike cloud, the myriads stood
In the red air before the Demon seen even by mortal men,

Who call it Fancy, or shut the gates of sense, or in their chambers
Sleep like the dead. But like a constellation ris'n and blazing
Over the rugged ocean, so the Angels of Albion hung
Over the frowning shadow like an aged King in arms of gold,
Who wept over a den, in which his only son outstretch'd
By rebels' hands was slain; his white beard wav'd in the wild wind.
On mountains & cliffs of snow the awful apparition hover'd,
And like the voices of religious dead heard in the mountains
When holy zeal scents the sweet valleys of ripe virgin bliss,
Such was the hollow voice that o'er America lamented.

Europe: A Prophecy

[INTRODUCTION]

"FIVE windows light the cavern'd Man: thro' one he breathes the air;
Thro' one hears music of the spheres; thro' one the eternal vine
Flourishes, that he may recieve the grapes; thro' one can look
And see small portions of the eternal world that ever groweth;
Thro' one himself pass out what time he please; but he will not,
For stolen joys are sweet & bread eaten in secret pleasant."

So sang a Fairy, mocking, as he sat on a streak'd Tulip,
Thinking none saw him: when he ceas'd I started from the trees
And caught him in my hat, as boys knock down a butterfly.
"How know you this," said I, "small Sir? where did you learn this song?"
Seeing himself in my possession, thus he answer'd me:
"My master, I am yours! command me, for I must obey."

"Then tell me, what is the material world, and is it dead?"
He, laughing, answer'd: "I will write a book on leaves of flowers,
If you will feed me on love-thoughts & give me now and then
A cup of sparkling poetic fancies; so, when I am tipsie,
I'll sing to you to this soft lute, and shew you all alive
The world, where every particle of dust breathes forth its joy."

I took him home in my warm bosom: as we went along
Wild flowers I gather'd, & he shew'd me each eternal flower:
He laugh'd aloud to see them whimper because they were
    pluck'd.
They hover'd round me like a cloud of incense: when I came
Into my parlour and sat down and took my pen to write,
My Fairy sat upon the table and dictated EUROPE.

PRELUDIUM

THE nameless shadowy female rose from out the breast of Orc,
Her snaky hair brandishing in the winds of Enitharmon;
And thus her voice arose:

"O mother Enitharmon, wilt thou bring forth other sons?
To cause my name to vanish, that my place may not be found,
For I am faint with travail,
Like the dark cloud disburden'd in the day of dismal thunder.

"My roots are brandish'd in the heavens, my fruits in earth
    beneath
Surge, foam and labour into life, first born & first consum'd!
Consumed and consuming!
Then why shouldst thou, accursed mother, bring me into life?

"I wrap my turban of thick clouds around my lab'ring head,
And fold the sheety waters as a mantle round my limbs;
Yet the red sun and moon
And all the overflowing stars rain down prolific pains.

"Unwilling I look up to heaven, unwilling count the stars:
Sitting in fathomless abyss of my immortal shrine
I sieze their burning power
And bring forth howling terrors, all devouring fiery kings,

"Devouring & devoured, roaming on dark and desolate moun-
    tains,
In forests of eternal death, shrieking in hollow trees.
Ah mother Enitharmon!
Stamp not with solid form this vig'rous progeny of fires.

"I bring forth from my teeming bosom myriads of flames,
And thou dost stamp them with a signet; then they roam
   abroad
And leave me void as death.
Ah! I am drown'd in shady woe and visionary joy.

"And who shall bind the infinite with an eternal band?
To compass it with swaddling bands? and who shall cherish it
With milk and honey?
I see it smile, & I roll inward, & my voice is past."

> She ceast, & roll'd her shady clouds
> Into the secret place.

A PROPHECY

THE deep of winter came,
What time the secret child
Descended thro' the orient gates of the eternal day:
War ceas'd, & all the troops like shadows fled to their abodes.

Then Enitharmon saw her sons & daughters rise around;
Like pearly clouds they meet together in the crystal house;
And Los, possessor of the moon, joy'd in the peaceful night,
Thus speaking, while his num'rous sons shook their bright fiery
   wings:

"Again the night is come
That strong Urthona takes his rest;
And Urizen, unloos'd from chains,
Glows like a meteor in the distant north.
Stretch forth your hands and strike the elemental strings!
Awake the thunders of the deep!

"The shrill winds wake,
Till all the sons of Urizen look out and envy Los.
Sieze all the spirits of life, and bind
Their warbling joys to our loud strings!
Bind all the nourishing sweets of earth
To give us bliss, that we may drink the sparkling wine of Los!
And let us laugh at war,

Despising toil and care,
Because the days and nights of joy in lucky hours renew.

"Arise, O Orc, from thy deep den!
First born of Enitharmon, rise!
And we will crown thy head with garlands of the ruddy vine;
For now thou art bound,
And I may see thee in the hour of bliss, my eldest born."

The horrent Demon rose surrounded with red stars of fire
Whirling about in furious circles round the immortal fiend.

Then Enitharmon down descended into his red light,
And thus her voice rose to her children: the distant heavens
    reply:

"Now comes the night of Enitharmon's joy!
Who shall I call? Who shall I send,
That Woman, lovely Woman, may have dominion?
Arise, O Rintrah, thee I call! & Palamabron, thee!
Go! tell the Human race that Woman's love is Sin;
That an Eternal life awaits the worms of sixty winters
In an allegorical abode where existence hath never come.
Forbid all Joy, & from her childhood shall the little female
Spread nets in every secret path.

"My weary eyelids draw towards the evening; my bliss is yet but
    new.

"Arise, O Rintrah, eldest born, second to none but Orc!
O lion Rintrah, raise thy fury from thy forests black!
Bring Palamabron, horned priest, skipping upon the mountains,
And silent Elynittria, the silver bowed queen.
Rintrah, where hast thou hid thy bride?
Weeps she in desart shades?
Alas! my Rintrah, bring the lovely jealous Ocalythron.

"Arise, my son! bring all thy brethren, O thou king of fire!
Prince of the sun! I see thee with thy innumerable race,
Thick as the summer stars;
But each, ramping, his golden mane shakes,
And thine eyes rejoice because of strength, O Rintrah, furious
    king!"

Enitharmon slept
Eighteen hundred years. Man was a Dream!
The night of Nature and their harps unstrung!
She slept in middle of her nightly song
Eighteen hundred years, a female dream.

Shadows of men in fleeting bands upon the winds
Divide the heavens of Europe
Till Albion's Angel, smitten with his own plagues, fled with his
    bands.
The cloud bears hard on Albion's shore,
Fill'd with immortal demons of futurity:
In council gather the smitten Angels of Albion;
The cloud bears hard upon the council house, down rushing
On the heads of Albion's Angels.

One hour they lay buried beneath the ruins of that hall;
But as the stars rise from the salt lake, they arise in pain,
In troubled mists, o'erclouded by the terrors of strugling times.

In thoughts perturb'd they rose from the bright ruins, silent
    following
The fiery King, who sought his ancient temple, serpent-form'd,
That stretches out its shady length along the Island white.
Round him roll'd his clouds of war; silent the Angel went
Along the infinite shores of Thames to golden Verulam.
There stand the venerable porches that high-towering rear
Their oak-surrounded pillars, form'd of massy stones, uncut
With tool, stones precious, such eternal in the heavens,
Of colours twelve, few known on earth, give light in the opake,
Plac'd in the order of the stars, when the five senses whelm'd
In deluge o'er the earth-born man; then turn'd the fluxile eyes
Into two stationary orbs, concentrating all things:
The ever-varying spiral ascents to the heavens of heavens
Were bended downward, and the nostrils' golden gates shut,
Turn'd outward, barr'd and petrify'd against the infinite.

Thought chang'd the infinite to a serpent, that which pitieth
To a devouring flame; and man fled from its face and hid
In forests of night: then all the eternal forests were divided
Into earths rolling in circles of space, that like an ocean rush'd
And overwhelmed all except this finite wall of flesh.

Then was the serpent temple form'd, image of infinite
Shut up in finite revolutions, and man became an Angel,
Heaven a mighty circle turning, God a tyrant crown'd.

Now arriv'd the ancient Guardian at the southern porch
That planted thick with trees of blackest leaf & in a vale
Obscure enclos'd the Stone of Night; oblique it stood, o'erhung
With purple flowers and berries red, image of that sweet south
Once open to the heavens, and elevated on the human neck,
Now overgrown with hair and cover'd with a stony roof.
Downward 'tis sunk beneath th' attractive north, that round
    the feet,
A raging whirlpool, draws the dizzy enquirer to his grave.

        Albion's Angel rose upon the Stone of Night.
        He saw Urizen on the Atlantic;
        And his brazen Book
        That Kings & Priests had copied on Earth,
        Expanded from North to South.

And the clouds & fires pale roll'd round in the night of Enithar-
    mon,
Round Albion's cliffs & London's walls: still Enitharmon slept.
Rolling volumes of grey mist involve Churches, Palaces, Tow-
    ers;
For Urizen unclasp'd his Book, feeding his soul with pity.
The youth of England, hid in gloom, curse the pain'd heavens,
    compell'd
Into the deadly night to see the form of Albion's Angel.
Their parents brought them forth, & aged ignorance preaches,
    canting,
On a vast rock, perciev'd by those senses that are clos'd from
    thought:
Bleak, dark, abrupt it stands & overshadows London city.
They saw his boney feet on the rock, the flesh consum'd in∙
    flames;
They saw the Serpent temple lifted above, shadowing the Island
    white;
They heard the voice of Albion's Angel howling in flames of
    Orc,
Seeking the trump of the last doom.

Above the rest the howl was heard from Westminster louder &
    louder:
The Guardian of the secret codes forsook his ancient mansion,
Driven out by the flames of Orc; his furr'd robes & false locks
Adhered and grew one with his flesh, and nerves & veins shot
    thro' them.
With dismal torment sick, hanging upon the wind, he fled
Groveling along Great George Street thro' the Park gate: all
    the soldiers
Fled from his sight: he drag'd his torments to the wilderness.

Thus was the howl thro' Europe!
For Orc rejoic'd to hear the howling shadows;
But Palamabron shot his lightnings, trenching down his wide
    back;
And Rintrah hung with all his legions in the nether deep.

Enitharmon laugh'd in her sleep to see (O woman's triumph!)
Every house a den, every man bound: the shadows are fill'd
With spectres, and the windows wove over with curses of iron:
Over the doors "Thou shalt not," & over the chimneys "Fear" is
    written:
With bands of iron round their necks fasten'd into the walls
The citizens, in leaden gyves the inhabitants of suburbs
Walk heavy; soft and bent are the bones of villagers.

Between the clouds of Urizen the flames of Orc roll heavy
Around the limbs of Albion's Guardian, his flesh consuming:
Howlings & hissings, shrieks & groans, & voices of despair
Arise around him in the cloudy heavens of Albion. Furious,
The red limb'd Angel siez'd in horror and torment
The Trump of the last doom; but he could not blow the iron
    tube!
Thrice he assay'd presumptuous to awake the dead to Judg-
    ment.

A mighty Spirit leap'd from the land of Albion,
Nam'd Newton: he siez'd the trump & blow'd the enormous
    blast!
Yellow as leaves of Autumn, the myriads of Angelic hosts
Fell thro' the wintry skies seeking their graves,
Rattling their hollow bones in howling and lamentation.

Then Enitharmon woke, nor knew that she had slept;
And eighteen hundred years were fled
As if they had not been.
She call'd her sons & daughters
To the sports of night
Within her crystal house,
And thus her song proceeds:

"Arise, Ethinthus! tho' the earth-worm call,
Let him call in vain,
Till the night of holy shadows
And human solitude is past!

"Ethinthus, queen of waters, how thou shinest in the sky!
My daughter, how do I rejoice! for thy children flock around
Like the gay fishes on the wave, when the cold moon drinks the
     dew.
Ethinthus! thou art sweet as comforts to my fainting soul,
For now thy waters warble round the feet of Enitharmon.

"Manathu-Varcyon! I behold thee flaming in my halls,
Light of thy mother's soul! I see thy lovely eagles round;
Thy golden wings are my delight, & thy flames of soft delusion.

"Where is my lureing bird of Eden? Leutha, silent love!
Leutha, the many colour'd bow delights upon thy wings:
Soft soul of flowers, Leutha!
Sweet smiling pestilence! I see thy blushing light;
Thy daughters, many changing,
Revolve like sweet perfumes ascending, O Leutha, silken queen!

"Where is the youthful Antamon, prince of the pearly dew?
O Antamon! why wilt thou leave thy mother Enitharmon?
Alone I see thee, crystal form,
Floating upon the bosom'd air
With lineaments of gratified desire.
My Antamon, the seven churches of Leutha seek thy love.

"I hear the soft Oothoon in Enitharmon's tents;
Why wilt thou give up woman's secrecy, my melancholy child?
Between two moments bliss is ripe.
O Theotormon! robb'd of joy, I see thy salt tears flow
Down the steps of my crystal house.

"Sotha & Thiralatha! secret dwellers of dreamful caves,
Arise and please the horrent fiend with your melodious songs;
Still all your thunders, golden-hoof'd, & bind your horses black.
Orc! smile upon my children!
Smile, son of my afflictions.
Arise, O Orc, and give our mountains joy of thy red light!"

She ceas'd; for All were forth at sport beneath the solemn
    moon
Waking the stars of Urizen with their immortal songs,
That nature felt thro' all her pores the enormous revelry
Till morning oped the eastern gate;
Then every one fled to his station, & Enitharmon wept.

But terrible Orc, when he beheld the morning in the east,
Shot from the heights of Enitharmon,
And in the vineyards of red France appear'd the light of his
    fury.

The sun glow'd fiery red!
The furious terrors flew around
On golden chariots raging with red wheels dropping with blood!
The Lions lash their wrathful tails!
The Tigers couch upon the prey & suck the ruddy tide,
And Enitharmon groans & cries in anguish and dismay.

Then Los arose: his head he rear'd in snaky thunders clad;
And with a cry that shook all nature to the utmost pole,
Call'd all his sons to the strife of blood.

FINIS

The (First) Book of Urizen

PRELUDIUM TO THE FIRST BOOK OF URIZEN

OF the primeval Priest's assum'd power,
When Eternals spurn'd back his religion
And gave him a place in the north,
Obscure, shadowy, void, solitary.

Eternals! I hear your call gladly.
Dictate swift winged words & fear not
To unfold your dark visions of torment.

CHAP: I

1. Lo, a shadow of horror is risen
In Eternity! Unknown, unprolific,
Self-clos'd, all-repelling: what Demon
Hath form'd this abominable void,
This soul-shudd'ring vacuum? Some said
"It is Urizen." But unknown, abstracted,
Brooding, secret, the dark power hid.

2. Times on times he divided & measur'd
Space by space in his ninefold darkness,
Unseen, unknown; changes appear'd
Like desolate mountains, rifted furious
By the black winds of perturbation.

3. For he strove in battles dire,
In unseen conflictions with shapes
Bred from his forsaken wilderness
Of beast, bird, fish, serpent & element,
Combustion, blast, vapour and cloud.

4. Dark, revolving in silent activity:
Unseen in tormenting passions:
An activity unknown and horrible,
A self-contemplating shadow,
In enormous labours occupied.

5. But Eternals beheld his vast forests;
Age on ages he lay, clos'd, unknown,
Brooding shut in the deep; all avoid
The petrific, abominable chaos.

6. His cold horrors silent, dark Urizen
Prepar'd; his ten thousands of thunders,
Rang'd in gloom'd array, stretch out across
The dread world; & the rolling of wheels,
As of swelling seas, sound in his clouds,

In his hills of stor'd snows, in his mountains
Of hail & ice; voices of terror
Are heard, like thunders of autumn
When the cloud blazes over the harvests.

CHAP: II

1. Earth was not: nor globes of attraction;
The will of the Immortal expanded
Or contracted his all flexible senses;
Death was not, but eternal life sprung.

2. The sound of a trumpet the heavens
Awoke, & vast clouds of blood roll'd
Round the dim rocks of Urizen, so nam'd
That solitary one in Immensity.

3. Shrill the trumpet: & myriads of Eternity
Muster around the bleak desarts,
Now fill'd with clouds, darkness, & waters,
That roll'd perplex'd, lab'ring; & utter'd
Words articulate bursting in thunders
That roll'd on the tops of his mountains:

4. "From the depths of dark solitude, From
The eternal abode in my holiness,
Hidden, set apart, in my stern counsels,
Reserv'd for the days of futurity,
I have sought for a joy without pain,
For a solid without fluctuation.
Why will you die, O Eternals?
Why live in unquenchable burnings?

5. "First I fought with the fire, consum'd
Inwards into a deep world within:
A void immense, wild, dark & deep,
Where nothing was: Nature's wide womb;
And self balanc'd, stretch'd o'er the void,
I alone, even I! the winds merciless
Bound; but condensing in torrents
They fall & fall; strong I repell'd

The vast waves, & arose on the waters
A wide world of solid obstruction.

6. "Here alone I, in books form'd of metals,
Have written the secrets of wisdom,
The secrets of dark contemplation,
By fightings and conflicts dire
With terrible monsters Sin-bred
Which the bosoms of all inhabit,
Seven deadly Sins of the soul.

7. "Lo! I unfold my darkness, and on
This rock place with strong hand the Book
Of eternal brass, written in my solitude:

8. "Laws of peace, of love, of unity,
Of pity, compassion, forgiveness;
Let each chuse one habitation,
His ancient infinite mansion,
One command, one joy, one desire,
One curse, one weight, one measure,
One King, one God, one Law."

CHAP: III

1. The voice ended: they saw his pale visage
Emerge from the darkness, his hand
On the rock of eternity unclasping
The Book of brass. Rage siez'd the strong,

2. Rage, fury, intense indignation,
In cataracts of fire, blood, & gall,
In whirlwinds of sulphurous smoke,
And enormous forms of energy,
All the seven deadly sins of the soul
In living creations appear'd,
In the flames of eternal fury.

3. Sund'ring, dark'ning, thund'ring,
Rent away with a terrible crash,
Eternity roll'd wide apart,
Wide asunder rolling;

Mountainous all around
Departing, departing, departing,
Leaving ruinous fragments of life
Hanging, frowning cliffs & all between,
An ocean of voidness unfathomable.

4. The roaring fires ran o'er the heav'ns
In whirlwinds & cataracts of blood,
And o'er the dark desarts of Urizen
Fires pour thro' the void on all sides
On Urizen's self-begotten armies.

5. But no light from the fires: all was darkness
In the flames of Eternal fury.

6. In fierce anguish & quenchless flames
To the desarts and rocks he ran raging
To hide; but he could not: combining,
He dug mountains & hills in vast strength,
He piled them in incessant labour,
In howlings & pangs & fierce madness,
Long periods in burning fires labouring
Till hoary, and age-broke, and aged,
In despair and the shadows of death.

7. And a roof vast, petrific around
On all sides he fram'd, like a womb,
Where thousands of rivers in veins
Of blood pour down the mountains to cool
The eternal fires, beating without
From Eternals; & like a black globe,
View'd by sons of Eternity standing
On the shore of the infinite ocean,
Like a human heart, strugling & beating,
The vast world of Urizen appear'd.

8. And Los, round the dark globe of Urizen,
Kept watch for Eternals to confine
The obscure separation alone;
For Eternity stood wide apart,
As the stars are apart from the earth.

9. Los wept, howling around the dark Demon,
And cursing his lot; for in anguish
Urizen was rent from his side,
And a fathomless void for his feet,
And intense fires for his dwelling.

10. But Urizen laid in a stony sleep,
Unorganiz'd, rent from Eternity.

11. The Eternals said: "What is this? Death.
Urizen is a clod of clay."

12. Los howl'd in a dismal stupor,
Groaning, gnashing, groaning,
Till the wrenching apart was healed.

13. But the wrenching of Urizen heal'd not.
Cold, featureless, flesh or clay,
Rifted with direful changes,
He lay in a dreamless night,

14. Till Los rouz'd his fires, affrighted
At the formless, unmeasurable death.

CHAP: IV [a]

1. Los, smitten with astonishment,
Frighten'd at the hurtling bones

2. And at the surging, sulphureous,
Perturbed Immortal, mad raging

3. In whirlwinds & pitch & nitre
Round the furious limbs of Los.

4. And Los formed nets & gins
And threw the nets round about.

5. He watch'd in shudd'ring fear
The dark changes, & bound every change
With rivets of iron & brass.

6. And these were the changes of Urizen:

CHAP: IV [b]

1. Ages on ages roll'd over him;
In stony sleep ages roll'd over him,
Like a dark waste stretching, chang'able,
By earthquakes riv'n, belching sullen fires:
On ages roll'd ages in ghastly
Sick torment; around him in whirlwinds
Of darkness the eternal Prophet howl'd,
Beating still on his rivets of iron,
Pouring sodor of iron; dividing
The horrible night into watches.

2. And Urizen (so his eternal name)
His prolific delight obscur'd more & more
In dark secresy, hiding in surgeing
Sulphureous fluid his phantasies.
The Eternal Prophet heav'd the dark bellows,
And turn'd restless the tongs, and the hammer
Incessant beat, forging chains new & new,
Numb'ring with links hours, days & years.

3. The Eternal mind, bounded, began to roll
Eddies of wrath ceaseless round & round,
And the sulphureous foam, surgeing thick,
Settled, a lake, bright & shining clear,
White as the snow on the mountains cold.

4. Forgetfulness, dumbness, necessity,
In chains of the mind locked up,
Like fetters of ice shrinking together,
Disorganiz'd, rent from Eternity,
Los beat on his fetters of iron,
And heated his furnaces, & pour'd
Iron sodor and sodor of brass.

5. Restless turn'd the Immortal inchain'd,
Heaving dolorous, anguish'd unbearable;
Till a roof, shaggy wild, inclos'd
In an orb his fountain of thought.

6. In a horrible, dreamful slumber,
Like the linked infernal chain,
A vast Spine writh'd in torment
Upon the winds, shooting pain'd
Ribs, like a bending cavern;
And bones of solidness froze
Over all his nerves of joy.
And a first Age passed over,
And a state of dismal woe.

7. From the caverns of his jointed Spine
Down sunk with fright a red
Round Globe, hot burning, deep,
Deep down into the Abyss;
Panting, Conglobing, Trembling,
Shooting out ten thousand branches
Around his solid bones.
And a second Age passed over,
And a state of dismal woe.

8. In harrowing fear rolling round,
His nervous brain shot branches
Round the branches of his heart
On high into two little orbs,
And fixed in two little caves,
Hiding carefully from the wind,
His Eyes beheld the deep.
And a third Age passed over,
And a state of dismal woe.

9. The pangs of hope began.
In heavy pain, striving, struggling,
Two Ears in close volutions
From beneath his orbs of vision
Shot spiring out and petrified
As they grew. And a fourth Age passed,
And a state of dismal woe.

10. In ghastly torment sick,
Hanging upon the wind,
Two Nostrils bend down to the deep.

And a fifth Age passed over,
And a state of dismal woe.

11. In ghastly torment sick,
Within his ribs bloated round,
A craving Hungry Cavern;
Thence arose his channel'd Throat.
And, like a red flame, a Tongue
Of thirst & of hunger appear'd.
And a sixth Age passed over,
And a state of dismal woe.

12. Enraged & stifled with torment,
He threw his right Arm to the north,
His left Arm to the south
Shooting out in anguish deep,
And his feet stamp'd the nether Abyss
In trembling & howling & dismay.
And a seventh Age passed over,
And a state of dismal woe.

CHAP: V

1. In terrors Los shrunk from his task:
His great hammer fell from his hand.
His fires beheld, and sickening
Hid their strong limbs in smoke;
For with noises, ruinous, loud,
With hurtlings & clashings & groans,
The Immortal endur'd his chains,
Tho' bound in a deadly sleep.

2. All the myriads of Eternity,
All the wisdom & joy of life
Roll like a sea around him,
Except what his little orbs
Of sight by degrees unfold.

3. And now his eternal life
Like a dream was obliterated.

4. Shudd'ring, the Eternal Prophet smote
With a stroke from his north to south region.
The bellows & hammer are silent now;
A nerveless silence his prophetic voice
Siez'd; a cold solitude & dark void
The Eternal Prophet & Urizen clos'd.

5. Ages on ages roll'd over them,
Cut off from life & light, frozen
Into horrible forms of deformity.
Los suffer'd his fires to decay;
Then he look'd back with anxious desire,
But the space, undivided by existence,
Struck horror into his soul.

6. Los wept obscur'd with mourning,
His bosom earthquak'd with sighs;
He saw Urizen deadly black
In his chains bound, & Pity began,

7. In anguish dividing & dividing,
For pity divides the soul
In pangs, eternity on eternity,
Life in cataracts pour'd down his cliffs.
The void shrunk the lymph into Nerves
Wand'ring wide on the bosom of night
And left a round globe of blood
Trembling upon the void.
Thus the Eternal Prophet was divided
Before the death image of Urizen;
For in changeable clouds and darkness,
In a winterly night beneath,
The Abyss of Los stretch'd immense;
And now seen, now obscur'd, to the eyes
Of Eternals the visions remote
Of the dark seperation appear'd:
As glasses discover Worlds
In the endless Abyss of space,
So the expanding eyes of Immortals
Beheld the dark visions of Los
And the globe of life blood trembling.

8. The globe of life blood trembled
Branching out into roots,
Fibrous, writhing upon the winds,
Fibres of blood, milk and tears,
In pangs, eternity on eternity.
At length in tears & cries imbodied,
A female form, trembling and pale,
Waves before his deathy face.

9. All Eternity shudder'd at sight
Of the first female now separate,
Pale as a cloud of snow
Waving before the face of Los.

10. Wonder, awe, fear, astonishment
Petrify the eternal myriads
At the first female form now separate.
They call'd her Pity, and fled.

11. "Spread a Tent with strong curtains around them.
Let cords & stakes bind in the Void,
That Eternals may no more behold them."

12. They began to weave curtains of darkness,
They erected large pillars round the Void,
With golden hooks fasten'd in the pillars;
With infinite labour the Eternals
A woof wove, and called it Science.

CHAP: VI

1. But Los saw the Female & pitied;
He embrac'd her; she wept, she refus'd;
In perverse and cruel delight
She fled from his arms, yet he follow'd.

2. Eternity shudder'd when they saw
Man begetting his likeness
On his own divided image.

3. A time passed over: the Eternals
Began to erect the tent,

When Enitharmon, sick,
Felt a Worm within her Womb.

4. Yet helpless it lay like a Worm
In the trembling womb
To be moulded into existence.

5. All day the worm lay on her bosom;
All night within her womb
The worm lay till it grew to a serpent,
With dolorous hissings & poisons
Round Enitharmon's loins folding.

6. Coil'd within Enitharmon's womb
The serpent grew, casting its scales;
With sharp pangs the hissings began
To change to a grating cry:
Many sorrows and dismal throes,
Many forms of fish, bird & beast
Brought forth an Infant form
Where was a worm before.

7. The Eternals their tent finished
Alarm'd with these gloomy visions,
When Enitharmon groaning
Produc'd a man Child to the light.

8. A shriek ran thro' Eternity,
And a paralytic stroke,
At the birth of the Human shadow.

9. Delving earth in his resistless way,
Howling, the Child with fierce flames
Issu'd from Enitharmon.

10. The Eternals closed the tent;
They beat down the stakes, the cords
Stretch'd for a work of eternity.
No more Los beheld Eternity.

11. In his hands he siez'd the infant,
He bathed him in springs of sorrow,
He gave him to Enitharmon.

CHAP: VII

1. They named the child Orc; he grew,
Fed with milk of Enitharmon.

2. Los awoke her. O sorrow & pain!
A tight'ning girdle grew
Around his bosom. In sobbings
He burst the girdle in twain;
But still another girdle
Oppress'd his bosom. In sobbings
Again he burst it. Again
Another girdle succeeds.
The girdle was form'd by day,
By night was burst in twain.

3. These falling down on the rock
Into an iron Chain
In each other link by link lock'd.

4. They took Orc to the top of a mountain.
O how Enitharmon wept!
They chain'd his young limbs to the rock
With the Chain of Jealousy
Beneath Urizen's deathful shadow.

5. The dead heard the voice of the child
And began to awake from sleep;
All things heard the voice of the child
And began to awake to life.

6. And Urizen, craving with hunger,
Stung with the odours of Nature,
Explor'd his dens around.

7. He form'd a line & a plummet
To divide the Abyss beneath;
He form'd a dividing rule;

8. He formed scales to weigh,
He formed massy weights;

He formed a brazen quadrant;
He formed golden compasses,
And began to explore the Abyss;
And he planted a garden of fruits.

9. But Los encircled Enitharmon
With fires of Prophecy
From the sight of Urizen & Orc.

10. And she bore an enormous race.

CHAP: VIII

1. Urizen explor'd his dens,
Mountain, moor & wilderness,
With a globe of fire lighting his journey,
A fearful journey, annoy'd
By cruel enormities, forms
Of life on his forsaken mountains.

2. And his world teem'd vast enormities,
Fright'ning, faithless, fawning
Portions of life, similitudes
Of a foot, or a hand, or a head,
Or a heart, or an eye; they swam mischevous,
Dread terrors, delighting in blood.

3. Most Urizen sicken'd to see
His eternal creations appear,
Sons & daughters of sorrow on mountains
Weeping, wailing. First Thiriel appear'd,
Astonish'd at his own existence,
Like a man from a cloud born; & Utha,
From the waters emerging, laments;
Grodna rent the deep earth, howling
Amaz'd; his heavens immense cracks
Like the ground parch'd with heat, then Fuzon
Flam'd out, first begotten, last born;
All his Eternal sons in like manner;
His daughters from green herbs & cattle,
From monsters & worms of the pit.

4. He in darkness clos'd view'd all his race,
And his soul sicken'd! he curs'd
Both sons & daughters; for he saw
That no flesh nor spirit could keep
His iron laws one moment.

5. For he saw that life liv'd upon death:
The Ox in the slaughter house moans,
The Dog at the wintry door;
And he wept & he called it Pity,
And his tears flowed down on the winds.

6. Cold he wander'd on high, over their cities
In weeping & pain & woe;
And wherever he wander'd, in sorrows
Upon the aged heavens,
A cold shadow follow'd behind him
Like a spider's web, moist, cold & dim,
Drawing out from his sorrowing soul,
The dungeon-like heaven dividing,
Where ever the footsteps of Urizen
Walked over the cities in sorrow;

7. Till a Web, dark & cold, throughout all
The tormented element stretch'd
From the sorrows of Urizen's soul.
And the Web is a Female in embrio.
None could break the Web, no wings of fire,

8. So twisted the cords, & so knotted
The meshes, twisted like to the human brain.

9. And all call'd it The Net of Religion.

CHAP: IX

1. Then the Inhabitants of those Cities
Felt their Nerves change into Marrow,
And hardening Bones began
In swift diseases and torments,
In throbbings & shootings & grindings

Thro' all the coasts; till weaken'd
The Senses inward rush'd, shrinking
Beneath the dark net of infection;

2. Till the shrunken eyes, clouded over,
Discern'd not the woven hipocrisy;
But the streaky slime in their heavens,
Brought together by narrowing perceptions,
Appear'd transparent air; for their eyes
Grew small like the eyes of a man,
And in reptile forms shrinking together,
Of seven feet stature they remain'd.

3. Six days they shrunk up from existence,
And on the seventh day they rested,
And they bless'd the seventh day, in sick hope,
And forgot their eternal life.

4. And their thirty cities divided
In form of a human heart.
No more could they rise at will
In the infinite void, but bound down
To earth by their narrowing perceptions
They lived a period of years;
Then left a noisom body
To the jaws of devouring darkness.

5. And their children wept, & built
Tombs in the desolate places,
And form'd laws of prudence, and call'd them
The eternal laws of God.

6. And the thirty cities remain'd,
Surrounded by salt floods, now call'd
Africa: its name was then Egypt.

7. The remaining sons of Urizen
Beheld their brethren shrink together
Beneath the Net of Urizen.
Perswasion was in vain;
For the ears of the inhabitants
Were wither'd & deafen'd & cold,

And their eyes could not discern
Their brethren of other cities.

8. So Fuzon call'd all together
The remaining children of Urizen,
And they left the pendulous earth.
They called it Egypt, & left it.

9. And the salt Ocean rolled englob'd.

THE END OF THE FIRST BOOK OF URIZEN

The Book of Ahania

CHAP: IST

1.

FUZON on a chariot iron-wing'd
On spiked flames rose; his hot visage
Flam'd furious; sparkles his hair & beard
Shot down his wide bosom and shoulders.
On clouds of smoke rages his chariot
And his right hand burns red in its cloud
Moulding into a vast Globe his wrath,
As the thunder-stone is moulded.
Son of Urizen's silent burnings:

2. "Shall we worship this Demon of smoke,"
Said Fuzon, "this abstract non-entity,
This cloudy God seated on waters,
Now seen, now obscur'd, King of sorrow?"

3. So he spoke in a fiery flame,
On Urizen frowning indignant,
The Globe of wrath shaking on high;
Roaring with fury he threw
The howling Globe; burning it flew
Length'ning into a hungry beam. Swiftly

4. Oppos'd to the exulting flam'd beam,
The broad Disk of Urizen upheav'd
Across the Void many a mile.

5. It was forg'd in mills where the winter
Beats incessant: ten winters the disk
Unremitting endur'd the cold hammer.

6. But the strong arm that sent it remember'd
The sounding beam: laughing, it tore through
That beaten mass, keeping its direction,
The cold loins of Urizen dividing.

7. Dire shriek'd his invisible Lust;
Deep groan'd Urizen! stretching his awful hand,
Ahania (so name his parted soul)
He siez'd on his mountains of Jealousy.
He groan'd anguish'd, & called her Sin,
Kissing her and weeping over her;
Then hid her in darkness, in silence,
Jealous, tho' she was invisible.

8. She fell down a faint shadow wand'ring
In chaos and circling dark Urizen,
As the moon anguish'd circles the earth,
Hopeless! abhorr'd! a death-shadow,
Unseen, unbodied, unknown,
The mother of Pestilence.

9. But the fiery beam of Fuzon
Was a pillar of fire to Egypt
Five hundred years wand'ring on earth,
Till Los siez'd it and beat in a mass
With the body of the sun.

CHAP: IID

1. But the forehead of Urizen gathering,
And his eyes pale with anguish, his lips
Blue & changing, in tears and bitter
Contrition he prepar'd his Bow,

2. Form'd of Ribs, that in his dark solitude,
When obscur'd in his forests, fell monsters
Arose. For his dire Contemplations
Rush'd down like floods from his mountains,

In torrents of mud settling thick,
With Eggs of unnatural production:
Forthwith hatching, some howl'd on his hills,
Some in vales, some aloft flew in air.

3. Of these, an enormous dread Serpent,
Scaled and poisonous horned,
Approach'd Urizen, even to his knees,
As he sat on his dark rooted Oak.

4. With his horns he push'd furious:
Great the conflict & great the jealousy
In cold poisons, but Urizen smote him.

5. First he poison'd the rocks with his blood,
Then polish'd his ribs, and his sinews
Dried, laid them apart till winter;
Then a Bow black prepar'd: on this Bow
A poisoned rock plac'd in silence.
He utter'd these words to the Bow:

6. "O Bow of the clouds of secresy!
O nerve of that lust-form'd monster!
Send this rock swift, invisible thro'
The black clouds on the bosom of Fuzon."

7. So saying, In torment of his wounds
He bent the enormous ribs slowly,
A circle of darkness! then fixed
The sinew in its rest; then the Rock,
Poisonous source, plac'd with art, lifting difficult
Its weighty bulk; silent the rock lay,

8. While Fuzon, his tygers unloosing,
Thought Urizen slain by his wrath.
"I am God!" said he, "eldest of things."

9. Sudden sings the rock; swift & invisible
On Fuzon flew, enter'd his bosom;
His beautiful visage, his tresses
That gave light to the mornings of heaven,
Were smitten with darkness, deform'd
And outstretch'd on the edge of the forest.

10. But the Rock fell upon the Earth,
Mount Sinai in Arabia.

CHAP: III

1. The Globe shook, and Urizen seated
On black clouds his sore wound anointed;
The ointment flow'd down on the void
Mix'd with blood—here the snake gets her poison.

2. With difficulty & great pain Urizen
Lifted on high the dead corse:
On his shoulders he bore it to where
A Tree hung over the Immensity.

3. For when Urizen shrunk away
From Eternals, he sat on a rock
Barren: a rock which himself
From redounding fancies had petrified.
Many tears fell on the rock,
Many sparks of vegetation.
Soon shot the pained root
Of Mystery under his heel:
It grew a thick tree: he wrote
In silence his book of iron,
Till the horrid plant bending its boughs
Grew to roots when it felt the earth,
And again sprung to many a tree.

4. Amaz'd started Urizen when
He beheld himself compassed round
And high roofed over with trees.
He arose, but the stems stood so thick
He with difficulty and great pain
Brought his Books, all but the Book
Of iron, from the dismal shade.

5. The Tree still grows over the Void
Enrooting itself all around,
An endless labyrinth of woe!

6. The corse of his first begotten
On the accursed Tree of Mystery,
On the topmost stem of this Tree,
Urizen nail'd Fuzon's corse.

CHAP: IV

1. Forth flew the arrows of pestilence
Round the pale living Corse on the tree.

2. For in Urizen's slumbers of abstraction
In the infinite ages of Eternity,
When his Nerves of Joy melted & flow'd,
A white Lake on the dark blue air
In perturb'd pain and dismal torment
Now stretching out, now swift conglobing,

3. Effluvia vapor'd above
In noxious clouds; these hover'd thick
Over the disorganiz'd Immortal,
Till petrific pain scurf'd o'er the Lakes
As the bones of man, solid & dark.

4. The clouds of disease hover'd wide
Around the Immortal in torment,
Perching around the hurtling bones,
Disease on disease, shape on shape
Winged screaming in blood & torment.

5. The Eternal Prophet beat on his anvils;
Enrag'd in the desolate darkness
He forg'd nets of iron around
And Los threw them around the bones.

6. The shapes screaming flutter'd vain:
Some combin'd into muscles & glands,
Some organs for craving and lust;
Most remain'd on the tormented void,
Urizen's army of horrors.

7. Round the pale living Corse on the Tree
Forty years flew the arrows of pestilence.

8. Wailing and terror and woe
Ran thro' all his dismal world;
Forty years all his sons & daughters
Felt their skulls harden; then Asia
Arose in the pendulous deep.

9. They reptilize upon the Earth.

10 Fuzon groan'd on the Tree.

CHAP: V

1. The lamenting voice of Ahania
Weeping upon the void!
And round the Tree of Fuzon,
Distant in solitary night,
Her voice was heard, but no form
Had she; but her tears from clouds
Eternal fell round the Tree.

2. And the voice cried: "Ah, Urizen! Love!
Flower of morning! I weep on the verge
Of Non-entity; how wide the Abyss
Between Ahania and thee!

3. "I lie on the verge of the deep;
I see thy dark clouds ascend;
I see thy black forests and floods,
A horrible waste to my eyes!

4. "Weeping I walk over rocks,
Over dens & thro' valleys of death.
Why didst thou despise Ahania
To cast me from thy bright presence
Into the World of Loneness?

5. "I cannot touch his hand,
Nor weep on his knees, nor hear
His voice & bow, nor see his eyes
And joy, nor hear his footsteps and
My heart leap at the lovely sound!
I cannot kiss the place

Whereon his bright feet have trod,
But I wander on the rocks
With hard necessity.

6. "Where is my golden palace?
Where my ivory bed?
Where the joy of my morning hour?
Where the sons of eternity singing

7. "To awake bright Urizen, my king,
To arise to the mountain sport,
To the bliss of eternal valleys;

8. "To awake my king in the morn,
To embrace Ahania's joy
On the bredth of his open bosom?
From my soft cloud of dew to fall
In showers of life on his harvests,

9. "When he gave my happy soul
To the sons of eternal joy,
When he took the daughters of life
Into my chambers of love,

10. "When I found babes of bliss on my beds
And bosoms of milk in my chambers
Fill'd with eternal seed.
O eternal births sung round Ahania
In interchange sweet of their joys!

11. "Swell'd with ripeness & fat with fatness,
Bursting on winds, my odors,
My ripe figs and rich pomegranates
In infant joy at thy feet,
O Urizen, sported and sang.

12. "Then thou with thy lap full of seed,
With thy hand full of generous fire
Walked forth from the clouds of morning,
On the virgins of springing joy,
On the human soul to cast
The seed of eternal science.

13. "The sweat poured down thy temples;
To Ahania return'd in evening,
The moisture awoke to birth
My mothers-joys, sleeping in bliss.

14. "But now alone over rocks, mountains,
Cast out from thy lovely bosom,
Cruel jealousy! selfish fear!
Self-destroying, how can delight
Renew in these chains of darkness,
Where bones of beasts are strown
On the bleak and snowy mountains,
Where bones from the birth are buried
Before they see the light?"

FINIS

The Song of Los

AFRICA

I WILL sing you a song of Los, the Eternal Prophet:
He sung it to four harps at the tables of Eternity.
In heart-formed Africa
Urizen faded! Ariston shudder'd!
And thus the Song began:

Adam stood in the garden of Eden
And Noah on the mountains of Ararat;
They saw Urizen give his Laws to the Nations
By the hands of the children of Los.

Adam shudder'd! Noah faded! black grew the sunny African
When Rintrah gave Abstract Philosophy to Brama in the East.
(Night spoke to the Cloud:
"Lo these Human form'd spirits, in smiling hipocrisy, War
Against one another; so let them War on, slaves to the eternal
      Elements.")
Noah shrunk beneath the waters;
Abram fled in fires from Chaldea;
Moses beheld upon Mount Sinai forms of dark delusion.

To Trismegistus, Palamabron gave an abstract Law:
To Pythagoras, Socrates & Plato.

Times rolled on o'er all the sons of Har: time after time
Orc on Mount Atlas howl'd, chain'd down with the Chain of
    Jealousy;
Then Oothoon hover'd over Judah & Jerusalem,
And Jesus heard her voice (a man of sorrows) he reciev'd
A Gospel from wretched Theotormon.

The human race began to wither, for the healthy built
Secluded places, fearing the joys of Love,
And the diseased only propagated.
So Antamon call'd up Leutha from her valleys of delight
And to Mahomet a loose Bible gave.
But in the North, to Odin, Sotha gave a Code of War,
Because of Diralada, thinking to reclaim his joy.

These were the Churches, Hospitals, Castles, Palaces,
Like nets & gins & traps to catch the joys of Eternity,
    And all the rest a desart;
Till, like a dream, Eternity was obliterated & erased.

Since that dread day when Har and Heva fled
Because their brethren & sisters liv'd in War & Lust;
And as they fled they shrunk
Into two narrow doleful forms
Creeping in reptile flesh upon
The bosom of the ground;
And all the vast of Nature shrunk
Before their shrunken eyes.

Thus the terrible race of Los & Enitharmon gave
Laws & Religions to the sons of Har, binding them more
And more to Earth, closing and restraining,
Till a Philosophy of Five Senses was complete.
Urizen wept & gave it into the hands of Newton & Locke.

Clouds roll heavy upon the Alps round Rousseau & Voltaire,
And on the mountains of Lebanon round the deceased Gods
Of Asia, & on the desarts of Africa round the Fallen Angels
The Guardian Prince of Albion burns in his nightly tent.

ASIA

The Kings of Asia heard
The howl rise up from Europe,
And each ran out from his Web,
From his ancient woven Den;
For the darkness of Asia was startled
At the thick-flaming, thought-creating fires of Orc.

And the Kings of Asia stood
And cried in bitterness of soul:

"Shall not the King call for Famine from the heath,
Nor the Priest for Pestilence from the fen,
To restrain, to dismay, to thin
The inhabitants of mountain and plain,
In the day of full-feeding prosperity
And the night of delicious songs?

"Shall not the Councellor throw his curb
Of Poverty on the laborious,
To fix the price of labour,
To invent allegoric riches?

"And the privy admonishers of men
Call for fires in the City,
For heaps of smoking ruins
In the night of prosperity & wantonness?

"To turn man from his path,
To restrain the child from the womb,
To cut off the bread from the city,
That the remnant may learn to obey,

"That the pride of the heart may fail,
That the lust of the eyes may be quench'd,
That the delicate ear in its infancy
May be dull'd, and the nostrils clos'd up,
To teach mortal worms the path
That leads from the gates of the Grave?"

Urizen heard them cry,
And his shudd'ring, waving wings
Went enormous above the red flames,
Drawing clouds of despair thro' the heavens
Of Europe as he went.
And his Books of brass, iron & gold
Melted over the land as he flew,
Heavy-waving, howling, weeping.

And he stood over Judea,
And stay'd in his ancient place,
And stretch'd his clouds over Jerusalem;

For Adam, a mouldering skeleton,
Lay bleach'd on the garden of Eden;
And Noah, as white as snow,
On the mountains of Ararat.

Then the thunders of Urizen bellow'd aloud
From his woven darkness above.

Orc, raging in European darkness,
Arose like a pillar of fire above the Alps,
Like a serpent of fiery flame!
        The sullen Earth
        Shrunk!

Forth from the dead dust, rattling bones to bones
Join; shaking convuls'd, the shiv'ring clay breathes,
And all flesh naked stands: Fathers and Friends,
Mothers & Infants, Kings & Warriors.

The Grave shrieks with delight & shakes
Her hollow womb & clasps the solid stem:
Her bosom swells with wild desire,
And milk & blood & glandous wine
In rivers rush & shout & dance,
On mountain, dale and plain.

The SONG of LOS is ended.

Urizen Wept.

PART THREE

MAJOR PROPHECIES

MAJOR PROPHECIES

Selections from The Four Zoas

From NIGHT THE FIRST

THE Song of the Aged Mother which shook the heavens with
    wrath,
Hearing the march of long resounding, strong heroic Verse
Marshall'd in order for the day of Intellectual Battle.
The heavens quake, the earth was moved & shudder'd, & the
    mountains
With all their woods, the streams & valleys wail'd in dismal fear.

Four Mighty Ones are in every Man; a Perfect Unity
Cannot Exist but from the Universal Brotherhood of Eden,
The Universal Man, to Whom be Glory Evermore. Amen.
What are the Natures of those Living Creatures the Heav'nly
    Father only
Knoweth. No Individual knoweth, nor can know in all Eternity.

Los was the fourth immortal starry one, & in the Earth
Of a bright Universe, Empery attended day & night,
Days & nights of revolving joy. Urthona was his name
In Eden; in the Auricular Nerves of Human Life,
Which is the Earth of Eden, he his Emanations propagated,
Fairies of Albion, afterwards Gods of the Heathen.
    Daughter of Beulah, Sing
His fall into Division & his Resurrection to Unity:
His fall into the Generation of decay & death, & his
Regeneration by the Resurrection from the dead.

Begin with Tharmas, Parent power, dark'ning in the West.

"Lost! Lost! Lost! are my Emanations! Enion, O Enion,
We are become a Victim to the Living. We hide in secret.
I have hidden Jerusalem in silent Contrition, O Pity Me.
I will build thee a Labyrinth also: O pity me. O Enion,
Why hast thou taken sweet Jerusalem from my inmost Soul?
Let her Lay secret in the soft recess of darkness & silence.
It is not Love I bear to Enitharmon. It is Pity.
She hath taken refuge in my bosom & I cannot cast her out.

"The Men have receiv'd their death wounds & their Emanations
     are fled
To me for refuge & I cannot turn them out for Pity's sake."

Enion said: "Thy fear has made me tremble, thy terrors have
     surrounded me.
All Love is lost: Terror succeeds, & Hatred instead of Love,
And stern demands of Right & Duty instead of Liberty.
Once thou wast to Me the loveliest son of heaven—But now
Why art thou Terrible? and yet I love thee in thy terror till
I am almost Extinct & soon shall be a shadow in Oblivion,
Unless some way can be found that I may look upon thee &
     live.
Hide me some shadowy semblance, secret whisp'ring in my Ear,
In secret of soft wings, in mazes of delusive beauty.
I have look'd into the secret soul of him I lov'd,
And in the Dark recesses found Sin & cannot return."

Trembling & pale sat Tharmas, weeping in his clouds.

"Why wilt thou Examine every little fibre of my soul,
Spreading them out before the sun like stalks of flax to dry?
The infant joy is beautiful, but its anatomy
Horrible, Ghast & Deadly; nought shalt thou find in it
But Death, Despair & Everlasting brooding Melancholy.
Thou wilt go mad with horror if thou dost Examine thus
Every moment of my secret hours. Yea, I know
That I have sinn'd, & that my Emanations are become harlots.
I am already distracted at their deeds, & if I look   .
Upon them more, Despair will bring self-murder on my soul.
O Enion, thou art thyself a root growing in hell,
Tho' thus heavenly beautiful to draw me to destruction.
Sometimes I think thou art a flower expanding,

Sometimes I think thou art fruit, breaking from its bud
In dreadful dolor & pain; & I am like an atom,
A Nothing, left in darkness; yet I am an identity:
I wish & feel & weep & groan. Ah, terrible! terrible!"

In Eden, Females sleep the winter in soft silken veils
Woven by their own hands to hide them in the darksom grave;
But Males immortal live renew'd by female deaths; in soft
Delight they die, & they revive in spring with music & songs.
Enion said: "Farewell, I die. I hide from thy searching eyes."

So saying, From her bosom weaving soft in sinewy threads
A tabernacle for Jerusalem, she sat among the Rocks
Singing her lamentation. Tharmas groan'd among his Clouds
Weeping; then bending from his Clouds, he stoop'd his inno-
cent head,
And stretching out his holy hand in the vast deep sublime,
Turn'd round the circle of Destiny with tears & bitter sighs
And said: "Return, O wanderer, when the day of Clouds is
o'er."

So saying, he sunk down into the sea, a pale white corse.
In torment he sunk down & flow'd among her filmy Woof,
His spectre issuing from his feet in flames of fire.
In gnawing pain drawn out by her lov'd fingers, every nerve
She counted, every vein & lacteal, threading them among
Her woof of terror. Terrified & drinking tears of woe
Shudd'ring she wove nine days & nights, sleepless; her food was
tears.
Wond'ring she saw her woof begin to animate, & not
As Garments woven subservient to her hands, but having a will
Of its own, perverse & wayward. Enion lov'd & wept.
Nine days she labour'd at her work, & nine dark sleepless
nights;
But on the tenth trembling morn, the Circle of Destiny com-
plete,
Round roll'd the sea, Englobing in a wat'ry Globe, self balanc'd.
A Frowning Continent appear'd where Enion in the desert,
Terrified in her own Creation, viewing her woven shadow,
Sat in a dread intoxication of Repentance & Contrition.
He spurn'd Enion with his foot; he sprang aloft in Clouds
Alighting in his drunken joy in a far distant Grove.

There is from Great Eternity a mild & pleasant rest
Nam'd Beulah, a soft Moony Universe, feminine, lovely,
Pure, mild & Gentle, given in mercy to those who sleep,
Eternally Created by the Lamb of God around,
On all sides, within & without the Universal Man.
The daughters of Beulah follow sleepers in all their dreams,
Creating spaces, lest they fall into Eternal Death.
The Circle of Destiny complete, they gave to it a space
And nam'd the space Ulro, & brooded over it in care & love.
They said: "The Spectre is in every man insane & most
Deform'd. Thro' the three heavens descending in fury & fire
We meet it with our songs & loving blandishments, & give
To it a form of vegetation. But this Spectre of Tharmas
Is Eternal Death. What shall we do? O God, pity & help!"
So spoke they, & clos'd the Gate of the Tongue in trembling
    fear.

                    .   .   .

And This is the Song sung at The Feast of Los & Enitharmon:

"Ephraim call'd out to Zion: 'Awake, O Brother Mountain!
Let us refuse the Plow & Spade, the heavy Roller & spiked
Harrow; burn all these Corn fields, throw down all these fences!
Fatten'd on Human blood & drunk with wine of life is better
    far
Than all these labours of the harvest & the vintage. See the
    river,
Red with the blood of Men, swells lustful round my rocky
    knees;
My clouds are not the clouds of verdant fields & groves of fruit,
But Clouds of Human Souls: my nostrils drink the lives of
    Men.'

"The Villages lament: they faint, outstretch'd upon the plain.
Wailing runs round the Valleys from the Mill & from the Barn.
But most the polish'd Palaces, dark, silent, bow with dread,
Hiding their books & pictures underneath the dens of Earth.

"The Cities send to one another saying: 'My sons are Mad
With wine of cruelty. Let us plat a scourge, O Sister City.'

Children are nourish'd for the Slaughter; once the Child was
    fed
With Milk, but wherefore now are Children fed with blood?

"The Horse is of more value than the Man. The Tyger fierce
Laughs at the Human form; the Lion mocks & thirsts for blood.
They cry, 'O Spider, spread thy web! Enlarge thy bones &, fill'd
With marrow, sinews & flesh, Exalt thyself, attain a voice.

" 'Call to thy dark arm'd hosts; for all the sons of Men muster
    together
To desolate their cities! Man shall be no more! Awake, O
    Hosts!'
The bow string sang upon the hills, 'Luvah & Vala ride
Triumphant in the bloody sky, & the Human form is no more.'

"The list'ning Stars heard, & the first beam of the morning
    started back:
He cried out to his Father 'depart! depart!' but sudden Siez'd,
And clad in steel, & his Horse proudly neigh'd; he smelt the
    battle
Afar off. Rushing back, redd'ning with rage, the Mighty Father

"Siez'd his bright sheephook studded with gems & gold; he swung
    it round
His head, shrill sounding in the sky; down rush'd the Sun with
    noise
Of war; the Mountains fled away; they sought a place beneath.
Vala remain'd in deserts of dark solitude, nor Sun nor Moon

"By night nor day to comfort her; she labour'd in thick smoke.
Tharmas endur'd not; he fled howling: then, a barren waste,
    sunk down
Conglobing in the dark confusion. Mean time Los was born
And thou, O Enitharmon! Hark, I hear the hammers of Los.

"They melt the bones of Vala & the bones of Luvah into
    wedges;
The innumerable sons & daughters of Luvah, clos'd in furnaces,
Melt into furrows; winter blows his bellows: Ice & snow
Tend the dire anvils: Mountains mourn, & Rivers faint & fail.

"There is no City, nor Cornfield, nor Orchard; all is Rock &
    Sand.
There is no Sun, nor Moon, nor Star, but rugged wintry rocks
Justling together in the void, suspended by inward fires.
Impatience now no longer can endure. Distracted Luvah,

"Bursting forth from the loins of Enitharmon, Thou fierce
    Terror,
Go howl in vain! Smite, smite his fetters! smite, O wintry ham-
    mers!
Smite, Spectre of Urthona! mock the fiend who drew us down
From heavens of joy into this deep. Now rage, but rage in
    vain!"

Thus sang the demons of the deep; the Clarions of war blew
    loud.
The Feast redounds, & Crown'd with roses & the circling vine
The Enormous Bride & Bridegroom sat; beside them Urizen,
With faded radiance sigh'd, forgetful of the flowing wine
And of Ahania, his Pure Bride; but she was distant far.

But Los & Enitharmon sat in discontent & scorn,
Craving the more, the more enjoying, drawing out sweet bliss
From all the turning wheels of heaven & the chariots of the
    Slain.

At distance, Far in Night repell'd, in direful hunger craving,
Summers & winters round revolving in the frightful deep,
Enion, blind & age-bent, wept upon the desolate wind:

"Why does the Raven cry aloud and no eye pities her?
Why fall the Sparrow & the Robin in the foodless winter?
Faint, shivering, they sit on leafless bush or frozen stone

"Wearied with seeking food across the snowy waste, the little
Heart cold, and the little tongue consum'd that once in thought-
    less joy
Gave songs of gratitude to waving cornfields round their nest.

"Why howl the Lion & the Wolf? why do they roam abroad?
Deluded by summer's heat, they sport in enormous love
And cast their young out to the hungry wilds & sandy deserts.

"Why is the Sheep given to the knife? the Lamb plays in the
    Sun:
He starts! he hears the foot of Man! he says: Take thou my
    wool,
But spare my life: but he knows not that winter cometh fast.

"The Spider sits in his labour'd Web, eager watching for the
    Fly.
Presently comes a famish'd Bird & takes away the Spider.
His Web is left all desolate that his little anxious heart
So careful wove & spread it out with sighs and weariness."

This was the Lamentation of Enion round the golden Feast.

From NIGHT THE SECOND

NIGHT passed, & Enitharmon, e'er the dawn, return'd in bliss.
She sang O'er Los reviving him to Life: his groans were ter-
    rible;
But thus she sang:
        "I sieze the sphery harp. I strike the strings.

"At the first sound the Golden sun arises from the deep
And shakes his awful hair,
The Eccho wakes the moon to unbind her silver locks,
The golden sun bears on my song
And nine bright spheres of harmony rise round the fiery king.

"The joy of woman is the death of her most best beloved
Who dies for Love of her
In torments of fierce jealousy & pangs of adoration.
The Lovers' night bears on my song
And the nine spheres rejoice beneath my powerful controll.

"They sing unceasing to the notes of my immortal hand.
The solemn, silent moon
Reverberates the living harmony upon my limbs,
The birds & beasts rejoice & play,
And every one seeks for his mate to prove his inmost joy.

"Furious & terrible they sport & red the nether deep;
The deep lifts up his rugged head,
And lost in infinite humming wings vanishes with a cry.
The fading cry is ever dying,
The living voice is ever living in its inmost joy.

"Arise, you little glancing wings & sing your infant joy!
Arise & drink your bliss!
For every thing that lives is holy; for the source of life
Descends to be a weeping babe;
For the Earthworm renews the moisture of the sandy plain.

"Now my left hand I stretch to earth beneath,
And strike the terrible string.
I wake sweet joy in dens of sorrow & I plant a smile
In forests of affliction,
And wake the bubbling springs of life in regions of dark death.

"O, I am weary! lay thine hand upon me or I faint,
I faint beneath these beams of thine,
For thou hast touch'd my five senses & they answer'd thee.
Now I am nothing, & I sink
And on the bed of silence sleep till thou awakest me."

Thus sang the Lovely one in Rapturous delusive trance.
Los heard, reviving; he siez'd her in his arms; delusive hopes
Kindling, she led him into shadows & thence fled outstretch'd
Upon the immense like a bright rainbow, weeping & smiling &
    fading.

Thus liv'd Los, driving Enion far into the deathful infinite
That he may also draw Ahania's spirit into her Vortex.
Ah, happy blindness! Enion sees not the terrors of the uncer-
    tain,
And thus she wails from the dark deep; the golden heavens
    tremble:

"I am made to sow the thistle for wheat, the nettle for a nour-
    ishing dainty.
I have planted a false oath in the earth; it has brought forth a
    poison tree.
I have chosen the serpent for a councellor, & the dog

For a schoolmaster to my children.
I have blotted out from light & living the dove & nightingale,
And I have caused the earth worm to beg from door to door.

"I have taught the thief a secret path into the house of the just.
I have taught pale artifice to spread his nets upon the morning.
My heavens are brass, my earth is iron, my moon a clod of clay,
My sun a pestilence burning at noon & a vapour of death in
    night.   .

"What is the price of Experience? do men buy it for a song?
Or wisdom for a dance in the street? No, it is bought with the
    price
Of all that a man hath, his house, his wife, his children.
Wisdom is sold in the desolate market where none come to
    buy,
And in the wither'd field where the farmer plows for bread in
    vain.

"It is an easy thing to triumph in the summer's sun
And in the vintage & to sing on the waggon loaded with corn.
It is an easy thing to talk of patience to the afflicted,
To speak the laws of prudence to the houseless wanderer,
To listen to the hungry raven's cry in wintry season
When the red blood is fill'd with wine & with the marrow of
    lambs.

"It is an easy thing to laugh at wrathful elements,
To hear the dog howl at the wintry door, the ox in the slaughter
    house moan;
To see a god on every wind & a blessing on every blast;
To hear sounds of love in the thunder storm that destroys our
    enemies' house;
To rejoice in the blight that covers his field, & the sickness that
    cuts off his children,
While our olive & vine sing & laugh round our door, & our chil-
    dren bring fruits & flowers.

"Then the groan & the dolor are quite forgotten, & the slave
    grinding at the mill,

And the captive in chains, & the poor in the prison, & the sol-
    dier in the field
When the shatter'd bone hath laid him groaning among the
    happier dead.

"It is an easy thing to rejoice in the tents of prosperity:
Thus could I sing & thus rejoice: but it is not so with me:"

From NIGHT THE FIFTH

INFECTED, Mad, he danc'd on his mountains high & dark as
    heaven,
Now fix'd into one stedfast bulk his features stonify,
From his mouth curses, & from his eyes sparks of blighting,
Beside the anvil cold he danc'd with the hammer of Urthona.
Terrific pale Enitharmon stretched on the dreary earth
Felt her immortal limbs freeze, stiffening, pale, inflexible.
His feet shrink with'ring from the deep, shrinking & withering,
And Enitharmon shrunk up, all their fibres with'ring beneath,
As plants wither'd by winter, leaves & stems & roots decaying
Melt into thin air, while the seed, driv'n by the furious wind,
Rests on the distant Mountain's top. So Los & Enitharmon,
Shrunk into fixed space, stood trembling on a Rocky cliff,
Yet mighty bulk & majesty & beauty remain'd, but unexpansive.
As far as highest Zenith from the lowest Nadir, so far shrunk
Los from the furnaces, a space immense, & left the cold
Prince of Light bound in chains of intellect among the fur-
    naces;
But all the furnaces were out & the bellows had ceast to blow.

He stood trembling & Enitharmon clung around his knees,
Their senses unexpansive in one stedfast bulk remain.
The night blew cold, & Enitharmon shriek'd on the dismal wind.
Her pale hands cling around her husband, & over her weak
    head
Shadows of Eternal Death sit in the leaden air.

But the soft pipe, the flute, the viol, organ, harp, & cymbal,
And the sweet sound of silver voices calm the weary couch
Of Enitharmon; but her groans drown the immortal harps.
Loud & more loud the living music floats upon the air,

Faint & more faint the daylight wanes; the wheels of turning
    darkness
Began in solemn revolutions. Earth, convuls'd with rending
    pangs,
Rock'd to & fro & cried sore at the groans of Enitharmon.
Still the faint harps & silver voices calm the weary couch,
But from the caves of deepest night, ascending in clouds of
    mist,
The winter spread his wide black wings across from pole to
    pole:
Grim frost beneath & terrible snow, link'd in a marriage chain,
Began a dismal dance. The winds around on pointed rocks
Settled like bats innumerable, ready to fly abroad.
The groans of Enitharmon shake the skies, the lab'ring Earth,
Till from her heart rending his way, a terrible child sprang
    forth
In thunder, smoke & sullen flames, & howlings & fury & blood.

.   .   .

His limbs bound down mock at his chains, for over them a
    flame
Of circling fire unceasing plays; to feed them with life & bring
The virtues of the Eternal worlds, ten thousand thousand spirits
Of life lament around the Demon, going forth & returning.
At his enormous call they flee into the heavens of heavens
And back return with wine & food, or dive into the deeps
To bring the thrilling joys of sense to quell his ceaseless rage.
His eyes, the lights of his large soul, contract or else expand:
Contracted they behold the secrets of the infinite mountains,
The veins of gold & silver & the hidden things of Vala,
Whatever grows from its pure bud or breathes a fragrant soul:
Expanded they behold the terrors of the Sun & Moon,
The Elemental Planets & the orbs of eccentric fire.
His nostrils breathe a fiery flame, his locks are like the forests
Of wild beasts; there the lion glares, the tyger & wolf howl
    there,
And there the Eagle hides her young in cliffs & precipices.
His bosom is like starry heaven expanded; all the stars
Sing round; there waves the harvest & the vintage rejoices; the
    springs
Flow into rivers of delight; there the spontaneous flowers
Drink, laugh & sing, the grasshopper, the Emmet and the Fly;

The golden Moth builds there a house & spreads her silken bed.
His loins inwove with silken fires are like a furnace fierce:
As the strong Bull in summer time when bees sing round the
    heath
Where the herds low after the shadow & after the water spring,
The num'rous flocks cover the mountains & shine along the
    valley.
His knees are rocks of adament & rubie & emerald:
Spirits of strength in Palaces rejoice in golden armour
Armed with spear & shield they drink & rejoice over the slain.
Such is the Demon, such his terror on the nether deep.

                    .   .   .

The Woes of Urizen shut up in the deep dens of Urthona:

"Ah! how shall Urizen the King submit to this dark mansion?
Ah! how is this? Once on the heights I stretch'd my throne sub-
    lime;
The mountains of Urizen, once of silver, where the sons of wis-
    dom dwelt,
And on whose tops the Virgins sang, are rocks of desolation.

"My fountains, once the haunt of swans, now breed the scaly
    tortoise,
The houses of my harpers are become a haunt of crows,
The gardens of wisdom are become a field of horrid graves,
And on the bones I drop my tears & water them in vain.

"Once how I walked from my palace in gardens of delight,
The sons of wisdom stood around, the harpers follow'd with
    harps,
Nine virgins cloth'd in light compos'd the song to their immor-
    tal voices,
And at my banquets of new wine my head was crown'd with
    joy.

"Then in my ivory pavilions I slumber'd in the noon
And walked in the silent night among sweet smelling flowers,
Till on my silver bed I slept & sweet dreams round me hover'd,
But now my land is darken'd & my wise men are departed.

"My songs are turned into cries of Lamentation
Heard on my Mountains, & deep sighs under my palace roofs,
Because the Steeds of Urizen, once swifter than the light,
Were kept back from my Lord & from his chariot of mercies.

"O did I keep the horses of the day in silver pastures!
O I refus'd the lord of day the horses of his prince!
O did I close my treasuries with roofs of solid stone
And darken all my Palace walls with envyings & hate!

"O Fool! to think that I could hide from his all piercing eyes
The gold & silver & costly stones, his holy workmanship!
O Fool! could I forget the light that filled my bright spheres
Was a reflection of his face who call'd me from the deep!

"I well remember, for I heard the mild & holy voice
Saying, 'O light, spring up & shine,' & I sprang up from the
    deep.
He gave me a silver scepter, & crown'd me with a golden
    crown,
& said, 'Go forth & guide my Son who wanders on the ocean.'

"I went not forth: I hid myself in black clouds of my wrath;
I call'd the stars around my feet in the night of councils dark;
The stars threw down their spears & fled naked away.
We fell. I siez'd thee, dark Urthona. In my left hand falling

"I siez'd thee, beauteous Luvah; thou art faded like a flower
And like a lilly is thy wife Valâ wither'd by winds.
When thou didst bear the golden cup at the immortal tables
Thy children smote their fiery wings, crown'd with the gold of
    heaven.

"Thy pure feet step'd on the steps divine, too pure for other
    feet,
And thy fair locks shadow'd thine eyes from the divine efful-
    gence,
Then thou didst keep with Strong Urthona the living gates of
    heaven,
But now thou art bow'd down with him, even to the gates of
    hell.

"Because thou gavest Urizen the wine of the Almighty
For Steeds of Light, that they might run in thy golden chariot
    of pride,
I gave to thee the Steeds, I pour'd the stolen wine
And drunken with the immortal draught fell from my throne
    sublime.

"I will arise, Explore these dens, & find that deep pulsation
That shakes my cavern with strong shudders; perhaps this is
    the night
Of Prophecy, & Luvah hath burst his way from Enitharmon.
When Thought is clos'd in Caves Then love shall shew its root
    in deepest Hell."

From NIGHT THE SIXTH

FOR Urizen beheld the terrors of the Abyss wandering among
The ruin'd spirits, once his children & the children of Luvah.
Scar'd at the sound of their own sigh that seems to shake the
    immense
They wander Moping, in their heart a sun, a dreary moon,
A Universe of fiery constellations in their brain,
An earth of wintry woe beneath their feet, & round their loins
Waters or winds or clouds or brooding lightnings & pestilential
    plagues.
Beyond the bounds of their own self their senses cannot pene-
    trate:
As the tree knows not what is outside of its leaves & bark
And yet it drinks the summer joy & fears the winter sorrow,
So, in the regions of the grave, none knows his dark compeer
Tho' he partakes of his dire woes & mutual returns the pang,
The throb, the dolor, the convulsion, in soul-sickening woes.

Not so clos'd kept the Prince of Light now darken'd, wand'ring
    among
The Ruin'd Spirits, once his Children & the Children of Luvah:
For Urizen beheld the terrors of the Abyss, wandering among

The horrid shapes & sights of torment in burning dungeons & in
Fetters of red hot iron; some with crowns of serpents & some
With monsters girding round their bosoms; some lying on beds
    of sulphur,
On racks & wheels; he beheld women marching o'er burning
    wastes
Of Sand in bands of hundreds & of fifties & of thousands,
    strucken with
Lightnings which blazed after them upon their shoulders in
    their march
In successive volleys with loud thunders: swift flew the King of
    Light
Over the burning desarts; Then, the desarts pass'd, involv'd in
    clouds
Of smoke with myriads moping in the stifling vapours, Swift
Flew the King, tho' flag'd his powers, labouring till over rocks
And Mountains faint weary he wander'd where multitudes
    were shut
Up in the solid mountains & in rocks which heav'd with their
    torments.
Then came he among fiery cities & castles built of burning
    steel.
Then he beheld the forms of tygers & of Lions, dishumaniz'd
    men.
Many in serpents & in worms, stretched out enormous length
Over the sullen mould & slimy tracks, obstruct his way
Drawn out from deep to deep, woven by ribb'd
And scaled monsters or arm'd in iron shell, or shell of brass
Or gold: a glittering torment shining & hissing in eternal pain;
Some, columns of fire or of water, sometimes stretch'd out in
    heighth,
Sometimes in length, sometimes englobing, wandering in vain
    seeking for ease.
His voice to them was but an inarticulate thunder, for their
    Ears
Were heavy & dull, & their eyes & nostrils closed up.
Oft he stood by a howling victim Questioning in words
Soothing or Furious; no one answer'd; every one wrap'd up
In his own sorrow howl'd regardless of his words, nor voice
Of sweet response could he obtain, tho' oft assay'd with tears.
He knew they were his Children ruin'd in his ruin'd world.

From NIGHT THE SEVENTH

(Later Version)

AND Urizen hung over Orc & view'd his terrible wrath;
Sitting upon an iron Crag, at length his words broke forth:

"Image of dread, whence art thou? whence is this most woful
   place?
Whence these fierce fires, but from thyself? No other living
   thing
In all this Chasm I behold. No other living thing
Dare thy most terrible wrath abide. Bound here to waste in
   pain
Thy vital substance in these fires that issue new & new
Around thee, sometimes like a flood, & sometimes like a rock
Of living pangs, thy horrible bed glowing with ceaseless fires
Beneath thee & around. Above, a shower of fire now beats,
Moulded to globes & arrowy wedges, rending thy bleeding
   limbs.
And now a whirling pillar of burning sands to overwhelm thee,
Steeping thy wounds in salts infernal & in bitter anguish.
And now a rock moves on the surface of this lake of fire
To bear thee down beneath the waves in stifling despair.
Pity for thee mov'd me to break my dark & long repose,
And to reveal myself before thee in a form of wisdom.
Yet thou dost laugh at all these tortures, & this horrible place:
Yet throw thy limbs these fires abroad that back return upon
   thee
While thou reposest, throwing rage on rage, feeding thyself
With visions of sweet bliss far other than this burning clime.
Sure thou art bath'd in rivers of delight, on verdant fields
Walking in joy, in bright Expanses sleeping on bright clouds
With visions of delight so lovely that they urge thy rage
Tenfold with fierce desire to rend thy chain & howl in fury
And dim oblivion of all woe, & desperate repose.
Or is thy joy founded on torment which others bear for thee?"

Orc answer'd: "Curse thy hoary brows! What dost thou in this
   deep?

Thy Pity I contemn. Scatter thy snows elsewhere.
I rage in the deep, for Lo, my feet & hands are nail'd to the
    burning rock,
Yet my fierce fires are better than thy snows. Shudd'ring thou
    sittest.
Thou art not chain'd. Why shouldst thou sit, cold grovelling
    demon of woe,
In tortures of dire coldness? now a Lake of waters deep
Sweeps over thee freezing to solid; still thou sit'st clos'd up
In that transparent rock as if in joy of thy bright prison,
Till, overburden'd with its own weight drawn out thro' im-
    mensity,
With a crash breaking across, the horrible mass comes down
Thund'ring, & hail & frozen iron hail'd from the Element
Rends thy white hair; yet thou dost, fix'd obdurate brooding, sit
Writing thy books. Anon a cloud, fill'd with a waste of snows
Covers thee, still obdurate, still resolv'd & writing still;
Tho' rocks roll o'er thee, tho' floods pour, tho' winds black as
    the sea
Cut thee in gashes, tho' the blood pours down around thy
    ankles,
Freezing thy feet to the hard rock, still thy pen obdurate
Traces the wonders of Futurity in horrible fear of the future.
I rage furious in the deep, for lo. my feet & hands are nail'd
To the hard rock, or thou shouldst feel my enmity & hate
In all the diseases of man falling upon thy grey accursed front."

Urizen answer'd: "Read my books, explore my Constellations,
Enquire of my Sons & they shall teach thee how to War.
Enquire of my Daughters, who, accurs'd in the dark depths,
Knead bread of Sorrow by my stern command; for I am God
Of all this dreadful ruin. Rise, O daughters, at my stern com-
    mand!"

Rending the Rocks, Eleth & Uveth rose, & Ona rose,
Terrific with their iron vessels, driving them across
In the dim air; they took the book of iron & plac'd above
On clouds of death, & sang their songs, kneading the bread of
    Orc.
Orc listen'd to the song, compell'd, hung'ring on the cold wind
That swagg'd heavy with the accursed dough; the hoar frost
    rag'd

Thro' Ona's sieve; the torrent rain poured from the iron pail
Of Eleth, & the icy hands of Uveth kneaded the bread.
The heavens bow with terror underneath their iron hands,
Singing at their dire work the words of Urizen's book of iron
While the enormous scrolls roll'd dreadful in the heavens
    above;
And still the burden of their song in tears was pour'd forth:
"The bread is kneaded, let us rest, O cruel father of children!"

But Urizen remitted not their labours upon his rock,
And Urizen Read in his book of brass in sounding tones:
"Listen, O Daughters, to my voice. Listen to the Words of Wis-
    dom,
So shall [you] govern over all; let Moral Duty tune your
    tongue,
But be your hearts harder than the nether millstone.
To bring the Shadow of Enitharmon beneath our wondrous
    tree,
That Los may Evaporate like smoke & be no more,
Draw down Enitharmon to the spectre of Urthona,
And let him have dominion over Los, the terrible shade.
Compell the poor to live upon a Crust of bread, by soft mild
    arts.
Smile when they frown, frown when they smile; & when a man
    looks pale
With labour & abstinence, say he looks healthy & happy;
And when his children sicken, let them die; there are enough
Born, even too many, & our Earth will be overrun
Without these arts. If you would make the poor live with tem-
    per[ance],
With pomp give every crust of bread you give; with gracious
    cunning
Magnify small gifts; reduce the man to want a gift, & then give
    with pomp.
Say he smiles if you hear him sigh. If pale, say he is ruddy.
Preach temperance: say he is overgorg'd & drowns his wit
In strong drink, tho' you know that bread & water are all
He can afford. Flatter his wife, pity his children, till we can
Reduce all to our will, as spaniels are taught with art.
Lo! how the heart & brain are formed in the breeding womb
Of Enitharmon: how it buds with life & forms the bones,
The little heart, the liver, & the red blood in its labyrinths;   •

By gratified desire, by strong devouring appetite, she fills
Los with ambitious fury that his race shall all devour."

         .   .   .

Then Los mourn'd on the dismal wind in his jealous lamentation:

"Why can I not Enjoy thy beauty, Lovely Enitharmon?
When I return from clouds of Grief in the wand'ring Elements
Where thou in thrilling joy, in beaming summer loveliness,
Delectable reposest, ruddy in my absence, flaming with beauty,
Cold pale in sorrow at my approach, trembling at my terrific
Forehead & eyes, thy lips decay like roses in the spring.
How art thou shrunk! thy grapes that burst in summer's vast
    Excess,
Shut up in little purple covering, faintly bud & die.
Thy olive trees that pour'd down oil upon a thousand hills,
Sickly look forth & scarcely stretch their branches to the plain.
Thy roses that expanded in the face of glowing morn,
Hid in a little silken veil scarce breathe & faintly shine.
Thy lillies that gave light what time the morning looked forth,
Hid in the Vales, faintly lament, & no one hears their voice.
All things beside the woful Los enjoy the delights of beauty!
Once how I sang & call'd the beasts & birds to their delight,
Nor knew that I, alone exempted from the joys of love,
Must war with secret monsters of the animating worlds.
O that I had not seen the day! then should I be at rest,
Nor felt the stingings of desire, nor longings after life,
For life is sweet to Los the wretched; to his winged woes
Is given a craving cry, that they may sit at night on barren
    rocks
And whet their beaks & snuff the air, & watch the opening
    dawn,
And shriek till, at the smells of blood, they stretch their boney
    wings
And cut the winds like arrows shot by troops of Destiny."

From NIGHT THE EIGHTH

AND thus Ahania cries aloud to the Caverns of the Grave:
"Will you keep a flock of wolves & lead them? will you take the
    wintry blast
For a covering to your limbs, or the summer pestilence for a
    tent to abide in?

Will you erect a lasting habitation in the mouldering Church
   yard?
Or a pillar & palace of Eternity in the jaws of the hungry
   grave?
Will you seek pleasure from the festering wound, or marry for a
   Wife
The ancient Leprosy? that the King & Priest may still feast on
   your decay
And the grave mock & laugh at the plow'd fields, saying,
'I am the nourisher, thou the destroyer; in my bosom is milk &
   wine,
And a fountain from my breasts; to me come all multitudes;
To my breath they obey; they worship me. I am a goddess &
   queen.'
But listen to Ahania, O ye sons of the Murder'd one,
Listen to her whose memory beholds your ancient days,
Listen to her whose eyes behold the dark body of corruptible
   death
Looking for Urizen in vain; in vain I seek for morning.
The Eternal Man sleeps in the Earth, nor feels the vig'rous sun
Nor silent moon, nor all the hosts of heaven move in his body.
His fiery halls are dark, & round his limbs the Serpent Orc
Fold without fold incompasses him, And his corrupting mem-
   bers
Vomit out the scaly monsters of the restless deep.
They come up in the rivers & annoy the nether parts
Of Man who lays upon the Shores, leaning his faded head
Upon the Oozy rock inwrapped with the weeds of death.
His eyes sink hollow in his head, his flesh cover'd with slime
And shrunk up to the bones; alas, that Man should come to
   this!
His strong bones beat with snows & hid within the caves of
   night,
Marrowless, bloodless,. falling into dust, driven by the winds.
O how the horrors of Eternal Death take hold on Man!
His faint groans shake the caves & issue thro' the desolate rocks,
And the strong Eagle, now with numbing cold blighted of
   feathers,
Once like the pride of the sun, now flagging on cold night,
Hovers with blasted wings aloft, watching with Eager Eye
Till Man shall leave a corruptible body; he, famish'd, hears him
   groan,

And now he fixes his strong talons in the pointed rock,
And now he beats the heavy air with his enormous wings.
Beside him lies the Lion dead, & in his belly worms
Feast on his death till universal death devours all,
And the pale horse seeks for the pool to lie him down & die,
But finds the pools filled with serpents devouring one another.
He droops his head & trembling stands, & his bright eyes decay.
These are the Visions of My Eyes, the Visions of Ahania."

Thus cries Ahania. Enion replies from the Caverns of the
    Grave:

"Fear not, O poor forsaken one! O land of briars & thorns
Where once the olive flourish'd & the Cedar spread his wings!
Once I wail'd desolate like thee; my fallow fields in fear
Cried to the Churchyards & the Earthworm came in dismal
    state.
I found him in my bosom, & I said the time of love
Appears upon the rocks & hills in silent shades; but soon
A voice came in the night, a midnight cry upon the mountains:
'Awake! the bridegroom cometh!' I awoke to sleep no more;
But an Eternal consummation is dark Enion,
The wat'ry Grave. O thou corn field! O thou vegetater happy!
More happy is the dark consumer; hope drowns all my torment,
For I am surrounded by a shadowy vortex drawing
The spectre quite away from Enion, that I die a death
Of better hope, altho' I consume in these raging waters.
The furrow'd field replies to the grave. I hear her reply to me:
'Behold the time approaches fast that thou shalt be as a thing
Forgotten; when one speaks of thee he will not be believ'd.
When a man gently fades away in his immortality,
When the mortal disappears in improved knowledge, cast
    away
The former things, so shall the Mortal gently fade away
And so become invisible to those who still remain.
Listen. I will tell thee what is done in the caverns of the grave.
The Lamb of God has rent the Veil of Mystery, soon to re-
    turn
In Clouds & Fires around the rock & the Mysterious tree.
And as the seed waits Eagerly watching for its flower & fruit,
Anxious its little soul looks out into the clear expanse
To see if hungry winds are abroad with their invisible array,

So Man looks out in tree & herb & fish & bird & beast
Collecting up the scatter'd portions of his immortal body
Into the Elemental forms of every thing that grows.
He tries the sullen north wind, riding on its angry furrows,
The sultry south when the sun rises, & the angry east
When the sun sets; when the clods harden & the cattle stand
Drooping & the birds hide in their silent nests, he stores his
      thoughts
As in a store house in his memory; he regulates the forms
Of all beneath & all above, & in the gentle West
Reposes where the Sun's heat dwells; he rises to the Sun
And to the Planets of the Night, & to the stars that gild
The Zodiac, & the stars that sullen stand to north & south.
He touches the remotest pole, & in the center weeps
That Man should Labour & sorrow, & learn & forget, & re-
      turn
To the dark valley whence he came, to begin his labour anew.
In pain he sighs, in pain he labours in his universe,
Sorrowing in birds over the deep, & howling in the wolf
Over the slain, & moaning in the cattle, & in the winds,
And weeping over Orc & Urizen in clouds & flaming fires,
And in the cries of birth & in the groans of death his voice
Is heard throughout the Universe; wherever a grass grows
Or a leaf buds, The Eternal Man is seen, is heard, is felt,
And all his sorrows, till he reassumes his ancient bliss.' "

Such are the words of Ahania & Enion. Los hears & weeps.

NIGHT THE NINTH

BEING

THE LAST JUDGMENT

AND Los & Enitharmon builded Jerusalem, weeping
Over the Sepulcher & over the Crucified body
Which, to their Phantom Eyes, appear'd still in the Sepulcher;
But Jesus stood beside them in the spirit, separating
Their spirit from their body. Terrified at Non Existence,
For such they deem'd the death of the body, Los his vegetable
      hands
Outstretch'd; his right hand, branching out in fibrous strength,

Siez'd the Sun; His left hand, like dark roots, cover'd the
  Moon,
And tore them down, cracking the heavens across from im-
  mense to immense.
Then fell the fires of Eternity with loud & shrill
Sound of Loud Trumpet thundering along from heaven to
  heaven
A mighty sound articulate: "Awake, ye dead, & come
To Judgment from the four winds! Awake & Come away!"
Folding like scrolls of the Enormous volume of Heaven &
  Earth,
With thunderous noise & dreadful shakings, rocking to & fro,
The heavens are shaken & the Earth removed from its place,
The foundations of the Eternal hills discover'd:
The thrones of Kings are shaken, they have lost their robes &
  crowns,
The poor smite their oppressors, they awake up to the harvest,
The naked warriors rush together down to the sea shore
Trembling before the multitudes of slaves now set at liberty:
They are become like wintry flocks, like forests strip'd of leaves:
The oppressed pursue like the wind; there is no room for es-
  cape.

The Spectre of Enitharmon, let loose on the troubled deep,
Wail'd shrill in the confusion, & the Spectre of Urthona
Reciev'd her in the darkening south; their bodies lost, they
  stood
Trembling & weak, a faint embrace, a fierce desire, as when
Two shadows mingle on a wall; they wail & shadowy tears
Fell down, & shadowy forms of joy mix'd with despair & grief—
Their bodies buried in the ruins of the Universe—
Mingled with the confusion. Who shall call them from the
  Grave?

Rahab & Tirzah wail aloud in the wild flames; they give up
  themselves to Consummation.

The books of Urizen unroll with dreadful noise; the folding
  Serpent
Of Orc began to Consume in fierce raving fire; his fierce flames
Issu'd on all sides, gathering strength in animating volumes,
Roaming abroad on all the winds, raging intense, reddening

Into resistless pillars of fire rolling round & round, gathering
Strength from the Earths consum'd & heavens & all hidden
    abysses,
Where'er the Eagle has Explor'd, or Lion or Tyger trod,
Or where the Comets of the night or stars of asterial day
Have shot their arrows or long beamed spears in wrath &
    fury.

And all the while the trumpet sounds, "Awake, ye dead, & come
To Judgment!" From the clotted gore & from the hollow den
Start forth the trembling millions into flames of mental fire,
Bathing their limbs in the bright visions of Eternity.
Then, like the doves from pillars of Smoke, the trembling fami-
    lies
Of women & children throughout every nation under heaven
Cling round the men in bands of twenties & of fifties, pale
As snow that falls around a leafless tree upon the green.
Their oppressors are fall'n, they have stricken them, they awake
    to life.
Yet pale the just man stands erect & looking up to heav'n.
Trembling & strucken by the Universal stroke, the trees unroot,
The rocks groan horrible & run about; the mountains &
Their rivers cry with a dismal cry; the cattle gather together,
Lowing they kneel before the heavens; the wild beasts of the
    forests
Tremble; the Lion shuddering asks the Leopard: "Feelest thou
The dread I feel, unknown before? My voice refuses to roar,
And in weak moans I speak to thee. This night,
Before the morning's dawn, the Eagle call'd the Vulture,
The Raven call'd the hawk, I heard them from my forests black,
Saying: 'Let us go up far, for soon, I smell upon the wind,
A terror coming from the south.' The Eagle & Hawk fled away
At dawn, & e'er the sun arose, the raven & Vulture follow'd.
Let us flee also to the north." They fled. The Sons of Men
Saw them depart in dismal droves. The trumpet sounded loud
And all the Sons of Eternity Descended into Beulah.

In the fierce flames the limbs of Mystery lay consuming with
    howling
And deep despair. Rattling go up the flames around the Syna-
    gogue

Of Satan. Loud the Serpent Orc rag'd thro' his twenty seven
Folds. The tree of Mystery went up in folding flames.
Blood issu'd out in rushing volumes, pouring in whirlpools fierce
From out the flood gates of the Sky. The Gates are burst; down
    pour
The torrents black upon the Earth; the blood pours down in-
    cessant.
Kings in their palaces lie drown'd. Shepherds, their flocks, their
    tents,
Roll down the mountains in black torrents. Cities, Villages,
High spires & Castles drown'd in the black deluge; shoal on
    shoal
Float the dead carcases of Men & Beasts, driven to & fro on
    waves
Of foaming blood beneath the black incessant sky, till all
Mystery's tyrants are cut off & not one left on Earth.

And when all Tyranny was cut off from the face of the Earth,
Around the dragon form of Urizen, & round his strong form,
The flames rolling intense thro' the wide Universe
Began to enter the Holy City. Ent'ring, the dismal clouds
In furrow'd lightnings break their way, the wild flames licking
    up
The Bloody Deluge: living flames winged with intellect
And Reason, round the Earth they march in order, flame by
    flame.
From the clotted gore & from the hollow den
Start forth the trembling millions into flames of mental fire,
Bathing their limbs in the bright visions of Eternity.

Beyond this Universal Confusion, beyond the remotest Pole
Where their vortexes began to operate, there stands
A Horrible rock far in the South; it was forsaken when
Urizen gave the horses of Light into the hands of Luvah.
On this rock lay the faded head of the Eternal Man
Enwrapped round with weeds of death, pale cold in sorrow &
    woe.
He lifts the blue lamps of his Eyes & cries with heavenly voice:
Bowing his head over the consuming Universe, he cried:
"O weakness & O weariness! O war within my members!
My sons, exiled from my breast, pass to & fro before me.

My birds are silent on my hills, flocks die beneath my
      branches.
My tents are fallen, my trumpets & the sweet sound of my harp
Is silent on my clouded hills that belch forth storms & fire.
My milk of cows & honey of bees & fruit of golden harvest
Are gather'd in the scorching heat & in the driving rain.
My robe is turned to confusion, & my bright gold to stone.
Where once I sat, I weary walk in misery & pain,
For from within my wither'd breast grown narrow with my
      woes
The Corn is turned to thistles & the apples into poison,
The birds of song to murderous crows, My joys to bitter groans,
The voices of children in my tents to cries of helpless infants,
And all exiled from the face of light & shine of morning
In this dark world, a narrow house, I wander up & down.
I hear Mystery howling in these flames of Consummation.
When shall the Man of future times become as in days of old?
O weary life! why sit I here & give up all my powers
To indolence, to the night of death, when indolence & mourn-
      ing
Sit hovering over my dark threshold? tho' I arise, look out
And scorn the war within my members, yet my heart is weak
And my head faint. Yet will I look again into the morning.
Whence is this sound of rage of Men drinking each other's
      blood,   -
Drunk with the smoking gore, & red, but not with nourishing
      wine?"

The Eternal Man sat on the Rocks & cried with awful voice:
"O Prince of Light, where art thou? I behold thee not as once
In those Eternal fields, in clouds of morning stepping forth
With harps & songs when bright Ahania sang before thy face
And all thy sons & daughters gather'd round my ample table.
See you not all this wracking furious confusion?
Come forth from slumbers of thy cold abstraction! Come forth,
Arise to Eternal births! Shake off thy cold repose,
Schoolmaster of souls, great opposer of change, arise!
That the Eternal worlds may see thy face in peace & joy,
That thou, dread form of Certainty, maist sit in town & village
While little children play around thy feet in gentle awe,
Fearing thy frown, loving thy smile, O Urizen, Prince of Light."

He call'd; the deep buried his voice & answer none return'd.
Then wrath burst round; the Eternal Man was wrath; again he
    cried:
"Arise, O stony form of death! O dragon of the Deeps!
Lie down before my feet, O Dragon! let Urizen arise.
O how couldst thou deform those beautiful proportions
Of life & person; for as the Person, so is his life proportion'd.
Let Luvah rage in the dark deep, even to Consummation,
For if thou feedest not his rage, it will subside in peace.
But if thou darest obstinate refuse my stern behest,
Thy crown & scepter I will sieze, & regulate all my members
In stern severity, & cast thee out into the indefinite
Where nothing lives, there to wander; & if thou returnest weary,
Weeping at the threshold of Existence, I will steel my heart
Against thee to Eternity, & never recieve thee more.
Thy self-destroying, beast form'd Science shall be thy eternal
    lot.
My anger against thee is greater than against this Luvah,
For war is energy Enslav'd, but thy religion,
The first author of this war & the distracting of honest minds
Into confused perturbation & strife & horrour & pride,
Is a deciet so detestable that I will cast thee out
If thou repentest not, & leave thee as a rotten branch to be
    burn'd
With Mystery the Harlot & with Satan for Ever & Ever.
Error can never be redeemed in all Eternity,
But Sin, Even Rahab, is redeem'd in blood & fury & jealousy—
That line of blood that stretch'd across the windows of the
    morning—   .
Redeem'd from Error's power. Wake, thou dragon of the
    deeps!"

Urizen wept in the dark deep, anxious his scaly form
To reassume the human; & he wept in the dark deep,
Saying: "O that I had never drunk the wine nor eat the bread
Of dark mortality, or cast my view into futurity, nor turn'd
My back, dark'ning the present, clouding with a cloud,
And building arches high, & cities, turrets & towers & domes
Whose smoke destroy'd the pleasant gardens, & whose running
    kennels
Chok'd the bright rivers; burd'ning with my Ships the angry
    deep;

Thro' Chaos seeking for delight, & in spaces remote
Seeking the Eternal which is always present to the wise;
Seeking for pleasure which unsought falls round the infant's
    path
And on the fleeces of mild flocks who neither care nor labour;
But I, the labourer of ages, whose unwearied hands
Are thus deform'd with hardness, with the sword & with the
    spear
And with the chisel & the mallet, I, whose labours vast
Order the nations, separating family by family,
Alone enjoy not. I alone, in misery supreme,
Ungratified give all my joy unto this Luvah & Vala.
Then Go, O dark futurity! I will cast thee forth from these
Heavens of my brain, nor will I look upon futurity more.
I cast futurity away, & turn my back upon that void
Which I have made; for lo! futurity is in this moment.
Let Orc consume, let Tharmas rage, let dark Urthona give
All strength to Los & Enitharmon, & let Los self-curs'd
Rend down this fabric, as a wall ruin'd & family extinct.
Rage Orc! Rage Tharmas! Urizen no longer curbs your rage."

So Urizen spoke; he shook his snows from off his shoulders &
    arose
As on a Pyramid of mist, his white robes scattering
The fleecy white: renew'd, he shook his aged mantles off
Into the fires. Then, glorious bright, Exulting in his joy,
He sounding rose into the heavens in naked majesty,
In radiant Youth; when Lo! like garlands in the Eastern sky
When vocal may comes dancing from the East, Ahania came
Exulting in her flight, as when a bubble rises up
On the surface of a lake, Ahania rose in joy.
Excess of Joy is worse than grief; her heart beat high, her blood
Burst its bright vessels: she fell down dead at the feet of
    Urizen
Outstretch'd, a smiling corse: they buried her in a silent cave.
Urizen dropped a tear; the Eternal Man Darken'd with sorrow.

The three daughters of Urizen guard Ahania's death couch;
Rising from the confusion in tears & howlings & despair,
Calling upon their father's Name, upon their Rivers dark.

And the Eternal Man said: "Hear my words, O Prince of Light.
Behold Jerusalem in whose bosom the Lamb of God
Is seen; tho' slain before her Gates, he self-renew'd remains
Eternal, & I thro' him awake from death's dark vale.
The times revolve; the time is coming when all these delights
Shall be renew'd, & all these Elements that now consume
Shall reflourish. Then bright Ahania shall awake from death,
A glorious Vision to thine Eyes, a Self-renewing Vision:
The spring, the summer, to be thine; then sleep the wintry days
In silken garments spun by her own hands against her funeral.
The winter thou shalt plow & lay thy stores into thy barns
Expecting to recieve Ahania in the spring with joy.
Immortal thou, Regenerate She, & all the lovely Sex
From her shall learn obedience & prepare for a wintry grave,
That spring may see them rise in tenfold joy & sweet delight.
Thus shall the male & female live the life of Eternity,
Because the Lamb of God Creates himself a bride & wife
That we his Children evermore may live in Jerusalem
Which now descendeth out of heaven, a City, yet a Woman,
Mother of myriads redeem'd & born in her spiritual palaces,
By a New Spiritual birth Regenerated from Death."

Urizen said: "I have Erred, & my Error remains with me.
What Chain encompasses? in what Lock is the river of light
    confin'd
That issues forth in the morning by measure & in the evening
    by carefulness?
Where shall we take our stand to view the infinite & un-
    bounded?
Or where are human feet? for Lo, our eyes are in the heavens."

He ceas'd, for riv'n link from link, the bursting Universe ex-
    plodes.
All things revers'd flew from their centers: rattling bones
To bones Join: shaking convuls'd, the shivering clay breathes:
Each speck of dust to the Earth's center nestles round & round
In pangs of an Eternal Birth: in torment & awe & fear,
All spirits deceas'd, let loose from reptile prisons, come in
    shoals:
Wild furies from the tyger's brain & from the lion's eyes,
And from the ox & ass come moping terrors, from the eagle

And raven: numerous as the leaves of autumn, every species
Flock to the trumpet, mutt'ring over the sides of the grave &
    crying
In the fierce wind round heaving rocks & mountains fill'd with
    groans.
On rifted rocks, suspended in the air by inward fires,
Many a woful company & many on clouds & waters,
Fathers & friends, Mothers & Infants, Kings & Warriors,
Priests & chain'd Captives, met together in a horrible fear;
And every one of the dead appears as he had liv'd before,
And all the marks remain of the slave's scourge & tyrant's
    Crown,
And of the Priest's o'ergorged Abdomen, & of the merchant's
    thin
Sinewy deception, & of the warrior's outbraving & thought-
    lessness
In lineaments too extended & in bones too strait & long.
They shew their wounds: they accuse: they sieze the opressor;
    howlings began
On the golden palace, songs & joy on the desart; the Cold
    babe
Stands in the furious air; he cries: "the children of six thousand
    years
Who died in infancy rage furious: a mighty multitude rage
    furious,
Naked & pale standing in the expecting air, to be deliver'd.
Rend limb from limb the warrior & the tyrant, reuniting in
    pain."

The furious wind still rends around; they flee in sluggish effort;
They beg, they intreat in vain now; they listened not to intreaty;
They view the flames red rolling on thro' the wide universe
From the dark jaws of death beneath & desolate shores remote,
These covering vaults of heaven & these trembling globes of
    earth.
One Planet calls to another & one star enquires of another:
"What flames are these, coming from the South? what noise,
    what dreadful rout
As of a battle in the heavens? hark! heard you not the trumpet
As of fierce battle?" While they spoke, the flames come on in-
    tense roaring.

They see him whom they have pierc'd, they wail because of
    him,
They magnify themselves no more against Jerusalem, Nor
Against her little ones; the innocent, accused before the Judges,
Shines with immortal glory; trembling, the judge springs from
    his throne
Hiding his face in the dust beneath the prisoner's feet & saying:
"Brother of Jesus, what have I done? intreat thy lord for me:
Perhaps I may be forgiven." While he speaks the flames roll on,
And after the flames appears the Cloud of the Son of Man
Descending from Jerusalem with power and great Glory.
All nations look up to the Cloud & behold him who was
    crucified.
The Prisoner answers: "You scourg'd my father to death be-
    fore my face
While I stood bound with cords & heavy chains. Your hipocrisy
Shall now avail you nought." So speaking, he dash'd him with
    his foot.

The Cloud is Blood, dazling upon the heavens, & in the cloud,
Above upon its volumes, is beheld a throne & a pavement
Of precious stones surrounded by twenty-four venerable patri-
    archs,
And these again surrounded by four Wonders of the Almighty,
Incomprehensible, pervading all, amidst & round about,
Fourfold, each in the other reflected; they are named Life's—
    in Eternity—
Four Starry Universes going forward from Eternity to
    Eternity.
And the Fall'n Man who was arisen upon the Rock of Ages
Beheld the Vision of God, & he arose up from the Rock,
And Urizen arose up with him, walking thro' the flames
To meet the Lord coming to Judgment; but the flames repell'd
    them
Still to the Rock; in vain they strove to Enter the Consum-
    mation
Together, for the Redeem'd Man could not enter the Consum-
    mation.

Then siez'd the sons of Urizen the Plow: they polish'd it
From rust of ages; all its ornaments of gold & silver & ivory
Reshone across the field immense where all the nations

Darken'd like Mould in the divided fallows where the weed
Triumphs in its own destruction; they took down the harness
From the blue walls of heaven, starry jingling, ornamented
With beautiful art, the study of angels, the workmanship of
    Demons
When Heaven & Hell in Emulation strove in sports of Glory.

The noise of rural works resounded thro' the heavens of
    heavens,
The horses neigh from the battle, the wild bulls from the sultry
    waste,
The tygers from the forests, & the lions from the sandy desarts.
They sing; they sieze the instruments of harmony; they throw
    away
The spear, the bow, the gun, the mortar; they level the forti-
    fications.
They beat the iron engines of destruction into wedges;
They give them to Urthona's sons; ringing the hammers sound
In dens of death to forge the spade, the mattock & the ax,
The heavy roller to break the clods, to pass over the nations.

The Sons of Urizen shout. Their father rose. The Eternal
    horses
Harness'd, They call'd to Urizen; the heavens moved at their
    call.
The limbs of Urizen shone with ardor. He laid his hand on the
    Plow,
Thro' dismal darkness drave the Plow of ages over Cities
And all their Villages; over Mountains & all their Vallies;
Over the graves & caverns of the dead; Over the Planets
And over the void spaces; over sun & moon & star & constel-
    lation.

Then Urizen commanded & they brought the Seed of Men.
The trembling souls of All the dead stood before Urizen,
Weak wailing in the troubled air. East, west, & north & south
He turn'd the horses loose & laid his Plow in the northern cor-
    ner
Of the wide Universal field, then step'd forth into the immense.

Then he began to sow the seed; he girded round his loins
With a bright girdle, & his skirt fill'd with immortal souls.
Howling & Wailing fly the souls from Urizen's strong hand,

For from the hand of Urizen the myriads fall like stars
Into their own appointed places, driven back by the winds.
The naked warriors rush together down to the sea shores:
They are become like wintry flocks, like forests strip'd of
    leaves;
The Kings & Princes of the Earth cry with a feeble cry,
Driven on the unproducing sands & on the harden'd rocks;
And all the while the flames of Orc follow the vent'rous feet
Of Urizen, & all the while the Trump of Tharmas sounds.
Weeping & wailing fly the souls from Urizen's strong hands—
The daughters of Urizen stand with Cups & measures of foam-
    ing wine
Immense upon the heavens with bread & delicate repasts—
Then follows the golden harrow in the midst of Mental fires.
To ravishing melody of flutes & harps & softest voice
The seed is harrow'd in, while flames heat the black mould &
    cause
The human harvest to begin. Towards the south first sprang
The myriads, & in silent fear they look out from their graves.

Then Urizen sits down to rest, & all his wearied sons
Take their repose on beds; they drink, they sing, they view the
    flames
Of Orc; in joy they view the human harvest springing up.
A time they give to sweet repose, till all the harvest is ripe.
And Lo, like the harvest Moon, Ahania cast off her death
    clothes;
She folded them up in care, in silence, & her bright'ning limbs
Bath'd in the clear spring of the rock; then from her darksome
    cave
Issu'd in majesty divine. Urizen rose up from his couch
On wings of tenfold joy, clapping his hands, his feet, his radiant
    wings
In the immense: as when the Sun dances upon the mountains
A shout of jubilee in lovely notes responds from daughter to
    daughter,
From son to son: as if the stars beaming innumerable
Thro' night should sing soft warbling, filling earth & heaven;
And bright Ahania took her seat by Urizen in songs & joy.

The Eternal Man also sat down upon the Couches of Beulah,
Sorrowful that he could not put off his new risen body

In mental flames; the flames refus'd, they drove him back to
    Beulah.
His body was redeem'd to be permanent thro' Mercy Divine.

And now fierce Orc had quite consum'd himself in Mental
    flames,
Expending all his energy against the fuel of fire.
The Regenerate Man stoop'd his head over the Universe & in
His holy hands reciev'd the flaming Demon & Demoness of
    smoke
And gave them to Urizen's hands; the Immortal frown'd, say-
    ing,

"Luvah & Vala, henceforth you are Servants; obey & live.
You shall forget your former state; return, & Love in peace,
Into your place, the place of seed, not in the brain or heart.
If Gods combine against Man, setting their dominion above
The Human form Divine, Thrown down from their high station
In the Eternal heavens of Human Imagination, buried beneath
In dark Oblivion, with incessant pangs, ages on ages,
In enmity & war first weaken'd, then in stern repentance
They must renew their brightness, & their disorganiz'd func-
    tions
Again reorganize, till they resume the image of the human,
Co-operating in the bliss of Man, obeying his Will,
Servants to the infinite & Eternal of the Human form."

Luvah & Vala descended & enter'd the Gates of Dark Urthona,
And walk'd from the hands of Urizen in the shadows of Vala's
    Garden
Where the impressions of Despair & Hope for ever vegetate
In flowers, in fruits, in fishes, birds & beasts & clouds & waters,
The land of doubt & shadows, sweet delusions, unform'd hopes.
They saw no more the terrible confusion of the wracking uni-
    verse.
They heard not, saw not, felt not all the terrible confusion,
For in their orbed senses, within clos'd up, they wander'd at
    will.
And those upon the Couches view'd them, in the dreams of
    Beulah,
As they repos'd from the terrible wide universal harvest.
Invisible Luvah in bright clouds hover'd over Vala's head,

And thus their ancient golden age renew'd; for Luvah spoke
With voice mild from his golden Cloud upon the breath of
   morning:

"Come forth, O Vala, from the grass & from the silent dew,
Rise from the dews of death, for the Eternal Man is Risen."

She rises among flowers & looks toward the Eastern clearness,
She walks yea runs, her feet are wing'd, on the tops of the
   bending grass,
Her garments rejoice in the vocal wind & her hair glistens with
   dew.

She answer'd thus: "Whose voice is this, in the voice of the
   nourishing air,
In the spirit of the morning, awaking the Soul from its grassy
   bed?
Where dost thou dwell? for it is thee I seek, & but for thee
I must have slept Eternally, nor have felt the dew of thy morn-
   ing.
Look how the opening dawn advances with vocal harmony!
Look how the beams foreshew the rising of some glorious
   power!
The sun is thine, he goeth forth in his majestic brightness.
O thou creating voice that callest! & who shall answer thee?"

"Where dost thou flee, O fair one? where doth thou seek thy
   happy place?"

"To yonder brightness, there I haste, for sure I came from
   thence
Or I must have slept eternally, nor have felt the dew of morning."

"Eternally thou must have slept, not have felt the morning
   dew,
But for yon nourishing sun; 'tis that by which thou art arisen.
The birds adore the sun: the beasts rise up & play in his beams,
And every flower & every leaf rejoices in his light.
Then, O thou fair one, sit thee down, for thou art as the grass,
Thou risest in the dew of morning & at night art folded up."

"Alas! am I but as a flower? then will I sit me down,
Then will I weep, then I'll complain & sigh for immortality,
And chide my maker, thee O sun, that raisedst me to fall."

So saying she sat down & wept beneath the apple trees.

"O be thou blotted out, thou Sun! that raisedst me to trouble,
That gavest me a heart to crave, & raisedst me, thy phantom,
To feel thy heat & see thy light & wander here alone,
Hopeless, if I am like the grass & so shall pass away."

"Rise, sluggish Soul, why sit'st thou here? why dost thou sit &
    weep?
Yon sun shall wax old & decay, but thou shalt ever flourish.
The fruit shall ripen & fall down, & the flowers consume away,
But thou shalt still survive; arise, O dry thy dewy tears."

"Hah! shall I still survive? whence came that sweet & comfort-
    ing voice?
And whence that voice of sorrow? O sun! thou art nothing
    now to me.
Go on thy course rejoicing, & let us both rejoice together.
I walk among his flocks & hear the bleating of his lambs.
O that I could behold his face & follow his pure feet!
I walk by the footsteps of his flocks; come hither, tender
    flocks.
Can you converse with a pure soul that seeketh for her maker?
You answer not: then am I set your mistress in this garden.
I'll watch you & attend your footsteps; you are not like the birds
That sing & fly in the bright air; but you do lick my feet
And let me touch your woolly backs; follow me as I sing,
For in my bosom a new song arises to my Lord:

"Rise up, O sun, most glorious minister & light of day.
Flow on, ye gentle airs, & bear the voice of my rejoicing.
Wave freshly, clear waters flowing around the tender grass;
And thou, sweet smelling ground, put forth thy life in fruits &
    flowers.
Follow me, O my flocks, & hear me sing my rapturous song.
I will cause my voice to be heard on the clouds that glitter in
    the sun.
I will call; & who shall answer me? I will sing; who shall reply?
For from my pleasant hills behold the living, living springs,

Running among my green pastures, delighting among my trees.
I am not here alone: my flocks, you are my brethren;
And you birds that sing & adorn the sky, you are my sisters.
I sing, & you reply to my song; I rejoice, & you are glad.
Follow me, O my flocks; we will now descend into the valley.
O how delicious are the grapes, flourishing in the sun!
How clear the spring of the rock, running among the golden
    sand!
How cool the breezes of the valley, & the arms of the branch-
    ing trees!
Cover us from the sun; come & let us sit in the shade.
My Luvah here hath plac'd me in a sweet & pleasant land,
And given me fruits & pleasant waters, & warm hills & cool
    valleys.
Here will I build myself a house, & here I'll call on his name,
Here I'll return when I am weary & take my pleasant rest."

So spoke the sinless soul, & laid her head on the downy fleece
Of a curl'd Ram who stretch'd himself in sleep beside his mis-
    tress,
And soft sleep fell upon her eyelids in the silent noon of day.

Then Luvah passed by, & saw the sinless soul,
And said: "Let a pleasant house arise to be the dwelling place
Of this immortal spirit growing in lower Paradise."
He spoke, & pillars were builded, & walls as white as ivory.
The grass she slept upon was pav'd with pavement as of pearl.
Beneath her rose a downy bed, & a cieling cover'd all.

Vala awoke. "When in the pleasant gates of sleep I enter'd,
I saw my Luvah like a spirit stand in the bright air.
Round him stood spirits like me, who rear'd me a bright house,
And here I see thee, house, remain in my most pleasant world.
My Luvah smil'd: I kneeled down: he laid his hand on my
    head,
And when he laid his hand upon me, from the gates of sleep I
    came
Into this bodily house to tend my flocks in my pleasant garden."

So saying, she arose & walked round her beautiful house,
And then from her white door she look'd to see her bleating
    lambs,

But her flocks were gone up from beneath the trees into the
    hills.

"I see the hand that leadeth me doth also lead my flocks."
She went up to her flocks & turned oft to see her shining house.
She stop'd to drink of the clear spring & eat the grapes & apples.
She bore the fruits in her lap; she gather'd flowers for her
    bosom.
She called to her flocks, saying, "Follow me, O my flocks!"

They follow'd her to the silent valley beneath the spreading
    trees.
And on the river's margin she ungirded her golden girdle;
She stood in the river & view'd herself within the wat'ry glass,
And her bright hair was wet with the waters: she rose up from
    the river,
And as she rose her eyes were open'd to the world of waters:
She saw Tharmas sitting upon the rocks beside the wavy sea.
He strok'd the water from his beard & mourn'd faint thro' the
    summer vales.

And Vala stood on the rocks of Tharmas & heard his mourn-
    ful voice:

"O Enion, my weary head is in the bed of death,
For weeds of death have wrap'd around my limbs in the hoary
    deeps.
I sit in the place of shells & mourn, & thou art clos'd in clouds.
When will the time of Clouds be past, & the dismal night of
    Tharmas?
Arise, O Enion! Arise & smile upon my head
As thou dost smile upon the barren mountains and they re-
    joice.
When wilt thou smile on Tharmas, O thou bringer of golden
    day?
Arise, O Enion, arise, for Lo, I have calm'd my seas."

So saying, his faint head he laid upon the Oozy rock,
And darkness cover'd all the deep; the light of Enion faded
Like a faint flame quivering upon the surface of the darkness.

Then Vala lifted up her hands to heaven to call on Enion.
She call'd, but none could answer her & the eccho her voice
    return'd:

"Where is the voice of God that call'd me from the silent dew?
Where is the Lord of Vala? dost thou hide in clefts of the rock?
Why shouldst thou hide thyself from Vala, from the soul that
    wanders desolate?"

She ceas'd, & light beamed round her like the glory of the
    morning,
And she arose out of the river & girded her golden girdle.
And now her feet step on the grassy bosom of the ground
Among her flocks, & she turn'd her eyes toward her pleasant
    house
And saw in the door way beneath the trees two little children
    playing.
She drew near to her house & her flocks follow'd her footsteps.
The children clung around her knees, she embrac'd them &
    wept over them.

"Thou, little Boy, art Tharmas, & thou, bright Girl, Enion.
How are ye thus renew'd & brought into the Gardens of Vala?"

She embrac'd them in tears, till the sun descended the western
    hills,
And then she enter'd her bright house, leading her mighty
    children.
And when night came, the flocks laid round the house beneath
    the trees.
She laid the children on the beds which she saw prepar'd in
    the house,
Then last, herself laid down & clos'd her Eyelids in soft slum-
    bers.

And in the morning, when the sun arose in the crystal sky,
Vala awoke & call'd the children from their gentle slumbers:

"Awake, O Enion, awake & let thine innocent Eyes
Enlighten all the Crystal house of Vala! awake! awake!
Awake, Tharmas, awake, awake thou child of dewy tears.
Open the orbs of thy blue eyes & smile upon my gardens."

The Children woke & smil'd on Vala; she kneel'd by the golden
    couch,
She pres'd them to her bosom & her pearly tears drop'd down.
"O my sweet Children! Enion, let Tharmas kiss thy Cheek.
Why dost thou turn thyself away from his sweet wat'ry eyes?
Tharmas, henceforth in Vala's bosom thou shalt find sweet
    peace.
O bless the lovely eyes of Tharmas & the Eyes of Enion!"

They rose; they went out wand'ring, sometimes together, some-
    times alone.
"Why weep'st thou, Tharmas, Child of tears, in the bright
    house of joy?
Doth Enion avoid the sight of thy blue heavenly Eyes?
And dost thou wander with my lambs & wet their innocent
    faces
With thy bright tears because the steps of Enion are in the
    gardens?
Arise, sweet boy, & let us follow the path of Enion."

So saying, they went down into the garden among the fruits.
And Enion sang among the flowers that grew among the trees,
And Vala said: "Go, Tharmas; weep not. Go to Enion."

He said: "O Vala, I am sick, & all this garden of Pleasure
Swims like a dream before my eyes; but the sweet smiling fruit
Revives me to new deaths. I fade, even as a water lilly
In the sun's heat, till in the night on the couch of Enion
I drink new life & feel the breath of sleeping Enion.
But in the morning she arises to avoid my Eyes,
Then my loins fade & in the house I sit me down & weep."

"Chear up thy Countenance, bright boy, & go to Enion.
Tell her that Vala waits her in the shadows of her garden."

He went with timid steps, & Enion, like the ruddy morn
When infant spring appears in swelling buds & opening flowers,
Behind her Veil withdraws; so Enion turn'd her modest head.

But Tharmas spoke: "Vala seeks thee, sweet Enion, in the
    shades.

Follow the steps of Tharmas, O thou brightness of the
gardens."
He took her hand reluctant; she follow'd in infant doubts.
Thus in Eternal Childhood, straying among Vala's flocks
In infant sorrow & joy alternate, Enion & Tharmas play'd
Round Vala in the Gardens of Vala & by her river's margin.
They are the shadows of Tharmas & of Enion in Vala's world.

And the sleepers who rested from their harvest work beheld
these visions.
Thus were the sleepers entertain'd upon the Couches of Beulah.

When Luvah & Vala were clos'd up in their world of shadowy
forms,
Darkness was all beneath the heavens: only a little light
Such as glows out from sleeping spirits, appear'd in the deeps
beneath.
As when the wind sweeps over a corn field, the noise of souls
Thro' all the immense, borne down by Clouds swagging in au-
tumnal heat,
Mutt'ring along from heaven to heaven, hoarse roll the human
forms
Beneath thick clouds, dreadful lightnings burst & thunders roll,
Down pour the torrent floods of heaven on all the human har-
vest.
Then Urizen, sitting at his repose on beds in the bright South,
Cried, "Times are Ended!" he exulted; he arose in joy; he
exulted;
He pour'd his light, & all his sons & daughters pour'd their light
To exhale the spirits of Luvah & Vala thro' the atmosphere.
And Luvah & Vala saw the Light; their spirits were exhal'd
In all their ancient innocence; the floods depart; the clouds
Dissipate or sink into the Seas of Tharmas. Luvah sat
Above on the bright heavens in peace; the Spirits of Men be-
neath
Cried out to be deliver'd, & the spirit of Luvah wept
Over the human harvest & over Vala, the sweet wanderer.
In pain the human harvest wav'd, in horrible groans of woe.
The Universal Groan went up; the Eternal Man was darken'd.

Then Urizen arose & took his sickle in his hand.
There is a brazen sickle, & a scythe of iron hid

Deep in the South, guarded by a few solitary stars.
This sickle Urizen took; the scythe his sons embrac'd
And went forth & began to reap; & all his joyful sons
Reap'd the wide Universe & bound in sheaves a wondrous harvest.
They took them into the wide barns with loud rejoicings & triumph
Of flute & harp & drum & trumpet, horn & clarion.

The feast was spread in the bright South, & the Regenerate Man
Sat at the feast rejoicing, & the wine of Eternity
Was serv'd round by the flames of Luvah all day & all the Night.
And when Morning began to dawn upon the distant hills,
A whirlwind rose up in the Center, & in the whirlwind a shriek,
And in the shriek a rattling of bones, & in the rattling of bones
A dolorous groan, & from the dolorous groan in tears
Rose Enion like a gentle light; & Enion spoke, saying:

"O Dreams of Death! the human form dissolving, companied
By beasts & worms & creeping things, & darkness & despair.
The clouds fall off from my wet brow, the dust from my cold limbs
Into the sea of Tharmas. Soon renew'd, a Golden Moth,
I shall cast off my death clothes & Embrace Tharmas again.
For Lo, the winter melted away upon the distant hills,
And all the black mould sings." She speaks to her infant race; her milk
Descends down on the sand; the thirsty sand drinks & rejoices
Wondering to behold the Emmet, the Grasshopper, the jointed worm.
The roots shoot thick thro' the solid rocks, bursting their way
They cry out in joys of existence; the broad stems
Rear on the mountains stem after stem; the scaly newt creeps
From the stone, & the armed fly springs from the rocky crevice,
The spider, The bat burst from the harden'd slime, crying
To one another: "What are we, & whence is our joy & delight?
Lo, the little moss begins to spring, & the tender weed
Creeps round our secret nest." Flocks brighten the Mountains,
Herds throng up the Valley, wild beasts fill the forests.

Joy thrill'd thro' all the Furious forms of Tharmas humaniz-
    ing.
Mild he Embrac'd her whom he sought; he rais'd her thro'
    the heavens,
Sounding his trumpet to awake the dead, on high her soar'd
Over the ruin'd worlds, the smoking tomb of the Eternal
    Prophet.

The Eternal Man arose. He welcom'd them to the Feast.
The feast was spread in the bright South, & the Eternal Man
Sat at the feast rejoicing, & the wine of Eternity
Was serv'd round by the flames of Luvah all day & all the
    night.

And Many Eternal Men sat at the golden feast to see
The female form now separate. They shudder'd at the horrible
    thing
Not born for the sport and amusement of Man, but born to
    drink up all his powers.
They wept to see their shadows; they said to one another: "This
    is Sin:
This is the Generative world;" they remember'd the days of
    old.

And One of the Eternals spoke. All was silent at the feast.

"Man is a Worm; wearied with joy, he seeks the caves of sleep
Among the Flowers of Beulah, in his selfish cold repose
Forsaking Brotherhood & Universal love, in selfish clay
Folding the pure wings of his mind, seeking the places dark
Abstracted from the roots of Science; then inclos'd around
In walls of Gold we cast him like a Seed into the Earth
Till times & spaces have pass'd over him; duly every morn
We visit him, covering with a Veil the immortal seed;
With windows from the inclement sky we cover him, & with
    walls
And hearths protect the selfish terror, till divided all
In families we see our shadows born, ⎤
    & thence we know   ⎟
That Man subsists by Brotherhood   ⎬ Ephesians iii. c. 10 v.
    & Universal Love.   ⎟
We fall on one another's necks,   ⎦
    more closely we embrace.

Not for ourselves, but for the Eternal family we live.
Man liveth not by Self alone, but in his brother's face
Each shall behold the Eternal Father & love & joy abound."

So spoke the Eternal at the Feast; they embrac'd the New born
    Man,
Calling him Brother, image of the Eternal Father; they sat
    down
At the immortal tables, sounding loud their instruments of
    joy,
Calling the Morning into Beulah; the Eternal Man rejoic'd.

When Morning dawn'd, The Eternals rose to labour at the
    Vintage.
Beneath they saw their sons & daughters, wond'ring inconciev-
    able
At the dark myriads in shadows in the worlds beneath.

The morning dawn'd. Urizen rose, & in his hand the Flail
Sounds on the Floor, heard terrible by all beneath the heavens.
Dismal loud redounding, the nether floor shakes with the
    sound,
And all Nations were threshed out, & the stars thresh'd from
    their husks.

Then Tharmas took the Winnowing fan; then winnowing wind
    furious
Above, veer'd round by violent whirlwind, driven west & south,
Tossed the Nations like chaff into the seas of Tharmas.

"O Mystery," Fierce Tharmas cries, "Behold thy end is come!
Art thou she that made the nations drunk with the cup of Reli-
    gion?
Go down, ye Kings & Councellors & Giant Warriors,
Go down into the depths, go down & hide yourselves beneath,
Go down with horse & Chariots & Trumpets of hoarse war.

"Lo, how the Pomp of Mystery goes down into the Caves!
Her great men howl & throw the dust, & rend their hoary hair.
Her delicate women & children shriek upon the bitter wind,
Spoil'd of their beauty, their hair rent & their skin shrivel'd up.

"Lo, darkness covers the long pomp of banners on the wind,
And black horses & armed men & miserable bound captives.
Where shall the graves recieve them all, & where shall be their
   place?
And who shall mourn for Mystery who never loos'd her Cap-
   tives?

"Let the slave, grinding at the mill, run out into the field;
Let him look up into the heavens & laugh in the bright air.
Let the inchained soul, shut up in darkness & in sighing,
Whose face has never seen a smile in thirty weary years,
Rise & look out: his chains are loose, his dungeon doors are
   open;
And let his wife & children return from the opressor's scourge.

"They look behind at every step & believe it is a dream.
Are these the slaves that groan'd along the streets of Mystery?
Where are your bonds & task masters? are these the prisoners?
Where are your chains? where are your tears? why do you
   look around?
If you are thirsty, there is the river: go, bathe your parched
   limbs,
The good of all the Land is before you, for Mystery is no
   more."

Then All the Slaves from every Earth in the wide Universe
Sing a New Song, drowning confusion in its happy notes,
While the flail of Urizen sounded loud, & the winnowing wind
   of Tharmas
So loud, so clear in the wide heavens; & the song that they
   sung was this,
Composed by an African Black from the little Earth of Sotha:

"Aha! Aha! how came I here so soon in my sweet native land?
How came I here? Methinks I am as I was in my youth
When in my father's house I sat & heard his chearing voice.
Methinks I see his flocks & herds & feel my limbs renew'd,
And Lo, my Brethren in their tents, & their little ones around
   them!"

The song arose to the Golden feast; the Eternal Man rejoic'd.
Then the Eternal Man said: "Luvah, the Vintage is ripe: arise!

The sons of Urizen shall gather the vintage with sharp hooks,
And all thy sons, O Luvah! bear away the families of Earth.
I hear the flail of Urizen; his barns are full; no room
Remains, & in the Vineyards stand the abounding sheaves be-
neath
The falling Grapes that odorous burst upon the winds. Arise
My flocks & herds, trample the Corn! my cattle, browze upon
The ripe Clusters! The shepherds shout for Luvah, prince of
Love.
Let the Bulls of Luvah tread the Corn & draw the loaded wag-
gon
Into the Barn while children glean the Ears around the door.
Then shall they lift their innocent hands & stroke his furious
nose,
And he shall lick the little girl's white neck & on her head
Scatter the perfume of his breath; while from his mountains
high
The lion of terror shall come down, & bending his bright mane
And crouching at their side, shall eat from the curl'd boy's
white lap
His golden food, and in the evening sleep before the door."

"Attempting to be more than Man We become less," said
Luvah
As he arose from the bright feast, drunk with the wine of ages.
His crown of thorns fell from his head, he hung his living Lyre
Behind the seat of the Eternal Man & took his way
Sounding the Song of Los, descending to the Vineyards bright.
His sons, arising from the feast with golden baskets, follow,
A fiery train, as when the Sun sings in the ripe vineyards.
Then Luvah stood before the Wine press; all his fiery sons
Brought up the loaded Waggons with shoutings; ramping tygers
play
In the jingling traces; furious lions sound the song of joy
To the golden wheels circling upon the pavement of heaven, &
all
The Villages of Luvah ring; the golden tiles of the villages
Reply to violins & tabors, to the pipe, flute, lyre & cymbal.
Then fell the Legions of Mystery in madd'ning confusion,
Down, down thro' the immense, with outcry, fury & despair,
Into the wine presses of Luvah; howling fell the clusters

Of human families thro' the deep; the wine presses were fill'd;
The blood of life flow'd plentiful. Odors of life arose
All round the heavenly arches, & the Odors rose singing this
    song:

"O terrible wine presses of Luvah! O caverns of the Grave!
How lovely the delights of those risen again from death!
O trembling joy! excess of joy is like Excess of grief."

So sang the Human Odors round the wine presses of Luvah;

But in the Wine presses is wailing, terror & despair.
Forsaken of their Elements they vanish & are no more,
No more but a desire of Being, a distracted, ravening desire,
Desiring like the hungry worm & like the gaping grave.
They plunge into the Elements; the Elements cast them forth
Or else consume their shadowy semblance. Yet they, obstinate
Tho' pained to distraction, cry, "O let us Exist! for
This dreadful Non Existence is worse than pains of Eternal
    Birth:
Eternal death who can Endure? let us consume in fires,
In waters stifling, or in air corroding, or in earth shut up.
The Pangs of Eternal birth are better than the Pangs of Eter-
    nal death."

How red the sons & daughters of Luvah! how they tread the
    Grapes!
Laughing & shouting, drunk with odors, many fall o'erwearied:
Drown'd in the wine is many a youth & maiden; those around
Lay them on skins of tygers or the spotted Leopard or wild Ass
Till they revive, or bury them in cool Grots making lamen-
    tation.

But in the Wine Presses the Human Grapes sing not nor
    dance,
They howl & writhe in shoals of torment, in fierce flames
    consuming,
In chains of iron & in dungeons circled with ceaseless fires,
In pits & dens & shades of death, in shapes of torment & woe;
The Plates, the Screws & Racks & Saws & cords & fires & floods,
The cruel joy of Luvah's daughters, lacerating with knives

And whips their Victims, & the deadly sport of Luvah's sons.
Timbrels & Violins sport round the Wine Presses. The little
Seed,
The sportive root, the Earthworm, the small beetle, the wise
Emmett,
Dance round the Wine Presses of Luvah; the Centipede is
there,
The ground Spider with many eyes, the Mole clothed in Velvet,
The Earwig arm'd, the tender maggot, emblem of Im-
mortality;
The slow slug, the grasshopper that sings & laughs & drinks:
The winter comes; he folds his slender bones without a murmur.
There is the Nettle that stings with soft down; & there
The indignant Thistle whose bitterness is bred in his milk
And who lives on the contempt of his neighbour; there all the
idle weeds,
That creep about the obscure places, shew their various limbs
Naked in all their beauty, dancing round the Wine Presses.
They dance around the dying & they drink the howl & groan;
They catch the shrieks in cups of gold; they hand them to one
another.
These are the sports of love & these the sweet delights of amo-
rous play:
Tears of the grape, the death sweat of the Cluster, the last sigh
Of the mild youth who listens to the luring songs of Luvah.
The Eternal Man darken'd with sorrow & a wintry mantle
Cover'd the Hills. He said, "O Tharmas, rise! & O Urthona!"
Then Tharmas & Urthona rose from the Golden feast, satiated
With Mirth & Joy: Urthona, limping from his fall, on Tharmas
lean'd,
In his right hand his hammer. Tharmas held his shepherd's
crook
Beset with gold, gold were the ornaments form'd by sons of
Urizen.
Then Enion & Ahania & Vala & the wife of dark Urthona
Rose from the feast, in joy ascending to their Golden Looms.
There the wing'd shuttle sang, the spindle & the distaff & the
Reel
Rang sweet the praise of industry. Thro' all the golden rooms
Heaven rang with winged Exultation. All beneath howl'd loud;
With tenfold rout & desolation roar'd the Chasms beneath

Where the wide woof flow'd down & where the Nations are
gather'd together.

Tharmas went down to the Wine presses & beheld the sons &
daughters
Of Luvah quite exhausted with the labour & quite fill'd
With new wine, that they began to torment one another and
to tread
The weak. Luvah & Vala slept on the floor, o'erwearied.
Urthona call'd his sons around him: Tharmas call'd his sons
Numerous; they took the wine, they separated the Lees,
And Luvah was put for dung on the ground by the Sons of
Tharmas & Urthona.
They formed heavens of sweetest woods, of gold & silver &
ivory,
Of glass & precious stones. They loaded all the waggons of
heaven
And took away the wine of ages with solemn songs & joy.

Luvah & Vala woke, & all the sons & daughters of Luvah
Awoke; they wept to one another & they reascended
To the Eternal Man in woe: he cast them wailing into
The world of shadows, thro' the air; till winter is over & gone;
But the Human Wine stood wondering; in all their delightful
Expanses
The elements subside; the heavens roll'd on with vocal har-
mony.

Then Los, who is Urthona, rose in all his regenerate power.
The Sea that roll'd & foam'd with darkness, & the shadows of
death
Vomited out & gave up all; the floods lift up their hands
Singing & shouting to the Man; they bow their hoary heads
And murmuring in their channels flow & circle round his feet.

Then Dark Urthona took the Corn out of the Stores of Urizen;
He ground it in his rumbling Mills. Terrible the distress
Of all the Nations of Earth, ground in the Mills of Urthona.
In his hand Tharmas takes the Storms: he turns the whirlwind
loose
Upon the wheels; the stormy seas howl at his dread command

And Eddying fierce rejoice in the fierce agitation of the wheels
Of Dark Urthona. Thunders, Earthquakes, Fires, Water floods,
Rejoice to one another; loud their voices shake the Abyss,
Their dread forms tending the dire mills. The grey hoar frost
    was there,
And his pale wife, the aged Snow; they watch over the fires,
They build the Ovens of Urthona. Nature in darkness groans
And Men are bound to sullen contemplation in the night:
Restless they turn on beds of sorrow; in their inmost brain
Feeling the crushing Wheels, they rise, they write the bitter
    words
Of Stern Philosophy & knead the bread of knowledge with
    tears & groans.

Such are the works of Dark Urthona. Tharmas sifts the corn.
Urthona made the Bread of Ages, & he placed it,
In golden & in silver baskets, in heavens of precious stone
And then took his repose in Winter, in the night of Time.

The Sun has left his blackness & has found a fresher morning,
And the mild moon rejoices in the clear & cloudless night,
And Man walks forth from midst of the fires: the evil is all
    consum'd.
His eyes behold the Angelic spheres arising night & day;
The stars consum'd like a lamp blown out, & in their stead, be-
    hold
The Expanding Eyes of Man behold the depths of wondrous
    worlds!
One Earth, one sea beneath; nor Erring Globes wander, but
    Stars
Of fire rise up nightly from the Ocean; & one Sun
Each morning, like a New born Man, issues with songs & joy
Calling the Plowman to his Labour & the Shepherd to his
    rest.
He walks upon the Eternal Mountains, raising his heavenly
    voice,
Conversing with the Animal forms of wisdom night & day,
That, risen from the Sea of fire, renew'd walk o'er the Earth;
For Tharmas brought his flocks upon the hills, & in the Vales
Around the Eternal Man's bright tent, the little Children play
Among the wooly flocks. The hammer of Urthona sounds

In the deep caves beneath; his limbs renew'd, his Lions roar
Around the Furnaces & in Evening sport upon the plains.
They raise their faces from the Earth, conversing with the
    Man:

"How is it we have walk'd thro' fires & yet are not consum'd?
How is it that all things are chang'd, even as in ancient times?"

The Sun arises from his dewy bed, & the fresh airs
Play in his smiling beams giving the seeds of life to grow,
And the fresh Earth beams forth ten thousand thousand springs
    of life.
Urthona is arisen in his strength, no longer now
Divided from Enitharmon, no longer the Spectre Los.
Where is the Spectre of Prophecy? where is the delusive Phan-
    tom?
Departed: & Urthona rises from the ruinous Walls
In all his ancient strength to form the golden armour of science
For intellectual War. The war of swords departed now,
The dark Religions are departed & sweet Science reigns.

END OF THE DREAM

Selections from MILTON

PREFACE

THE Stolen and Perverted Writings of Homer & Ovid, of Plato & Cicero, which all men ought to contemn, are set up by artifice against the Sublime of the Bible; but when the New Age is at leisure to Pronounce, all will be set right, & those Grand Works of the more ancient & consciously & professedly Inspired Men will hold their proper rank, & the Daughters of Memory shall become the Daughters of Inspiration. Shakspeare & Milton were both curb'd by the general malady & infection from the silly Greek & Latin slaves of the Sword.

Rouze up, O Young Men of the New Age! set your foreheads against the ignorant Hirelings! For we have Hirelings in the Camp, the Court & the University, who would, if they could, for ever depress Mental & prolong Corporeal War. Painters! on you I call. Sculptors! Architects! Suffer not the fashonable Fools to depress your powers by the prices they pretend to give for contemptible works, or the expensive advertizing boasts that they make of such works; believe Christ & his Apostles that there is a Class of Men whose whole delight is in Destroying. We do not want either Greek or Roman Models if we are but just & true to our own Imaginations, those Worlds of Eternity in which we shall live for ever in JESUS OUR LORD.

> And did those feet in ancient time
> Walk upon England's mountains green?
> And was the holy Lamb of God
> On England's pleasant pastures seen?
>
> And did the Countenance Divine
> Shine forth upon our clouded hills?
> And was Jerusalem builded here
> Among these dark Satanic Mills?

Bring me my Bow of burning gold:
Bring me my Arrows of desire:
Bring me my Spear: O clouds unfold!
Bring me my Chariot of fire.

I will not cease from Mental Fight,
Nor shall my Sword sleep in my hand
Till we have built Jerusalem
In England's green & pleasant Land.

"Would to God that all the Lord's people were Prophets."
NUMBERS, xi. ch., 29 v.

From BOOK THE FIRST

DAUGHTERS of Beulah! Muses who inspire the Poet's Song,
Record the journey of immortal Milton thro' your Realms
Of terror & mild moony lustre in soft sexual delusions
Of varied beauty, to delight the wanderer and repose
His burning thirst & freezing hunger! Come into my hand,
By your mild power descending down the Nerves of my right
    arm
From out the portals of my Brain, where by your ministry
The Eternal Great Humanity Divine planted his Paradise
And in it caus'd the Spectres of the Dead to take sweet forms
In likeness of himself. Tell also of the False Tongue! vegetated
Beneath your land of shadows, of its sacrifices and
Its offerings: even till Jesus, the image of the Invisible God,
Became its prey, a curse, an offering and an atonement
For Death Eternal in the heavens of Albion & before the Gates
Of Jerusalem his Emanation, in the heavens beneath Beulah.

.   .   .

Then Milton rose up from the heavens of Albion ardorous.
The whole Assembly wept prophetic, seeing in Milton's face
And in his lineaments divine the shades of Death & Ulro:
He took off the robe of the promise & ungirded himself from
    the oath of God.

And Milton said: "I go to Eternal Death! The Nations still
Follow after the detestable Gods of Priam, in pomp

Of warlike selfhood contradicting and blaspheming.
When will the Resurrection come to deliver the sleeping body
From corruptibility? O when, Lord Jesus, wilt thou come?
Tarry no longer, for my soul lies at the gates of death.
I will arise and look forth for the morning of the grave:
I will go down to the sepulcher to see if morning breaks:
I will go down to self annihilation and eternal death,
Lest the Last Judgment come & find me unannihilate
And I be siez'd & giv'n into the hands of my own Selfhood.
The Lamb of God is seen thro' mists & shadows, hov'ring
Over the sepulchers in clouds of Jehovah & winds of Elohim,
A disk of blood distant, & heav'ns & earths roll dark between.
What do I here before the Judgment? without my Emanation?
With the daughters of memory & not with the daughters of
    inspiration?
I in my Selfhood am that Satan: I am that Evil One!
He is my Spectre! in my obedience to loose him from my Hells,
To claim the Hells, my Furnaces, I go to Eternal Death."

And Milton said: "I go to Eternal Death!" Eternity shudder'd,
For he took the outside course among the graves of the dead,
A mournful shade. Eternity shudder'd at the image of eternal
    death.

Then on the verge of Beulah he beheld his own Shadow,
A mournful form double, hermaphroditic, male & female
In one wonderful body; and he enter'd into it
In direful pain, for the dread shadow twenty-seven fold
Reach'd to the depths of direst Hell & thence to Albion's land,
Which is this earth of vegetation on which now I write.

The Seven Angels of the Presence wept over Milton's Shadow.

As when a man dreams he reflects not that his body sleeps,
Else he would wake, so seem'd he entering his Shadow: but
With him the Spirits of the Seven Angels of the Presence
Entering, they gave him still perceptions of his Sleeping Body
Which now arose and walk'd with them in Eden, as an Eighth
Image Divine tho' darken'd and tho' walking as one walks
In sleep, and the Seven comforted and supported him.

Like as a Polypus that vegetates beneath the deep,
They saw his Shadow vegetated underneath the Couch
Of death: for when he enter'd into his Shadow, Himself,
His real and immortal Self, was, as appear'd to those
Who dwell in immortality, as One sleeping on a couch
Of gold, and those in immortality gave forth their Emanations
Like Females of sweet beauty to guard round him & to feed
His lips with food of Eden in his cold and dim repose:
But to himself he seem'd a wanderer lost in dreary night.

Onwards his Shadow kept its course among the Spectres call'd
Satan, but swift as lightning passing them, startled the shades
Of Hell beheld him in a trail of light as of a comet
That travels into Chaos: so Milton went guarded within.

The nature of infinity is this: That every thing has its
Own Vortex, and when once a traveller thro' Eternity
Has pass'd that Vortex, he percieves it roll backward behind
His path, into a globe itself infolding like a sun,
Or like a moon, or like a universe of starry majesty,
While he keeps onwards in his wondrous journey on the earth,
Or like a human form, a friend with whom he liv'd benevolent.
As the eye of man views both the east & west encompassing
Its vortex, and the north & south with all their starry host,
Also the rising sun & setting moon he views surrounding
His corn-fields and his valleys of five hundred acres square,
Thus is the earth one infinite plane, and not as apparent
To the weak traveller confin'd beneath the moony shade.
Thus is the heaven a vortex pass'd already, and the earth
A vortex not yet pass'd by the traveller thro' Eternity.

First Milton saw Albion upon the Rock of Ages,
Deadly pale outstretch'd and snowy cold, storm cover'd,
A Giant form of perfect beauty outstretch'd on the rock
In solemn death: the Sea of Time & Space thunder'd aloud
Against the rock, which was inwrapped with the weeds of
    death.
Hovering over the cold bosom in its vortex Milton bent down
To the bosom of death: what was underneath soon seem'd
    above:
A cloudy heaven mingled with stormy seas in loudest ruin;

But as a wintry globe descends precipitant thro' Beulah bursting
With thunders loud and terrible, so Milton's shadow fell
Precipitant, loud thund'ring into the Sea of Time & Space.

Then first I saw him in the Zenith as a falling star
Descending perpendicular, swift as the swallow or swift:
And on my left foot falling on the tarsus, enter'd there:
But from my left foot a black cloud redounding spread over
    Europe.

Then Milton knew that the Three Heavens of Beulah were
    beheld
By him on earth in his bright pilgrimage of sixty years
In those three females whom his wives, & those three whom his
    Daughters
Had represented and contain'd, that they might be resum'd
By giving up Selfhood: & they distant view'd his journey
In their eternal spheres, now Human, tho' their Bodies remain
    clos'd
In the dark Ulro till the Judgment: also Milton knew they and
Himself was Human, tho' now wandering thro' Death's Vale
In conflict with those Female forms, which in blood & jealousy
Surrounded him, dividing & uniting without end or number.

                    .   .   .

But Milton entering my Foot, I saw in the nether
Regions of the Imagination—also all men on Earth
And all in Heaven saw in the nether regions of the Imagination
In Ulro beneath Beulah—the vast breach of Milton's descent.
But I knew not that it was Milton, for man cannot know
What passes in his members till periods of Space & Time
Reveal the secrets of Eternity: for more extensive
Than any other earthly things are Man's earthly lineaments.
And all this Vegetable World appear'd on my left Foot
As a bright sandal form'd immortal of precious stones & gold.
I stooped down & bound it on to walk forward thro' Eternity.

There is in Eden a sweet River of milk & liquid pearl
Nam'd Ololon, on whose mild banks dwelt those who Milton
    drove
Down into Ulro: and they wept in long resounding song
For seven days of eternity, and the river's living banks,

The mountains, wail'd, & every plant that grew, in solemn sighs
  lamented.

When Luvah's bulls each morning drag the sulphur Sun out of
  the Deep
Harness'd with starry harness, black & shining, kept by black
  slaves
That work all night at the starry harness, Strong and vigorous
They drag the unwilling Orb: at this time all the Family
Of Eden heard the lamentation and Providence began.
But when the clarions of day sounded, they drown'd the lamen-
  tations,
And when night came, all was silent in Ololon, & all refus'd to
  lament
In the still night, fearing lest they should others molest.

Seven mornings Los heard them, as the poor bird within the
  shell
Hears its impatient parent bird, and Enitharmon heard them
But saw them not, for the blue Mundane Shell inclos'd them in.

And they lamented that they had in wrath & fury & fire
Driven Milton into the Ulro; for now they knew too late
That it was Milton the Awakener: they had not heard the Bard
Whose song call'd Milton to the attempt; and Los heard these
  laments.
He heard them call in prayer all the Divine Family,
And he beheld the Cloud of Milton stretching over Europe.

But all the Family Divine collected as Four Suns
In the Four Points of heaven, East, West & North & South,
Enlarging and enlarging till their Disks approach'd each other,
And when they touch'd, closed together Southward in One Sun
Over Ololon; and as One Man who weeps over his brother
In a dark tomb, so all the Family Divine wept over Ololon,

Saying: "Milton goes to Eternal Death!" so saying they groan'd
  in spirit
And were troubled; and again the Divine Family groaned in
  spirit.

And Ololon said: "Let us descend also, and let us give
Ourselves to death in Ulro among the Transgressors.

Is Virtue a Punisher? O no! how is this wondrous thing,
This World beneath, unseen before, this refuge from the wars
Of Great Eternity! unnatural refuge! unknown by us till now?
Or are these the pangs of repentance? let us enter into them."

Then the Divine Family said: "Six Thousand Years are now
Accomplished in this World of Sorrow. Milton's Angel knew
The Universal Dictate, and you also feel this Dictate.
And now you know this World of Sorrow and feel Pity. Obey
The Dictate! Watch over this World, and with your brooding
    wings
Renew it to Eternal Life. Lo! I am with you alway.
But you cannot renew Milton: he goes to Eternal Death."

So spake the Family Divine as One Man, even Jesus,
Uniting in One with Ololon, & the appearance of One Man,
Jesus the Saviour, appear'd coming in the Clouds of Ololon.

Tho' driven away with the Seven Starry Ones into the Ulro,
Yet the Divine Vision remains Every-where For-ever. Amen.
And Ololon lamented for Milton with a great lamentation.

While Los heard indistinct in fear, what time I bound my san-
    dals
On to walk forward thro' Eternity, Los descended to me:
And Los behind me stood, a terrible flaming Sun, just close
Behind my back. I turned round in terror, and behold!
Los stood in that fierce glowing fire, & he also stoop'd down
And bound my sandals on in Udan-Adan; trembling I stood
Exceedingly with fear & terror, standing in the Vale
Of Lambeth; but he kissed me and wish'd me health,
And I became One Man with him arising in my strength.
'Twas too late now to recede. Los had enter'd into my soul:
His terrors now possess'd me whole! I arose in fury & strength.

"I am that Shadowy Prophet who Six Thousand Years ago
Fell from my station in the Eternal bosom. Six Thousand Years
Are finish'd. I return! both Time & Space obey my will.
I in Six Thousand Years walk up and down; for not one Mo-
    ment
Of Time is lost, nor one Event of Space unpermanent,
But all remain: every fabric of Six Thousand Years

Remains permanent, tho' on the Earth where Satan
Fell and was cut off, all things vanish & are seen no more,
They vanish not from me & mine, we guard them first & last.
The generations of men run on in the tide of Time,
But leave their destin'd lineaments permanent for ever & ever."

So spoke Los as we went along to his supreme abodes.

.   .   .

And Los stood & cried to the Labourers of the Vintage in voice
of awe:

"Fellow Labourers! The Great Vintage & Harvest is now upon
Earth.
The whole extent of the Globe is explored. Every scatter'd
Atom
Of Human Intellect now is flocking to the sound of the Trum-
pet.
All the Wisdom which was hidden in caves & dens from ancient
Time is now sought out from Animal & Vegetable & Mineral.
The Awakener is come outstretch'd over Europe: the Vision of
God is fulfilled:
The Ancient Man upon the Rock of Albion Awakes,
He listens to the sounds of War astonish'd & ashamed,
He sees his Children mock at Faith and deny Providence.
Therefore you must bind the Sheaves not by Nations or Fam-
ilies,
You shall bind them in Three Classes, according to their
Classes
So shall you bind them, Separating What has been Mixed
Since Men began to be Wove into Nations by Rahab & Tirzah,
Since Albion's Death & Satan's Cutting off from our awful
Fields,
When under pretence to benevolence the Elect Subdu'd All
From the Foundation of the World. The Elect is one Class:
You
Shall bind them separate: they cannot Believe in Eternal Life
Except by Miracle & a New Birth. The other two Classes,
The Reprobate who never cease to Believe, and the Redeem'd
Who live in doubts & fears perpetually tormented by the Elect,
These you shall bind in a twin-bundle for the Consummation:
But the Elect must be saved from fires of Eternal Death,

To be formed into the Churches of Beulah that they destroy
    not the Earth.
For in every Nation & every Family the Three Classes are born,
And in every Species of Earth, Metal, Tree, Fish, Bird & Beast.
We form the Mundane Egg, that Spectres coming by fury or
    amity,
All is the same, & every one remains in his own energy.
Go forth Reapers with rejoicing; you sowed in tears,
But the time of your refreshing cometh: only a little moment
Still abstain from pleasure & rest in the labours of eternity,
And you shall Reap the whole Earth from Pole to Pole, from
    Sea to Sea,
Beginning at Jerusalem's Inner Court, Lambeth, ruin'd and
    given
To the detestable Gods of Priam, to Apollo, and at the Asylum
Given to Hercules, who labour in Tirzah's Looms for bread,
Who set Pleasure against Duty, who Create Olympic crowns
To make Learning a burden & the Work of the Holy Spirit,
    Strife:
The Thor & cruel Odin who first rear'd the Polar Caves.
Lambeth mourns, calling Jerusalem: she weeps & looks abroad
For the Lord's coming, that Jerusalem may overspread all
    Nations.
Crave not for the mortal & perishing delights, but leave them
To the weak, and pity the weak as your infant care. Break not
Forth in your wrath, lest you also are vegetated by Tirzah.
Wait till the Judgment is past, till the Creation is consumed,
And then rush forward with me into the glorious spiritual
Vegetation, the Supper of the Lamb & his Bride, and the
Awaking of Albion our friend and ancient companion."

           ·   ·   ·

But the Wine-press of Los is eastward of Golgonooza before
    the Seat
Of Satan: Luvah laid the foundation & Urizen finish'd it in howl-
    ing woe.
How red the sons & daughters of Luvah! here they tread the
    grapes:
Laughing & shouting, drunk with odours many fell o'erwearied,
Drown'd in the wine is many a youth & maiden: those around
Lay them on skins of Tygers & of the spotted Leopard & the
    Wild Ass

Till they revive, or bury them in cool grots, making lamentation.

This Wine-press is call'd War on Earth: it is the Printing-Press
Of Los, and here he lays his words in order above the mortal
brain,
As cogs are form'd in a wheel to turn the cogs of the adverse
wheel.

Timbrels & violins sport round the Wine-presses; the little Seed,
The sportive Root, the Earth-worm, the gold Beetle, the wise
Emmet
Dance round the Wine-presses of Luvah: the Centipede is
there,
The ground Spider with many eyes, the Mole clothed in velvet,
The ambitious Spider in his sullen web, the lucky golden Spin-
ner,
The Earwig arm'd, the tender Maggot, emblem of immortality,
The Flea, Louse, Bug, the Tape-Worm, all the Armies of Dis-
ease,
Visible or invisible to the slothful vegetating Man.
The slow Slug, the Grasshopper that sings & laughs & drinks:
Winter comes, he folds his slender bones without a murmur.
The cruel Scorpion is there, the Gnat, Wasp, Hornet & the
Honey Bee,
The Toad & venomous Newt, the Serpent cloth'd in gems &
gold.
They throw off their gorgeous raiment: they rejoice with loud
jubilee
Around the Wine-presses of Luvah, naked & drunk with wine.

There is the Nettle that stings with soft down, and there
The indignant Thistle whose bitterness is bred in his milk,
Who feeds on contempt of his neighbour: there all the idle
Weeds
That creep around the obscure places shew their various limbs
Naked in all their beauty dancing round the Wine-presses.

But in the Wine-presses the Human grapes sing not nor dance:
They howl & writhe in shoals of torment, in fierce flames con-
suming,
In chains of iron & in dungeons circled with ceaseless fires,

In pits & dens & shades of death, in shapes of torment & woe:
The plates & screws & wracks & saws & cords & fires & cisterns,
The cruel joys of Luvah's Daughters, lacerating with knives
And whips their Victims, & the deadly sport of Luvah's Sons.

They dance around the dying & they drink the howl & groan,
They catch the shrieks in cups of gold, they hand them to one
    another:
These are the sports of love, & these the sweet delights of
    amorous play,
Tears of the grape, the death sweat of the cluster, the last sigh
Of the mild youth who listens to the lureing songs of Luvah.

                            .   .   .

But others of the Sons of Los build Moments & Minutes &
    Hours
And Days & Months & Years & Ages & Periods, wondrous
    buildings;
And every Moment has a Couch of gold for soft repose,
(A Moment equals a pulsation of the artery),
And between every two Moments stands a Daughter of Beulah
To feed the Sleepers on their Couches with maternal care.
And every Minute has an azure Tent with silken Veils:
And every Hour has a bright golden Gate carved with skill:
And every Day & Night has Walls of brass & Gates of adamant,
Shining like precious Stones & ornamented with appropriate
    signs:
And every Month a silver paved Terrace builded high:
And every Year invulnerable Barriers with high Towers:
And every Age is Moated deep with Bridges of silver & gold:
And every Seven Ages is Incircled with a Flaming Fire.
Now Seven Ages is amounting to Two Hundred Years.
Each has its Guard, each Moment, Minute, Hour, Day, Month
    & Year.
All are the work of Fairy hands of the·Four Elements:
The Guard are Angels of Providence on duty evermore.
Every Time less than a pulsation of the artery
Is equal in its period & value to Six Thousand Years,
For in this Period the Poet's Work is Done, and all the Great
Events of Time start forth & are conciev'd in such a Period,
Within a Moment, a Pulsation of the Artery.

The Sky is an immortal Tent built by the Sons of Los:
And every Space that a Man views around his dwelling-place
Standing on his own roof or in his garden on a mount
Of twenty-five cubits in height, such space is his Universe:
And on its verge the Sun rises & sets, the Clouds bow
To meet the flat Earth & the Sea in such order'd Space:
The Starry heavens reach no further, but here bend and set
On all sides, & the two Poles turn on their valves of gold;
And if he move his dwelling-place, his heavens also move
Where'er he goes, & all his neighbourhood bewail his loss.
Such are the Spaces called Earth & such its dimension.
As to that false appearance which appears to the reasoner
As of a Globe rolling thro' Voidness, it is a delusion of Ulro.
The Microscope knows not of this nor the Telescope: they alter
The ratio of the Spectator's Organs, but leave Objects un-
    touch'd.
For every Space larger than a red Globule of Man's blood
Is visionary, and is created by the Hammer of Los:
And every Space smaller than a Globule of Man's blood opens
Into Eternity of which this vegetable Earth is but a shadow.
The red Globule is the unwearied Sun by Los created
To measure Time and Space to mortal Men every morning.
Bowlahoola & Allamanda are placed on each side
Of that Pulsation & that Globule, terrible their power.

From BOOK THE SECOND

INTO this pleasant Shadow all the weak & weary
Like Women & Children were taken away as on wings
Of dovelike softness, & shadowy habitations prepared for them.
But every Man return'd & went still going forward thro'
The Bosom of the Father in Eternity on Eternity,
Neither did any lack or fall into Error without
A Shadow to repose in all the Days of happy Eternity.

Into this pleasant Shadow, Beulah, all Ololon descended,
And when the Daughters of Beulah heard the lamentation
All Beulah wept, for they saw the Lord coming in the Clouds.
And the Shadows of Beulah terminate in rocky Albion.

And all Nations wept in affliction, Family by Family:
Germany wept towards France & Italy, England wept & trembled
Towards America, India rose up from his golden bed
As one awaken'd in the night; they saw the Lord coming
In the Clouds of Ololon with Power & Great Glory.

And all the Living Creatures of the Four Elements wail'd
With bitter wailing; these in the aggregate are named Satan
And Rahab: they know not of Regeneration, but only of Generation:
The Fairies, Nymphs, Gnomes & Genii of the Four Elements,
Unforgiving & unalterable, these cannot be Regenerated
But must be Created, for they know only of Generation:
These are the Gods of the Kingdoms of the Earth, in contrarious
And cruel opposition, Element against Element, opposed in War
Not Mental, as the Wars of Eternity, but a Corporeal Strife
In Los's Halls, continual labouring in the Furnaces of Golgonooza.
Orc howls on the Atlantic: Enitharmon trembles: All Beulah weeps.

Thou hearest the Nightingale begin the Song of Spring.
The Lark sitting upon his earthly bed, just as the morn
Appears, listens silent; then springing from the waving Cornfield, loud
He leads the Choir of Day: trill, trill, trill, trill,
Mounting upon the wings of light into the Great Expanse,
Reecchoing against the lovely blue & shining heavenly Shell,
His little throat labours with inspiration; every feather
On throat & breast & wings vibrates with the effluence Divine.
All Nature listens silent to him, & the awful Sun
Stands still upon the Mountain looking on this little Bird
With eyes of soft humility & wonder, love & awe,
Then loud from their green covert all the Birds begin their Song:
The Thrush, the Linnet & the Goldfinch, Robin & the Wren
Awake the Sun from his sweet reverie upon the Mountain.
The Nightingale again assays his song, & thro' the day
And thro' the night warbles luxuriant, every Bird of Song

Attending his loud harmony with admiration & love.
This is a Vision of the lamentation of Beulah over Ololon.

Thou percievest the Flowers put forth their precious Odours,
And none can tell how from so small a center comes such
    sweets,
Forgetting that within that Center Eternity expands
Its ever during doors that Og & Anak fiercely guard.
First, e'er the morning breaks, joy opens in the flowery bosoms,
Joy even to tears, which the Sun rising dries; first the Wild
    Thyme
And Meadow-sweet, downy & soft waving among the reeds,
Light springing on the air, lead the sweet Dance: they wake
The Honeysuckle sleeping on the Oak; the flaunting beauty
Revels along upon the wind; the White-thorn, lovely May,
Opens her many lovely eyes listening; the Rose still sleeps,
None dare to wake her; soon she bursts her crimson curtain'd
    bed
And comes forth in the majesty of beauty; every Flower,
The Pink, the Jessamine, the Wall-flower, the Carnation,
The Jonquil, the mild Lilly, opes her heavens; every Tree
And Flower & Herb soon fill the air with an innumerable
    Dance,
Yet all in order sweet & lovely. Men are sick with Love.
Such is a Vision of the lamentation of Beulah over Ololon.

      •   •   •

There is a Moment in each Day that Satan cannot find,
Nor can his Watch Fiends find it; but the Industrious find
This Moment & it multiply, & when it once is found
It renovates every Moment of the Day if rightly placed.
In this Moment Ololon descended to Los & Enitharmon
Unseen beyond the Mundane Shell, Southward in Milton's track.

Just in this Moment, when the morning odours rise abroad
And first from the Wild Thyme, stands a Fountain in a rock
Of crystal flowing into two Streams: one flows thro' Gol-
    gonooza
And thro' Beulah to Eden beneath Los's western Wall:
The other flows thro' the Aerial Void & all the Churches,
Meeting again in Golgonooza beyond Satan's Seat.

The Wild Thyme is Los's Messenger to Eden, a mighty Demon,
Terrible, deadly & poisonous his presence in Ulro dark;
Therefore he appears only a small Root creeping in grass
Covering over the Rock of Odours his bright purple mantle
Beside the Fount above the Lark's nest in Golgonooza.
Luvah slept here in death & here is Luvah's empty Tomb.
Ololon sat beside this Fountain on the Rock of Odours.

Just at the place to where the Lark mounts is a Crystal Gate:
It is the entrance of the First Heaven, named Luther; for
The Lark is Los's Messenger thro' the Twenty-seven Churches,
That the Seven Eyes of God, who walk even to Satan's Seat
Thro' all the Twenty-seven Heavens, may not slumber nor
   sleep.
But the Lark's Nest is at the Gate of Los, at the eastern
Gate of wide Golgonooza, & the Lark is Los's Messenger.
When on the highest lift of his light pinions he arrives
At that bright Gate, another Lark meets him, & back to back
They touch their pinions, tip tip, and each descend
To their respective Earths & there all night consult with Angels
Of Providence & with the eyes of God all night in slumbers
Inspired, & at the dawn of day send out another Lark
Into another Heaven to carry news upon his wings.
Thus are the Messengers dispatch'd till they reach the Earth
   again
In the East Gate of Golgonooza, & the Twenty-eighth bright
Lark met the Female Ololon descending into my Garden.
Thus it appears to Mortal eyes & those of the Ulro Heavens,
But not thus to Immortals: the Lark is a mighty Angel.

For Ololon step'd into the Polypus within the Mundane Shell.
They could not step into Vegetable Worlds without becoming
The enemies of Humanity, except in a Female Form,
And as One Female Ololon and all its mighty Hosts
Appear'd, a Virgin of twelve years: nor time nor space was
To the perception of the Virgin Ololon, but as the
Flash of lightning, but more quick the Virgin in my Garden
Before my Cottage stood, for the Satanic Space is delusion.

For when Los join'd with me he took me in his fi'ry whirlwind:
My Vegetated portion was hurried from Lambeth's shades,
He set me down in Felpham's Vale & prepar'd a beautiful

Cottage for me, that in three years I might write all these Visions
To display Nature's cruel holiness, the deceits of Natural Religion.
Walking in my Cottage Garden, sudden I beheld
The Virgin Ololon & address'd her as a Daughter of Beulah:

"Virgin of Providence, fear not to enter into my Cottage.
What is thy message to thy friend? What am I now to do?
Is it again to plunge into deeper affliction? behold me
Ready to obey, but pity thou my Shadow of Delight:
Enter my Cottage, comfort her, for she is sick with fatigue."

The Virgin answer'd: "Knowest thou of Milton who descended
Driven from Eternity? him I seek, terrified at my Act
In Great Eternity which thou knowest: I come him to seek."

    .   .   .

I also stood in Satan's bosom & beheld its desolations:
A ruin'd Man, a ruin'd building of God, not made with hands:
Its plains of burning sand, its mountains of marble terrible:
Its pits & declivities flowing with molten ore & fountains
Of pitch & nitre: its ruin'd palaces & cities & mighty works:
Its furnaces of affliction, in which his Angels & Emanations
Labour with blacken'd visages among its stupendous ruins,
Arches & pryamids & porches, colonades & domes,
In which dwells Mystery, Babylon; here is her secret place,
From hence she comes forth on the Churches in delight;
Here is her Cup fill'd with its poisons in these horrid vales,
And here her scarlet Veil woven in pestilence & war;
Here is Jerusalem bound in chains in the Dens of Babylon.

In the Eastern porch of Satan's Universe Milton stood & said:

"Satan! my Spectre! I know my power thee to annihilate
And be a greater in thy place & be thy Tabernacle,
A covering for thee to do thy will, till one greater comes
And smites me as I smote thee & becomes my covering.
Such are the Laws of thy false Heav'ns; but Laws of Eternity
Are not such; know thou, I come to Self Annihilation.
Such are the Laws of Eternity, that each shall mutually
Annihilate himself for others' good, as I for thee.

Thy purpose & the purpose of thy Priests & of thy Churches
Is to impress on men the fear of death, to teach
Trembling & fear, terror, constriction, abject selfishness.
Mine is to teach Men to despise death & to go on
In fearless majesty annihilating Self, laughing to scorn
The Laws & terrors, shaking down thy Synagogues as webs.
I come to discover before Heav'n & Hell the Self righteousness
In all its Hypocritic turpitude, opening to every eye
These wonders of Satan's holiness, shewing to the Earth
The Idol Virtues of the Natural Heart, & Satan's Seat
Explore in all its Selfish Natural Virtue, & put off
In Self annihilation all that is not of God alone,
To put off Self & all I have, ever & ever. Amen."

Satan heard, Coming in a cloud, with trumpets & flaming fire,
Saying: "I am God the judge of all, the living & the dead.
Fall therefore down & worship me, submit thy supreme
Dictate to my eternal Will, & to my dictate bow.
I hold the Balances of Right & Just & mine the Sword.
Seven Angels bear my Name & in those Seven I appear,
But I alone am God & I alone in Heav'n & Earth
Of all that live dare utter this, others tremble & bow,
Till All Things become One Great Satan, in Holiness
Oppos'd to Mercy, and the Divine Delusion, Jesus, be no more."

      .   .   .

But turning toward Ololon in terrible majesty Milton
Replied: "Obey thou the Words of the Inspired Man.
All that can be annihilated must be annihilated
That the Children of Jerusalem may be saved from slavery.
There is a Negation, & there is a Contrary:
The Negation must be destroy'd to redeem the Contraries.
The Negation is the Spectre, the Reasoning Power in Man:
This is a false Body, an Incrustation over my Immortal
Spirit, a Selfhood which must be put off & annihilated alway.
To cleanse the Face of my Spirit by Self-examination,
To bathe in the Waters of Life, to wash off the Not Human,
I come in Self-annihilation & the grandeur of Inspiration,
To cast off Rational Demonstration by Faith in the Saviour,
To cast off the rotten rags of Memory by Inspiration,
To cast off Bacon, Locke & Newton from Albion's covering,
To take off his filthy garments & clothe him with Imagination,

To cast aside from Poetry all that is not Inspiration,
That it no longer shall dare to mock with the aspersion of
    Madness
Cast on the Inspired by the tame high finisher of paltry Blots
Indefinite, or paltry Rhymes, or paltry Harmonies,
Who creeps into State Government like a catterpiller to de-
    stroy;
To cast off the idiot Questioner who is always questioning
But never capable of answering, who sits with a sly grin
Silent plotting when to question, like a thief in a cave,
Who publishes doubt & calls it knowledge, whose Science is
    Despair,
Whose pretence to knowledge is Envy, whose whole Science is
To destroy the wisdom of ages to gratify ravenous Envy
That rages round him like a Wolf day & night without rest:
He smiles with condescension, he talks of Benevolence & Vir-
    tue,
And those who act with Benevolence & Virtue they murder
    time on time.
These are the destroyers of Jerusalem, these are the murderers
Of Jesus, who deny the Faith & mock at Eternal Life,
Who pretend to Poetry that they may destroy Imagination
By imitation of Nature's Images drawn from Remembrance.
These are the Sexual Garments, the Abomination of Desola-
    tion,
Hiding the Human Lineaments as with an Ark & Curtains
Which Jesus rent & now shall wholly purge away with Fire
Till Generation is swallow'd up in Regeneration."

Then trembled the Virgin Ololon & reply'd in clouds of despair:

"Is this our Feminine Portion, the Six-fold Miltonic Female?
Terribly this Portion trembles before thee, O awful Man.
Altho' our Human Power can sustain the severe contentions
Of Friendship, our Sexual cannot, but flies into the Ulro.
Hence arose all our terrors in Eternity; & now remembrance
Returns upon us; are we Contraries, O Milton, Thou & I?
O Immortal, how were we led to War the Wars of Death?
Is this the Void Outside of Existence, which if enter'd into
Becomes a Womb? & is this the Death Couch of Albion?
Thou goest to Eternal Death & all must go with thee."

So saying, the Virgin divided Six-fold, & with a shriek
Dolorous that ran thro' all Creation, a Double Six-fold Wonder
Away from Ololon she divided & fled into the depths
Of Milton's Shadow, as a Dove upon the stormy Sea.

Then as a Moony Ark Ololon descended to Felpham's Vale
In clouds of blood, in streams of gore, with dreadful thunder-
    ings
Into the Fires of Intellect that rejoic'd in Felpham's Vale
Around the Starry Eight; with one accord the Starry Eight be-
    came
One Man, Jesus the Saviour, wonderful! round his limbs
The Clouds of Ololon folded as a Garment dipped in blood,
Written within & without in woven letters, & the Writing
Is the Divine Revelation in the Litteral expression,
A Garment of War. I heard it nam'd the Woof of Six Thousand
    Years.

And I beheld the Twenty-four Cities of Albion
Arise upon their Thrones to Judge the Nations of the Earth;
And the Immortal Four in whom the Twenty-four appear Four-
    fold
Arose around Albion's body. Jesus wept & walked forth
From Felpham's Vale clothed in Clouds of blood, to enter into
Albion's Bosom, the bosom of death, & the Four surrounded
    him
In the Column of Fire in Felpham's Vale; then to their mouths
    the Four
Applied their Four Trumpets & them sounded to the Four
    winds.

Terror struck in the Vale I stood at that immortal sound.
My bones trembled, I fell outstretch'd upon the path
A moment, & my Soul return'd into its mortal state
To Resurrection & Judgment in the Vegetable Body,
And my sweet Shadow of Delight stood trembling by my side.

Immediately the Lark mounted with a loud trill from Felpham's
    Vale,
And the Wild Thyme from Wimbleton's green & impurpled
    Hills,
And Los & Enitharmon rose over the Hills of Surrey:

Their clouds roll over London with a south wind; soft Oothoon
Pants in the Vales of Lambeth, weeping o'er her Human Har-
    vest.
Los listens to the Cry of the Poor Man, his Cloud
Over London in volume terrific low bended in anger.

Rintrah & Palamabron view the Human Harvest beneath.
Their Wine-presses & Barns stand open, the Ovens are prepar'd,
The Waggons ready; terrific Lions & Tygers sport & play.
All Animals upon the Earth are prepar'd in all their strength
To go forth to the Great Harvest & Vintage of the Nations.

FINIS

Selections from *JERUSALEM*

From PART ONE

Of the Measure in which the following Poem is written.

We who dwell on Earth can do nothing of ourselves; every thing is conducted by Spirits, no less than Digestion or Sleep. *I fear the best . . . in Jesus whom we . . .* When this Verse was first dictated to me, I consider'd a Monotonous Cadence, like that used by Milton & Shakespeare & all writers of English Blank Verse, derived from the modern bondage of Rhyming, to be a necessary and indispensible part of Verse. But I soon found that in the mouth of a true Orator such monotony was not only awkward, but as much a bondage as rhyme itself. I therefore have produced a variety in every line, both of cadences & number of syllables. Every word and every letter is studied and put into its fit place; the terrific numbers are reserved for the terrific parts, the mild & gentle for the mild & gentle parts, and the prosaic for inferior parts; all are necessary to each other. Poetry Fetter'd Fetters the Human Race. Nations are Destroy'd or Flourish in proportion as Their Poetry, Painting and Music are Destroy'd or Flourish! The Primeval State of Man was Wisdom, Art and Science.

OF the Sleep of Ulro! and of the passage through
Eternal Death! and of the awaking to Eternal Life.

This theme calls me in sleep night after night, & ev'ry morn
Awakes me at sun-rise; then I see the Saviour over me
Spreading his beams of love & dictating the words of this mild
    song.

"Awake! awake O sleeper of the land of shadows, wake! expand!
I am in you and you in me, mutual in love divine:
Fibres of love from man to man thro' Albion's pleasant land.
In all the dark Atlantic vale down from the hills of Surrey
A black water accumulates; return Albion! return!
Thy brethren call thee, and thy fathers and thy sons,
Thy nurses and thy mothers, thy sisters and thy daughters
Weep at thy soul's disease, and the Divine Vision is darken'd,
Thy Emanation that was wont to play before thy face,
Beaming forth with her daughters into the Divine bosom:

"Where hast thou hidden thy Emanation, lovely Jerusalem,
From the vision and fruition of the Holy-one?
I am not a God afar off, I am a brother and friend:
Within your bosoms I reside, and you reside in me:
Lo! we are One, forgiving all Evil, Not seeking recompense.
Ye are my members, O ye sleepers of Beulah, land of shades!"

But the perturbed Man away turns down the valleys dark:
"Phantom of the over heated brain! shadow of immortality!
Seeking to keep my soul a victim to thy Love! which binds
Man, the enemy of man, into deceitful friendships,
Jerusalem is not! her daughters are indefinite:
By demonstration man alone can live, and not by faith.
My mountains are my own, and I will keep them to myself:
The Malvern and the Cheviot, the Wolds, Plinlimmon & Snowdon
Are mine: here will I build my Laws of Moral Virtue.
Humanity shall be no more, but war & princedom & victory!"

.   .   .

And this is the manner of the Sons of Albion in their strength:
They take the Two Contraries which are call'd Qualities, with which
Every Substance is clothed: they name them Good & Evil;
From them they make an Abstract, which is a Negation
Not only of the Substance from which it is derived,
A murderer of its own Body, but also a murderer
Of every Divine Member: it is the Reasoning Power,
An Abstract objecting power that Negatives every thing.

This is the Spectre of Man, the Holy Reasoning Power,
And in its Holiness is closed the Abomination of Desolation.

Therefore Los stands in London building Golgonooza,
Compelling his Spectre to labours mighty; trembling in fear
The Spectre weeps, but Los unmov'd by tears or threats re-
    mains.

"I must Create a System or be enslav'd by another Man's.
I will not Reason & Compare: my business is to Create."

So Los in fury & strength, in indignation & burning wrath.
Shudd'ring the Spectre howls, his howlings terrify the night,
He stamps around the Anvil, beating blows of stern despair,
He curses Heaven & Earth, Day & Night & Sun & Moon,
He curses Forest, Spring & River, Desart & sandy Waste,
Cities & Nations, Families & Peoples, Tongues & Laws,
Driven to desperation by Los's terrors & threatening fears.

Los cries, "Obey my voice & never deviate from my will
And I will be merciful to thee! be thou invisible to all
To whom I make thee invisible, but chief to my own Children.
O Spectre of Urthona! Reason not against their dear approach
Nor them obstruct with thy temptations of doubt & despair.
O Shame, O strong & mighty Shame, I break thy brazen fetters!
If thou refuse, thy present torments will seem southern breezes
To what thou shalt endure if thou obey not my great will."

The Spectre answer'd: "Art thou not asham'd of those thy Sins
That thou callest thy Children? lo, the Law of God commands
That they be offered upon his Altar! O cruelty & torment,
For thine are also mine! I have kept silent hitherto
Concerning my chief delight, but thou hast broken silence.
Now I will speak my mind! Where is my lovely Enitharmon?
O thou my enemy, where is my Great Sin? She is also thine.
I said: now is my grief at worst, incapable of being
Surpassed; but every moment it accumulates more & more,
It continues accumulating to eternity; the joys of God advance,
For he is Righteous, he is not a Being of Pity & Compassion,
He cannot feel Distress, he feeds on Sacrifice & Offering,
Delighting in cries & tears & clothed in holiness & solitude;
But my griefs advance also, for ever & ever without end.

O that I could cease to be! Despair! I am Despair,
Created to be the great example of horror & agony; also my
Prayer is vain. I called for compassion; compassion mock'd;
Mercy & pity threw the grave stone over me, & with lead
And iron bound it over me for ever. Life lives on my
Consuming & the Almighty hath made me his Contrary
To be all evil, all reversed & for ever dead, knowing
And seeing life, yet living not; how can I then behold
And not tremble? how can I be beheld & not abhorr'd?"

So spoke the Spectre shudd'ring, & dark tears ran down his
    shadowy face,
Which Los wiped off, but comfort none could give, or beam of
    hope.
Yet ceas'd he not from labouring at the roarings of his Forge,
With iron & brass Building Golgonooza in great contendings,
Till his Sons & Daughters came forth from the Furnaces
At the sublime Labours: for Los compell'd the invisible Spectre
To labours mighty with vast strength, with his mighty chains,
In pulsations of time, & extensions of space like Urns of Beu-
    lah,
With great labour upon his anvils, & in his ladles the Ore
He lifted, pouring it into the clay ground prepar'd with art,
Striving with Systems to deliver Individuals from those Systems,
That whenever any Spectre began to devour the Dead,
He might feel the pain as if a man gnaw'd his own tender
    nerves.

            .   .   .

What are those golden builders doing? where was the burying-
    place
Of soft Ethinthus? near Tyburn's fatal Tree? is that
Mild Zion's hill's most ancient promontory, near mournful
Ever weeping Paddington? is that Calvary and Golgotha
Becoming a building of pity and compassion? Lo!
The stones are pity, and the bricks, well wrought affections
Enamel'd with love & kindness, & the tiles engraven gold,
Labour of merciful hands: the beams & rafters are forgiveness:
The mortar & cement of the work, tears of honesty: the nails
And the screws & iron braces are well wrought blandishments
And well contrived words, firm fixing, never forgotten,
Always comforting the remembrance: the floors, humility:

The cielings, devotion: the hearths, thanksgiving.
Prepare the furniture, O Lambeth, in thy pitying looms,
The curtains, woven tears & sighs wrought into lovely forms
For comfort; there the secret furniture of Jerusalem's chamber
Is wrought. Lambeth! the Bride, the Lamb's Wife, loveth thee.
Thou art one with her & knowest not of self in thy supreme
    joy.
Go on, builders in hope, tho' Jerusalem wanders far away
Without the gate of Los, among the dark Satanic wheels.

Fourfold the Sons of Los in their divisions, and fourfold
The great City of Golgonooza: fourfold toward the north,
And toward the south fourfold, & fourfold toward the east &
    west,
Each within other toward the four points: that toward
Eden, and that toward the World of Generation,
And that toward Beulah, and that toward Ulro.
Ulro is the space of the terrible starry wheels of Albion's sons,
But that toward Eden is walled up till time of renovation,
Yet it is perfect in its building, ornaments & perfection.

                    .   .   .

The Vegetative Universe opens like a flower from the Earth's
    center
In which is Eternity. It expands in Stars to the Mundane Shell
And there it meets Eternity again, both within and without,
And the abstract Voids between the Stars are the Satanic
    .Wheels.

There is the Cave, the Rock, the Tree, the Lake of Udan Adan,
The Forest and the Marsh and the Pits of bitumen deadly,
The Rocks of solid fire, the Ice valleys, the Plains
Of burning sand, the rivers, cataract & Lakes of Fire,
The Islands of the fiery Lakes, the Trees of Malice, Revenge
And black Anxiety, and the Cities of the Salamandrine men,
(But whatever is visible to the Generated Man
Is a Creation of mercy & love from the Satanic Void).
The land of darkness flamed, but no light & no repose:
The land of snows of trembling & of iron hail incessant:
The land of earthquakes, and the land of woven labyrinths:
The land of snares & traps & wheels & pit-falls & dire mills:
The Voids, the Solids, & the land of clouds & regions of waters

With their inhabitants, in the Twenty-seven Heavens beneath
    Beulah:
Self-righteousness conglomerating against the Divine Vision:
A Concave Earth wondrous, Chasmal, Abyssal, Incoherent,
Forming the Mundane Shell: above, beneath, on all sides sur-
    rounding
Golgonooza. Los walks round the walls night and day.

He views the City of Golgonooza & its smaller Cities,
The Looms & Mills & Prisons & Work-houses of Og & Anak,
The Amalekite, the Canaanite, the Moabite, the Egyptian,
And all that has existed in the space of six thousand years,
Permanent & not lost, not lost nor vanish'd, & every little act,
Word, work & wish that has existed, all remaining still
In those Churches ever consuming & ever building by the Spec-
    tres
Of all the inhabitants of the Earth wailing to be Created,
Shadowy to those who dwell not in them, meer possibilities,
But to those who enter into them they seem the only sub-
    stances;
For every thing exists & not one sigh nor smile nor tear,
One hair nor particle of dust, not one can pass away.

       •   •   •

I see the Four-fold Man, The Humanity in deadly sleep
And its fallen Emanation, The Spectre & its cruel Shadow.
I see the Past, Present & Future existing all at once
Before me. O Divine Spirit, sustain me on thy wings,
That I may awake Albion from his long & cold repose;
For Bacon & Newton, sheath'd in dismal steel, their terrors
    hang
Like iron scourges over Albion: Reasonings like vast Serpents
Infold around my limbs, bruising my minute articulations.

I turn my eyes to the Schools & Universities of Europe
And there behold the Loom of Locke, whose Woof rages dire,
Wash'd by the Water-wheels of Newton: black the cloth
In heavy wreathes folds over every Nation: cruel Works
Of many Wheels I view, wheel without wheel, with cogs tyran-
    nic
Moving by compulsion each other, not as those in Eden, which,
Wheel within Wheel, in freedom revolve in harmony & peace.

       •   •   •

From every-one of the Four Regions of Human Majesty
There is an Outside spread Without & an Outside spread
    Within,
Beyond the Outline of Identity both ways, which meet in One,
An orbed Void of doubt, despair, hunger & thirst & sorrow.
Here the Twelve Sons of Albion, join'd in dark Assembly,
Jealous of Jerusalem's children, asham'd of her little-ones,
(For Vala produc'd the Bodies, Jerusalem gave the Souls)
Became as Three Immense Wheels turning upon one-another
Into Non-Entity, and their thunders hoarse appall the Dead
To murder their own Souls, to build a Kingdom among the
    Dead.

"Cast, Cast ye Jerusalem forth! The Shadow of delusions!
The Harlot daughter! Mother of pity and dishonourable for-
    giveness!
Our Father Albion's sin and shame! But father now no more,
Nor sons, nor hateful peace & love, nor soft complacencies,
With transgressors meeting in brotherhood around the table
Or in the porch or garden. No more the sinful delights
Of age and youth, and boy and girl, and animal and herb,
And river and mountain, and city & village, and house & family,
Beneath the Oak & Palm, beneath the Vine and Fig-tree,
In self-denial!—But War and deadly contention Between
Father and Son, and light and love! All bold asperities
Of Haters met in deadly strife, rending the house & garden,
The unforgiving porches, the tables of enmity, and beds
And chambers of trembling & suspition, hatreds of age & youth,
And boy & girl, & animal & herb, & river & mountain,
And city & village, and house & family, That the Perfect
May live in glory, redeem'd by Sacrifice of the Lamb
And of his children before sinful Jerusalem, to build
Babylon the City of Vala, the Goddess Virgin-Mother.
She is our Mother! Nature! Jerusalem is our Harlot-Sister
Return'd with Children of pollution to defile our House
With Sin and Shame. Cast, Cast her into the Potter's field!
Her little-ones She must slay upon our Altars, and her aged
Parents must be carried into captivity: to redeem her Soul,
To be for a Shame & a Curse, and to be our Slave for ever."

So cry Hand & Hyle, the eldest of the fathers of Albion's
Little-ones, to destroy the Divine Saviour, the Friend of Sin-
    ners,

Building Castles in desolated places and strong Fortifications.
Soon Hand mightily devour'd & absorb'd Albion's Twelve Sons.
Out from his bosom a mighty Polypus, vegetating in darkness;
And Hyle & Coban were his two chosen ones for Emissaries
In War: forth from his bosom they went and return'd,
Like Wheels from a great Wheel reflected in the Deep.
Hoarse turn'd the Starry Wheels rending a way in Albion's
    Loins:
Beyond the Night of Beulah, In a dark & unknown Night:
Outstretch'd his Giant beauty on the ground in pain & tears:
His Children exil'd from his breast pass to and fro before him,
His birds are silent on his hills, flocks die beneath his branches,
His tents are fall'n; his trumpets and the sweet sound of his
    harp
Are silent on his clouded hills that belch forth storms & fire.
His milk of Cows & honey of Bees & fruit of golden harvest
Is gather'd in the scorching heat & in the driving rain.
Where once he sat, he weary walks in misery and pain,
His Giant beauty and perfection fallen into dust,
Till, from within his wither'd breast, grown narrow with his
    woes,
The corn is turn'd to thistles & the apples into poison,
The birds of song to murderous crows, his joys to bitter groans,
The voices of children in his tents to cries of helpless infants,
And self-exiled from the face of light & shine of morning,
In the dark world, a narrow house! he wanders up and down
Seeking for rest and finding none! and hidden far within,
His Eon weeping in the cold and desolated Earth.

.   .   .

But when they saw Albion fall'n upon mild Lambeth's vale,
Astonish'd, Terrified, they hover'd over his Giant limbs.
Then thus Jerusalem spoke, while Vala wove the veil of tears,
Weeping in pleadings of Love, in the web of despair:

"Wherefore hast thou shut me into the winter of human life,
And clos'd up the sweet regions of youth and virgin innocence
Where we live forgetting error, not pondering on evil,
Among my lambs & brooks of water, among my warbling birds:
Where we delight in innocence before the face of the Lamb,
Going in and out before him in his love and sweet affection?"

Vala replied weeping & trembling, hiding in her veil:

"When winter rends the hungry family and the snow falls
Upon the ways of men hiding the paths of man and beast,
Then mourns the wanderer: then he repents his wanderings &
    eyes
The distant forest: then the slave groans in the dungeon of
    stone,
The captive in the mill of the stranger, sold for scanty hire.
They view their former life: they number moments over and
    over,
Stringing them on their remembrance as on a thread of sorrow.
Thou art my sister and my daughter: thy shame is mine also:
Ask me not of my griefs! thou knowest all my griefs."

Jerusalem answer'd with soft tears over the valleys:

"O Vala, what is Sin, that thou shudderest and weepest
At sight of thy once lov'd Jerusalem? What is Sin but a little
Error & fault that is soon forgiven? but mercy is not a Sin,
Nor pity nor love nor kind forgiveness. O, if I have Sinned
Forgive & pity me! O, unfold thy Veil in mercy & love!
Slay not my little ones, beloved Virgin daughter of Babylon,
Slay not my infant loves & graces, beautiful daughter of Moab!
I cannot put off the human form. I strive but strive in vain.
When Albion rent thy beautiful net of gold and silver twine,
Thou hadst woven it with art, thou hadst caught me in the
    bands
Of love, thou refusedst to let me go: Albion beheld thy beauty,
Beautiful thro' our Love's comeliness, beautiful thro' pity.
The Veil shone with thy brightness in the eyes of Albion
Because it inclos'd pity & love, because we lov'd one-another.
Albion lov'd thee: he rent thy Veil: he embrac'd thee: he lov'd
    thee!
Astonish'd at his beauty & perfection, thou forgavest his furious
    love.
I redounded from Albion's bosom in my virgin loveliness:
The Lamb of God reciev'd me in his arms, he smil'd upon us:
He made me his Bride & Wife: he gave thee to Albion.
Then was a time of love. O why is it passed away!"

Then Albion broke silence and with groans reply'd:

"O Vala! O Jerusalem! do you delight in my groans!
You, O lovely forms, you have prepared my death-cup.
The disease of Shame covers me from head to feet. I have no
    hope.
Every boil upon my body is a separate & deadly Sin.
Doubt first assail'd me, then Shame took possession of me.
Shame divides Families, Shame hath divided Albion in sunder.
First fled my Sons & then my Daughters, then my Wild Anima-
    tions,
My Cattle next, last ev'n the Dog of my Gate; the Forests fled,
The Corn-fields & the breathing Gardens outside separated,
The Sea, the Stars, the Sun, the Moon, driv'n forth by my disease.
All is Eternal Death unless you can weave a chaste
Body over an unchaste Mind! Vala! O that thou wert pure!
That the deep wound of Sin might be clos'd up with the Needle
And with the Loom, to cover Gwendolen & Ragan with costly
    Robes
Of Natural Virtue, for their Spiritual forms without a Veil
Wither in Luvah's Sepulcher. I thrust him from my presence,
And all my Children follow'd his loud howlings into the Deep.

        .   .   .

Then Vala answer'd spreading her scarlet Veil over Albion:

"Albion thy fear has made me tremble; thy terrors have sur-
    rounded me:
Thy Sons have nail'd me on the Gates, piercing my hands &
    feet,
Till Skofield's Nimrod, the mighty Huntsman Jehovah, came
With Cush his Son & took me down. He in a golden Ark
Bears me before his Armies, tho' my shadow hovers here.
The flesh of multitudes fed & nourish'd me in my childhood,
My morn & evening food were prepar'd in Battles of Men.
Great is the cry of the Hounds of Nimrod along the Valley
Of Vision, they scent the odor of War in the Valley of Vision.
All Love is lost! terror succeeds, & Hatred instead of Love,
And stern demands of Right & Duty instead of Liberty.
Once thou wast to me the loveliest Son of heaven, but now
Where shall I hide from thy dread countenance & searching
    eyes?
I have looked into the secret Soul of him I loved,
And in the dark recesses found Sin & can never return."

Albion again utter'd his voice beneath the silent Moon:

"I brought Love into light of day, to pride in chaste beauty,
I brought Love into light, & fancied Innocence is no more."

Then spoke Jerusalem: "O Albion! my Father Albion!
Why wilt thou number every little fibre of my Soul,
Spreading them out before the Sun like stalks of flax to dry?
The Infant Joy is beautiful, but its anatomy
Horrible, ghast & deadly! nought shalt thou find in it
But dark despair & everlasting brooding melancholy!"

Then Albion turn'd his face toward Jerusalem & spoke:

"Hide thou, Jerusalem, in impalpable voidness, not to be
Touch'd by the hand nor seen with the eye. O Jerusalem,
Would thou wert not & that thy place might never be found!
But come, O Vala, with knife & cup, drain my blood
To the last drop, then hide me in thy Scarlet Tabernacle;
For I see Luvah whom I slew, I behold him in my Spectre
As I behold Jerusalem in thee, O Vala, dark and cold."

Jerusalem then stretch'd her hand toward the Moon & spoke:

"Why should Punishment Weave the Veil with Iron Wheels of
    War
When Forgiveness might it Weave with Wings of Cherubim?"

FROM PART TWO

To the Jews

JERUSALEM the Emanation of the Giant Albion! Can it be? Is
it a Truth that the Learned have explored? Was Britain the
Primitive Seat of the Patriarchal Religion? If it is true, my
title-page is also True, that Jerusalem was & is the Emanation
of the Giant Albion. It is True and cannot be controverted. Ye
are united, O ye Inhabitants of Earth, in One Religion, The
Religion of Jesus, the most Ancient, the Eternal & the Everlasting Gospel. The Wicked will turn it to Wickedness, the
Righteous to Righteousness. Amen! Huzza! Selah!

"All things Begin & End in Albion's Ancient Druid Rocky Shore."

Your Ancestors derived their origin from Abraham, Heber, Shem and Noah, who were Druids, as the Druid Temples (which are the Patriarchal Pillars & Oak Groves) over the whole Earth witness to this day.

You have a tradition, that Man anciently contain'd in his mighty limbs all things in Heaven & Earth: this you recieved from the Druids.

"But now the Starry Heavens are fled from the mighty limbs of Albion."

Albion was the Parent of the Druids, & in his Chaotic State of Sleep, Satan & Adam & the whole World was Created by the Elohim.

> The fields from Islington to Marybone,
> To Primrose Hill and Saint John's Wood,
>   Were builded over with pillars of gold,
> And there Jerusalem's pillars stood.

> Her Little-ones ran on the fields,
> The Lamb of God among them seen,
>   And fair Jerusalem his Bride,
> Among the little meadows green.

> Pancrass & Kentish-town repose
> Among her golden pillars high,
>   Among her golden arches which
> Shine upon the starry sky.

> The Jew's-harp-house & the Green Man,
> The Ponds where Boys to bathe delight,
>   The fields of Cows by Willan's farm,
> Shine in Jerusalem's pleasant sight.

> She walks upon our meadows green,
> The Lamb of God walks by her side,
>   And every English Child is seen
> Children of Jesus & his Bride.

Forgiving trespasses and sins
Lest Babylon with cruel Og
    With Moral & Self-righteous Law
Should Crucify in Satan's Synagogue!

What are those golden Builders doing
Near mournful ever-weeping Paddington,
    Standing above that mighty Ruin
Where Satan the first victory won,

Where Albion slept beneath the Fatal Tree,
And the Druids' golden Knife
    Rioted in human gore,
In Offerings of Human Life?

They groan'd aloud on London Stone,
They groan'd aloud on Tyburn's Brook,
    Albion gave his deadly groan,
And all the Atlantic Mountains shook.

Albion's Spectre from his Loins
Tore forth in all the pomp of War:
    Satan his name: in flames of fire
He stretch'd his Druid Pillars far.

Jerusalem fell from Lambeth's Vale
Down thro' Poplar & Old Bow,
    Thro' Malden & across the Sea,
In War & howling, death & woe.

The Rhine was red with human blood,
The Danube roll'd a purple tide,
    On the Euphrates Satan stood,
And over Asia stretch'd his pride.

He wither'd up sweet Zion's Hill
From every Nation of the Earth;
    He wither'd up Jerusalem's Gates,
And in a dark Land gave her birth.

He wither'd up the Human Form
By laws of sacrifice for sin,

Till it became a Mortal Worm,
But O! translucent all within.

The Divine Vision still was seen,
Still was the Human Form Divine,
    Weeping in weak & mortal clay,
O Jesus, still the Form was thine.

And thine the Human Face, & thine
The Human Hands & Feet & Breath,
    Entering thro' the Gates of Birth
And passing thro' the Gates of Death.

And O thou Lamb of God, whom I
Slew in my dark self-righteous pride,
    Art thou return'd to Albion's Land?
And is Jerusalem thy Bride?

Come to my arms & never more
Depart, but dwell for ever here:
    Create my Spirit to thy Love:
Subdue my Spectre to thy Fear.

Spectre of Albion! warlike Fiend!
In clouds of blood & ruin roll'd,
    I here reclaim thee as my own.
My Selfhood! Satan! arm'd in gold.

Is this thy soft Family-Love,
Thy cruel Patriarchal pride,
    Planting thy Family alone,
Destroying all the World beside?

A man's worst enemies are those
Of his own house & family;
    And he who makes his law a curse,
By his own law shall surely die.

In my Exchanges every Land
Shall walk, & mine in every Land,
    Mutual shall build Jerusalem,
Both heart in heart & hand in hand.

If Humility is Christianity, you, O Jews, are the true Christians. If your tradition that Man contained in his Limbs all Animals is True, & they were separated from him by cruel Sacrifices, and when compulsory cruel Sacrifices had brought Humanity into a Feminine Tabernacle in the loins of Abraham & David, the Lamb of God, the Saviour became apparent on Earth as the Prophets had foretold, The Return of Israel is a Return to Mental Sacrifice & War. Take up the Cross, O Israel, & follow Jesus.

EVERY ornament of perfection and every labour of love
In all the Garden of Eden & in all the golden mountains
Was become an envied horror and a remembrance of jealousy,
And every Act a Crime, and Albion the punisher & judge.

And Albion spoke from his secret seat and said:

"All these ornaments are crimes, they are made by the labours
Of loves, of unnatural consanguinities and friendships
Horrid to think of when enquired deeply into; and all
These hills & valleys are accursed witnesses of Sin.

"I therefore condense them into solid rocks, stedfast,
A foundation and certainty and demonstrative truth,
That Man be separate from Man, & here I plant my seat."

Cold snows drifted around him: ice cover'd his loins around.
He sat by Tyburn's brook, and underneath his heel shot up
A deadly Tree: he nam'd it Moral Virtue and the Law
Of God who dwells in Chaos hidden from the human sight.

The Tree spread over him its cold shadows, (Albion groan'd)
They bent down, they felt the earth, and again enrooting
Shot into many a Tree, an endless labyrinth of woe.

From willing sacrifice of Self, to sacrifice of (miscall'd) Enemies
For Atonement. Albion began to erect twelve Altars
Of rough unhewn rocks, before the Potter's Furnace.
He nam'd them Justice and Truth. And Albion's Sons
Must have become the first Victims, being the first transgressors,

But they fled to the mountains to seek ransom, building A
    Strong
Fortification against the Divine Humanity and Mercy,
In Shame & Jealousy to annihilate Jerusalem.

Then the Divine Vision like a silent Sun appear'd above
Albion's dark rocks, setting behind the Gardens of Kensington
On Tyburn's River in clouds of blood, where was mild Zion
    Hill's
Most ancient promontory; and in the Sun a Human Form
    appear'd,
And thus the Voice Divine went forth upon the rocks of Al-
    bion:

"I elected Albion for my glory: I gave to him the Nations
Of the whole Earth. He was the Angel of my Presence, and all
The Sons of God were Albion's Sons, and Jerusalem was my
    joy.
The Reactor hath hid himself thro' envy. I behold him,
But you cannot behold him till he be reveal'd in his System.
Albion's Reactor must have a Place prepar'd. Albion must Sleep
The Sleep of Death till the Man of Sin & Repentance be re-
    veal'd.
Hidden in Albion's Forests he lurks: he admits of no Reply
From Albion, but hath founded his Reaction into a Law
Of Action, for Obedience to destroy the Contraries of Man.
He hath compell'd Albion to become a Punisher & hath pos-
    sess'd
Himself of Albion's Forests & Wilds, and Jerusalem is taken,
The City of the Woods in the Forest of Ephratah is taken!
London is a stone of her ruins, Oxford is the dust of her walls,
Sussex & Kent are her scatter'd garments, Ireland her holy
    place,
And the murder'd bodies of her little ones are Scotland and
    Wales.
The Cities of the Nations are the smoke of her consummation,
The Nations are her dust, ground by the chariot wheels
Of her lordly conquerors, her palaces levell'd with the dust.
I come that I may find a way for my banished ones to return.
Fear not, O little Flock, I come. Albion shall rise again."

So saying, the mild Sun inclos'd the Human Family.

Forthwith from Albion's dark'ning locks came two Immortal
    forms,
Saying: "We alone are escaped, O merciful Lord and Saviour,
We flee from the interiors of Albion's hills and mountains,
From his Valleys Eastward from Amalek, Canaan & Moab,
Beneath his vast ranges of hills surrounding Jerusalem.

"Albion walk'd on the steps of fire before his Halls,
And Vala walk'd with him in dreams of soft deluding slumber;
He looked up & saw the Prince of Light with splendor faded.
Then Albion ascended mourning into the porches of his Palace,
Above him rose a Shadow from his wearied intellect,
Of living gold, pure, perfect, holy; in white linen pure he hov-
    er'd,
A sweet entrancing self-delusion, a wat'ry vision of Albion.
Soft exulting in existence, all the Man absorbing.

"Albion fell upon his face prostrate before the wat'ry Shadow,
Saying: 'O Lord, whence is this change? thou knowest I am
    nothing!'
And Vala trembled & cover'd her face, & her locks were spread
    on the pavement.

"We heard, astonish'd at the Vision, & our hearts tremble
    within us;
We heard the voice of slumberous Albion, and thus he spake,
Idolatrous to his own Shadow, words of eternity uttering:

" 'O I am nothing when I enter into judgment with thee!
If thou withdraw thy breath, I die & vanish into Hades;
If thou dost lay thine hand upon me, behold I am silent;
If thou withhold thine hand, I perish like a fallen leaf.
O I am nothing, and to nothing must return again!
If thou withdraw thy breath, Behold, I am oblivion.'

"He ceas'd: the shadowy voice was silent: but the cloud hover'd
    over their heads
In golden wreathes, the sorrow of Man, & the balmy drops fell
    down.
And lo! that son of Man, that Shadowy Spirit of mild Albion,
Luvah, descended from the cloud; in terror Albion rose:
Indignant rose the awful Man & turn'd his back on Vala.

"We heard the voice of Albion starting from his sleep:

" 'Whence is this voice crying, Enion! that soundeth in my ears?
O cruel pity! O dark deceit! can love seek for dominion?'

"And Luvah strove to gain dominion over Albion:
They strove together above the Body where Vala was inclos'd
And the dark Body of Albion left prostrate upon the crystal
    pavement,
Cover'd with boils from head to foot, the terrible smitings of
    Luvah.

"Then frown'd the fallen Man and put forth Luvah from his
    presence,
Saying, 'Go and Die the Death of Man for Vala the sweet
    wanderer.
I will turn the volutions of your ears outward, and bend your
    nostrils
Downward, and your fluxile eyes englob'd roll round in fear;
Your with'ring lips and tongue shrink up into a narrow circle,
Till into narrow forms you creep: go take your fiery way,
And learn what 'tis to absorb the Man, you Spirits of Pity &
    Love.'

"They heard the voice and fled swift as the winter's setting sun.
And now the human blood foam'd high; the Spirits Luvah &
    Vala
Went down the Human Heart, where Paradise & its joys
    abounded,
In jealous fears & fury & rage, & flames roll round their fervid
    feet,
And the vast form of Nature like a serpent play'd before them.
And as they fled in folding fires & thunders of the deep,
Vala shrunk in like the dark sea that leaves its slimy banks;
And from her bosom Luvah fell far as the east and west,
And the vast form of Nature like a serpent roll'd between,
Whether of Jerusalem's or Vala's ruins congenerated, we know
    not:
All is confusion, all is tumult, & we alone are escaped."
So spoke the fugitives; they join'd the Divine Family, trembling.

.   .   .

Then spoke the Spectrous Chaos to Albion, dark'ning cold,
From the back & loins where dwell the Spectrous Dead:

"I am your Rational Power, O Albion, & that Human Form
You call Divine is but a Worm seventy inches long
That creeps forth in a night & is dried in the morning sun,
In fortuitous concourse of memorys accumulated & lost.
It plows the Earth in its own conceit, it overwhelms the Hills
Beneath its winding labyrinths, till a stone of the brook
Stops it in midst of its pride among its hills & rivers.
Battersea & Chelsea mourn, London & Canterbury tremble:
Their place shall not be found as the wind passes over.
The ancient Cities of the Earth remove as a traveller,
And shall Albion's Cities remain when I pass over them
With my deluge of forgotten remembrances over the tablet?"

So spoke the Spectre to Albion: he is the Great Selfhood,
Satan, Worship'd as God by the Mighty Ones of the Earth,
Having a white Dot call'd a Center, from which branches out
A Circle in continual gyrations: this became a Heart
From which sprang numerous branches varying their motions,
Producing many Heads, three or seven or ten, & hands & feet
Innumerable at will of the unfortunate contemplator
Who becomes his food: such is the way of the Devouring
    Power.

And this is the cause of the appearance in the frowning Chaos:
Albion's Emanation, which he had hidden in Jealousy,
Appear'd now in the frowning Chaos, prolific upon the Chaos,
Reflecting back to Albion in Sexual Reasoning Hermaphroditic.

Albion spoke: "Who art thou that appearest in gloomy pomp
Involving the Divine Vision in colours of autumn ripeness?
I never saw thee till this time, nor beheld life abstracted,
Nor darkness immingled with light on my furrow'd field.
Whence camest thou? who art thou, O loveliest? the Divine
    Vision
Is as nothing before thee: faded is all life and joy."

Vala replied in clouds of tears, Albion's garment embracing:

"I was a City & a Temple built by Albion's Children.
I was a Garden planted with beauty. I allured on hill & valley
The River of Life to flow against my walls & among my trees.
Vala was Albion's Bride & Wife in great Eternity,
The loveliest of the daughters of Eternity when in daybreak
I emanated from Luvah over the Towers of Jerusalem,
And in her Courts among her little Children offering up
The Sacrifice of fanatic love! why loved I Jerusalem?
Why was I one with her, embracing in the Vision of Jesus?

"Wherefore did I, loving, create love, which never yet
Immingled God & Man, when thou & I hid the Divine Vision
In cloud of secret gloom which, behold, involves me round
      about?
Know me now Albion: look upon me. I alone am Beauty.
The Imaginative Human Form is but a breathing of Vala:
I breathe him forth into the Heaven from my secret Cave,
Born of the Woman, to obey the Woman, O Albion the mighty,
For the Divine appearance is Brotherhood, but I am Love
Elevate into the Region of Brotherhood with my red fires."

"Art thou Vala?" replied Albion, "image of my repose!
O how I tremble! how my members pour down milky fear!
A dewy garment covers me all over, all manhood is gone!
At thy word & at thy look, death enrobes me about
From head to feet, a garment of death & eternal fear.
Is not that Sun thy husband & that Moon thy glimmering Veil?
Are not the Stars of heaven thy Children? art thou not Baby-
      lon?
Art thou Nature, Mother of all? is Jerusalem thy Daughter?
Why have thou elevate inward, O dweller of outward cham-
      bers,
From grot & cave beneath the Moon, dim region of death
Where I laid my Plow in the hot noon, where my hot team fed,
Where implements of War are forged, the Plow to go over the
      Nations,
In pain girding me round like a rib of iron in heaven? O Vala!
In Eternity they neither marry nor are given in marriage.
Albion, the high Cliff of the Atlantic, is become a barren
      Land."

Los stood at his Anvil: he heard the contentions of Vala;
He heav'd his thund'ring Bellows upon the valleys of Middle-
     sex,
He open'd his Furnaces before Vala; then Albion frown'd in
     anger
On his Rock, ere yet the Starry Heavens were fled away
From his awful Members; and thus Los cried aloud
To the Sons of Albion & to Hand the eldest Son of Albion:

"I hear the screech of Childbirth loud pealing, & the groans
Of Death in Albion's clouds dreadful utter'd over all the Earth.
What may Man be? who can tell! but what may Woman be
To have power over Man from Cradle to corruptible Grave?
There is a Throne in every Man, it is the Throne of God;
This, Woman has claim'd as her own, & Man is no more!
Albion is the Tabernacle of Vala & her Temple,
And not the Tabernacle & Temple of the Most High.
O Albion, why wilt thou Create a Female Will?
To hide the most evident God in a hidden covert, even
In the shadows of a Woman & a secluded Holy Place,
That we may pry after him as after a stolen treasure,
Hidden among the Dead & mured up from the paths of life."

                    .   .   .

And many of the Eternal Ones laughed after their manner:

"Have you known the Judgment that is arisen among the
Zoas of Albion, where a Man dare hardly to embrace
His own Wife for the terrors of Chastity that they call
By the name of Morality? their Daughters govern all
In hidden deceit! they are Vegetable, only fit for burning.
Art & Science cannot exist but by Naked Beauty display'd."

Then those in Great Eternity who contemplate on Death
Said thus: "What seems to Be, Is, To those to whom
It seems to Be, & is productive of the most dreadful
Consequences to those to whom it seems to Be, even of
Torments, Despair, Eternal Death; but the Divine Mercy
Steps beyond and Redeems Man in the Body of Jesus. Amen.
And Length, Bredth, Highth again Obey the Divine Vision.
     Hallelujah."

                    .   .   .

Then Los grew furious, raging: "Why stand we here trembling
  around
Calling on God for help, and not ourselves, in whom God
  dwells,
Stretching a hand to save the falling Man? are we not Four
Beholding Albion upon the Precipice ready to fall into Non-
  Entity?
Seeing these Heavens & Hells conglobing in the Void, Heavens
  over Hells
Brooding in holy hypocritic lust, drinking the cries of pain
From howling victims of Law, building Heavens Twenty-seven-
  fold,
Swell'd & bloated General Forms repugnant to the Divine-
Humanity who is the Only General and Universal Form,
To which all Lineaments tend & seek with love & sympathy.
All broad & general principles belong to benevolence
Who protects minute particulars every one in their own iden-
  tity;
But here the affectionate touch of the tongue is clos'd in by
  deadly teeth,
And the soft smile of friendship & the open dawn of benevo-
  lence
Become a net & a trap, & every energy render'd cruel,
Till the existence of friendship & benevolence is denied:
The wine of the Spirit & the vineyards of the Holy-One
Here turn into poisonous stupor & deadly intoxication.
That they may be condemn'd by Law & the Lamb of God be
  slain;
And the two Sources of Life in Eternity, Hunting and War,
Are become the Sources of dark & bitter Death & of corroding
  Hell.
The open heart is shut up in integuments of frozen silence
That the spear that lights it forth may shatter the ribs & bosom.
A pretence of Art to destroy Art; a pretence of Liberty
To destroy Liberty; a pretence of Religion to destroy Religion.
Oshea and Caleb fight: they contend in the valleys of Peor,
In the terrible Family Contentions of those who love each
  other.
The Armies of Balaam weep—no women come to the field:
Dead corses lay before them, & not as in Wars of old;
For the Soldier who fights for Truth calls his enemy his
  brother:

They fight & contend for life & not for eternal death;
But here the Soldier strikes, & a dead corse falls at his feet,
Nor Daughter nor Sister nor Mother come forth to embosom
    the Slain;
But Death, Eternal Death, remains in the Valleys of Peor.
The English are scatter'd over the face of the Nations: are
    these
Jerusalem's children? Hark! hear the Giants of Albion cry at
    night:
'We smell the blood of the English! we delight in their blood
    on our Altars.
The living & the dead shall be ground in our rumbling Mills
For bread of the Sons of Albion, of the Giants Hand & Sco-
    field.' "

.   .   .

"Come & mourn over Albion, the White Cliff of the Atlantic,
The Mountain of Giants: all the Giants of Albion are become
Weak, wither'd, darken'd, & Jerusalem is cast forth from Albion.
They deny that they ever knew Jerusalem, or ever dwelt in
    Shiloh.
The Gigantic roots & twigs of the vegetating Sons of Albion,
Fill'd with the little-ones, are consumed in the Fires of their
    Altars.
The vegetating Cities are burned & consumed from the Earth,
And the Bodies in which all Animals & Vegetations, the Earth
    & Heaven
Were contain'd in the All Glorious Imagination, are wither'd &
    darken'd.
The golden Gate of Havilah and all the Garden of God
Was caught up with the Sun in one day of fury and war.
The Lungs, the Heart, the Liver, shrunk away far distant from
    Man
And left a little slimy substance floating upon the tides.
In one night the Atlantic Continent was caught up with the
    Moon
And became an Opake Globe far distant, clad with moony
    beams.
The Visions of Eternity, by reason of narrowed perceptions,
Are become weak Visions of Time & Space, fix'd into fur-
    rows of death,

Till deep dissimulation is the only defence an honest man has
left.
O Polypus of Death! O Spectre over Europe and Asia,
Withering the Human Form by Laws of·Sacrifice for Sin!
By Laws of Chastity & Abhorrence I am wither'd up:
Striving to create a Heaven in which all shall be pure & holy
In their Own Selfhoods: in Natural Selfish Chastity to banish
Pity
And dear Mutual Forgiveness, & to become One Great Satan
Inslav'd to the most powerful Selfhood: to murder the Divine
Humanity
In whose sight all are as the dust & who chargeth his Angels
with folly!
Ah! weak & wide astray! Ah! shut in narrow doleful form!
Creeping in reptile flesh upon the bosom of the ground!
The Eye of Man, a little narrow orb, clos'd up & dark,
Scarcely beholding the Great Light, conversing with the
ground:
The Ear, a little shell, in small volutions shutting out
True Harmonies & comprehending great as very small:
The Nostrils, bent down to the earth & clos'd with senseless
flesh
That odours cannot them expand, nor joy on them exult:
The Tongue, a little moisture fills, a little food it cloys,
A little sound it utters, & its cries are faintly heard.
Therefore they are removed: therefore they have taken root
In Egypt & Philistea, in Moab & Edom & Aram."

. . .

Expanding on wing, the Daughters of Beulah replied in sweet
response:

"Come, O thou Lamb of God, and take away the remembrance
of Sin.
To Sin & to hide the Sin in sweet deceit is lovely!
To Sin in the open face of day is cruel & pitiless! But
To record the Sin for a reproach, to let the Sun go down
In a remembrance of the Sin, is a Woe & a Horror,
A brooder of an Evil Day and a Sun rising in blood!
Come then, O Lamb of God, and take away the remembrance
of Sin."

From PART THREE

Rahab is an ⎱   TO THE DEISTS.   ⎧ The   Spiritual
Eternal State. ⎰   ⎪ States of the Soul
                                                 ⎨ are all Eternal.
                                                 ⎪ Distinguish be-
                                                 ⎪ tween the Man &
                                                 ⎩ his present State.

HE never can be a Friend to the Human Race who is the
Preacher of Natural Morality or Natural Religion; he is a flatterer who means to betray, to perpetuate Tyrant Pride & the
Laws of that Babylon which he foresees shall shortly be destroyed, with the Spiritual and not the Natural Sword. He is
in the State named Rahab, which State must be put off before
he can be the Friend of Man.

You, O Deists, profess yourselves the Enemies of Christianity,
and you are so: you are also the Enemies of the Human Race
& of Universal Nature. Man is born a Spectre or Satan & is
altogether an Evil, & requires a New Selfhood continually, &
must continually be changed into his direct Contrary. But your
Greek Philosophy (which is a remnant of Druidism) teaches
that Man is Righteous in his Vegetated Spectre: an Opinion of
fatal & accursed consequence, to Man, as the Ancients saw
plainly by Revelation to the intire abrogation of Experimental
Theory; and many believed what they saw and Prophecied of
Jesus.

Man must & will have Some Religion: if he has not the Religion of Jesus, he will have the Religion of Satan & will erect
the Synagogue of Satan, calling the Prince of this World, God,
and destroying all who do not worship Satan under the Name
of God. Will any one say, "Where are those who worship Satan
under the Name of God?" Where are they? Listen! Every Religion that Preaches Vengence for Sin is the Religion of the
Enemy & Avenger and not of the Forgiver of Sin, and their
God is Satan, Named by the Divine Name. Your Religion, O
Deists! Deism, is the Worship of the God of this World by the
means of what you call Natural Religion and Natural Philosophy, and of Natural Morality or Self-Righteousness, the Selfish
Virtues of the Natural Heart. This was the Religion of the

Pharisees who murder'd Jesus. Deism is the same & ends in the same.

Voltaire, Rousseau, Gibbon, Hume, charge the Spiritually Religious with Hypocrisy; but how a Monk, or a Methodist either, can be a Hypocrite, I cannot concieve. We are Men of like passions with others & pretend not to be holier than others; therefore, when a Religious Man falls into Sin, he ought not to be call'd a Hypocrite; this title is more properly to be given to a Player who falls into Sin, whose profession is Virtue & morality & the making Men Self-Righteous. Foote in calling Whitefield, Hypocrite, was himself one; for Whitefield pretended not to be holier than others, but confessed his Sins before all the World. Voltaire! Rousseau! You cannot escape my charge that you are Pharisees & Hypocrites, for you are constantly talking of the Virtues of the Human Heart and particularly of your own, that you may accuse others, & especially the Religious, whose errors you, by this display of pretended Virtue, chiefly design to expose. Rousseau thought Men Good by Nature: he found them Evil & found no friend. Friendship cannot exist without Forgiveness of Sins continually. The Book written by Rousseau call'd his Confessions, is an apology & cloke for his sin & not a confession.

But you also charge the poor Monks & Religious with being the causes of War, while you acquit & flatter the Alexanders & Caesars, the Lewis's & Fredericks, who alone are its causes & its actors. But the Religion of Jesus, Forgiveness of Sin, can never be the cause of a War nor of a single Martyrdom.

Those who Martyr others or who cause War are Deists, but never can be Forgivers of Sin. The Glory of Christianity is To Conquer by Forgiveness. All the Destruction, therefore, in Christian Europe has arisen from Deism, which is Natural Religion.

I saw a Monk of Charlemaine
Arise before my sight:
I talk'd with the Grey Monk as we stood
In beams of infernal light.

Gibbon arose with a lash of steel,
And Voltaire with a wracking wheel:
The Schools, in clouds of learning roll'd,
Arose with War in iron & gold.

"Thou lazy Monk," they sound afar,
"In vain condemning glorious War;
   And in your Cell you shall ever dwell:
Rise, War, & bind him in his Cell!"

The blood red ran from the Grey Monk's side,
His hands & feet were wounded wide,
   His body bent, his arms & knees
Like to the roots of ancient trees.

When Satan first the black bow bent
And the Moral Law from the Gospel rent,
   He forg'd the Law into a Sword
And spill'd the blood of mercy's Lord.

Titus! Constantine! Charlemaine!
O Voltaire! Rousseau! Gibbon! Vain
   Your Grecian Mocks & Roman Sword
Against this image of his Lord!

For a Tear is an Intellectual thing,
And a Sigh is the Sword of an Angel King,
   And the bitter groan of a Martyr's woe
Is an Arrow from the Almightie's Bow.

     •   •   •

In Great Eternity every particular Form gives forth or Ema-
   nates
Its own peculiar Light, & the Form is the Divine Vision
And the Light is his Garment. This is Jerusalem in every Man,
A Tent & Tabernacle of Mutual Forgiveness, Male & Female
   Clothings.
And Jerusalem is called Liberty among the Children of Albion.

But Albion fell down, a Rocky fragment from Eternity hurl'd
By his own Spectre, who is the Reasoning Power in every Man,
Into his own Chaos, which is the Memory between Man & Man.

The silent broodings of deadly revenge springing from the
All powerful parental affection, fills Albion from head to foot.
Seeing his Sons assimilate with Luvah, bound in the bonds

Of spiritual Hate, from which springs Sexual Love as iron
    chains,
He tosses like a cloud outstretch'd among Jerusalem's Ruins
Which overspread all the Earth; he groans among his ruin'd
    porches.
But the Spectre, like a hoar frost & a Mildew, rose over Albion,
Saying, "I am God, O Sons of Men! I am your Rational Power!
Am I not Bacon & Newton & Locke who teach Humility to
    Man,
Who teach Doubt & Experiment? & my two Wings, Voltaire,
    Rousseau?
Where is that Friend of Sinners? that Rebel against my Laws
Who teaches Belief to the Nations & an unknown Eternal Life?
Come hither into the Desert & turn these stones to bread.
Vain foolish Man! wilt thou believe without Experiment
And build a World of Phantasy upon my Great Abyss,
A World of Shapes in craving lust & devouring appetite?"

.   .   .

And the Great Voice of the Atlantic howled over the Druid
    Altars,
Weeping over his Children in Stone-henge, in Malden & Col-
    chester,
Round the Rocky Peak of Derbyshire, London Stone & Rosa-
    mond's Bower:

"What is a Wife & what is a Harlot? What is a Church & What
Is a Theatre? are they Two & not One? can they Exist
    Separate?
Are not Religion & Politics the Same Thing? Brotherhood is
    Religion,
O Demonstrations of Reason Dividing Families in Cruelty &
    Pride!"

.   .   .

And one Daughter of Los sat at the fiery Reel, & another
Sat at the shining Loom with her Sisters attending round,
Terrible their distress, & their sorrow cannot be utter'd;
And another Daughter of Los sat at the Spinning Wheel,
Endless their labour, with bitter food, void of sleep;
Tho' hungry, they labour: they rouze themselves anxious

Hour after hour labouring at the Whirling Wheel,
Many Wheels & as many lovely Daughters sit weeping.

Yet the intoxicating delight that they take in their work
Obliterates every other evil; none pities their tears,
Yet they regard not pity & they expect no one to pity,
For they labour for life & love regardless of any one
But the poor Spectres that they work for always, incessantly.

They are mock'd by every one that passes by; they regard not,
They labour, & when their Wheels are broken by scorn &
    malice
They mend them sorrowing with many tears & afflictions.

Other Daughters Weave on the Cushion & Pillow Network fine
That Rahab & Tirzah may exist & live & breathe & love.
Ah, that it could be as the Daughters of Beulah wish!

Other Daughters of Los, labouring at Looms less fine,
Create the Silk-worm & the Spider & the Catterpiller
To assist in their most grievous work of pity & compassion;
And others Create the wooly Lamb & the downy Fowl
To assist in the work; the Lamb bleats, the Sea-fowl cries:
Men understand not the distress & the labour & sorrow
That in the Interior Worlds is carried on in fear & trembling,
Weaving the shudd'ring fears & loves of Albion's Families.
Thunderous rage the Spindles of iron, & the iron Distaff
Maddens in the fury of their hands, weaving in bitter tears
The Veil of Goats-hair & Purple & Scarlet & fine twined Linen.

                    .   .   .

"Behold, in the Visions of Elohim Jehovah, behold Joseph & Mary
And be comforted, O Jerusalem, in the Visions of Jehovah
    Elohim."

She looked & saw Joseph the Carpenter in Nazareth & Mary
His espoused Wife. And Mary said, "If thou put me away from
    thee
Dost thou not murder me?" Joseph spoke in anger & fury,
    "Should I
Marry a Harlot & an Adulteress?" Mary answer'd, "Art thou
    more pure

Than thy Maker who forgiveth Sins & calls again Her that is
   Lost?
Tho' She hates, he calls her again in love. I love my dear
   Joseph,
But he driveth me away from his presence; yet I hear the voice
   of God
In the voice of my Husband: tho' he is angry for a moment, he
   will not
Utterly cast me away; if I were pure, never could I taste the
   sweets
Of the Forgiveness of Sins; if I were holy, I never could be-
   hold the tears
Of love of him who loves me in the midst of his anger in fur-
   nace of fire."

"Ah my Mary!" said Joseph, weeping over & embracing her
   closely in
His arms: "Doth he forgive Jerusalem, & not exact Purity
   from her who is
Polluted? I heard his voice in my sleep & his Angel in my
   dream,
Saying, 'Doth Jehovah Forgive a Debt only on condition that
   it shall
Be Payed? Doth he Forgive Pollution only on conditions of
   Purity?
That Debt is not Forgiven! That Pollution is not Forgiven!
Such is the Forgiveness of the Gods, the Moral Virtues of the
Heathen whose tender Mercies are Cruelty. But Jehovah's Sal-
   vation
Is without Money & without Price, in the Continual Forgiveness
   of Sins,
In the Perpetual Mutual Sacrifice in Great Eternity; for behold,
There is none that liveth & Sinneth not! And this is the Cove-
   nant
Of Jehovah: If you Forgive one-another, so shall Jehovah For-
   give You,
That He Himself may Dwell among You. Fear not then to
   take
To thee Mary thy Wife, for she is with Child by the Holy
   Ghost.' "

.   .   .

Then All the Daughters of Albion became One before Los,
  even Vala.
And she put forth her hand upon the Looms in dreadful howl-
  ings
Till she vegetated into a hungry Stomach & a devouring
  Tongue.
Her Hand is a Court of Justice: her Feet two Armies in Battle:
Storms & Pestilence in her Locks, & in her Loins Earthquake
And Fire & the Ruin of Cities & Nations & Families & Tongues.

She cries: "The Human is but a Worm, & thou, O Male! Thou
  art
Thyself Female, a Male, a breeder of Seed, a Son & Husband:
  & Lo,
The Human Divine is Woman's Shadow, a Vapor in the sum-
  mer's heat.
Go assume Papal dignity, thou Spectre, thou Male Harlot!
  Arthur,
Divide into the Kings of Europe in times remote, O Woman-
  born
And   Woman-nourish'd   &   Woman-educated   &   Woman-
  scorn'd!"

"Wherefore art thou living," said Los, "& Man cannot live in
  thy presence?
Art thou Vala the Wife of Albion, O thou lovely Daughter of
  Luvah?
All Quarrels arise from Reasoning: the secret Murder and
The violent Man-slaughter, these are the Spectre's double Cave,
The Sexual Death living on accusation of Sin & Judgment,
To freeze Love & Innocence into the gold & silver of the Mer-
  chant.
Without Forgiveness of Sin, Love is Itself Eternal Death."

Then the Spectre drew Vala into his bosom, magnificent, terrific,
Glittering with precious stones & gold, with Garments of blood
  & fire.
He wept in deadly wrath of the Spectre, in self-contradicting
  agony,
Crimson with Wrath & green with Jealousy, dazling with Love,

And Jealousy immingled, & the purple of the violet darken'd
    deep,
Over the Plow of Nations thund'ring in the hand of Albion's
    Spectre.

A dark Hermaphrodite they stood frowning upon London's
    River;
And the Distaff & Spindle in the hands of Vala, with the Flax of
Human Miseries, turn'd fierce with the Lives of Men along the
    Valley
As Reuben fled before the Daughters of Albion, Taxing the
    Nations.

Derby Peak yawn'd a horrid Chasm at the Cries of Gwendolen
    & at
The stamping feet of Ragan upon the flaming Treddles of her
    Loom
That drop with crimson gore with the Loves of Albion &
    Canaan,
Opening along the Valley of Rephaim, weaving over the Caves
    of Machpelah,
To decide Two Worlds with a great decision, a World of
    Mercy and
A World of Justice, the World of Mercy for Salvation:
To cast Luvah into the Wrath and Albion into the Pity,
In the Two Contraries of Humanity & in the Four Regions.

For in the depths of Albion's bosom in the eastern heaven
They sound the clarions strong, they chain the howling Cap-
    tives,
They cast the lots into the helmet, they give the oath of blood
    in Lambeth,
They vote the death of Luvah & they nail'd him to Albion's
    Tree in Bath,
They stain'd him with poisonous blue, they inwove him in cruel
    roots
To die a death of Six thousand years bound round with vegeta-
    tion.
The sun was black & the moon roll'd a useless globe thro'
    Britain.

Then left the Sons of Urizen the plow & harrow, the loom,
The hammer & the chisel & the rule & compasses; from London
    fleeing,
They forg'd the sword on Cheviot, the chariot of war & the
    battle-ax,
The trumpet fitted to mortal battle, & the flute of summer in
    Annandale;
And all the Arts of Life they chang'd into the Arts of Death
    in Albion.
The hour-glass contemn'd because its simple workmanship
Was like the workmanship of the plowman, & the water wheel
That raises water into cisterns, broken & burn'd with fire
Because its workmanship was like the workmanship of the
    shepherd;
And in their stead, intricate wheels invented, wheel without
    wheel,
To perplex youth in their outgoings & to bind to labours in
    Albion
Of day & night the myriads of eternity: that they may grind
And polish brass & iron hour after hour, laborious task,
Kept ignorant of its use: that they might spend the days of wis-
    dom
In sorrowful drudgery to obtain a scanty pittance of bread,
In ignorance to view a small portion & think that All,
And call it Demonstration, blind to all the simple rules of life.

"Now, now the battle rages round thy tender limbs, O Vala!
Now smile among thy bitter tears, now put on all thy beauty.
Is not the wound of the sword sweet & the broken bone de-
    lightful?
Wilt thou now smile among the scythes when the wounded
    groan in the field?
We were carried away in thousands from London & in tens
Of thousands from Westminster & Marybone, in ships clos'd
    up,
Chain'd hand & foot, compell'd to fight under the iron whips
Of our captains, fearing our officers more than the enemy.
Lift up thy blue eyes, Vala, & put on thy sapphire shoes!
O melancholy Magdalen, behold the morning over Malden
    break!
Gird on thy flaming zone, descend into the sepulcher of Can-
    terbury.

Scatter the blood from thy golden brow, the tears from thy
  silver locks;
Shake off the waters from thy wings & the dust from thy white
  garments.
Remember all thy feigned terrors on the secret couch of Lam-
  beth's Vale
When the sun rose in glowing morn, with arms of mighty hosts
Marching to battle, who was wont to rise with Urizen's harps
Girt as a sower with his seed to scatter life abroad over Albion.
Arise, O Vala, bring the bow of Urizen, bring the swift arrows
  of light.
How rag'd the golden horses of Urizen, compell'd to the chariot
  of love!
Compell'd to leave the plow to the ox, to snuff up the winds of
  desolation,
To trample the corn fields in boastful neighings, this is no gentle
  harp,
This is no warbling brook nor shadow of a mirtle tree,
But blood and wounds and dismal cries and shadows of the
  oak,
And hearts laid open to the light by the broad grizly sword,
And bowels, hid in hammer'd steel, rip'd quivering on the
  ground.
Call forth thy smiles of soft deceit: call forth thy cloudy tears.
We hear thy sighs in trumpets shrill when morn shall blood
  renew."

So sang the Spectre Sons of Albion round Luvah's Stone of
  Trial,
Mocking and deriding at the writhings of their Victim on Salis-
  bury,
Drinking his Emanations in intoxicating bliss, rejoicing in Giant
  dance;
For a Spectre has no Emanation but what he imbibes from
  decieving
A Victim: Then he becomes her Priest & she his Tabernacle
And his Oak Grove, till the Victim rend the woven Veil
In the end of his sleep when Jesus calls him from his grave.

                    .   .   .

The Daughters of Albion clothed in garments of needle work
Strip them off from their shoulders and bosoms, they lay aside
Their garments, they sit naked upon the Stone of trial.

The Knife of flint passes over the howling Victim: his blood
Gushes & stains the fair side of the fair Daughters of Albion.
They put aside his curls, they divide his seven locks upon
His forehead, they bind his forehead with thorns of iron,
They put into his hand a reed, they mock, Saying: "Behold
The King of Canaan whose are seven hundred chariots of iron!"
They take off his vesture whole with their Knives of flint,
But they cut asunder his inner garments, searching with
Their cruel fingers for his heart, & there they enter in pomp,
In many tears, & there they erect a temple & an altar.
They pour cold water on his brain in front, to cause
Lids to grow over his eyes in veils of tears, and caverns
To freeze over his nostrils, while they feed his tongue from cups
And dishes of painted clay. Glowing with beauty & cruelty
They obscure the sun & the moon: no eye can look upon
    them.

Ah! alas! at the sight of the Victim & at sight of those who are
    smitten,
All who see become what they behold; their eyes are cover'd
With veils of tears and their nostrils & tongues shrunk up,
Their ear bent outwards; as their Victim, so are they, in the
    pangs
Of unconquerable fear amidst delights of revenge Earth-shak-
    ing.
And as their eye & ear shrunk, the heavens shrunk away:
The Divine Vision became first a burning flame, then a column
Of fire, then an awful fiery wheel surrounding earth & heaven,
And then a globe of blood wandering distant in an unknown
    night.
Afar into the unknown night the mountains fled away,
Six months of mortality, a summer, & six months of mortality,
    a winter.
The Human form began to be alter'd by the Daughters of
    Albion
And the perceptions to be dissipated into the Indefinite, Be-
    coming
A mighty Polypus nam'd Albion's Tree; they tie the Veins
And Nerves into two knots & the Seed into a double knot.
They look forth: the Sun is shrunk: the Heavens are shrunk
Away into the far remote, and the Trees & Mountains
    wither'd

Into indefinite cloudy shadows in darkness & separation.
By Invisible Hatreds adjoin'd, they seem remote and separate
From each other, and yet are a Mighty Polypus in the Deep!
As the Misletoe grows on the Oak, so Albion's Tree on Eternity. Lo!
He who will not comingle in Love must be adjoin'd by Hate.

.   .   .

The inhabitants are sick to death: they labour to divide into Days
And Nights the uncertain Periods, and into Weeks & Months. In vain
They send the Dove & Raven & in vain the Serpent over the mountains
And in vain the Eagle & Lion over the four-fold wilderness:
They return not, but generate in rocky places desolate:
They return not, but build a habitation separate from Man.
The Sun forgets his course like a drunken man; he hesitates
Upon the Cheselden hills, thinking to sleep on the Severn.
In vain: he is hurried afar into an unknown Night:
He bleeds in torrents of blood as he rolls thro' heaven above.
He chokes up the paths of the sky; the Moon is leprous as snow,
Trembling & descending down, seeking to rest on high Mona,
Scattering her leprous snows in flakes of disease over Albion.
The Stars flee remote; the heaven is iron, the earth is sulphur,
And all the mountains & hills shrink up like a withering gourd
As the Senses of Men shrink together under the Knife of flint
In the hands of Albion's Daughters among the Druid Temples,
By those who drink their blood & the blood of their Covenant.

.   .   .

And thus the Warriors cry, in the hot day of Victory, in Songs:

"Look! the beautiful Daughter of Albion sits naked upon the Stone,
Her panting Victim beside her: her heart is drunk with blood
Tho' her brain is not drunk with wine: she goes forth from Albion
In pride of beauty, in cruelty of holiness, in the brightness
Of her tabernacle & her ark & secret place: the beautiful Daughter

Of Albion delights the eyes of the Kings: their hearts & the
Hearts of their Warriors glow hot before Thor & Friga. O
    Molech!
O Chemosh! O Bacchus! O Venus! O Double God of Genera-
    tion!
The Heavens are cut like a mantle around from the Cliffs of
    Albion
Across Europe, across Africa: in howlings & deadly War,
A sheet & veil & curtain of blood is let down from Heaven
Across the hills of Ephraim & down Mount Olivet to
The Valley of the Jebusite. Molech rejoices in heaven,
He sees the Twelve Daughters naked upon the Twelve Stones
Themselves condensing to rocks & into the Ribs of a Man.
Lo, they shoot forth in tender Nerves across Europe & Asia.
Lo, they rest upon the Tribes, where their panting Victims lie.
Molech rushes into the Kings, in love to the beautiful Daugh-
    ters,
But they frown & delight in cruelty, refusing all other joy.
Bring your Offerings, your first begotten, pamper'd with milk
    & blood,
Your first born of seven years old, be they Males or Females,
To the beautiful Daughters of Albion! they sport before the
    Kings
Clothed in the skin of the Victim! blood, human blood is the
    life
And delightful food of the Warrior; the well fed Warrior's flesh
Of him who is slain in War fills the Valleys of Ephraim with
Breeding Women walking in pride & bringing forth under green
    trees
With pleasure, without pain, for their food is blood of the Cap-
    tive.
Molech rejoices thro' the Land from Havilah to Shur: he re-
    joices
In moral law & its severe penalties; loud Shaddai & Jehovah
Thunder above, when they see the Twelve panting Victims
On the Twelve Stones of Power, & the beautiful Daughters of
    Albion:
'If you dare rend their Veil with your spear, you are healed of
    Love.'
From the Hills of Camberwell & Wimbledon, from the Val-
    leys
Of Walton & Esher, from Stone-henge & from Malden's Cove,

Jerusalem's Pillars fall in the rendings of fierce War.

Over France & Germany, upon the Rhine & Danube,

Reuben & Benjamin flee: they hide in the Valley of Rephaim.

Why trembles the Warrior's limbs when he beholds thy beauty

Spotted with Victims' blood? by the fires of thy secret taber-
     nacle

And thy ark & holy place, at thy frowns, at thy dire revenge,

Smitten as Uzzah of old, his armour is soften'd, his spear

And sword faint in his hand from Albion across Great Tartary.

O beautiful Daughter of Albion! cruelty is thy delight.

O Virgin of terrible eyes who dwellest by Valleys of springs

Beneath the Mountains of Lebanon in the City of Rehob in
     Hamath,

Taught to touch the harp, to dance in the Circle of Warriors

Before the Kings of Canaan, to cut the flesh from the Victim,

To roast the flesh in fire, to examine the Infant's limbs

In cruelties of holiness, to refuse the joys of love, to bring

The Spies from Egypt, to raise jealousy in the bosoms of the
     Twelve

Kings of Canaan, then let the Spies depart to Meribah Kadesh,

To the place of the Amalekite: I am drunk with unsatiated love,

I must rush again to War, for the Virgin has frown'd & refus'd.

Sometimes I curse & sometimes bless thy fascinating beauty.

Once Man was occupied in intellectual pleasures & energies,

But now my Soul is harrow'd with grief & fear & love & desire,

And now I hate & now I love, & Intellect is no more.

There is no time for any thing but the torments of love &
     desire.

The Feminine & Masculine Shadows, soft, mild & ever varying

In beauty, are Shadows now no more, but Rocks in Horeb."

.   .   .

And now the Spectres of the Dead awake in Beulah; all

The Jealousies become Murderous, uniting together in Rahab

A Religion of Chastity, forming a Commerce to sell Loves,

With Moral Law an Equal Balance not going down with de-
     cision.

Therefore the Male severe & cruel, fill'd with stern Revenge,

Mutual Hate returns & mutual Deceit & mutual Fear.

Hence the Infernal Veil grows in the disobedient Female,

Which Jesus rends & the whole Druid Law removes away

From the Inner Sanctuary, a False Holiness hid within the
    Center.
For the Sanctuary of Eden is in the Camp, in the Outline,
In the Circumference, & every Minute Particular is Holy:
Embraces are Cominglings from the Head even to the Feet,
And not a pompous High Priest entering by a Secret Place.

                          .   .   .

The Spectre is the Reasoning Power in Man, & when separated
From Imagination and closing itself as in steel in a Ratio
Of the Things of Memory, It thence frames Laws & Moralities
To destroy Imagination, the Divine Body, by Martyrdoms &
    Wars.

Teach me, O Holy Spirit, the Testimony of Jesus! let me
Comprehend wonderous things out of the Divine Law!
I behold Babylon in the opening Streets of London. I behold
Jerusalem in ruins wandering about from house to house.
This I behold: the shudderings of death attend my steps.
I walk up and down in Six Thousand Years: their Events are
    present before me
To tell how Los in grief & anger, whirling round his Hammer
    on high,
Drave the Sons & Daughters of Albion from their ancient
    mountains.
They became the Twelve Gods of Asia Opposing the Divine
    Vision.

From PART FOUR

TO THE CHRISTIANS

Devils are	I give you the end of a golden
False Religions.	string,
"Saul, Saul,	Only wind it into a ball,
Why persecutest thou me?"	It will lead you in at Heaven's gate
	Built in Jerusalem's wall.

WE are told to abstain from fleshly desires that we may lose
no time from the Work of the Lord: Every moment lost is a

moment that cannot be redeemed; every pleasure that intermingles with the duty of our station is a folly unredeemable, & is planted like the seed of a wild flower among our wheat: All the tortures of repentance are tortures of self-reproach on account of our leaving the Divine Harvest to the Enemy, the struggles of intanglement with incoherent roots. I know of no other Christianity and of no other Gospel than the liberty both of body & mind to exercise the Divine Arts of Imagination, Imagination, the real & eternal World of which this Vegetable Universe is but a faint shadow, & in which we shall live in our Eternal or Imaginative Bodies when these Vegetable Mortal Bodies are no more. The Apostles knew of no other Gospel. What were all their spiritual gifts? What is the Divine Spirit? is the Holy Ghost any other than an Intellectual Fountain? What is the Harvest of the Gospel & its Labours? What is that Talent which it is a curse to hide? What are the Treasures of Heaven which we are to lay up for ourselves, are they any other than Mental Studies & Performances? What are all the Gifts of the Gospel, are they not all Mental Gifts? Is God a Spirit who must be worshipped in Spirit & in Truth, and are not the Gifts of the Spirit Every-thing to Man? O ye Religious, discountenance every one among you who shall pretend to despise Art & Science! I call upon you in the Name of Jesus! What is the Life of Man but Art & Science? is it Meat & Drink? is not the Body more than Raiment? What is Mortality but the things relating to the Body which Dies? What is Immortality but the things relating to the Spirit which Lives Eternally? What is the Joy of Heaven but Improvement in the things of the Spirit? What are the Pains of Hell but Ignorance, Bodily Lust, Idleness & devastation of the things of the Spirit? Answer this to yourselves, & expel from among you those who pretend to despise the labours of Art & Science, which alone are the labours of the Gospel. Is not this plain & manifest to the thought? Can you think at all & not pronounce heartily That to Labour in Knowledge is to Build up Jerusalem, and to Despise Knowledge is to Despise Jerusalem & her Builders. And remember: He who despises & mocks a Mental Gift in another, calling it pride & selfishness & sin, mocks Jesus the giver of every Mental Gift, which always appear to the ignorance-loving Hypocrite as Sins; but that which is a Sin in the sight of cruel Man is not so in the sight of our kind God. Let every Christian, as much as in him lies, engage himself openly &

publicly before all the World in some Mental pursuit for the
Building up of Jerusalem.

I stood among my valleys of the south
And saw a flame of fire, even as a Wheel
Of fire surrounding all the heavens: it went
From west to east, against the current of
Creation, and devour'd all things in its loud
Fury & thundering course round heaven & earth.
By it the Sun was roll'd into an orb,
By it the Moon faded into a globe
Travelling thro' the night; for, from its dire
And restless fury, Man himself shrunk up
Into a little root a fathom long.
And I asked a Watcher & a Holy-One
Its Name; he answered: "It is the Wheel of Religion."
I wept & said: "Is this the law of Jesus,
This terrible devouring sword turning every way?"
He answer'd: "Jesus died because he strove
Against the current of this Wheel; its Name
Is Caiaphas, the dark preacher of Death,
Of sin, of sorrow & of punishment:
Opposing Nature! It is Natural Religion;
But Jesus is the bright Preacher of Life
Creating Nature from this fiery Law
By self-denial & forgiveness of Sin.
Go therefore, cast out devils in Christ's name,
Heal thou the sick of spiritual disease,
Pity the evil, for thou art not sent
To smite with terror & with punishments
Those that are sick, like to the Pharisees
Crucifying & encompassing sea & land
For proselytes to tyranny & wrath;
But to the Publicans & Harlots go,
Teach them True Happiness, but let no curse
Go forth out of thy mouth to blight their peace;
For Hell is open'd to Heaven: thine eyes beheld
The dungeons burst & the Prisoners set free."

England! awake! awake! awake!
Jerusalem thy Sister calls!

Why wilt thou sleep the sleep of death
    And close her from thy ancient walls?

Thy hills & valleys felt her feet
    Gently upon their bosoms move:
Thy gates beheld sweet Zion's ways:
    Then was a time of joy and love.

And now the time returns again:
    Our souls exult, & London's towers
Recieve the Lamb of God to dwell
    In England's green & pleasant bowers.

        .   .   .

"Albion gave me to the whole Earth to walk up & down, to pour
Joy upon every mountain, to teach songs to the shepherd & plowman.
I taught the ships of the sea to sing the songs of Zion.
Italy saw me in sublime astonishment: France was wholly mine
As my garden & as my secret bath: Spain was my heavenly couch,
I slept in his golden hills; the Lamb of God met me there,
There we walked as in our secret chamber among our little ones,
They looked upon our loves with joy, they beheld our secret joys
With holy raptures of adoration, rap'd sublime in the Visions of God.
Germany, Poland & the North wooed my footsteps, they found
My gates in all their mountains & my curtains in all their vales;
The furniture of their houses was the furniture of my chamber.
Turkey & Grecia saw my instruments of music; they arose,
They siez'd the harp, the flute, the mellow horn of Jerusalem's joy;
They sounded thanksgivings in my courts. Egypt & Lybia heard,
The swarthy sons of Ethiopia stood round the Lamb of God
Enquiring for Jerusalem: he led them up my steps to my altar.
And thou, America! I once beheld thee, but now behold no more

Thy golden mountains where my Cherubim & Seraphim re-
    joic'd
Together among my little-ones. But now my Altars run with
    blood,
My fires are corrupt, my incense is a cloudy pestilence
Of seven diseases! Once a continual cloud of salvation rose
From all my myriads, once the Four-fold World rejoic'd among
The pillars of Jerusalem between my winged Cherubim;
But now I am clos'd out from them in the narrow passages
Of the valleys of destruction into a dark land of pitch & bitu-
    men,
From Albion's Tomb afar and from the four-fold wonders
    of God
Shrunk to a narrow doleful form in the dark land of Cabul.
There is Reuben & Gad & Joseph & Judah & Levi clos'd up
In narrow vales. I walk & count the bones of my beloveds
Along the Valley of Destruction, among these Druid Temples
Which overspread all the Earth in patriarchal pomp & cruel
    pride.
Tell me, O Vala, thy purposes; tell me wherefore thy shuttles
Drop with the gore of the slain, why Euphrates is red with
    blood,
Wherefore in dreadful majesty & beauty outside appears
Thy Masculine from thy Feminine, hardening against the
    heavens
To devour the Human! Why dost thou weep upon the wind
    among
These cruel Druid Temples? O Vala! Humanity is far above
Sexual organization & the Visions of the Night of Beulah
Where Sexes wander in dreams of bliss among the Emanations,
Where the Masculine & Feminine are nurs'd into Youth &
    Maiden
By the tears & smiles of Beulah's Daughters till the time of
    Sleep is past.
Wherefore then do you realize these nets of beauty & delusion
In open day, to draw the souls of the Dead into the light
Till Albion is shut out from every Nation under Heaven?
Encompass'd by the frozen Net and by the rooted Tree
I walk weeping in pangs of a Mother's torment for her Chil-
    dren.
I walk in affliction. I am a worm and no living soul!

A worm going to eternal torment, rais'd up in a night
To an eternal night of pain, lost! lost! lost! for ever!"

.   .   .

Terrified Los sat to behold, trembling & weeping & howling:
"I care not whether a Man is Good or Evil; all that I care
Is whether he is a Wise Man or a Fool. Go, put off Holiness
And put on Intellect, or my thund'rous Hammer shall drive
   thee
To wrath which thou condemnest, till thou obey my voice."

So Los terrified cries, trembling & weeping & howling: "Be-
   holding,
What do I see! The Briton, Saxon, Roman, Norman amalgam-
   ating
In my Furnaces into One Nation, the English, & taking refuge
In the Loins of Albion. The Canaanite united with the fugitive
Hebrew, whom she divided into Twelve & sold into Egypt,
Then scatter'd the Egyptian & Hebrew to the four Winds.
This sinful Nation Created in our Furnaces & Looms is Albion."

So Los spoke. Enitharmon answer'd in great terror in Lambeth's Vale:

"The Poet's Song draws to its period, & Enitharmon is no
   more;
For if he be that Albion, I can never weave him in my Looms,
But when he touches the first fibrous thread, like filmy dew
My Looms will be no more & I annihilate vanish for ever.
Then thou wilt Create another Female according to thy Will."

Los answer'd swift as the shuttle of gold: "Sexes must vanish &
   cease
To be when Albion arises from his dread repose, O lovely Eni-
   tharmon:
When all their Crimes, their Punishments, their Accusations of
   Sin,
All their Jealousies, Revenges, Murders, hidings of Cruelty in
   Deceit
Appear only in the Outward Spheres of Visionary Space and
   Time,

In the shadows of Possibility, by Mutual Forgiveness for ever-
    more,
And in the Vision & in the Prophecy, that we may Foresee &
    Avoid
The terrors of Creation & Redemption & Judgment."

          ·   ·   ·

Then Los again took up his speech as Enitharmon ceast:

"Fear not, my Sons, this Waking Death; he is become One
    with me.
Behold him here! We shall not Die! we shall be united in Jesus.
Will you suffer this Satan, this Body of Doubt that Seems but
    Is Not,
To occupy the very threshold of Eternal Life? if Bacon, New-
    ton, Locke
Deny a Conscience in Man & the Communion of Saints &
    Angels,
Contemning the Divine Vision & Fruition, Worshiping the
    Deus
Of the Heathen, the God of This World, & the Goddess Nature,
Mystery, Babylon the Great, The Druid Dragon & hidden
    Harlot,
Is it not that Signal of the Morning which was told us in the
    Beginning?"

          ·   ·   ·

Then Jesus appeared standing by Albion as the Good Shepherd
By the lost Sheep that he hath found, & Albion knew that it
Was the Lord, the Universal Humanity; & Albion saw his Form
A Man, & they conversed as Man with Man in Ages of Eter-
    nity.
And the Divine Appearance was the likeness & similitude of
    Los.

Albion said: "O Lord, what can I do? my Selfhood cruel
Marches against thee, deceitful, from Sinai & from Edom
Into the Wilderness of Judah, to meet thee in his pride.
I behold the Visions of my deadly Sleep of Six Thousand Years
Dazling around thy skirts like a Serpent of precious stones &
    gold.
I know it is my Self, O my Divine Creator & Redeemer."

Jesus replied: "Fear not Albion: unless I die thou canst not
    live;
But if I die I shall arise again & thou with me.
This is Friendship & Brotherhood: without it Man is Not."

So Jesus spoke: the Covering Cherub coming on in darkness
Overshadow'd them, & Jesus said: "Thus do Men in Eternity
One for another to put off, by forgiveness, every sin."

Albion reply'd: "Cannot Man exist without Mysterious
Offering of Self for Another? is this Friendship & Brother-
    hood?
I see thee in the likeness & similitude of Los my Friend."

Jesus said: "Wouldest thou love one who never died
For thee, or ever die for one who had not died for thee?
And if God dieth not for Man & giveth not himself
Eternally for Man, Man could not exist; for Man is Love
As God is Love: every kindness to another is a little Death
In the Divine Image, nor can Man exist but by Brotherhood."

So saying the Cloud overshadowing divided them asunder.
Albion stood in terror, not for himself but for his Friend
Divine; & Self was lost in the contemplation of faith
And wonder at the Divine Mercy & at Los's sublime honour.

"Do I sleep amidst danger to Friends? O my Cities & Counties,
Do you sleep? rouze up, rouze up! Eternal Death is abroad!"

So Albion spoke & threw himself into the Furnaces of affliction.
All was a Vision, all a Dream: the Furnaces became
Fountains of Living Waters flowing from the Humanity Divine.
And all the Cities of Albion rose from their Slumbers, and All
The Sons & Daughters of Albion on soft clouds, waking from
    Sleep.
Soon all around remote the Heavens burnt with flaming fires,
And Urizen & Luvah & Tharmas & Urthona arose into
Albion's Bosom. Then Albion stood before Jesus in the Clouds
Of Heaven, Fourfold among the Visions of God in Eternity.

"Awake, Awake, Jerusalem! O lovely Emanation of Albion,
Awake and overspread all Nations as in Ancient Time;

For lo! the Night of Death is past and the Eternal Day
Appears upon our Hills. Awake, Jerusalem, and come away!"

So spake the Vision of Albion, & in him so spake in my hear-
  ing
The Universal Father. Then Albion stretch'd his hand into
  Infinitude
And took his Bow. Fourfold the Vision; for bright beaming
  Urizen
Lay'd his hand on the South & took a breathing Bow of carved
  Gold:
Luvah his hand stretch'd to the East & bore a Silver Bow,
  bright shining:
Tharmas Westward a Bow of Brass, pure flaming, richly
  wrought:
Urthona Northward in thick storms a Bow of Iron, terrible
  thundering.

And the Bow is a Male & Female, & the Quiver of the Arrows
  of Love
Are the Children of this Bow, a Bow of Mercy & Loving kind-
  ness laying
Open the hidden Heart in Wars of mutual Benevolence, Wars
  of Love:
And the Hand of Man grasps firm between the Male & Female
  Loves.
And he Clothed himself in Bow & Arrows, in awful state, Four-
  fold,
In the midst of his Twenty-eight Cities, each with his Bow
  breathing.
Then each an Arrow flaming from his Quiver fitted carefully;
They drew fourfold the unreprovable String, bending thro' the
  wide Heavens
The horned Bow Fourfold; loud sounding flew the flaming Ar-
  row fourfold.

Murmuring the Bowstring breathes with ardor. Clouds roll
  round the horns
Of the wide Bow; loud sounding Winds sport on the Mountains' Brows.
The Druid Spectre was Annihilate, loud thund'ring rejoicing
  terrific, vanishing,

Fourfold Annihilation; & at the clangor of the Arrows of Intellect

The innumerable Chariots of the Almighty appear'd in Heaven,

And Bacon & Newton & Locke, & Milton & Shakspear & Chaucer,

A Sun of blood red wrath surrounding heaven, on all sides around,

Glorious, incomprehensible by Mortal Man, & each Chariot was Sexual Threefold.

And every Man stood Fourfold; each Four Faces had: One to the West,

One toward the East, One to the South, One to the North, the Horses Fourfold.

And the dim Chaos brighten'd beneath, above, around: Eyed as the Peacock,

According to the Human Nerves of Sensation, the Four Rivers of the Water of Life.

South stood the Nerves of the Eye; East in Rivers of bliss, the Nerves of the

Expansive Nostrils; West flow'd the Parent Sense, the Tongue; North stood

The labyrinthine Ear: Circumscribing & Circumcising the excrementitious

Husk & Covering, into Vacuum evaporating, revealing the lineaments of Man,

Driving outward the Body of Death in an Eternal Death & Resurrection,

Awaking it to Life among the Flowers of Beulah, rejoicing in Unity

In the Four Senses, in the Outline, the Circumference & Form, for ever

In Forgiveness of Sins which is Self Annihilation; it is the Covenant of Jehovah.

The Four Living Creatures, Chariots of Humanity Divine Incomprehensible,

In beautiful Paradises expand. These are the Four Rivers of Paradise

And the Four Faces of Humanity, fronting the Four Cardinal Points

Of Heaven, going forward, forward irresistible from Eternity
    to Eternity.

And they conversed together in Visionary forms dramatic
    which bright
Redounded from their Tongues in thunderous majesty, in
    Visions
In new Expanses, creating exemplars of Memory and of In-
    tellect,
Creating Space, Creating Time, according to the wonders Di-
    vine
Of Human Imagination throughout all the Three Regions
    immense
Of Childhood, Manhood & Old Age; & the all tremendous un-
    fathomable Non Ens
Of Death was seen in regenerations terrific or complacent,
    varying
According to the subject of discourse; & every Word & every
    Character
Was Human according to the Expansion or Contraction, the
    Translucence or
Opakeness of Nervous fibres: such was the variation of Time &
    Space
Which vary according as the Organs of Perception vary; &
    they walked
To & fro in Eternity as One Man, reflecting each in each &
    clearly seen
And seeing, according to fitness & order. And I heard Jehovah
    speak
Terrific from his Holy Place, & saw the Words of the Mutual
    Covenant Divine
On Chariots of gold & jewels, with Living Creatures, starry &
    flaming
With every Colour, Lion, Tyger, Horse, Elephant, Eagle, Dove,
    Fly, Worm
And the all wondrous Serpent clothed in gems & rich array,
    Humanize
In the Forgiveness of Sins according to thy Covenant, Jehovah.
    They Cry:

"Where is the Covenant of Priam, the Moral Virtues of the
    Heathen?

Where is the Tree of Good & Evil that rooted beneath the
    cruel heel
Of Albions Spectre, the Patriarch Druid? where are all his
    Human Sacrifice
For Sin in War & in the Druid Temples of the Accuser of Sin,
    beneath
The Oak Groves of Albion that cover'd the whole Earth be-
    neath his Spectre?
Where are the Kingdoms of the World & all their glory that
    grew on Desolation,
The Fruit of Albion's Poverty Tree, when the Triple Headed
    Gog-Magog Giant
Of Albion Taxed the Nations into Desolation & then gave the
    Spectrous Oath?"

Such is the Cry from all the Earth, from the Living Creatures
    of the Earth
And from the great City of Golgonooza in the Shadowy Gener-
    ation,
And from the Thirty-two Nations of the Earth among the
    Living Creatures.
All Human Forms identified, even Tree, Metal, Earth & Stone:
    all
Human Forms identified, living, going forth & returning
    wearied
Into the Planetary lives of Years, Months, Days & Hours; re-
    posing,
And then Awaking into his Bosom in the Life of Immortality.

And I heard the Name of their Emanations: they are named
    Jerusalem.

THE END OF THE SONG OF JERUSALEM

PART FOUR

LATER WORKS

LATER WORKS

The Everlasting Gospel

THERE is not one Moral Virtue that Jesus Inculcated but Plato & Cicero did Inculcate before him; what then did Christ inculcate? Forgiveness of Sins. This alone is the Gospel, & this is the Life & Immortality brought to light by Jesus, Even the Covenant of Jehovah, which is This: If you forgive one another your Trespasses, so shall Jehovah forgive you, That he himself may dwell among you; but if you Avenge, you Murder the Divine Image, & he cannot dwell among you; because you Murder him he arises again, & you deny that he is Arisen, & are blind to Spirit.

1

If Moral Virtue was Christianity,
Christ's Pretensions were all Vanity,
And Cai[a]phas & Pilate, Men
Praise Worthy, & the Lion's Den
And not the Sheepfold, Allegories
Of God & Heaven & their Glories.
The Moral Christian is the Cause
Of the Unbeliever & his Laws.
The Roman Virtues, Warlike Fame,
Take Jesus' & Jehovah's Name;
For what is Antichrist but those
Who against Sinners Heaven close
With Iron bars, in Virtuous State,
And Rhadamanthus at the Gate?

2

What can this Gospel of Jesus be?
What Life & Immortality,
What was it that he brought to Light
That Plato & Cicero did not write?

The Heathen Deities wrote them all,
These Moral Virtues, great & small.
What is the Accusation of Sin
But Moral Virtues' deadly Gin?
The Moral Virtues in their Pride
Did o'er the World triumphant ride
In Wars & Sacrifice for Sin,
And Souls to Hell ran trooping in.
The Accuser, Holy God of All
This Pharisaic Worldly Ball,
Amidst them in his Glory Beams
Upon the Rivers & the Streams.
Then Jesus rose & said to Me,
"Thy Sins are all forgiven thee."
Loud Pilate Howl'd, loud Cai[a]phas yell'd,
When they the Gospel Light beheld.
It was when Jesus said to Me,
"Thy Sins are all forgiven thee."
The Christian trumpets loud proclaim
Thro' all the World in Jesus' name
Mutual forgiveness of each Vice,
And oped the Gates of Paradise.
The Moral Virtues in Great fear
Formed the Cross & Nails & Spear,
And the Accuser standing by
Cried out, "Crucify! Crucify!
Our Moral Virtues ne'er can be,
Nor Warlike pomp & Majesty;
For Moral Virtues all begin
In the Accusations of Sin,
And all the Heroic Virtues End
In destroying the Sinners' Friend.
Am I not Lucifer the Great,
And you my daughters in Great State,
The fruit of my Mysterious Tree
Of Good & Evil & Misery
And Death & Hell, which now begin
On everyone who Forgives Sin?"

a

THE Vision of Christ that thou dost see
Is my Vision's Greatest Enemy:

Thine has a great hook nose like thine,
Mine has a snub nose like to mine:
Thine is the friend of All Mankind,
Mine speaks in parables to the Blind:
Thine loves the same world that mine hates,
Thy Heaven doors are my Hell Gates.
Socrates taught what Meletus
Loath'd as a Nation's bitterest Curse,
And Caiaphas was in his own Mind
A benefactor to Mankind:
Both read the Bible day & night,
But thou read'st black where I read white.

b

Was Jesus gentle, or did he
Give any marks of Gentility?
When twelve years old he ran away
And left his Parents in dismay.
When after three days' sorrow found,
Loud as Sinai's trumpet sound:
"No Earthly Parents I confess—
My Heavenly Father's business!
Ye understand not what I say,
And, angry, force me to obey."
Obedience is a duty then,
And favour gains with God & Men.
John from the Wilderness loud cried;
Satan gloried in his Pride.
"Come," said Satan, "come away,
I'll soon see if you'll obey!
John for disobedience bled,
But you can turn the stones to bread.
God's high king & God's high Priest
Shall Plant their Glories in your breast
If Caiaphas you will obey,
If Herod you with bloody Prey
Feed with the sacrifice, & be
Obedient, fall down, worship me."
Thunders & lightnings broke around,
And Jesus' voice in thunders' sound:
"Thus I seize the Spiritual Prey.
Ye smiters with disease, make way.

I come your King & God to sieze.
Is God a smiter with disease?"
The God of this World raged in vain:
He bound Old Satan in his Chain,
And bursting forth, his furious ire
Became a Chariot of fire.
Throughout the land he took his course,
And traced diseases to their source:
He curs'd the Scribe & Pharisee,
Trampling down Hipocrisy:
Where'er his Chariot took its way,
There Gates of death let in the day,
Broke down from every Chain & Bar;
And Satan in his Spiritual War
Drag'd at his Chariot wheels: loud howl'd
The God of this World: louder roll'd
The Chariot Wheels, & louder still
His voice was heard from Zion's hill,
And in his hand the Scourge shone bright;
He scourg'd the Merchant Canaanite
From out the Temple of his Mind,
And in his Body tight does bind
Satan & all his Hellish Crew;
And thus with wrath he did subdue
The Serpent Bulk of Nature's dross,
Till He had nail'd it to the Cross.
He took on Sin in the Virgin's Womb,
And put it off on the Cross & Tomb
To be Worship'd by the Church of Rome.

c

Was Jesus Humble? or did he
Give any proofs of Humility?
When but a Child he ran away
And left his Parents in dismay.
When they had wonder'd three days long
These were the words upon his Tongue:
"No Earthly Parents I confess:
I am doing my Father's business."
When the rich learned Pharisee
Came to consult him secretly,
Upon his heart with Iron pen

He wrote, "Ye must be born again."
He was too Proud to take a bribe;
He spoke with authority, not like a Scribe.
He says with most consummate Art,
"Follow me, I am meek & lowly of heart,"
As that is the only way to Escape
The Miser's net & the Glutton's trap.
He who loves his Enemies, hates his Friends;
This is surely not what Jesus intends;
He must mean the meer love of Civility,
And so he must mean concerning Humility;
But he acts with triumphant, honest pride,
And this is the Reason Jesus died.
If he had been Antichrist, Creeping Jesus,
He'd have done anything to please us:
Gone sneaking into the Synagogues
And not used the Elders & Priests like Dogs,
But humble as a Lamb or an Ass,
Obey himself to Caiaphas.
God wants not Man to humble himself:
This is the Trick of the Ancient Elf.
Humble toward God, Haughty toward Man,
This is the Race that Jesus ran,
And when he humbled himself to God,
Then descended the cruel rod.
"If thou humblest thyself, thou humblest me;
Thou also dwelst in Eternity.
Thou art a man, God is no more,
Thine own Humanity learn to Adore
And thy Revenge Abroad display
In terrors at the Last Judgment day.
God's Mercy & Long Suffering
Are but the Sinner to Judgment to bring.
Thou on the Cross for them shalt pray
And take Revenge at the last Day.

"Do what you will, this Life's a Fiction
And is made up of Contradiction."

d

Was Jesus Humble? or did he
Give any Proofs of Humility?

Boast of high Things with Humble tone,
And give with Charity a Stone?
When but a Child he ran away
And left his Parents in dismay.
When they had wander'd three days long
These were the words upon his tongue:
"No Earthly Parents I confess:
I am doing my Father's business."
When the rich learned Pharisee
Came to consult him secretly,
Upon his heart with Iron pen
He wrote, "Ye must be born again."
He was too proud to take a bribe;
He spoke with authority, not like a Scribe.
He says with most consummate Art,
"Follow me, I am meek & lowly of heart,"
As that is the only way to escape
The Miser's net & the Glutton's trap.
What can be done with such desperate Fools
Who follow after the Heathen Schools?
I was standing by when Jesus died;
What I call'd Humility, they call'd Pride.
He who loves his Enemies betrays his Friends;
This surely is not what Jesus intends,
But the sneaking Pride of Heroic Schools,
And the Scribes' & Pharisees' Virtuous Rules;
For he acts with honest, triumphant Pride,
And this is the cause that Jesus died.
He did not die with Christian Ease,
Asking pardon of his Enemies:
If he had, Caiaphas would forgive;
Sneaking submission can always live.
He had only to say that God was the devil,
And the Devil was God, like a Christian Civil:
Mild Christian regrets to the devil confess
For affronting him thrice in the Wilderness;
He had soon been bloody Caesar's Elf,
And at last he would have been Caesar himself.
Like dr. Priestly & Bacon & Newton—
Poor Spiritual Knowledge is not worth a button!
For thus the Gospel Sir Isaac confutes:
"God can only be known by his Attributes;

And as for the Indwelling of the Holy Ghost
Or of Christ & his Father, it's all a boast
And Pride & Vanity of the imagination;
That disdains to follow this World's Fashion."
To teach doubt & Experiment
Certainly was not what Christ meant.
What was he doing all that time,
From twelve years old to manly prime?
Was he then Idle, or the Less
About his Father's business?
Or was his wisdom held in scorn
Before his wrath began to burn
In Miracles throughout the Land,
That quite unnerv'd Caiaphas' hand?
If he had been Antichrist, Creeping Jesus,
He'd have done any thing to please us—
Gone sneaking into Synagogues
And not us'd the Elders & Priests like Dogs,
But Humble as a Lamb or Ass
Obey'd himself to Caiaphas.
God wants not Man to Humble himself:
This is the trick of the ancient Elf.
This is the Race that Jesus ran:
Humble to God, Haughty to Man,
Cursing the Rulers before the People
Even to the temple's highest Steeple;
And when he Humbled himself to God,
Then descended the Cruel Rod.
"If thou humblest thyself, thou humblest me;
Thou also dwell'st in Eternity.
Thou art a Man, God is no more,
Thy own humanity learn to adore,
For that is my Spirit of Life.
Awake, arise to Spiritual Strife
And thy Revenge abroad display
In terrors at the Last Judgment day
God's Mercy & Long Suffering
Is but the Sinner to Judgment to bring.
Thou on the Cross for them shalt pray
And take Revenge at the Last Day.
This Corporeal life's a fiction
And is made up of Contradiction."

Jesus replied & thunders hurl'd:
"I never will Pray for the World.
Once I did so when I pray'd in the Garden;
I wish'd to take with me a Bodily Pardon."
Can that which was of woman born
In the absence of the Morn,
When the Soul fell into Sleep
And Archangels round it weep,
Shooting out against the Light
Fibres of a deadly night,
Reasoning upon its own dark Fiction,
In doubt which is Self Contradiction?
Humility is only doubt,
And does the Sun & Moon blot out,
Rooting over with thorns & stems
The buried Soul & all its Gems.
This Life's dim Windows of the Soul
Distorts the Heavens from Pole to Pole
And leads you to Believe a Lie
When you see with, not thro', the Eye
That was born in a night to perish in a night,
When the Soul slept in the beams of Light.
Was Jesus Chaste? or did he, &c.

e

Was Jesus Chaste? or did he
Give any Lessons of Chastity?
The morning blush'd fiery red:
Mary was found in Adulterous bed;
Earth groan'd beneath, & Heaven above
Trembled at discovery of Love.
Jesus was sitting in Moses' Chair,
They brought the trembling Woman There.
Moses commands she be stoned to death,
What was the sound of Jesus' breath?
He laid His hand on Moses' Law:
The Ancient Heavens, in Silent Awe
Writ with Curses from Pole to Pole,
All away began to roll:
The Earth trembling & Naked lay
In secret bed of Mortal Clay,

On Sinai felt the hand divine
Putting back the bloody shrine,
And she heard the breath of God
As she heard by Eden's flood:
"Good & Evil are no more!
Sinai's trumpets, cease to roar!
Cease, finger of God, to write!
The Heavens are not clean in thy Sight.
Thou art Good, & thou Alone;
Nor may the sinner cast one stone.
To be Good only, is to be
A God or else a Pharisee.
Thou Angel of the Presence Divine
That didst create this Body of Mine,
Wherefore hast thou writ these Laws
And Created Hell's dark jaws?
My Presence I will take from thee:
A Cold Leper thou shalt be.
Tho' thou wast so pure & bright
That Heaven was Impure in thy Sight,
Tho' thy Oath turn'd Heaven Pale,
Tho' thy Covenant built Hell's Jail,
Tho' thou didst all to Chaos roll
With the Serpent for its soul,
Still the breath Divine does move
And the breath Divine is Love.
Mary, Fear Not! Let me see
The Seven Devils that torment thee:
Hide not from my Sight thy Sin,
That forgiveness thou maist win.
Has no Man Condemned thee?"
"No Man, Lord:" "then what is he
Who shall Accuse thee? Come Ye forth,
Fallen fiends of Heav'nly birth
That have forgot your Ancient love
And driven away my trembling Dove.
You shall bow before her feet;
You shall lick the dust for Meat;
And tho' you cannot Love, but Hate,
Shall be beggars at Love's Gate.
What was thy love? Let me see it;

Was it love or dark deceit?"
"Love too long from Me has fled;
'Twas dark deceit, to Earn my bread;
'Twas Covet, or 'twas Custom, or
Some trifle not worth caring for;
That they may call a shame & Sin
Love's temple that God dwelleth in,
And hide in secret hidden shrine
The Naked Human form divine,
And render that a Lawless thing
On which the Soul Expands its wing.
But this, O Lord, this was my Sin
When first I let these devils in
In dark pretence to Chastity:
Blaspheming Love, blaspheming thee.
Thence Rose Secret Adulteries,
And thence did Covet also rise.
My sin thou hast forgiven me,
Canst thou forgive my Blasphemy?
Canst thou return to this dark Hell,
And in my burning bosom dwell?
And canst thou die that I may live?
And canst thou Pity & forgive?"
Then Roll'd the shadowy Man away
From the Limbs of Jesus, to make them his prey,
An Ever devouring appetite
Glittering with festering venoms bright,
Crying, "Crucify this cause of distress,
Who don't keep the secrets of holiness!
All Mental Powers by Diseases we bind,
But he heals the deaf & the dumb & the Blind.
Whom God has afflicted for Secret Ends,
He Comforts & Heals & calls them Friends."
But, when Jesus was Crucified,
Then was perfected his glitt'ring pride:
In three Nights he devour'd his prey,
And still he devours the Body of Clay;
For dust & Clay is the Serpent's meat,
Which never was made for Man to Eat.

I am sure this Jesus will not do
Either for Englishman or Jew.

g

Seeing this False Christ, In fury & Passion
I made my Voice heard all over the Nation.
What are those, &c. . . .

h

This was spoke by My Spectre to Voltaire, Bacon, &c.

Did Jesus teach doubt? or did he
Give any lessons of Philosophy,
Charge Visionaries with decieving,
Or call Men wise for not Believing?

i

Was Jesus Born of a Virgin Pure
With narrow Soul & looks demure?
If he intended to take on Sin
The Mother should an Harlot been,
Just such a one as Magdalen
With seven devils in her Pen;
Or were Jew Virgins still more Curst,
And more sucking devils nurst?
Or what was it which he took on
That he might bring Salvation?
A Body subject to be Tempted,
From neither pain nor grief Exempted?
Or such a body as might not feel
The passions that with Sinners deal?
Yes, but they say he never fell.
Ask Caiaphas; for he can tell.
"He mock'd the Sabbath, & he mock'd
The Sabbath's God, & he unlock'd
The Evil spirits from their Shrines,
And turn'd Fishermen to Divines;
O'erturn'd the Tent of Secret Sins,
& its Golden cords & Pins—
'Tis the Bloody Shrine of War
Pinn'd around from Star to Star,
Halls of justice, hating Vice,
Where the devil Combs his lice.
He turn'd the devils into Swine

That he might tempt the Jews to dine;
Since which, a Pig has got a look
That for a Jew may be mistook.
'Obey your parents.'—What says he?
'Woman, what have I to do with thee?
No Earthly Parents I confess:
I am doing my Father's Business.'
He scorn'd Earth's Parents, scorn'd Earth's God,
And mock'd the one & the other's Rod;
His Seventy Disciples sent
Against Religion & Government:
They by the Sword of Justice fell
And him their Cruel Murderer tell.
He left his Father's trade to roam
A wand'ring Vagrant without Home;
And thus he others' labour stole
That he might live above Controll.
The Publicans & Harlots he
Selected for his Company,
And from the Adulteress turn'd away
God's righteous Law, that lost its Prey."

Aphorisms on the Laocoon Group

Sentences engraved about the plate:

IF Morality was Christianity, Socrates was the Saviour.

Art Degraded, Imagination Denied, War Governed the
Nations.

Spiritual War: Israel deliver'd from Egypt, is Art deliver'd
from Nature & Imitation.

A Poet, a Painter, a Musician, an Architect: the Man Or
Woman who is not one of these is not a Christian.
You must leave Fathers & Mothers & Houses & Lands if they
stand in the way of Art.
Prayer is the Study of Art.
Praise is the Practise of Art.
Fasting &c., all relate to Art.

The outward Ceremony is Antichrist.

The Eternal Body of Man is The Imagination, that is,
God himself ⎫
The Divine Body ⎰ ישוע , Jesus: we are his Members.

It manifests itself in his Works of Art (In Eternity All is Vision).

The True Christian Charity not dependent on Money (the life's blood of Poor Families), that is, on Caesar or Empire or Natural Religion: Money, which is The Great Satan or Reason, the Root of Good & Evil In The Accusation of Sin.

Good & Evil are Riches & Poverty, a Tree of Misery, propagating Generation & Death.

Where any view of Money exists, Art cannot be carried on, but War only (Read Matthew, c. x: 9 & 10 v.) by pretences to the Two Impossibilities, Chastity & Abstinence, Gods of the Heathen.

He repented that he had made Adam (of the Female, the Adamah) & it grieved him at his heart.

What can be Created Can be Destroyed.

Adam is only The Natural Man & not the Soul or Imagination.

Hebrew Art is called Sin by the Deist Science.

All that we See is Vision, from Generated Organs gone as soon as come, Permanent in The Imagination, Consider'd as Nothing by the Natural Man.

Art can never exist without Naked Beauty displayed.

The Gods of Greece & Egypt were Mathematical Diagrams —See Plato's Works.

Divine Union Deriding, And Denying Immediate Communion with God, The Spoilers say, "Where are his Works That he did in the Wilderness? Lo, what are these? Whence came they?" These are not the Works Of Egypt nor Babylon, Whose Gods are the Powers Of this World, Goddess Nature,

Who first spoil & then destroy Imaginative Art; For their Glory is War and Dominion.

Empire against Art—See Virgil's Eneid, Lib. VI, v. 848.

Satan's Wife, The Goddess Nature, is War & Misery, & Heroism a Miser.

For every Pleasure Money Is Useless.

There are States in which all Visionary Men are accounted Mad Men; such are Greece & Rome: Such is Empire or Tax—See Luke, Ch. 2, v. 1.

Without Unceasing Practise nothing can be done, Practise is Art. If you leave off you are Lost.

Jesus & his Apostles & Disciples were all Artists. Their Works were destroy'd by the Seven Angels of the Seven Churches in Asia, Antichrist Science.

The Old & New Testaments are the Great Code of Art.

Art is the Tree of Life, God is Jesus.

Science is the Tree of Death.

The Whole Business of Man Is The Arts, & All Things Common. No Secresy in Art.

The unproductive Man is not a Christian, much less the Destroyer.

Christianity is Art & not Money. Money is its Curse.

What we call Antique Gems are the Gems of Aaron's Breast Plate.

Is not every Vice possible to Man described in the Bible openly?

All is not Sin that Satan calls so: all the Loves & Graces of Eternity.

On Homer's Poetry & on Virgil

ON HOMER'S POETRY

EVERY Poem must necessarily be a perfect Unity, but why Homer's is peculiarly so, I cannot tell; he has told the story of Bellerophon & omitted the Judgment of Paris, which is not only a part, but a principal part, of Homer's subject.

But when a Work has Unity, it is as much in a Part as in the Whole: the Torso is as much a Unity as the Laocoon.

As Unity is the cloke of folly, so Goodness is the cloke of knavery. Those who will have Unity exclusively in Homer come out with a Moral like a sting in the tail. Aristotle says Characters are either Good or Bad; now Goodness or Badness has nothing to do with Character: an Apple tree, a Pear tree, a Horse, a Lion are Characters, but a Good Apple tree or a Bad is an Apple tree still; a Horse is not more a Lion for being a Bad Horse: that is its Character: its Goodness or Badness is another consideration.

It is the same with the Moral of a whole Poem as with the Moral Goodness of its parts. Unity & Morality are secondary considerations, & belong to Philosophy & not to Poetry, to Exception & not to Rule, to Accident & not to Substance; the Ancients call'd it eating of the tree of good & evil.

The Classics! it is the Classics, & not Goths nor Monks, that Desolate Europe with Wars.

ON VIRGIL

SACRED Truth has pronounced that Greece & Rome, as Babylon & Egypt, so far from being parents of Arts & Sciences as they pretend, were destroyers of all Art. Homer, Virgil, & Ovid confirm this opinion & make us reverence The Word of God, the only light of antiquity that remains unperverted by War. Virgil in the Eneid, Book vi, line 848, says "Let others study Art: Rome has somewhat better to do, namely War & Dominion."

Rome & Greece swept Art into their maw & destroy'd it; a
Warlike State never can produce Art. It will Rob & Plunder &
accumulate into one place, & Translate & Copy & Buy & Sell &
Criticise, but not Make. Grecian is Mathematic Form: Gothic
is Living Form. Mathematic Form is Eternal in the Reasoning
Memory: Living Form is Eternal Existence.

The Ghost of Abel

A REVELATION IN THE VISIONS OF
JEHOVAH SEEN BY WILLIAM BLAKE

TO LORD BYRON in the Wilderness:

> What doest thou here, Elijah?
Can a Poet doubt the Visions of Jehovah? Nature has no Outline, but Imagination has. Nature has no Tune, but Imagination has. Nature has no Supernatural & dissolves: Imagination
is Eternity.

SCENE—*A rocky Country.* EVE *fainted over the dead body of*
ABEL, *which lays near a Grave.* ADAM *kneels by her.*
JEHOVAH *stands above.*

Jehovah. Adam!

Adam.   I will not hear thee more, thou Spiritual Voice.
Is this Death?

Jehovah.   Adam!

Adam.   It is in vain. I will not hear thee
Henceforth! Is this thy Promise, that the Woman's Seed
Should bruise the Serpent's head? Is this the Serpent? Ah!
Seven times, O Eve, thou hast fainted over the Dead. Ah!
Ah!

                    EVE *revives.*

Eve. Is this the Promise of Jehovah! O, it is all a vain delusion,
This Death & this Life & this Jehovah!

Jehovah.   Woman, lift thine eyes!

A Voice is heard coming on.

Voice. O Earth, cover not thou my Blood! cover not thou my
Blood!

Enter the Ghost *of* ABEL.

Eve. Thou Visionary Phantasm, thou art not the real Abel.

Abel. Among the Elohim, a Human Victim I wander: I am
their House,

    Prince of the Air, & our dimensions compass Zenith & Nadir.

    Vain is thy Covenant, O Jehovah! I am the Accuser &
Avenger

Of Blood. O Earth, Cover not thou the Blood of Abel.

Jehovah. What Vengence dost thou require?

Abel.   Life for Life! Life
for Life!

Jehovah. He who shall take Cain's life must also Die, O Abel!

    And who is he! Adam, wilt thou, or Eve, thou do this?

Adam. It is all a Vain delusion of the all creative Imagination.

    Eve, come away, & let us not believe these vain delusions.

    Abel is dead, & Cain slew him. We shall also Die a Death,

    And then, what then? be, as poor Abel, a Thought, or as

    This! O, what shall I call thee, Form Divine, Father of
Mercies,

That appearest to my Spiritual Vision? Eve, seest thou also?

Eve. I see him plainly with my Mind's Eye. I see also Abel
living,

    Tho' terribly afflicted, as We also are, yet Jehovah sees him

    Alive & not Dead; were it not better to believe Vision

    With all our might & strength, tho' we are fallen & lost?

Adam. Eve, thou hast spoken truly: let us kneel before his feet.

They Kneel before JEHOVAH.

Abel. Are these the Sacrifices of Eternity, O Jehovah, a Broken
Spirit

    And a Contrite Heart? O, I cannot Forgive! the Accuser
hath

    Enter'd into Me as into his House, & I loathe thy Taber-
nacles.

    As thou hast said, so is it come to pass: My desire is unto
Cain,

    And He doth rule over Me; therefore My Soul in fumes of
Blood

Cries for Vengeance, Sacrifice on Sacrifice, Blood on Blood!

Jehovah. Lo, I have given you a Lamb for an Atonement instead

Of the Transgressor, or no Flesh or Spirit could ever Live.

Abel. Compelled I cry, O Earth, cover not the Blood of Abel!

ABEL *sinks down into the Grave, from which arises* SATAN, *Armed in glittering scales, with a Crown & a Spear.*

Satan. I will have Human Blood & not the blood of Bulls or Goats,
And no Atonement, O Jehovah! the Elohim live on Sacrifice
Of Men: hence I am God of Men: Thou Human, O Jehovah!
By the Rock & Oak of the Druid, creeping Misletoe & Thorn,
Cain's City built with Human Blood, not Blood of Bulls & Goats,
Thou shalt Thyself be Sacrificed to Me, thy God, on Calvary.
Jehovah. Such is My Will   *Thunders.*
               that Thou Thyself go to Eternal Death
In Self Annihilation, even till Satan, Self-subdu'd, Put off Satan
Into the Bottomless Abyss, whose torment arises for ever & ever.

On each side a Chorus of Angels entering Sing the following:

The Elohim of the Heathen Swore Vengeance for Sin! Then Thou stood'st
Forth, O Elohim Jehovah! in the midst of the darkness of the Oath, All Clothed
In Thy Covenant of the Forgiveness of Sins: Death, O Holy! Is this Brotherhood.
The Elohim saw their Oath Eternal Fire: they rolled apart trembling over The
Mercy Seat, each in his station fixt in the Firmament by Peace, Brotherhood and Love.

The Curtain falls.

1822. Blake's Original Stereotype was 1788.

PART FIVE

PROSE   .

PROSE

An Island in the Moon

IN the Moon is a certain Island near by a mighty continent, which small island seems to have some affinity to England, &, what is more extraordinary, the people are so much alike, & their language so much the same, that you would think you was among your friends. In this Island dwells three Philosophers—Suction the Epicurean, Quid the Cynic, & Sipsop the Pythagorean. I call them by the names of those sects, tho' the sects are not ever mention'd there, as being quite out of date; however, the things still remain, and the vanities are the same. The three Philosophers sat together thinking of nothing. In comes Etruscan Column the Antiquarian, & after an abundance of Enquiries to no purpose, sat himself down & described something that nobody listen'd to. So they were employ'd when Mrs. Gimblet came in. The corners of her mouth seem'd—I don't know how, but very odd, as if she hoped you had not an ill opinion of her,—to be sure, we are all poor creatures! Well, she seated [herself] & seem'd to listen with great attention while the Antiquarian seem'd to be talking of virtuous cats. But it was not so; she was thinking of the shape of her eyes & mouth, & he was thinking of his eternal fame. The three Philosophers at this time were each endeavouring to conceal his laughter (not at them but) at his own imagination.

This was the situation of this improving company when, in a great hurry, Inflammable Gass the Wind-finder enter'd. They seem'd to rise & salute each other. Etruscan Column & Inflammable Gass fix'd their eyes on each other; their tongues went in question & answer, but their thoughts were otherwise employ'd. "I don't like his eyes," said Etruscan Column. "He's a foolish puppy," said Inflammable Gass, smiling on him. The 3 Philosophers—the Cynic smiling, the Epicurean seeming studying the flame of the candle, & the Pythagorean playing with the cat—listen'd with open mouths to the edifying discourses.

337

"Sir," said the Antiquarian, "I have seen these works, & I do affirm that they are no such thing. They seem to me to be the most wretched, paltry, flimsy stuff that ever——"

"What d'ye say? What d'ye say?" said Inflammable Gass. "Why—why, I wish I could see you write so."

"Sir," said the Antiquarian, "according to my opinion the author is an errant blockhead."

"Your reason—Your reason?" said Inflammable Gass. "Why —why, I think it very abominable to call a man a blockhead that you know nothing of."

"Reason, Sir?" said the Antiquarian. "I'll give you an example for your reason. As I was walking along the street I saw a vast number of swallows on the rails of an old Gothic square. They seem'd to be going on their passage, as Pliny says. As I was looking up, a little *outré* fellow, pulling me by the sleeve, cries, 'Pray, Sir, who do all they belong to?' I turn'd myself about with great contempt. Said I, 'Go along, you fool!' 'Fool!' said he, 'who do you call fool? I only ask'd you a civil question.' I had a great mind to have thrash'd the fellow, only he was bigger than I."

Here Etruscan Column left off—Inflammable Gass, recollecting himself [said], "Indeed I do not think the man was a fool, for he seems to me to have been desirous of enquiring into the works of nature!"

"Ha! Ha! Ha!" said the Pythagorean.

It was re-echo'd by Inflammable Gass to overthrow the argument.

Etruscan Column then, starting up & clenching both his fists, was prepared to give a formal answer to the company. But Obtuse Angle, entering the room, having made a gentle bow, proceeded to empty his pockets of a vast number of papers, turned about & sat down, wiped his face with his pocket handkerchief, & shutting his eyes, began to scratch his head.

"Well, gentlemen," said he, "what is the cause of strife?"

The Cynic answer'd, "They are only quarreling about Voltaire."

"Yes," said the Epicurean, "& having a bit of fun with him."

"And," said the Pythagorean, "endeavoring to incorporate their souls with their bodies."

Obtuse Angle, giving a grin, said, "Voltaire understood nothing of the Mathematics, and a man must be a fool i'faith not to understand the Mathematics."

Inflammable Gass, turning round hastily in his chair, said, "Mathematics! He found out a number of Queries in Philosophy."

Obtuse Angle, shutting his eyes & saying that he always understood better when he shut his eyes, [replied], "In the first place, it is of no use for a man to make Queries, but to solve them; for a man may be a fool & make Queries, but a man must have good sound sense to solve them. A query & an answer are as different as a strait line & a crooked one. Secondly——"

"I—I—I—aye! Secondly, Voltaire's a fool," says the Epicurean.

"Pooh!" says the Mathematician, scratching his head with double violence, "It is not worth Quarreling about."

The Antiquarian here got up, &, hemming twice to shew the strength of his Lungs, said, "But, my Good Sir, Voltaire was immersed in matter, & seems to have understood very little but what he saw before his eyes, like the Animal upon the Pythagorean's lap, always playing with its own tail."

"Ha! Ha! Ha!" said Inflammable Gass. "He was the Glory of France. I have got a bottle of air that would spread a Plague."

Here the Antiquarian shrugg'd up his shoulders, & was silent while Inflammable Gass talk'd for half an hour.

When Steelyard, the lawgiver, coming in stalking—with an act of parliament in his hand, said that it was a shameful thing that acts of parliament should be in a free state, it had so engrossed his mind that he did not salute the company.

Mrs. Gimblet drew her mouth downwards.

CHAP 2d

TILLY LALLY, the Siptippidist, Aradobo, the Dean of Morocco, Miss Gittipin, Mrs. Nannicantipot, Mrs. Sistagatist, Gibble Gabble, the wife of Inflammable Gass, & Little Scopprell enter'd the room.

(If I have not presented you with every character in the piece, call me Ass.)

CHAP 3d

IN the Moon, as Phebus stood over his oriental Gardening, "O ay, come, I'll sing you a song," said the Cynic.

" 'The trumpeter shit in his hat,' " said the Epicurean.
"———& clapt it on his head," said the Pythagorean.
"I'll begin again," said the Cynic.

> "Little Phebus came strutting in
> With his fat belly & his round chin,
> What is it you would please to have?
> Ho! Ho!
> I won't let it go at only so & so."

Mrs. Gimblet look'd as if they meant her. Tilly Lally laught like a cherry clapper. Aradobo ask'd, "Who was Phebus, Sir?"

Obtuse Angle answer'd quickly, "He was the God of Physic, Painting, Perspective, Geometry, Geography, Astronomy, Cookery, Chymistry, Mechanics, Tactics, Pathology, Ohrascology, Theology, Mythology, Astrology, Osteology, Somatology—in short, every art & science adorn'd him as beads round his neck."

Here Aradobo look'd Astonish'd & ask'd if he understood Engraving.

Obtuse Angle Answer'd, indeed he did.

"Well," said the other, "he was as great as Chatterton."

Tilly Lally turn'd round to Obtuse Angle & ask'd who it was that was as great as Chatterton.

"Hay! How should I know?" Answer'd Obtuse Angle. "Who was it, Aradobo?"

"Why sir," said he, "the Gentleman that the song was about."

"Ah," said Tilly Lally, "I did not hear it. What was it, Obtuse Angle?"

"Pooh," said he. "Nonsense!"

"Mhm," said Tilly Lally.

"It was Phebus," said the Epicurean.

"Ah, that was the Gentleman," said Aradobo.

"Pray, Sir," said Tilly Lally, "who was Phebus?"

Obtuse Angle answer'd, "The heathen in the old ages us'd to have Gods that they worship'd, & they us'd to sacrifice to them. You have read about that in the Bible."

"Ah," said Aradobo, "I thought I had read of Phebus in the Bible."

"Aradobo, you should always think before you speak," said Obtuse Angle.

"Ha! Ha! Ha! He means Pharaoh," said Tilly Lally.

"I am asham'd of you,—making use of the names in the Bible," said Mrs. Sistagatist.

"I'll tell you what, Mrs. Sinagain. I don't think there's any harm in it," said Tilly Lally.

"No," said Inflammable Gass. "I have got a camera obscura at home. What was it you was talking about?"

"Law!" said Tilly Lally. "What has that to do with Pharoah?"

"Pho! nonsense! hang Pharoh & all his hosts," said the Pythagorean. "Sing away, Quid."

Then the Cynic sung—

> "Honour & Genius is all I ask
> And I ask the Gods no more.

"No more, No more, ⎱   the three Philosophers
No more, No more." ⎰   bear Chorus.

Here Aradobo sucked his under lip.

CHAP 4

"HANG names!" said the Pythagorean, "What's Pharoh better than Phebus, or Phebus than Pharoh?"

"Hang them both," said the Cynic.

"Don't be prophane," said Mrs. Sistagatist.

"Why?" said Mrs. Nannicantipot, "I don't think it's prophane to say 'Hang Pharoh.' "

"Oh," said Mrs. Sinagain. "I'm sure you ought to hold your tongue, for you never say any thing about the scriptures, & you hinder your husband from going to church."

"Ha, ha!" said Inflammable Gass. "What! don't you like to go to church?"

"No," said Mrs. Nannicantipot. "I think a person may be as good at home."

"If I had not a place of profit that forces me to go to church," said Inflammable Gass, "I'd see the parsons all hang'd, —a parcel of lying——"

"O!" said Mrs. Sistagatist. "If it was not for churches & chapels I should not have liv'd so long. There was I, up in a Morning at four o'clock, when I was a Girl. I would run like the dickins till I was all in a heat. I would stand till I was ready to sink into the earth. Ah, Mr. Huffcap would kick the bottom of the Pulpit out with Passion—would tear off the sleeve of his Gown & set his wig on fire & throw it at the people. He'd cry & stamp & kick & sweat, and all for the good of their souls."

"I'm sure he must be a wicked villain," said Mrs. Nannicanti-pot, "a passionate wretch. If I was a man I'd wait at the bottom of the pulpit stairs & knock him down & run away!"

"You would, you Ignorant jade? I wish I could see you hit any of the ministers! You deserve to have your ears boxed, you do."

"I'm sure this is not religion," answers the other.

Then Mr. Inflammable Gass ran & shov'd his head into the fire & set his hair all in a flame, & ran about the room,——No, no, he did not; I was only making a fool of you.

CHAP 5

OBTUSE ANGLE, Scopprell, Aradobo, & Tilly Lally are all met in Obtuse Angle's study.

"Pray," said Aradobo, "is Chatterton a Mathematician?"

"No," said Obtuse Angle. "How can you be so foolish as to think he was?"

"Oh, I did not think he was—I only ask'd," said Aradobo.

"How could you think he was not, & ask if he was?" said Obtuse Angle.

"Oh no, Sir. I did not think he was, before you told me, but afterwards I thought he was not."

Obtuse Angle said, "In the first place you thought he was, & then afterwards when I said he was not, you thought he was not. Why, I know that——"

"Oh no, sir, I thought that he was not, but I ask'd to know whether he was."

"How can that be?" said Obtuse Angle. "How could you ask & think that he was not?"

"Why," said he, "it came into my head that he was not."

"Why then," said Obtuse Angle, "you said that he was."

"Did I say so? Law! I did not think I said that."

"Did not he?" said Obtuse Angle.

"Yes," said Scopprell.

"But I meant——" said Aradobo, "I—I—I can't think. Law! Sir, I wish you'd tell me how it is."

Then Obtuse Angle put his chin in his hand & said, "Whenever you think, you must always think for yourself."

"How, sir?" said Aradobo. "Whenever I think, I must think myself? I think I do. In the first place——" said he with a grin.

"Poo! Poo!" said Obtuse Angle. "Don't be a fool."

Then Tilly Lally took up a Quadrant & ask'd, "Is not this a sun-dial?"

"Yes," said Scopprell, "but it's broke."

At this moment the three Philosophers enter'd, and low'ring darkness hover'd over the assembly.

"Come," said the Epicurean, "let's have some rum & water, & hang the mathematics! Come, Aradobo! Say some thing."

Then Aradobo began, "In the first place I think, I think in the first place that Chatterton was clever at Fissie Follogy, Pistinology, Aridology, Arography, Transmography, Phizography, Hogamy, Hatomy, & hall that, but, in the first place, he eat every little, wickly—that is, he slept very little, which he brought into a consumsion; & what was that that he took? Fissic or somethink,—& so died!"

So all the people in the book enter'd into the room, & they could not talk any more to the present purpose.

CHAP 6

THEY all went home & left the Philosophers. Then Suction Ask'd if Pindar was not a better Poet than Ghiotto was a Painter.

"Plutarch has not the life of Ghiotto," said Sipsop.

"No," said Quid, "to be sure, he was an Italian."

"Well," said Suction, "that is not any proof."

"Plutarch was a nasty ignorant puppy," said Quid. "I hate your sneaking rascals. There's Aradobo in ten or twelve years will be a far superior genius."

"Ah!" said the Pythagorean, "Aradobo will make a very clever fellow."

"Why," said Quid, "I think that any natural fool would make a clever fellow, if he was properly brought up."

"Ah, hang your reasoning!" said the Epicurean. "I hate reasoning. I do everything by my feelings."

"Ah!" said Sipsop, "I only wish Jack Tearguts had had the cutting of Plutarch. He understands Anatomy better than any of the Ancients. He'll plunge his knife up to the hilt in a single drive and thrust his fist in, and all in the space of a Quarter of an hour. He does not mind their crying, tho' they cry ever so.

He'll swear at them & keep them down with his fist, & tell
them that he'll scrape their bones if they don't lay still & be
quiet. What the devil should the people in the hospital that
have it done for nothing make such a piece of work for?"

"Hang that," said Suction; "let us have a song."

Then the Cynic sang—

1.

"When old corruption first begun,
    Adorn'd in yellow vest,
He committed on flesh a whoredom—
    O, what a wicked beast!

2.

"From then a callow babe did spring,
    And old corruption smil'd
To think his race should never end,
    For now he had a child.

3.

"He call'd him surgery, & fed
    The babe with his own milk,
For flesh & he could ne'er agree,
    She would not let him suck.

4.

"And this he always kept in mind,
    And form'd a crooked knife,
And ran about with bloody hands
    To seek his mother's life.

5.

"And as he ran to seek his mother
    He met with a dead woman,
He fell in love & married her,
    A deed which is not common.

6.

"She soon grew pregnant & brought forth
    Scurvy & spott'd fever.
The father grin'd & skipt about,
    And said, 'I'm made for ever!

7.

" 'For now I have procur'd these imps
    I'll try experiments.'
With that he tied poor scurvy down
    & stopt up all its vents.

8.

"And when the child began to swell,
    He shouted out aloud,
'I've found the dropsy out, & soon
    Shall do the world more good.'

9.

"He took up fever by the neck
    And cut out all its spots,
And thro' the holes which he had made
    He first discover'd guts."

"Ah," said Sipsop, "you think we are rascals—& we think
you are rascals. I do as I chuse. What is it to any body what I
do? I am always unhappy too. When I think of Surgery—I
don't know. I do it because I like it. My father does what he
likes & so do I. I think, somehow, I'll leave it off. There was a
woman having her cancer cut, & she shriek'd so that I was
quite sick."

CHAP 7

"GOOD-NIGHT," said Sipsop.

"Good-night," said the other two.

Then Quid & Suction were left alone. Then said Quid, "I
think that Homer is bombast, & Shakespeare is too wild, &
Milton has no feelings: they might be easily outdone. Chatterton never writ those poems! A parcel of fools, going to Bristol!
If I was to go, I'd find it out in a minute, but I've found it out
already."

"If I don't knock them all up next year in the Exhibition, I'll
be hang'd," said Suction. "Hang Philosophy! I would not give
a farthing for it! Do all by your feelings, and never think at all
about it. I'm hang'd if I don't get up to-morrow morning by
four o'clock & work Sir Joshua."

"Before ten years are at an end," said Quid, "how I will work those poor milksop devils,—an ignorant pack of wretches!"

So they went to bed.

CHAP 8

STEELYARD the Lawgiver, sitting at his table, taking extracts from Hervey's Meditations among the tombs & Young's Night thoughts.

"He is not able to hurt me," said he, "more than making me Constable or taking away the parish business. Hah!

" 'My crop of corn is but a field of tares',

says Jerome. Happiness is not for us, poor crawling reptiles of the earth. Talk of happiness & happiness! It's no such thing. Every person has a something.

"Hear then the pride & knowledge of a Sailor,
His sprit sail, fore sail, main sail, & his mizen.
A poor frail man! God wot, I know none frailer.
I know no greater sinner than John Taylor.

If I had only myself to care for I'd soon make Double Elephant look foolish, & Filligreework. I hope [I] shall live to see—

" 'The wreck of matter & the crush of worlds',

as Young says."

Obtuse Angle enter'd the Room.

"What news, Mr. Steelyard?"

"I am reading Thison & Aspasio," said he.

Obtuse Angle took up the books one by one.

"I don't find it here," said he.

"O no," said the other, "it was the meditations!"

Obtuse Angle took up the book & read till the other was quite tir'd out.

Then Scopprell & Miss Gittipin coming in, Scopprell took up a book & read the following passage:—

"An Easy of Huming Understanding, by John Lookye Gent."

"John Locke," said Obtuse Angle.

"O, ay—Lock," said Scopprell.

"Now here," said Miss Gittipin,—"I never saw such company in my life. You are always talking of your books. I like to be where we talk. You had better take a walk, that we may have some pleasure. I am sure I never see any pleasure. There's Double Elephant's Girls, they have their own way; & there's Miss Filligreework, she goes out in her coaches, & her footman & her maids, & Stormonts & Balloon hats, & a pair of Gloves every day, & the Sorrows of Werter, & Robinsons, & the Queen of France's Puss colour, & my Cousin Gibble Gabble says that I am like nobody else. I might as well be in a nunnery. There they go in Postchaises & Stages to Vauxhall & Ranelagh. And I hardly know what a coach is, except when I go to Mr. Jacko's. He knows what riding is, & his wife is the most agreeable woman. You hardly know she has a tongue in her head, and he is the funniest fellow, & I do believe he'll go in partnership with his master, & they have black servants lodge at their house. I never saw such a place in my life. He says he has six & twenty rooms in his house, and I believe it, & he is not such a liar as Quid thinks he is."

"Poo! Poo! Hold your tongue. Hold your tongue," said the Lawgiver.

This quite provok'd Miss Gittipin, to interrupt her in her favourite topic, & she proceeded to use every Provoking speech that ever she could, & he bore it more like a Saint than a Lawgiver, and with great solemnity he address'd the company in these words:—

"They call women the weakest vessel, but I think they are the strongest. A girl has always more tongue than a boy. I have seen a little brat no higher than a nettle, & she had as much tongue as a city clark; but a boy would be such a fool, not have any thing to say, and if anybody ask'd him a question he would put his head into a hole & hide it. I am sure I take but little pleasure. You have as much pleasure as I have. There I stand & bear every fool's insult. If I had only myself to care for, I'd wring off their noses."

To this Scopprell answer'd, "I think the Ladies' discourses, Mr. Steelyard, are some of them more improving than any book. That is the way I have got some of my knowledge."

"Then," said Miss Gittipin, "Mr. Scopprell, do you know the song of Phebe and Jellicoe?"

"No, Miss," said Scopprell.

Then she repeated these verses, while Steelyard walk'd about the room:

> "Phebe, dressed like beautie's Queen,
> Jellicoe in faint pea green,
> Sitting all beneath a grot
> Where the little lambkins trot;

> "Maidens dancing, loves a-sporting,
> All the country folks a-courting,
> Susan, Johnny, Bet, & Joe
> Lightly tripping on a row.

> "Happy people, who can be
> In happiness compar'd with ye?
> The Pilgrim with his crook & hat
> Sees your happiness compleat."

"A charming song, indeed, Miss," said Scopprell. Here they receiv'd a summons for a merry making at the Philosopher's house.

CHAP 9

"I SAY, this evening we'll get drunk—I say—dash!—an Anthem, an Anthem!" said Suction.

> "Lo the Bat with Leathern wing,
> Winking & blinking,
> Winking & blinking,
> Winking & blinking,
> Like Doctor Johnson."

Quid. " 'Oho', said Dr. Johnson
> To Scipio Africanus,
> 'If you don't own me a Philosopher,
> I'll kick your Roman Anus'."

Suction. " 'Aha', To Dr. Johnson
> Said Scipio Africanus,
> 'Lift up my Roman Petticoat
> And kiss my Roman Anus'."

> "And the Cellar goes down with a step."
> (Grand Chorus).

"Ho, Ho, Ho, Ho, Ho, Ho, Ho, Hooooo, my poooooor siiides! I, I should die if I was to live here!" said Scopprell. "Ho, Ho, Ho, Ho, Ho!"

> 1st *Vo.* "Want Matches?"
> 2nd *Vo.* "Yes, yes, yes."
> 1st *Vo.* "Want Matches?"
> 2nd *Vo.* "No."

> 1st *Vo.* "Want Matches?"
> 2nd *Vo.* "Yes, yes, yes."
> 1st *Vo.* "Want Matches?"
> 2nd *Vo.* "No."

Here was great confusion & disorder. Aradobo said that the boys in the street sing something very pretty & funny about London—O no, about Matches. Then Mrs. Nannicantipot sung:

> "I cry my matches as far as Guild hall;
> God bless the duke & his aldermen all!"

Then sung Scopprell:

> "I ask the Gods no more,—
> no more, no more."

"Then," said Suction, "come, Mr. Lawgiver, your song"; and the Lawgiver sung:

> "As I walk'd forth one may morning
> To see the fields so pleasant & so gay,
> O there did I spy a young maiden sweet,
> Among the Violets that smell so sweet,
>   Smell so sweet,
>   Smell so sweet,
> Among the Violets that smell so sweet."

"Hang your Violets! Here's your Rum & water. O ay," said Tilly Lally, "Joe Bradley & I was going along one day in the sugar-house. Joe Bradley saw—for he had but one eye—saw a treacle jar. So he goes of his blind side & dips his hand up to the

shoulder in treacle. 'Here, lick, lick, lick, lick!' said he. Ha! Ha!
Ha! Ha! For he had but one eye. Ha! Ha! Ha! Ho!"

Then sung Scopprell:

> "And I ask the Gods no more,—
>   no more, no more,
>   no more, no more.

"Miss Gittipin," said he, "you sing like a harpsichord. Let
your bounty descend to our fair ears and favour us with a fine
song."

Then she sung:

> "This frog he would a-wooing ride,
>   Kitty alone—Kitty alone,—
> This frog he would a-wooing ride,—
>   Kitty alone & I!
> Sing cock I cary, Kitty alone,
>   Kitty alone,—Kitty alone,—
> Cock I cary, Kitty alone,—
>   Kitty alone & I!"

"Charming! Truly elegant!" said Scopprell.

> "And I ask the gods no more!"

"Hang your serious songs!" said Sipsop, & he sung as follows:—

> "Fa ra so bo ro
>   Fa ra bo ra
> Sa ba ra ra ba rare roro
> Sa ra ra ra bo ro ro ro
>   Radara
> Sarapodo no flo ro."

"Hang Italian songs! Let's have English!" said Quid. "English
genius for ever! Here I go:

> "Hail Matrimony, made of Love,
> To thy wide gates how great a drove
>   On purpose to be yok'd do come!
> Widows & maids & youths also,

That lightly trip on beauty's toe,
   Or sit on beauty's bum.

"Hail, finger-footed lovely Creatures!
The females of our human Natures,
   Formed to suckle all Mankind.
'Tis you that come in time of need;
Without you we should never Breed,
   Or any Comfort find.

"For if a Damsel's blind or lame,
Or Nature's hand has crooked her frame,
   Or if she's deaf, or is wall eyed,
Yet if her heart is well inclined,
Some tender lover she shall find
   That panteth for a Bride.

"The universal Poultice this,
To cure whatever is amiss
   In damsel or in widow gay.
It makes them smile, it makes them skip,
Like Birds just cured of the pip,
   They chirp, & hop away.

"Then come ye maidens, come ye swains,
Come & be cured of all your pains
   In Matrimony's Golden cage."

"Go & be hanged!" said Scopprell. "How can you have the
face to make game of matrimony?"

Then Quid call'd upon Obtuse Angle for a Song, & he, wiping his face & looking on the corner of the ceiling, sang:

         "To be, or not to be
         Of great capacity,
            Like Sir Isaac Newton,
         Or Locke, or Doctor South,
         Or Sherlock upon death?
            I'd rather be Sutton.

         "For he did build a house
         For aged men & youth,

With walls of brick & stone.
He furnish'd it within
With whatever he could win,
    And all his own.

"He drew out of the Stocks
His money in a box,
    And sent his servant
To Green the Bricklayer
And to the Carpenter:
    He was so fervent.

"The chimneys were three score,
The windows many more,
    And for convenience
He sinks & gutters made
And all the way he pav'd
    To hinder pestilence.

"Was not this a good man,
Whose life was but a span,
    Whose name was Sutton,—
As Locke, or Doctor South,
Or Sherlock upon Death,
    Or Sir Isaac Newton?"

The Lawgiver was very attentive & beg'd to have it sung
over again & again, till the company were tired & insisted on
the Lawgiver singing a song himself, which he readily complied
with.

"This city & this country has brought forth many mayors,
To sit in state & give forth laws out of their old oak chairs,
With face as brown as any nut with drinking of strong ale;
Good English hospitality, O then it did not fail!

"With scarlet gowns & broad gold lace would make a yeoman
        sweat,
With stockings roll'd above their knees & shoes as black as jet,
With eating beef & drinking beer, O they were stout & hale!
Good English hospitality, O then it did not fail!

"Thus sitting at the table wide, the Mayor & Aldermen
Were fit to give law to the city; each eat as much as ten.
The hungry poor enter'd the hall, to eat good beef & ale.
Good English hospitality, O then it did not fail!"

Here they gave a shout, & the company broke up.

CHAP 10

THUS these happy Islanders spent their time. But felicity does
not last long, for being met at the house of Inflammable Gass
the windfinder, the following affairs happen'd.

"Come, Flammable," said Gibble Gabble, "& let's enjoy ourselves. Bring the Puppets."

"Hay,—Hay," said he, "you—sho—why—ya, ya. How can
you be so foolish? Ha! Ha! Ha! She calls the experiments puppets!"

Then he went up stairs & loaded the maid with glasses, &
brass tubes, & magic pictures.

"Here, ladies & gentlemen," said he, "I'll shew you a louse,
or a flea, or a butterfly, or a cockchafer, the blade bone of a
tittleback. No, no. Here's a bottle of wind that I took up in the
boghouse, and—O dear, O dear, the water's got into the sliders!
Look here, Gibble Gabble! Lend me your handkerchief, Tilly
Lally."

Tilly Lally took out his handkerchief, which smear'd the
glass worse than ever. Then he screw'd it on. Then he took the
sliders, & then he set up the glasses for the Ladies to view
the pictures. Thus he was employ'd, & quite out of breath. While
Tilly Lally & Scopprell were pumping at the air-pump, Smack
went the glass.

"Hang!" said Tilly Lally.

Inflammable Gass turn'd short round & threw down the table
& Glasses, & Pictures, & broke the bottles of wind, & let out
the Pestilence. He saw the Pestilence fly out of the bottle, &
cried out, while he ran out of the room:

"Come out! Come out! We are putrified! We are corrupted!
Our lungs are destroy'd with the Flogiston. This will spread a
plague all thro' the Island!"

He was downstairs the very first. On the back of him came
all the others in a heap.

So they need not bidding go.

CHAP 11

ANOTHER merry meeting at the house of Steelyard the Law-giver. After supper, Steelyard & Obtuse Angle had pump'd In-flammable Gass quite dry. They play'd at forfeits, & try'd every method to get good humour.

Said Miss Gittipin, "Pray, Mr. Obtuse Angle, sing us a song." Then he sung:

"Upon a holy thursday, their innocent faces clean,
The children walking two & two in grey & blue & green,
Grey headed beadles walk'd before with wands as white as snow,
Till into the high dome of Paul's they like thames' waters flow.

"O what a multitude they seem'd, these flowers of London town!
Seated in companies, they sit with radiance all their own.
The hum of multitudes were there, but multitudes of lambs,
Thousands of little girls & boys raising their innocent hands.

"Then like a mighty wind they raise to heav'n the voice of song,
Or like harmonious thunderings the seats of heav'n among.
Beneath them sit the rev'rend men, the guardians of the poor;
Then cherish pity lest you drive an angel from your door."

After this they all sat silent for a quarter of an hour, & Mrs. Nannicantipot said, "It puts me in Mind of my mother's song,

"When the tongues of children are heard on the green,
    And laughing is heard on the hill,
My heart is at rest within my breast,
    And every thing else is still.

" 'Then come home, my children, the sun is gone down,
    And the dews of night arise;
Come, Come, leave off play, & let us away
    Till the morning appears in the skies.'

" 'No, No, let us play, for it is yet day,
    And we cannot go to sleep

Besides in the sky the little birds fly,
    And the meadows are cover'd with sheep.'

" 'Well, Well, go & play till the light fades away,
    And then go home to bed.'
The little ones leaped, & shouted, & laugh'd,
    And all the hills ecchoed."

Then sung Quid:

"O father, father, where are you going?
    Oh do not walk so fast;
Oh, speak, father, speak to your little boy,
    Or else I shall be lost.

"The night it was dark & no father was there,
    And the child was wet with dew.
The mire was deep, & the child did weep,
    And away the vapour flew."

Here nobody could sing any longer, till Tilly Lally pluck'd up
a spirit & he sung:

"I say, you Joe,
Throw us the ball.
I've a good mind to go,
And leave you all.

"I never saw such a bowler,
To bowl the ball in a tansey,
And to clean it with my handkercher
Without saying a word.

"That Bill's a foolish fellow,
He has given me a black eye.
He does not know how to handle a bat
Any more than a dog or a cat.

"He has knock'd down the wicket
And broke the stumps,
And runs without shoes to save his pumps."

Here a laugh began, and Miss Gittipin sung:

> "Leave, O leave me to my sorrows,
>   Here I'll sit & fade away;
> Till I'm nothing but a spirit,
>   And I lose this form of clay.

> "Then if chance along this forest
>   Any walk in pathless ways,
> Thro' the gloom he'll see my shadow,
>   Hear my voice upon the Breeze."

The Lawgiver all the while sat delighted to see them in such a serious humour. "Mr. Scopprell," said he, "you must be acquainted with a great many songs."

"Oh, dear sir! Ho, Ho, Ho, I am no singer. I must beg of one of these tender-hearted ladies to sing for me."

They all declined, & he was forced to sing himself:

> "There's Dr. Clash
>   And Signior Falalasole:
> O they sweep in the cash
>   Into their purse hole.
>   Fa me la sol, La me fa sol.

> "Great A, little A,
>   Bouncing B.
> Play away, Play away,
>   You're out of the key.
>   Fa me la sol, La me fa sol.

> "Musicians should have
>   A pair of very good ears,
> And Long fingers & thumbs,
>   And not like clumsy bears.
>   Fa me la sol, La me fa sol.

> "Gentlemen, Gentlemen!
>   Rap, rap, rap,
> Fiddle, Fiddle, Fiddle,
>   Clap, Clap, Clap.
>   Fa me la sol, La me fa sol."

"Hm," said the Lawgiver, "Funny enough! Let's have Handel's water piece." Then Sipsop sung:

"A crowned king,
On a white horse sitting,
With his trumpets sounding,
And Banners flying,
Thro' the clouds of smoke he makes his way,
And the shout of his thousands fills his heart with rejoicing &
    victory:
And the shout of his thousands fills his heart with rejoicing &
    victory.
Victory! Victory! 'twas William, the prince of Orange,—

[Part of the manuscript is missing here]

"—thus Illuminating the Manuscript."

"Ay," said she, "that would be excellent."

"Then," said he, "I would have all the writing Engraved instead of Printed, & at every other leaf a high finish'd print—all in three Volumes folio—& sell them a hundred pounds apiece. They would print off two thousand."

"Then," said she, "whoever will not have them will be ignorant fools & will not deserve to live."

"Don't you think I have something of the Goat's face?" says he.

"Very like a Goat's face," she answer'd.

"I think your face," said he, "is like that noble beast the Tyger. Oh, I was at Mrs. Sicknacker's, & I was speaking of my abilities, but their nasty hearts, poor devils, are eat up with envy. They envy me my abilities, & all the women envy your abilities."

"My dear, they hate people who are of higher abilities than their nasty, filthy selves. But do you outface them, & then strangers will see that you have an opinion."

"Now I think we should do as much good as we can when we are at Mr. Femality's. Do you snap, & take me up, and I will fall into such a passion. I'll hollow and stamp, & frighten all the People there, & show them what truth is."

At this Instant Obtuse Angle came in.

"Oh, I am glad you are come," said Quid.

A DESCRIPTIVE CATALOGUE OF PICTURES, POETICAL AND HISTORICAL INVENTIONS, PAINTED BY WILLIAM BLAKE IN WATER COLOURS, BEING THE ANCIENT METHOD OF FRESCO PAINTING RESTORED: AND DRAWINGS, FOR PUBLIC INSPECTION, AND FOR SALE BY PRIVATE CONTRACT

CONDITIONS OF SALE

I. *One third of the price to be paid at the time of Purchase, and the remainder on Delivery.*
II. *The Pictures and Drawings to remain in the Exhibition till its close, which will be on the 29th of September 1809; and the Picture of the Canterbury Pilgrims, which is to be engraved, will be Sold only on condition of its remaining in the Artist's hands twelve months, when it will be delivered to the Buyer.*

PREFACE

THE eye that can prefer the Colouring of Titian and Rubens to that of Michael Angelo and Rafael, ought to be modest and to doubt its own powers. Connoisseurs talk as if Rafael and Michael Angelo had never seen the colouring of Titian or Correggio: They ought to know that Correggio was born two years before Michael Angelo, and Titian but four years after. Both Rafael and Michael Angelo knew the Venetian, and contemned and rejected all he did with the utmost disdain, as that which is fabricated for the purpose to destroy art.

Mr. B. appeals to the Public, from the judgment of those narrow blinking eyes, that have too long governed art in a dark corner. The eyes of stupid cunning never will be pleased with the work any more than with the look of self-devoting genius. The quarrel of the Florentine with the Venetian is not because he does not understand Drawing, but because he does not understand Colouring. How should he, he who does not know how to draw a hand or a foot, know how to colour it?

Colouring does not depend on where the Colours are put,

358

but on where the lights and darks are put, and all depends on Form or Outline, on where that is put; where that is wrong, the Colouring never can be right; and it is always wrong in Titian and Correggio, Rubens and Rembrandt. Till we get rid of Titian and Correggio, Rubens and Rembrandt, We never shall equal Rafael and Albert Durer, Michael Angelo, and Julio Romano.

INDEX TO THE CATALOGUE

NUMBER I.

The spiritual form of Nelson guiding Leviathan, in whose wreathings are infolded the Nations of the Earth.

Clearness and precision have been the chief objects in painting these Pictures. Clear colours unmudded by oil, and firm and determinate lineaments unbroken by shadows, which ought to display and not to hide form, as is the practice of the latter schools of Italy and Flanders.

NUMBER II, ITS COMPANION.

The spiritual form of Pitt, guiding Behemoth; he is that Angel
who, pleased to perform the Almighty's orders, rides on the
whirlwind, directing the storms of war: He is ordering the
Reaper to reap the Vine of the Earth, and the Plowman to
Plow up the Cities and Towers.

This Picture also is a proof of the power of colours unsullied
with oil or with any cloggy vehicle. Oil has falsely been supposed to give strength to colours: but a little consideration must
shew the fallacy of this opinion. Oil will not drink or absorb
colour enough to stand the test of very little time and of the
air. It deadens every colour it is mixed with, at its first mixture,
and in a little time becomes a yellow mask over all that it
touches. Let the works of modern Artists since Rubens' time
witness the villainy of some one of that time, who first brought
oil Painting into general opinion and practice: since which we
have never had a Picture painted, that could shew itself by
the side of an earlier production. Whether Rubens or Vandyke,
or both, were guilty of this villainy, is to be enquired in another
work on Painting, and who first forged the silly story and
known falshood, about John of Bruges inventing oil colours: in
the meantime let it be observed, that before Vandyke's time,
and in his time all the genuine Pictures are on Plaster or Whit-
ing grounds and none since.

The two pictures of Nelson and Pitt are compositions of a
mythological cast, similar to those Apotheoses of Persian, Hindoo, and Egyptian Antiquity, which are still preserved on rude
monuments, being copies from some stupendous originals now
lost or perhaps buried till some happier age. The Artist having
been taken in vision into the ancient republics, monarchies, and
patriarchates of Asia has seen those wonderful originals, called
in the Sacred Scriptures the Cherubim, which were sculptured
and painted on walls of Temples, Towers, Cities, Palaces, and
erected in the highly cultivated states of Egypt, Moab, Edom,
Aram, among the Rivers of Paradise, being originals from
which the Greeks and Hetrurians copied Hercules Farnese,
Venus of Medicis, Apollo Belvidere, and all the grand works of
ancient art. They were executed in a very superior style to those

justly admired copies, being with their accompaniments terrific and grand in the highest degree. The Artist has endeavoured to emulate the grandeur of those seen in his vision, and to apply it to modern Heroes, on a smaller scale.

No man can believe that either Homer's Mythology, or Ovid's, were the production of Greece or of Latium; neither will any one believe, that the Greek statues, as they are called, were the invention of Greek Artists; perhaps the Torso is the only original work remaining; all the rest are evidently copies, though fine ones, from greater works of the Asiatic Patriarchs. The Greek Muses are daughters of Mnemosyne, or Memory, and not of Inspiration or Imagination, therefore not authors of such sublime conceptions. Those wonderful originals seen in my visions, were some of them one hundred feet in height; some were painted as pictures, and some carved as basso relievos, and some as groupes of statues, all containing mythological and recondite meaning, where more is meant than meets the eye. The Artist wishes it was now the fashion to make such monuments, and then he should not doubt of having a national commission to execute these two Pictures on a scale that is suitable to the grandeur of the nation, who is the parent of his heroes, in high finished fresco, where the colours would be as pure and as permanent as precious stones, though the figures were one hundred feet in height.

All Frescoes are as high finished as miniatures or enamels, and they are known to be unchangeable; but oil, being a body itself, will drink or absorb very little colour, and changing yellow, and at length brown, destroys every colour it is mixed with, especially every delicate colour. It turns every permanent white to a yellow and brown putty, and has compelled the use of that destroyer of colour, white lead; which, when its protecting oil is evaporated, will become lead again. This is an awful thing to say to oil Painters; they may call it madness, but it is true. All genuine old little pictures, called Cabinet Pictures, are in fresco and not in oil. Oil was not used, except by blundering ignorance, till after Vandyke's time, but the art of fresco painting being lost, oil became a fetter to genius, and a dungeon to art. But one convincing proof among many others, that these assertions are true is, that real gold and silver cannot be used with oil, as they are in all the old pictures and in Mr. B.'s frescoes.

NUMBER III.

Sir Jeffery Chaucer and the nine and twenty Pilgrims on their journey to Canterbury.

The time chosen is early morning, before sunrise, when the jolly company are just quitting the Tabarde Inn. The Knight and Squire with the Squire's Yeoman lead the Procession; next follow the youthful Abbess, her nun and three priests; her greyhounds attend her—

> "Of small hounds had she, that she fed
> With roast flesh, milk and wastel bread."

Next follow the Friar and Monk; then the Tapiser, the Pardoner, and the Somner and Manciple. After these "Our Host", who occupies the center of the cavalcade, directs them to the Knight as the person who would be likely to commence their task of each telling a tale in their order. After the Host follows the Shipman, the Haberdasher, the Dyer, the Franklin, the Physician, the Plowman, the Lawyer, the poor Parson, the Merchant, the Wife of Bath, the Miller, the Cook, the Oxford Scholar, Chaucer himself, and the Reeve comes as Chaucer has described:

> "And ever he rode hinderest of the rout."

These last are issuing from the gateway of the Inn; the Cook and the Wife of Bath are both taking their morning's draft of comfort. Spectators stand at the gateway of the Inn, and are composed of an old Man, a Woman, and Children.

The Landscape is an eastward view of the country, from the Tabarde Inn, in Southwark, as it may be supposed to have appeared in Chaucer's time, interspersed with cottages and villages; the first beams of the Sun are seen above the horizon; some buildings and spires indicate the situation of the great City; the Inn is a gothic building, which Thynne in his Glossary says was the lodging of the Abbot of Hyde, by Winchester. On the Inn is inscribed its title, and a proper advantage is taken of this circumstance to describe the subject of the Picture. The words written over the gateway of the Inn are as follow: "The Tabarde Inn, by Henry Baillie, the lodgynge-house for

Pilgrims, who journey to Saint Thomas's Shrine at Canterbury."

The characters of Chaucer's Pilgrims are the characters which compose all ages and nations: as one age falls, another rises, different to mortal sight, but to immortals only the same; for we see the same characters repeated again and again, in animals, vegetables, minerals, and in men; nothing new occurs in identical existence; Accident ever varies, Substance can never suffer change nor decay.

Of Chaucer's characters, as described in his Canterbury Tales, some of the names or titles are altered by time, but the characters themselves for ever remain unaltered, and consequently they are the physiognomies or lineaments of universal human life, beyond which Nature never steps. Names alter, things never alter. I have known multitudes of those who would have been monks in the age of monkery, who in this deistical age are deists. As Newton numbered the stars, and as Linneus numbered the plants, so Chaucer numbered the classes of men.

The Painter has consequently varied the heads and forms of his personages into all Nature's varieties; the Horses he has also varied to accord to their Riders; the costume is correct according to authentic monuments.

The Knight and Squire with the Squire's Yeoman lead the procession, as Chaucer has also placed them first in his prologue. The Knight is a true Hero, a good, great, and wise man; his whole length portrait on horseback, as written by Chaucer, cannot be surpassed. He has spent his life in the field; has ever been a conqueror, and is that species of character which in every age stands as the guardian of man against the oppressor. His son is like him with the germ of perhaps greater perfection still, as he blends literature and the arts with his warlike studies. Their dress and their horses are of the first rate, without ostentation, and with all the true grandeur that unaffected simplicity when in high rank always displays. The Squire's Yeoman is also a great character, a man perfectly knowing in his profession:

"And in his hand he bare a mighty bow."

Chaucer describes here a mighty man; one who in war is the worthy attendant on noble heroes.

The Prioress follows these with her female chaplain:

> "Another Nonne also with her had she,
> That was her Chaplaine, and Priests three."

This Lady is described also as of the first rank, rich and honoured. She has certain peculiarities and little delicate affectations, not unbecoming in her, being accompanied with what is truly grand and really polite; her person and face Chaucer has described with minuteness; it is very elegant, and was the beauty of our ancestors, till after Elizabeth's time, when voluptuousness and folly began to be accounted beautiful.

Her companion and her three priests were no doubt all perfectly delineated in those parts of Chaucer's work which are now lost; we ought to suppose them suitable attendants on rank and fashion.

The Monk follows these with the Friar. The Painter has also grouped with these the Pardoner and the Sompnour and the Manciple, and has here also introduced one of the rich citizens of London: Characters likely to ride in company, all being above the common rank in life or attendants on those who were so.

For the Monk is described by Chaucer as a man of the first rank in society, noble, rich, and expensively attended; he is a leader of the age, with certain humorous accompaniments in his character, that do not degrade, but render him an object of dignified mirth, but also with other accompaniments not so respectable.

The Friar is a character also of a mixed kind:

> "A friar there was, a wanton and a merry."

but in his office he is said to be a "full solemn man": eloquent, amorous, witty, and satyrical; young, handsome, and rich; he is a complete rogue, with constitutional gaiety enough to make him a master of all the pleasures of the world.

> "His neck was white as the flour de lis,
> Thereto strong he was as a champioun."

It is necessary here to speak of Chaucer's own character, that I may set certain mistaken critics right in their conception of the humour and fun that occurs on the journey. Chaucer is himself the great poetical observer of men, who in every age is born to record and eternize its acts. This he does as a master, as a father, and superior, who looks down on their little follies from the Emperor to the Miller; sometimes with severity, oftener with joke and sport.

Accordingly Chaucer has made his Monk a great tragedian, one who studied poetical art. So much so, that the generous Knight is, in the compassionate dictates of his soul, compelled to cry out:

" 'Ho,' quoth the Knyght,—'good Sir, no more of this;
That ye have said is right ynough I wis;
And mokell more, for little heaviness
Is right enough for much folk, as I guesse.
I say, for me, it is a great disease,
Whereas men have been in wealth and ease,
To heare of their sudden fall, alas,
And the contrary is joy and solas.' "

The Monk's definition of tragedy in the proem to his tale is worth repeating:

"Tragedie is to tell a certain story,
As old books us maken memory,
Of hem that stood in great prosperity,
And be fallen out of high degree,
Into miserie, and ended wretchedly."

Though a man of luxury, pride and pleasure, he is a master of art and learning, though affecting to despise it. Those who can think that the proud Huntsman and Noble Housekeeper, Chaucer's monk, is intended for a buffoon or a burlesque character, know little of Chaucer.

For the Host who follows this group, and holds the center of the cavalcade, is a first rate character, and his jokes are no trifles; they are always, though uttered with audacity, and equally free with the Lord and the Peasant, they are always substantially and weightily expressive of knowledge and experience; Henry Baillie, the keeper of the greatest Inn of the greatest City, for such was the Tabarde Inn in Southwark, near London: our Host was also a leader of the age.

By way of illustration, I instance Shakspeare's Witches in Macbeth. Those who dress them for the stage, consider them as wretched old women, and not as Shakspeare intended, the Goddesses of Destiny; this shews how Chaucer has been misunderstood in his sublime work. Shakspeare's Fairies also are the rulers of the vegetable world, and so are Chaucer's; let them be so considered, and then the poet will be understood, and not else.

But I have omitted to speak of a very prominent character, the Pardoner, the Age's Knave, who always commands and domineers over the high and low vulgar. This man is sent in every age for a rod and scourge, and for a blight, for a trial of men, to divide the classes of men; he is the most holy sanctuary, and he is suffered by Providence for wise ends, and has also his great use, and his grand leading destiny.

His companion, the Sompnour, is also a Devil of the first magnitude, grand, terrific, rich and honoured in the rank of which he holds the destiny. The uses to Society are perhaps equal of the Devil and of the Angel, their sublimity, who can dispute.

> "In daunger had he at his own gise,
> The young girls of his diocese,
> And he knew well their counsel, &c."

The principal figure in the next groupe is the Good Parson; an Apostle, a real Messenger of Heaven, sent in every age for its light and its warmth. This man is beloved and venerated by all, and neglected by all; He serves all, and is served by none, he is, according to Christ's definition, the greatest of his age. Yet he is a Poor Parson of a town. Read Chaucer's description of the Good Parson, and bow the head and the knee to him, who, in every age, sends us such a burning and a shining light. Search, O ye rich and powerful, for these men and obey their counsel, then shall the golden age return: But alas! you will not easily distinguish him from the Friar or the Pardoner; they, also, are "full solemn men," and their counsel you will continue to follow.

I have placed by his side the Sergeant at Lawe, who appears delighted to ride in his company, and between him and his brother, the Plowman; as I wish men of Law would always ride with them, and take their counsel, especially in all difficult points. Chaucer's Lawyer is a character of great venerableness, a Judge, and a real master of the jurisprudence of his age.

The Doctor of Physic is in this groupe, and the Franklin, the voluptuous country gentleman, contrasted with the Physician, and on his other hand, with two Citizens of London. Chaucer's characters live age after age. Every age is a Canterbury Pilgrimage; we all pass on, each sustaining one or other of these characters; nor can a child be born, who is not one of these characters of Chaucer. The Doctor of Physic is described as the first of his profession; perfect, learned, completely Master and Doctor in his art. Thus the reader will observe, that Chaucer makes every one of his characters perfect in his kind; every one is an Antique Statue; the image of a class, and not of an imperfect individual.

This groupe also would furnish substantial matter, on which volumes might be written. The Franklin is one who keeps open table, who is the genius of eating and drinking, the Bacchus; as the Doctor of Physic is the Esculapius, the Host is the Silenus, the Squire is the Apollo, the Miller is the Hercules, &c. Chaucer's characters are a description of the eternal Principles that exist in all ages. The Franklin is voluptuousness itself, most nobly pourtrayed:

"It snewed in his house of meat and drink."

The Plowman is simplicity itself, with wisdom and strength for its stamina. Chaucer has divided the ancient character of Hercules between his Miller and his Plowman. Benevolence is the plowman's great characteristic; he is thin with excessive labour, and not with old age, as some have supposed:

"He would thresh, and thereto dike and delve
For Christe's sake, for every poore wight,
Withouten hire, if it lay in his might."

Visions of these eternal principles or characters of human life appear to poets, in all ages; the Grecian gods were the ancient Cherubim of Phoenicia; but the Greeks, and since them the Moderns, have neglected to subdue the gods of Priam. These gods are visions of the eternal attributes, or divine names, which, when erected into gods, become destructive to humanity. They ought to be the servants, and not the masters of man, or of society. They ought to be made to sacrifice to Man, and not man compelled to sacrifice to them; for when separated from man or humanity, who is Jesus the Saviour, the vine of eternity, they are thieves and rebels, they are destroyers.

The Plowman of Chaucer is Hercules in his supreme eternal state, divested of his spectrous shadow; which' is the Miller, a terrible fellow, such as exists in all times and places for the trial of men, to astonish every neighbourhood with brutal strength and courage, to get rich and powerful to curb the pride of Man.

The Reeve and the Manciple are two characters of the most consummate worldly wisdom. The Shipman, or Sailor, is a similar genius of Ulyssean art; but with the highest courage superadded.

The Citizens and their Cook are each leaders of a class. Chaucer has been somehow made to number four citizens, which would make his whole company, himself included, thirty-one. But he says there was but nine and twenty in his company:

"Full nine and twenty in a company."

The Webbe, or Weaver, and the Tapiser, or Tapestry Weaver, appear to me to be the same person; but this is only an opinion, for full nine and twenty may signify one more, or less. But I dare say that Chaucer wrote "A Webbe Dyer", that is, a Cloth Dyer:

"A Webbe Dyer, and a Tapiser."

The Merchant cannot be one of the Three Citizens, as his dress is different, and his character is more marked, whereas Chaucer says of his rich citizens:

"All were yclothed in o liverie."

The characters of Women Chaucer has divided into two classes, the Lady Prioress and the Wife of Bath. Are not these leaders of the ages of men? The lady prioress, in some ages, predominates; and in some the wife of Bath, in whose character Chaucer has been equally minute and exact, because she is also a scourge and a blight. I shall say no more of her, nor expose what Chaucer has left hidden; let the young reader study what he has said of her: it is useful as a scare-crow. There are of such characters born too many for the peace of the world.

I come at length to the Clerk of Oxenford. This character varies from that of Chaucer, as the contemplative philosopher varies from the poetical genius. There are always these two classes of learned sages, the poetical and the philosophical. The painter has put them side by side, as if the youthful clerk had put himself under the tuition of the mature poet. Let the Philosopher always be the servant and scholar of inspiration and all will be happy.

Such are the characters that compose this Picture, which was painted in self-defence against the insolent and envious imputation of unfitness for finished and scientific art; and this imputation, most artfully and industriously endeavoured to be propagated among the public by ignorant hirelings. The painter courts comparison with his competitors, who, having received fourteen hundred guineas and more, from the profits of his designs in that well-known work, Designs for Blair's Grave, have left him to shift for himself, while others, more obedient to an employer's opinions and directions, are employed, at a great expence, to produce works, in succession to his, by which they acquired public patronage. This has hitherto been his lot —to get patronage for others and then to be left and neglected, and his work, which gained that patronage, cried down as eccentricity and madness; as unfinished and neglected by the artist's violent temper; he is sure the works now exhibited will give the lie to such aspersions.

Those who say that men are led by interest are knaves. A knavish character will often say, "of what interest is it to me to do so and so?" I answer, "of none at all, but the contrary, as you well know. It is of malice and envy that you have done this; hence I am aware of you, because I know that you act, not from interest, but from malice, even to your own destruction." It is therefore become a duty which Mr. B. owes to the Public, who have always recognized him, and patronized him, however hidden by artifices, that he should not suffer such things to be done, or be hindered from the public Exhibition of his finished productions by any calumnies in future.

The character and expression in this picture could never have been produced with Rubens's light and shadow, or with Rembrandt's, or anything Venetian or Flemish. The Venetian and Flemish practice is broken lines, broken masses, and broken colours. Mr. B.'s practice is unbroken lines, unbroken masses, and unbroken colours. Their art is to lose form; his art is to find form, and to keep it. His arts are opposite to theirs in all things.

As there is a class of men whose whole delight is the destruction of men, so there is a class of artist, whose whole art and science is fabricated for the purpose of destroying art. Who these are is soon known: "by their works ye shall know them." All who endeavour to raise up a style against Rafael, Mich. Angelo, and the Antique; those who separate Painting from Drawing; who look if a picture is well Drawn, and, if it is, immediately cry out that it cannot be well Coloured,—those are the men.

But to shew the stupidity of this class of men nothing need be done but to examine my rival's prospectus.

The two first characters in Chaucer, the Knight and the Squire, he has put among his rabble; and indeed his prospectus calls the Squire the fop of Chaucer's age. Now hear Chaucer:

> "Of his Stature, he was of even length,
> And wonderly deliver, and of great strength;
> And he had be sometime in Chivauchy,
> In Flanders, in Artois, and in Picardy,
> And borne him well, as of so litele space."

Was this a fop?

> "Well could he sit a horse, and faire ride,
> He could songs make, and eke well indite
> Just, and eke dance, pourtray, and well write."

Was this a fop?

> "Curteis he was, and meek, and serviceable;
> And kerft before his fader at the table."

Was this a fop?

It is the same with all his characters; he has done all by chance, or perhaps his fortune,—money, money. According to his prospectus he has Three Monks; these he cannot find in Chaucer, who has only One Monk, and that no vulgar character, as he has endeavoured to make him. When men cannot read they should not pretend to paint. To be sure Chaucer is a little difficult to him who has only blundered over novels, and catchpenny trifles of booksellers. Yet a little pains ought to be taken even by the ignorant and weak. He has put The Reeve, a vulgar fellow, between his Knight and Squire, as if he was resolved to go contrary in every thing to Chaucer, who says of the Reeve:

"And ever he rode hinderest of the rout."

In this manner he has jumbled his dumb dollies together and is praised by his equals for it; for both himself and his friend are equally masters of Chaucer's language. They both think that the Wife of Bath is a young, beautiful, blooming damsel, and H—— says, that she is the Fair Wife of Bath, and that the Spring appears in her Cheeks. Now hear what Chaucer has made her say of herself, who is no modest one:

" 'But Lord when it remembereth me
Upon my youth and on my jollity
It tickleth me about the heart root,
Unto this day it doth my heart boot,
That I have had my world as in my time;
But age, alas, that all will envenime
Hath me bireft my beauty and my pith
Let go; farewell: the Devil go therewith,
The flower is gone; there is no more to tell.
The bran, as best I can, I now mote sell;
And yet to be right merry will I fond,—
Now forth to tell of my fourth husband'."

She has had four husbands, a fit subject for this painter; yet the painter ought to be very much offended with his friend H——, who has called his "a common scene", "and very ordinary forms", which is the truest part of all, for it is so, and very wretchedly so indeed. What merit can there be in a picture of which such words are spoken with truth?

But the prospectus says that the Painter has represented Chaucer himself as a knave, who thrusts himself among honest people, to make game of and laugh at them; though I must do justice to the painter, and say that he has made him look more like a fool than a knave. But it appears in all the writings of

Chaucer, and particularly in his Canterbury Tales, that he was very devout, and paid respect to true enthusiastic superstition. He has laughed at his knaves and fools, as I do now. But he has respected his True Pilgrims, who are a majority of his company, and are not thrown together in the random manner that Mr. S—— has done. Chaucer has no where called the Plowman old, worn out with age and labour, as the prospectus has represented him, and says that the picture has done so too. He is worn down with labour, but not with age. How spots of brown and yellow, smeared about at random, can be either young or old, I cannot see. It may be an old man; it may be a young one; it may be any thing that a prospectus pleases. But I know that where there are no lineaments there can be no character. And what connoisseurs call touch, I know by experience, must be the destruction of all character and expression, as it is of every lineament.

The scene of Mr. S——'s Picture is by Dulwich Hills, which was not the way to Canterbury; but perhaps the painter thought he would give them a ride round about, because they were a burlesque set of scare-crows, not worth any man's respect or care.

But the painter's thoughts being always upon gold, he has introduced a character that Chaucer has not; namely, a Goldsmith; for so the prospectus tells us. Why he introduced a Goldsmith, and what is the wit of it, the prospectus does not explain. But it takes care to mention the reserve and modesty of the Painter; this makes a good epigram enough:

> The fox, the owl, the spider, and the mole,
> By sweet reserve and modesty get fat.

But the prospectus tells us, that the painter has introduced a Sea Captain; Chaucer has a Ship-man, a Sailor, a Trading Master of a Vessel, called by courtesy Captain, as every master of a boat is; but this does not make him a Sea Captain. Chaucer has purposely omitted such a personage, as it only exists in certain periods: it is the soldier by sea. He who would be a Soldier in inland nations is a sea captain in commercial nations.

All is misconceived, and its mis-execution is equal to its misconception. I have no objection to Rubens and Rembrandt being employed, or even to their living in a palace; but it shall not be at the expence of Rafael and Michael Angelo living in a cottage, and in contempt and derision. I have been scorned long enough by these fellows, who owe me all that they have; it shall be so no longer.

> I found them blind, I taught them how to see;
> And, now, they know me not, nor yet themselves.

NUMBER IV.

The Bard, from Gray.

> "On a rock, whose haughty brow
> Frown'd o'er old Conway's foaming flood,
> Robed in the sable garb of woe,
> With haggard eyes the Poet stood;
> Loose his beard, and hoary hair
> Stream'd like a meteor to the troubled air.

> "Weave the warp, and weave the woof,
> The winding sheet of Edward's race."

Weaving the winding sheet of Edward's race by means of sounds of spiritual music and its accompanying expressions of articulate speech is a bold, and daring, and most masterly conception, that the public have embraced and approved with avidity. Poetry consists in these conceptions; and shall Painting be confined to the sordid drudgery of fac-simile representations of merely mortal and perishing substances, and not be as poetry and music are, elevated into its own proper sphere of invention and visionary conception? No, it shall not be so! Painting, as well as poetry and music, exists and exults in immortal thoughts. If Mr. B.'s Canterbury Pilgrims had been done by any other power than that of the poetic visionary, it would have been just as dull as his adversary's.

The Spirits of the murdered bards assist in weaving the deadly woof:

> "With me in dreadful harmony they join
> And weave, with bloody hands, the tissue of thy line."

The connoisseurs and artists who have made objections to Mr. B.'s mode of representing spirits with real bodies, would do well to consider that the Venus, the Minerva, the Jupiter, the Apollo, which they admire in Greek statues are all of them representations of spiritual existences, of Gods immortal, to the mortal perishing organ of sight; and yet they are embodied and organized in solid marble. Mr. B. requires the same latitude, and all is well. The Prophets describe what they saw in Vision as real and existing men, whom they saw with their imaginative and immortal organs; the Apostles the same; the clearer the organ the more distinct the object. A Spirit and a Vision are not, as the modern philosophy supposes, a cloudy vapour, or a nothing: they are organized and minutely articulated beyond all that the mortal and perishing nature can produce. He who does not imagine in stronger and better lineaments, and in stronger and better light than his perishing and mortal eye can see, does not imagine at all. The painter of this work asserts that all his imaginations appear to him infinitely more perfect and more minutely organized than any thing seen by his mortal eye. Spirits are organized men. Moderns wish to draw figures without lines, and with great and heavy shadows; are not shadows more unmeaning than lines, and more heavy? O who can doubt this!

King Edward and his Queen Elenor are prostrated, with their horses, at the foot of a rock on which the Bard stands; prostrated by the terrors of his harp on the margin of the river Conway, whose waves bear up a corse of a slaughtered bard at the foot of the rock. The armies of Edward are seen winding among the mountains.

"He wound with toilsome march his long array."

Mortimer and Gloucester lie spell bound behind their king. The execution of this picture is also in Water Colours, or Fresco.

NUMBER V.

The Ancient Britons

In the last Battle of King Arthur, only Three Britons escaped; these were the Strongest Man, the Beautifullest Man, and the Ugliest Man; these three marched through the field unsubdued, as Gods, and the Sun of Britain set, but shall arise

again with tenfold splendor when Arthur shall awake from
sleep, and resume his dominion over earth and ocean.

The three general classes of men who are represented by
the most Beautiful, the most Strong, and the most Ugly, could
not be represented by any historical facts but those of our
own country, the Ancient Britons, without violating costume.
The Britons (say historians) were naked civilized men, learned,
studious, abstruse in thought and contemplation; naked, simple,
plain in their acts and manners; wiser than after-ages. They
were overwhelmed by brutal arms, all but a small remnant;
Strength, Beauty, and Ugliness escaped the wreck, and remain
for ever unsubdued, age after age.

The British Antiquities are now in the Artist's hands; all his
visionary contemplations, relating to his own country and its
ancient glory, when it was, as it again shall be, the source of
learning and inspiration. Arthur was a name for the constellation Arcturus, or Boötes, the keeper of the North Pole. And
all the fables of Arthur and his round table; of the warlike
naked Britons; of Merlin; of Arthur's conquest of the whole
world; of his death, or sleep, and promise to return again; of
the Druid monuments or temples; of the pavement of Watling-
street; of London stone; of the caverns in Cornwall, Wales,
Derbyshire, and Scotland; of the Giants of Ireland and Britain;
of the elemental beings called by us by the general name of
Fairies; and of these three who escaped, namely Beauty,
Strength, and Ugliness. Mr. B. has in his hands poems of the
highest antiquity. Adam was a Druid, and Noah; also Abraham
was called to succeed the Druidical age, which began to turn
allegoric and mental signification into corporeal command,
whereby human sacrifice would have depopulated the earth.
All these things are written in Eden. The artist is an inhabitant
of that happy country; and if every thing goes on as it has
begun, the world of vegetation and generation may expect to be
opened again to Heaven, through Eden, as it was in the beginning.

The Strong Man represents the human sublime. The Beautiful Man represents the human pathetic, which was in the
wars of Eden divided into male and female. The Ugly Man
represents the human reason. They were originally one man,
who was fourfold; he was self-divided, and his real humanity

slain on the stems of generation, and the form of the fourth was like the Son of God. How he became divided is a subject of great sublimity and pathos. The Artist has written it under inspiration, and will, if God please, publish it; it is voluminous, and contains the ancient history of Britain, and the world of Satan and of Adam.

In the mean time he has painted this Picture, which supposes \that in the reign of that British Prince, who lived in the fifth century, there were remains of those naked Heroes in the Welch Mountains; they are there now, Gray saw them in the person of his bard on Snowdon; there they dwell in naked simplicity; happy is he who can see and converse with them above the shadows of generation and death. The giant Albion, was Patriarch of the Atlantic; he is the Atlas of the Greeks, one of those the Greeks called Titans. The stories of Arthur are the acts of Albion, applied to a Prince of the fifth century, who conquered Europe, and held the Empire of the world in the dark age, which the Romans never again recovered. In this Picture, believing with Milton the ancient British History, Mr. B. has done as all the ancients did, and as all the moderns who are worthy of fame, given the historical fact in its poetical vigour so as it always happens, and not in that dull way that some Historians pretend, who, being weakly organized themselves, cannot see either miracle or prodigy; all is to them a dull round of probabilities and possibilities; but the history of all times and places is nothing else but improbabilities and impossibilities; what we should say was impossible if we did not see it always before our eyes.

The antiquities of every Nation under Heaven, is no less sacred than that of the Jews. They are the same thing, as Jacob Bryant and all antiquaries have proved. How other antiquities came to be neglected and disbelieved, while those of the Jews are collected and arranged, is an enquiry worthy both of the Antiquarian and the Divine. All had originally one language, and one religion: this was the religion of Jesus, the Everlasting Gospel. Antiquity preaches the Gospel of Jesus. The reasoning historian, turner and twister of causes and consequences, such as Hume, Gibbon, and Voltaire, cannot with all their artifice turn or twist one fact or disarrange self evident action and reality. Reasons and opinions concerning acts are not history. Acts themselves alone are history, and these are neither the exclusive property of Hume, Gibbon, nor Voltaire, Echard, Rapin, Plutarch, nor Herodotus. Tell me the Acts, O historian, and leave me to reason upon them as I please; away with your reasoning and your rubbish! All that is not action is not worth reading. Tell me the What; I do not want you to tell me the Why, and the How; I can find that out myself, as well as you can, and I will not be fooled by you into opinions, that you please to impose, to disbelieve what you think improbable or impossible. His opinions, who does not see spiritual agency, is not worth any man's reading; he who rejects a fact because it is improbable, must reject all History and retain doubts only.

It has been said to the Artist, "take the Apollo for the model of your beautiful Man, and the Hercules for your strong Man, and the Dancing Fawn for your Ugly Man." Now he comes to his trial. He knows that what he does is not inferior to the grandest Antiques. Superior they cannot be, for human power cannot go beyond either what he does, or what they have done; it is the gift of God, it is inspiration and vision. He had resolved to emulate those precious remains of antiquity; he has done so and the result you behold; his ideas of strength and beauty have not been greatly different. Poetry as it exists now on earth, in the various remains of ancient authors, Music as it exists in old tunes or melodies, Painting and Sculpture as it exists in the remains of Antiquity and in the works of more modern genius, is Inspiration, and cannot be surpassed; it is perfect and eternal. Milton, Shakspeare, Michael Angelo, Rafael, the finest specimens of Ancient Sculpture and Painting and Architecture, Gothic, Grecian, Hindoo and Egyptian, are the extent of the human mind. The human mind cannot go beyond the gift of God, the Holy Ghost. To suppose that Art can go beyond the finest specimens of Art that are now in the world, is not knowing what Art is; it is being blind to the gifts of the spirit.

It will be necessary for the Painter to say something concerning his ideas of Beauty, Strength and Ugliness.

The Beauty that is annexed and appended to folly, is a lamentable accident and error of the mortal and perishing life; it does but seldom happen; but with this unnatural mixture the sublime Artist can have nothing to do; it is fit for the burlesque. The Beauty proper for sublime art is lineaments, or forms and features that are capable of being the receptacles of intellect; accordingly the Painter has given in his Beautiful Man, his own idea of intellectual Beauty. The face and limbs that deviates or alters least, from infancy to old age, is the face and limbs of greatest Beauty and perfection.

The Ugly, likewise, when accompanied and annexed to imbecility and disease, is a subject for burlesque and not for historical grandeur; the Artist has imagined his Ugly Man, one approaching to the beast in features and form, his forehead small, without frontals; his jaws large; his nose high on the ridge, and narrow; his chest, and the stamina of his make, comparatively little, and his joints and his extremities large; his eyes, with scarce any whites, narrow and cunning, and every thing tending toward what is truly Ugly, the incapability of intellect.

The Artist has considered his strong Man as a receptacle of Wisdom, a sublime energizer; his features and limbs do not spindle out into length without strength, nor are they too large and unwieldy for his brain and bosom. Strength consists in accumulation of power to the principal seat, and from thence a regular gradation and subordination; strength is compactness, not extent nor bulk.

The strong Man acts from conscious superiority, and marches on in fearless dependence on the divine decrees, raging with the inspirations of a prophetic mind. The Beautiful Man acts from duty and anxious solicitude for the fates of those for whom he combats. The Ugly Man acts from love of carnage, and delight in the savage barbarities of war, rushing with sportive precipitation into the very jaws of the affrighted enemy.

The Roman Soldiers rolled together in a heap before them: "Like the rolling thing before the whirlwind"; each shew a different character, and a different expression of fear, or revenge, or envy, or blank horror, or amazement, or devout wonder and unresisting awe.

The dead and the dying, Britons naked, mingled with armed Romans, strew the field beneath. Among these the last of the Bards who were capable of attending warlike deeds, is seen falling, outstretched among the dead and the dying, singing to his harp in the pains of death.

Distant among the mountains are Druid Temples, similar to Stone Henge. The Sun sets behind the mountains, bloody with the day of battle.

The flush of health in flesh exposed to the open air, nourished by the spirits of forests and floods in that ancient happy period, which history has recorded, cannot be like the sickly daubs of Titian or Rubens. Where will the copier of nature as it now is, find a civilized man, who is accustomed to go naked? Imagination only can furnish us with colouring appropriate, such as is found in the Frescos of Rafael and Michael Angelo: the disposition of forms always directs colouring in works of true art. As to a modern Man, stripped from his load of cloathing he is like a dead corpse. Hence Reubens, Titian, Correggio and all of that class, are like leather and chalk; their men are like leather, and their women like chalk, for the disposition of their forms will not admit of grand colouring; in Mr. B.'s Britons the blood is seen to circulate in their limbs; he defies competition in colouring.

NUMBER VI.

"A Spirit vaulting from a cloud to turn and wind a fiery Pegasus."—*Shakspeare. The Horse of Intellect is leaping from the cliffs of Memory and Reasoning; it is a barren Rock: it is also called the Barren Waste of Locke and Newton.*

This Picture was done many years ago, and was one of the first Mr. B. ever did in Fresco; fortunately, or rather, providentially, he left it unblotted and unblurred, although molested continually by blotting and blurring demons; but he was also compelled to leave it unfinished, for reasons that will be shewn in the following.

NUMBER VII.

The Goats, an experiment Picture.

The subject is taken from the Missionary Voyage, and varied from the literal fact for the sake of picturesque scenery. The savage girls had dressed themselves with vine leaves, and some goats on board the missionary ship stripped them off presently. This Picture was painted at intervals, for experiment with the colours, and is laboured to a superabundant blackness; it has, however, that about it, which may be worthy the attention of the Artist and Connoisseur for reasons that follow.

NUMBER VIII.

The spiritual Preceptor, an experiment Picture.

The subject is taken from the Visions of Emanuel Swedenborg, Universal Theology, No. 623. The Learned, who strive to
ascend into Heaven by means of learning, appear to Children
like dead horses, when repelled by the celestial spheres. The
works of this visionary are well worthy the attention of Painters and Poets; they are foundations for grand things; the reason they have not been more attended to is because corporeal
demons have gained a predominance; who the leaders of these
are, will be shewn below. Unworthy Men who gain fame
among Men, continue to govern mankind after death, and in
their spiritual bodies oppose the spirits of those who worthily
are famous; and, as Swedenborg observes, by entering into
disease and excrement, drunkenness and concupiscence, they
possess themselves of the bodies of mortal men, and shut the
doors of mind and of thought by placing Learning above Inspiration. O Artist! you may disbelieve all this, but it shall be at
your own peril.

NUMBER IX.

Satan calling up his Legions, from Milton's Paradise Lost; a
composition for a more perfect Picture afterward executed
for a Lady of high rank. An experiment Picture.

This Picture was likewise painted at intervals, for experiment
on colours without any oily vehicle; it may be worthy of attention, not only on account of its composition, but of the great
labour which has been bestowed on it, that is, three or four
times as much as would have finished a more perfect Picture;
the labour has destroyed the lineaments; it was with difficulty
brought back again to a certain effect, which it had at first,
when all the lineaments were perfect.
These Pictures, among numerous others painted for experiment, were the result of temptations and perturbations, labouring to destroy Imaginative power, by means of that infernal
machine called Chiaro Oscuro, in the hands of Venetian and
Flemish Demons, whose enmity to the Painter himself, and to

all Artists who study in the Florentine and Roman Schools, may be removed by an exhibition and exposure of their vile tricks. They cause that every thing in art shall become a Machine. They cause that the execution shall be all blocked up with brown shadows. They put the original Artist in fear and doubt of his own original conception. The spirit of Titian was particularly active in raising doubts concerning the possibility of executing without a model, and when once he had raised the doubt, it became easy for him to snatch away the vision time after time, for, when the Artist took his pencil to execute his ideas, his power of imagination weakened so much and darkened, that memory of nature, and of Pictures of the various schools possessed his mind, instead of appropriate execution resulting from the inventions; like walking in another man's style, or speaking, or looking in another man's style and manner, unappropriate and repugnant to your own individual character; tormenting the true Artist, till he leaves the Florentine, and adopts the Venetian practice, or does as Mr. B. has done, has the courage to suffer poverty and disgrace, till he ultimately conquers.

Rubens is a most outrageous demon, and by infusing the remembrances of his Pictures and style of execution, hinders all power of individual thought: so that the man who is possessed by this demon loses all admiration of any other Artist but Rubens and those who were his imitators and journeymen; he causes to the Florentine and Roman Artist fear to execute; and though the original conception was all fire and animation, he loads it with hellish brownness, and blocks up all its gates of light except one, and that one he closes with iron bars, till the victim is obliged to give up the Florentine and Roman practice and adopt the Venetian and Flemish.

Correggio is a soft and effeminate, and consequently a most cruel demon, whose whole delight is to cause endless labour to whoever suffers him to enter his mind. The story that is told in all Lives of the Painters about Correggio being poor and but badly paid for his Pictures is altogether false; he was a petty Prince in Italy, and employed numerous Journeymen in manufacturing (as Rubens and Titian did) the Pictures that go under his name. The manual labour in these Pictures of Correggio is immense, and was paid for originally at the immense prices that those who keep manufactories of art always charge to their employers, while they themselves pay their journeymen little enough. But though Correggio was not poor, he will make any true artist so who permits him to enter his mind, and take possession of his affections; he infuses a love of soft and even tints without boundaries, and of endless reflected lights that confuse one another, and hinder all correct drawing from appearing to be correct; for if one of Rafael or Michael Angelo's figures was to be traced, and Correggio's reflections and refractions to be added to it, there would soon be an end of proportion and strength, and it would be weak, and pappy, and lumbering, and thick headed, like his own works; but then it would have softness and evenness by a twelvemonth's labour, where a month would with judgment have finished it better and higher; and the poor wretch who executed it, would be the Correggio that the life writers have written of: a drudge and a miserable man, compelled to softness by poverty. I say again, O Artist, you may disbelieve all this, but it shall be at your own peril.

Note. These experiment Pictures have been bruized and knocked about without mercy, to try all experiments.

NUMBER X.

The Bramins.—A Drawing.

The subject is, Mr. Wilkin translating the Geeta; an ideal design, suggested by the first publication of that part of the Hindoo Scriptures translated by Mr. Wilkin. I understand that my Costume is incorrect, but in this I plead the authority of the ancients, who often deviated from the Habits to preserve the Manners, as in the instance of the Laocoön, who, though a priest, is represented naked.

NUMBER XI.

The Body of Abel found by Adam and Eve; Cain, who was about to bury it, fleeing from the face of his Parents.—A Drawing.

NUMBER XII.

The Soldiers casting lots for Christ's Garment.—A Drawing.

NUMBER XIII.

Jacob's Ladder.—A Drawing.

NUMBER XIV.

*The Angels hovering over the Body of Jesus in the Sepulchre.—
A Drawing.*

The above four drawings the Artist wishes were in Fresco on
an enlarged scale to ornament the altars of churches, and to
make England, like Italy, respected by respectable men of other
countries on account of Art. It is not the want of Genius that
can hereafter be laid to our charge; the Artist who has done
these Pictures and Drawings will take care of that; let those
who govern the Nation take care of the other. The times require that every one should speak out boldly; England expects
that every man should do his duty, in Arts, as well as in Arms
or in the Senate.

NUMBER XV.

Ruth.—A Drawing.

This Design is taken from that most pathetic passage in the
Book of Ruth where Naomi, having taken leave of her daughters in law with intent to return to her own country, Ruth cannot leave her, but says, "Whither thou goest I will go; and
where thou lodgest I will lodge; thy people shall be my people,
and thy God my God; where thou diest I will die, and there
will I be buried; God do so to me and more also, if ought but
death part thee and me."
The distinction that is made in modern times between a
Painting and a Drawing proceeds from ignorance of art. The
merit of a Picture is the same as the merit of a Drawing. The
dawber dawbs his Drawings; he who draws his Drawings draws
his Pictures. There is no difference between Rafael's Cartoons
and his Frescos, or Pictures, except that the Frescos, or Pictures, are more finished. When Mr. B. formerly painted in oil
colours his Pictures were shewn to certain painters and con-

noisseurs, who said that they were very admirable Drawings on canvass, but not Pictures; but they said the same of Rafael's Pictures. Mr. B. thought this the greatest of compliments, though it was meant otherwise. If losing and obliterating the outline constitutes a Picture, Mr. B. will never be so foolish as to do one. Such art of losing the outlines is the art of Venice and Flanders; it loses all character, and leaves what some people call expression; but this is a false notion of expression; expression cannot exist without character as its stamina; and neither character nor expression can exist without firm and determinate outline. Fresco Painting is susceptible of higher finishing than Drawing on Paper, or than any other method of Painting. But he must have a strange organization of sight who does not prefer a Drawing on Paper to a Dawbing in Oil by the same master, supposing both to be done with equal care.

The great and golden rule of art, as well as of life, is this: That the more distinct, sharp, and wirey the bounding line, the more perfect the work of art, and the less keen and sharp, the greater is the evidence of weak imitation, plagiarism, and bungling. Great inventors, in all ages, knew this: Protogenes and Apelles knew each other by this line. Rafael and Michael Angelo and Albert Dürer are known by this and this alone. The want of this determinate and bounding form evidences the want of idea in the artist's mind, and the pretence of the plagiary in all its branches. How do we distinguish the oak from the beech, the horse from the ox, but by the bounding outline? How do we distinguish one face or countenance from another, but by the bounding line and its infinite inflexions and movements? What is it that builds a house and plants a garden, but the definite and determinate? What is it that distinguishes honesty from knavery, but the hard and wirey line of rectitude and certainty in the actions and intentions? Leave out this line, and you leave out life itself; all is chaos again, and the line of the almighty must be drawn out upon it before man or beast can exist. Talk no more then of Correggio, or Rembrandt, or any other of those plagiaries of Venice or Flanders. They were but the lame imitators of lines drawn by their predecessors, and their works prove themselves contemptible, disarranged imitations, and blundering, misapplied copies.

NUMBER XVI.

The Penance of Jane Shore in St. Paul's Church.—A Drawing.

This Drawing was done above Thirty Years ago, and proves to the Author, and he thinks will prove to any discerning eye, that the productions of our youth and of our maturer age are equal in all essential points. If a man is master of his profession, he cannot be ignorant that he is so; and if he is not employed by those who pretend to encourage art, he will employ himself, and laugh in secret at the pretences of the ignorant, while he has every night dropped into his shoe, as soon as he puts it off, and puts out the candle, and gets into bed, a reward for the labours of the day, such as the world cannot give, and patience and time await to give him all that the world can give.

FINIS

A Vision of the Last Judgment

P. 70.

THE Last Judgment [will be] when all those are Cast away who trouble Religion with Questions concerning Good & Evil or Eating of the Tree of those Knowledges or Reasonings which hinder the Vision of God, turning all into a Consuming Fire. When Imagination, Art & Science & all Intellectual Gifts, all the Gifts of the Holy Ghost, are look'd upon as of no use & only Contention remains to Man, then the Last Judgment begins, & its Vision is seen by the Imaginative Eye of Every one according to the situation he holds.

P. 68.

The Last Judgment is not Fable or Allegory, but Vision. Fable or Allegory are a totally distinct & inferior kind of Poetry. Vision or Imagination is a Representation of what Eternally Exists, Really & Unchangeably. Fable or Allegory is Form'd by the daughters of Memory. Imagination is surrounded by the daughters of Inspiration, who in the aggregate are call'd Jerusalem. Fable is allegory, but what Critics call The Fable, is Vision itself. The Hebrew Bible & the Gospel of Jesus are not Allegory, but Eternal Vision or Imagination of All that Exists. Note here that Fable or Allegory is seldom without some Vision. Pilgrim's Progress is full of it, the Greek Poets the same; but Allegory & Vision ought to be known as Two Distinct Things, & so call'd for the Sake of Eternal Life. Plato has made Socrates say that Poets & Prophets do not know or Understand what they write or Utter; this is a most Pernicious Falshood. If they do not, pray is an inferior kind to be call'd Knowing? Plato confutes himself.

386

PP. 68-69.

The Last Judgment is one of these Stupendous Visions. I have represented it as I saw it; to different People it appears differently as every thing else does; for tho' on Earth things seem Permanent, they are less permanent than a Shadow, as we all know too well.

The Nature of Visionary Fancy, or Imagination, is very little known, & the Eternal nature & permanence of its ever Existent Images is consider'd as less permanent than the things of Vegetative & Generative Nature; yet the Oak dies as well as the Lettuce, but Its Eternal Image & Individuality never dies, but renews by its seed; just so the Imaginative Image returns by the seed of Contemplative Thought; the Writings of the Prophets illustrate these conceptions of the Visionary Fancy by their various sublime & Divine Images as seen in the Worlds of Vision.

PP. 71-72.

The Learned m . . . or Heroes; this is an . . . & not Spiritual . . . while the Bible . . . of Virtue & Vice . . . as they are Ex . . . is the Real Di . . . Things. The . . . when they Assert that Jupiter usurped the Throne of his Father, Saturn, & brought on an Iron Age & Begat on Mnemosyne, or Memory, The Greek Muses, which are not Inspiration as the Bible is. Reality was Forgot, & the Vanities of Time & Space only Remember'd & call'd Reality. Such is the Mighty difference between Allegoric Fable & Spiritual Mystery. Let it here be Noted that the Greek Fables originated in Spiritual Mystery & Real Visions, which are lost & clouded in Fable & Allegory, while the Hebrew Bible & the Greek Gospel are Genuine, Preserv'd by the Saviour's Mercy. The Nature of my Work is Visionary or Imaginative; it is an Endeavour to Restore what the Ancients call'd the Golden Age.

PP. 69-70.

This world of Imagination is the world of Eternity; it is the divine bosom into which we shall all go after the death of the Vegetated body. This World of Imagination is Infinite & Eternal, whereas the world of Generation, or Vegetation, is Finite & Temporal. There Exist in that Eternal World the Permanent Realities of Every Thing which we see reflected in this Vegetable Glass of Nature. All Things are comprehended in their Eternal Forms in the divine body of the Saviour, the True Vine

of Eternity, The Human Imagination, who appear'd to Me as
Coming to Judgment among his Saints & throwing off the Temporal that the Eternal might be Establish'd; around him were
seen the Images of Existences according to a certain order Suited
to my Imaginative Eye as follows.

> *Query, the Above ought to follow the description.*
> *Here follows the description of the Picture:*

P. 76.

Jesus seated between the Two Pillars, Jachin & Boaz, with
the Word of divine Revelation on his knees, & on each side the
four & twenty Elders sitting in judgment; the Heavens opening
around him by unfolding the clouds around his throne. The Old
H[eave]n & O[ld] Earth are passing away & the N[ew]
H[eaven] & N[ew] Earth descending. The Just arise on his
right & the wicked on his Left hand. A sea of fire issues from
before the throne. Adam & Eve appear first, before the Judgment seat in humiliation. Abel surrounded by Innocents, &
Cain, with the flint in his hand with which he slew his brother,
falling with the head downward. From the Cloud on which Eve
stands, Satan is seen falling headlong wound round by the tail
of the serpent whose bulk, nail'd to the Cross round which he
wreathes, is falling into the Abyss. Sin is also represented as a
female bound in one of the Serpent's folds, surrounded by her
fiends. Death is Chain'd to the Cross, & Time falls together
with death, dragged down by a demon crown'd with Laurel;
another demon with a Key has the charge of Sin & is dragging
her down by the hair; beside them a figure is seen, scaled with
iron scales from head to feet, precipitating himself into the
Abyss with the Sword & Balances: he is Og, King of Bashan.

On the Right, Beneath the Cloud on which Abel Kneels, is
Abraham with Sarah & Isaac, also Hagar & Ishmael. Abel
kneels on a bloody Cloud &c. (*to come in here as two
leaves forward*).

P. 80.

Abel kneels on a bloody cloud descriptive of those Churches
before the flood, that they were fill'd with blood & fire & vapour
of smoke; even till Abraham's time the vapor & heat was not
extinguish'd; these States Exist now. Man Passes on, but States

remain for Ever; he passes thro' them like a traveller who may as well suppose that the places he has passed thro' exist no more, as a Man may suppose that the States he has pass'd thro' Exist no more. Every thing is Eternal.

P. 79.

In Eternity one Thing never Changes into another Thing. Each Identity is Eternal: consequently Apuleius's Golden Ass & Ovid's Metamorphosis & others of the like kind are Fable; yet they contain Vision in a sublime degree, being derived from real Vision in More ancient Writings. Lot's Wife being Changed into [a] Pillar of Salt alludes to the Mortal Body being render'd a Permanent Statue, but not Changed or Transformed into Another Identity while it retains its own Individuality. A Man can never become Ass nor Horse; some are born with shapes of Men, who may be both, but Eternal Identity is one thing & Corporeal Vegetation is another thing. Changing Water into Wine by Jesus & into Blood by Moses relates to Vegetable Nature also.

PP. 76-77.

Ishmael is Mahomed, & on the left, beneath the falling figure of Cain, is Moses casting his tables of stone into the deeps. It ought to be understood that the Persons, Moses & Abraham, are not here meant, but the States Signified by those Names, the Individuals being representatives or Visions of those States as they were reveal'd to Mortal Man in the Series of Divine Revelations as they are written in the Bible; these various States I have seen in my Imagination; when distant they appear as One Man, but as you approach they appear Multitudes of Nations. Abraham hovers above his posterity, which appear as Multitudes of Children ascending from the Earth, surrounded by Stars, as it was said: "As the Stars of Heaven for Multitude." Jacob & his Twelve Sons hover beneath the feet of Abraham & recieve their children from the Earth. I have seen, when at a distance, Multitudes of Men in Harmony appear like a single Infant, sometimes in the Arms of a Female; this represented the Church.

But to proceed with the description of those on the Left hand—beneath the Cloud on which Moses kneels is two figures, a Male & Female, chain'd together by the feet; they represent those who perish'd by the flood; beneath them a multitude of their associates are seen falling headlong; by the side of them is a Mighty fiend with a Book in his hand, which is Shut; he represents the person nam'd in Isaiah, xxii c. & 20v., Eliakim, the Son of Hilkiah: he drags Satan down headlong: he is crown'd with oak; by the side of the Scaled figure representing Og, King of Bashan, is a Figure with a Basket, emptying out the vanities of Riches & Worldly Honours: he is Araunah, the Jebusite, master of the threshing floor; above him are two figures, elevated on a Cloud, representing the Pharisees who plead their own Righteousness before the throne; they are weighed down by two fiends. Beneath the Man with the Basket are three fiery fiends with grey beards & scourges of fire: they represent Cruel Laws; they scourge a groupe of figures down into the deeps; beneath them are various figures in attitudes of contention representing various States of Misery, which, alas, every one on Earth is liable to enter into, & against which we should all watch. The Ladies will be pleas'd to see that I have represented the Furies by Three Men & not by three Women. It is not because I think the Ancients wrong, but they will be pleas'd to remember that mine is Vision & not Fable. The Spectator may suppose them Clergymen in the Pulpit, scourging Sin instead of Forgiving it.

The Earth beneath these falling Groupes of figures is rocky & burning, and seems as if convuls'd by Earthquakes; a Great City on fire is seen in the distance; the armies are fleeing upon the Mountains. On the foreground, hell is opened & many figures are descending into it down stone steps & beside a Gate beneath a rock where sin & death are to be closed Eternally by that Fiend who carries the key in one hand & drags them down with the other. On the rock & above the Gate a fiend with wings urges the wicked onwards with fiery darts; he is Hazael, the Syrian, who drives abroad all those who rebell against their Saviour; beneath the steps [is] Babylon, represented by a King crowned, Grasping his Sword and his Sceptre: he is just awaken'd out of his Grave; around him are other Kingdoms arising to Judgment, represented in this Picture as Single Personages according to the descriptions in the Prophets. The Figure dragging up a Woman by her hair represents the Inquisition, as do those contending on the sides of the Pit, & in Particular the Man strangling two women represents a Cruel Church.

P. 78.

Two persons, one in Purple, the other in Scarlet, are descending down the steps into the Pit; these are Caiaphas & Pilate—Two States where all those reside who Calumniate & Murder under Pretence of Holiness & Justice. Caiaphas has a Blue Flame like a Miter on his head. Pilate has bloody hands that never can be cleansed; the Females behind them represent the Females belonging to such States, who are under perpetual terrors & vain dreams, plots & secret deceit. Those figures that descend into the Flames before Caiaphas & Pilate are Judas & those of his Class. Achitophel is also here with the cord in his hand.

PP. 80-81.

Between the Figures of Adam & Eve appears a fiery Gulph descending from the sea of fire before the throne; in this Cataract Four Angels descend headlong with four trumpets to awake the dead; beneath these is the Seat of the Harlot, nam'd Mystery in the Revelations. She is siezed by Two Beings each with three heads; they represent Vegetative Existence; as it is written in Revelations, they strip her naked & burn her with fire; it represents the Eternal Consummation of Vegetable Life & Death with its Lusts. The wreathed Torches in their hands represents Eternal Fire which is the fire of Generation or Vegetation; it is an Eternal Consummation. Those who are blessed with Imaginative Vision see This Eternal Female & tremble at what others fear not, while they despise & laugh at what others fear. Her Kings & Councellors & Warriors descend in Flames, Lamenting & looking upon her in astonishment & Terror, & Hell is open'd beneath her Seat on the Left hand. Beneath her feet is a flaming Cavern in which is seen the Great Red Dragon with seven heads & ten Horns; he has Satan's book of Accusations lying on the Rock open before him; he is bound in chains by Two strong demons; they are Gog & Magog, who have been compell'd to subdue their Master (Ezekiel, xxxviii c, 8 v.) with their Hammer & Tongs, about to new-Create the Seven-Headed Kingdoms. The Graves beneath are open'd, & the dead awake & obey the call of the Trumpet; those on the Right hand awake in joy, those on the Left in Horror; beneath the Dragon's Cavern a Skeleton begins to Animate, starting into life at the Trumpet's sound, while the Wicked contend with each other on the brink of perdition. On the Right a Youthful couple are awaked by their Children; an Aged patriarch is awaked by his aged wife—He is Albion, our Ancestor, patriarch of the Atlantic Continent, whose History Preceded that of the Hebrews & in whose Sleep, or Chaos, Creation began; at their head the Aged Woman is Brittannica, the Wife of Albion: Jerusalem is their daughter. Little Infants creep out of the flowery mould into the Green fields of the blessed who in various joyful companies embrace & ascend to meet Eternity.

The Persons who ascend to Meet the Lord, coming in the Clouds with power & great Glory, are representations of those States described in the Bible under the Names of the Fathers before & after the Flood. Noah is seen in the Midst of these, canopied by a Rainbow, on his right hand Shem & on his Left Japhet; these three Persons represent Poetry, Painting & Music, the three Powers in Man of conversing with Paradise, which the flood did not Sweep away. Above Noah is the Church Universal, represented by a Woman Surrounded by Infants. There is such a State in Eternity: it is composed of the Innocent civilized Heathen & the Uncivilized Savage, who, having not the Law, do by Nature the things contain'd in the Law. This State appears like a Female crown'd with stars, driven into the Wilderness; she has the Moon under her feet. The Aged Figure with Wings, having a writing tablet & taking account of the numbers who arise, is That Angel of the Divine Presence mention'd in Exodus, xiv c., 19 v. & in other Places; this Angel is frequently call'd by the Name of Jehovah Elohim, The "I am" of the Oaks of Albion.

Around Noah & beneath him are various figures Risen into the Air; among these are Three Females, representing those who are not of the dead but of those found alive at the Last Judgment; they appear to be innocently gay & thoughtless, not being among the condemn'd because ignorant of crime in the midst of a corrupted Age; the Virgin Mary was of this Class. A Mother Meets her numerous Family in the Arms of their Father; these are representations of the Greek Learned & Wise, as also of those of other Nations, such as Egypt & Babylon, in which were multitudes who shall meet the Lord coming in the Clouds.

The Children of Abraham, or Hebrew Church, are represented as a Stream of Figures, on which are seen Stars somewhat like the Milky way; they ascend from the Earth where

Figures kneel Embracing above the Graves, & Represent Religion, or Civilized Life such as it is in the Christian Church, who are the Offspring of the Hebrew.

PP. 82-84.

Just above the graves & above the spot where the Infants creep out of the Ground stand two, a Man & Woman; these are the Primitive Christians. The two Figures in purifying flames by the side of the dragon's cavern represents the Latter state of the Church when on the verge of Perdition, yet protected by a Flaming Sword. Multitudes are seen ascending from the Green fields of the blessed in which a Gothic Church is representative of true Art, Call'd Gothic in All Ages by those who follow'd the Fashion, as that is call'd which is without Shape or Fashion. On the right hand of Noah a Woman with Children Represents the State Call'd Laban the Syrian; it is the Remains of Civilization in the State from whence Abraham was taken. Also on the right hand of Noah A Female descends to meet her Lover or Husband, representative of that Love, call'd Friendship, which Looks for no other heaven than their Beloved & in him sees all reflected as in a Glass of Eternal Diamond.

On the right hand of these rise the diffident & Humble, & on their left a solitary Woman with her infant: these are caught up by three aged Men who appear as suddenly emerging from the blue sky for their help. These three Aged Men represent divine Providence as oppos'd to, & distinct from, divine vengeance, represented by three Aged men on the side of the Picture among the Wicked, with scourges of fire.

If the Spectator could enter into these Images in his Imagination, approaching them on the Fiery Chariot of his Contemplative Thought, if he could Enter into Noah's Rainbow or into his bosom, or could make a Friend & Companion of one of these Images of wonder, which always intreats him to leave mortal things (as he must know), then would he arise from his Grave, then would he meet the Lord in the Air & then he would be happy. General Knowledge is Remote Knowledge; it is in Particulars that Wisdom consists & Happiness too. Both in Art & in Life, General Masses are as Much Art as a Pasteboard Man is Human. Every Man has Eyes, Nose & Mouth; this Every Idiot knows, but he who enters into & discriminates most minutely the Manners & Intentions, the Characters in all their branches, is the alone Wise or Sensible Man, & on this discrimination All Art is founded. I intreat, then, that the Spectator will attend to the Hands & Feet, to the Lineaments of the Countenances; they are all descriptive of Character, & not a line is drawn without intention, & that most discriminate & particular. As Poetry admits not a Letter that is Insignificant, so Painting admits not a Grain of Sand or a Blade of Grass Insignificant—much less an Insignificant Blur or Mark.

Above the Head of Noah is Seth; this State call'd Seth is Male & Female in a higher state of Happiness & wisdom than Noah, being nearer the State of Innocence; beneath the feet of Seth two figures represent the two Seasons of Spring & Autumn, while beneath the feet of Noah four Seasons represent the Changed State made by the flood.

By the side of Seth is Elijah; he comprehends all the Prophetic Characters; he is seen on his fiery Chariot, bowing before the throne of the Saviour; in like manner The figures of Seth & his wife comprehends the Fathers before the flood & their Generations; when seen remote they appear as One Man; a little below Seth on his right are Two Figures, a Male & Female, with numerous Children; these represent those who were not in the Line of the Church & yet were Saved from among the Antediluvians who Perished; between Seth & these a female figure represents the Solitary State of those who, previous to the Flood, walked with God.

All these arise toward the opening Cloud before the Throne, led onward by triumphant Groupes of Infants, & the Morning Stars sing together. Between Seth & Elijah three Female Figures crown'd with Garlands Represent Learning & Science, which accompanied Adam out of Eden.

The Cloud that opens, rolling apart before the throne & before the New Heaven & the New Earth, is Composed of Various Groupes of Figures, particularly the Four Living Creatures mention'd in Revelations as Surrounding the Throne; these I suppose to have the chief agency in removing the old heavens & the old Earth to make way for the New Heaven & the New Earth, to descend from the throne of God & of the Lamb; that Living Creature on the Left of the Throne Gives to the Seven Angels the Seven Vials of the wrath of God, with which they, hovering over the deeps beneath, pour out upon the wicked their Plagues; the Other Living Creatures are descending with a Shout & with the Sound of the Trumpet, directing the Combats in the upper Elements; in the two Corners of the Picture, on the Left hand Apollyon is foiled before the Sword of Michael, & on the Right the Two Witnesses are subduing their Enemies.

On the Cloud are open'd the Books of Remembrance of Life & of Death: before that of Life, on the Right, some figures bow in humiliation; before that of Death, on the Left, the Pharisees are pleading their own Righteousness; the one shines with beams of Light, the other utters Lightnings & tempests.

A Last Judgment is Necessary because Fools flourish. Nations Flourish under Wise Rulers & are depress'd under foolish Rulers; it is the same with Individuals as Nations; works of Art can only be produc'd in Perfection where the Man is either in Affluence or is Above the Care of it. Poverty is the Fool's Rod, which at last is turn'd on his own back; this is A Last Judgment—when Men of Real Art Govern & Pretenders Fall. Some People & not a few Artists have asserted that the Painter of this Picture would not have done so well if he had been properly Encourag'd. Let those who think so, reflect on the State of Nations under Poverty & their incapability of Art; tho' Art is Above Either, the Argument is better for Affluence than Poverty; & tho' he would not have been a greater Artist, yet he would have produc'd Greater works of Art in proportion to his means. A Last Judgment is not for the purpose of making Bad Men better, but for the Purpose of hindering them from opressing the Good with Poverty & Pain by means of Such Vile Arguments & Insinuations.

Around the Throne Heaven is open'd & the Nature of Eternal Things Display'd, All Springing from the Divine Humanity. All beams from him & as he himself has said, All dwells in him. He is the Bread & the Wine; he is the Water of Life; accordingly on Each Side of the opening Heaven appears an Apostle; that on the Right Represents Baptism, that on the Left Represents the Lord's Supper. All Life consists of these Two, Throwing off Error & Knaves from our company continually & Recieving Truth or Wise Men into our Company continually. He who is out of the Church & opposes it is no less an Agent of Religion than he who is in it; to be an Error & to be Cast out is a part of God's design. No man can Embrace True Art till he has Explor'd & cast out False Art (such is the Nature of Mortal Things), or he will be himself Cast out by those who have Already Embraced True Art. Thus My Picture is a History of Art & Science, the Foundation of Society, Which is

Humanity itself. What are all the Gifts of the Spirit but Mental Gifts? Whenever any Individual Rejects Error & Embraces Truth, a Last Judgment passes upon that Individual.

P. 85.

Over the Head of the Saviour & Redeemer The Holy Spirit, like a Dove, is surrounded by a blue Heaven in which are the two Cherubim that bow'd over the Ark, for here the temple is open'd in Heaven & the Ark of the Covenant is as a Dove of Peace. The Curtains are drawn apart, Christ having rent the Veil. The Candlestick & the Table of Shew-bread appear on Each side; a Glorification of Angels with Harps surround the Dove.

The Temple stands on the Mount of God; from it flows on each side the River of Life, on whose banks Grows the tree of Life, among whose branches temples & Pinnacles, tents & pavilions, Gardens & Groves, display Paradise with its Inhabitants walking up & down in Conversations concerning Mental Delights. Here they are &c. (*as three leaves on*).

PP. 90-91.

Here they are no longer talking of what is Good & Evil, or of what is Right or Wrong, & puzzling themselves in Satan's Labyrinth, But are Conversing with Eternal Realities as they Exist in the Human Imagination. We are in a World of Generation & death, & this world we must cast off if we would be Painters such as Rafael, Mich. Angelo & the Ancient Sculptors; if we do not cast off this world we shall be only Venetian Painters, who will be cast off & Lost from Art.

P. 85.

Jesus is surrounded by Beams of Glory in which are seen all around him Infants emanating from him; these represent the Eternal Births of Intellect from the divine Humanity. A Rainbow surrounds the throne & the Glory, in which youthful Nuptials recieve the infants in their hands. In Eternity Woman is the Emanation of Man; she has No Will of her own. There is no such thing in Eternity as a Female Will, & Queens.

On the Side next Baptism are seen those call'd in the Bible Nursing Fathers & Nursing Mothers; they represent Education. On the Side next the Lord's Supper The Holy Family, consisting of Mary, Joseph, John the Baptist, Zacharias & Elizabeth, recieving the Bread & Wine, among other Spirits of the Just made perfect. Beneath these a Cloud of Women & Children are taken up, fleeing from the rolling Cloud which separates the Wicked from the Seats of Bliss. These represent those who, tho' willing, were too weak to Reject Error without the Assistance & Countenance of those Already in the Truth; for a Man Can only Reject Error by the Advice of a Friend or by the Immediate Inspiration of God; it is for this Reason among many others that I have put the Lord's Supper on the Left hand of the Throne, for it appears so at the Last Judgment, for a Protection.

PP. 91-92.

Many suppose that before the Creation All was Solitude & Chaos. This is the most pernicious Idea that can enter the Mind, as it takes away all sublimity from the Bible & Limits All Existence to Creation & to Chaos, To the Time & Space fixed by the Corporeal Vegetative Eye, & leaves the Man who entertains such an Idea the habitation of Unbelieving demons. Eternity Exists, and All things in Eternity, Independent of Creation which was an act of Mercy. I have represented those who are in Eternity by some in a Cloud within the Rainbow that Surrounds the Throne; they merely appear as in a Cloud when any thing of Creation, Redemption or Judgment are the Subjects of Contemplation, tho' their Whole Contemplation is concerning these things; the Reason they so appear is The Humiliation of the Reason & doubting Self-hood, & the Giving all up to Inspiration. By this it will be seen that I do not consider either the Just or the Wicked to be in a Supreme State, but to be every one of them States of the Sleep which the Soul may fall into in its deadly dreams of Good & Evil when it leaves Paradise following the Serpent.

P. 91 (*sideways*).

The Greeks represent Chronos or Time as a very Aged Man; this is Fable, but the Real Vision of Time is in Eternal Youth. I have, however, somewhat accomodated my Figure of Time to the common opinion, as I myself am also infected with it & my Visions also infected, & I see Time aged, alas, too much so.

Allegories are things that Relate to Moral Virtues. Moral Virtues do not Exist; they are Allegories & dissimulations. But Time & Space are Real Beings, a Male & a Female. Time is a Man, Space is a Woman, & her Masculine Portion is Death.

PP. 86, 90.

The Combats of Good & Evil is Eating of the Tree of Knowledge. The Combats of Truth & Error is Eating of the Tree of Life; these are not only Universal, but Particular. Each are Personified. There is not an Error but it has a Man for its Agent, that is, it is a Man. There is not a Truth but it has also a Man. Good & Evil are Qualities in Every Man, whether a Good or Evil Man. These are Enemies & destroy one another by every Means in their power, both of deceit & of open Violence. The deist & the Christian are but the Results of these Opposing Natures. Many are deists who would in certain Circumstances have been Christians in outward appearance. Voltaire was one of this number; he was as intolerant as an Inquisitor. Manners make the Man, not Habits. It is the same in Art: by their Works ye shall know them; the Knave who is Converted to Deism & the Knave who is Converted to Christianity is still a Knave, but he himself will not know it, tho' Every body else does. Christ comes, as he came at first, to deliver those who were bound under the Knave, not to deliver the Knave. He Comes to deliver Man, the Accused, & not Satan, the Accuser. We do not find any where that Satan is Accused of Sin; he is only accused of Unbelief & thereby drawing Man into Sin that he may accuse him. Such is the Last Judgment—a deliverance from Satan's Accusation. Satan thinks that Sin is displeasing to God; he ought to know that Nothing is displeasing to God but Unbelief & Eating of the Tree of Knowledge of Good & Evil.

P. 87.

Men are admitted into Heaven not because they have curbed & govern'd their Passions or have No Passions, but because they have Cultivated their Understandings. The Treasures of Heaven are not Negations of Passion, but Realities of Intellect, from which all the Passions Emanate Uncurbed in their Eternal Glory. The Fool shall not enter into Heaven let him be ever so Holy. Holiness is not The Price of Enterance into Heaven. Those who are cast out are All Those who, having no Passions of their own because No Intellect, Have spent their lives in Curbing & Governing other People's by the Various arts of Poverty & Cruelty of all kinds. Wo, Wo, Wo to you Hypocrites. Even Murder, the Courts of Justice, more merciful than the Church, are compell'd to allow is not done in Passion, but in Cool Blooded design & Intention.

The Modern Church Crucifies Christ with the Head Downwards.

PP. 92-95.

Many Persons, such as Paine & Voltaire, with some of the Ancient Greeks, say: "we will not converse concerning Good & Evil; we will live in Paradise & Liberty." You may do so in Spirit, but not in the Mortal Body as you pretend, till after the Last Judgment; for in Paradise they have no Corporeal & Mortal Body—that originated with the Fall & was call'd Death & cannot be removed but by a Last Judgment. While we are in the world of Mortality we Must Suffer. The Whole Creation Groans to be deliver'd; there will always be as many Hypocrites born as Honest Men, & they will always have superior Power in Mortal Things. You cannot have Liberty in this World without what you call Moral Virtue, & you cannot have Moral Virtue without the Slavery of that half of the Human Race who hate what you call Moral Virtue.

The Nature of Hatred & Envy & of All the Mischiefs in the World are here depicted. No one Envies or Hates one of his Own Party; even the devils love one another in their Way; they torment one another for other reasons than Hate or Envy; these are only employ'd against the Just. Neither can Seth Envy Noah, or Elijah Envy Abraham, but they may both of them Envy the Success of Satan or of Og or Molech. The Horse never Envies the Peacock, nor the Sheep the Goat, but they Envy a Rival in Life & Existence whose ways & means exceed their own, let him be of what Class of Animals he will; a dog will envy a Cat who is pamper'd at the expense of his comfort, as I have often seen. The Bible never tells us that devils torment one another thro' Envy; it is thro' this that they torment the Just—but for what do they torment one another? I answer: For the Coercive Laws of Hell, Moral Hypocrisy. They torment a Hypocrite when he is discover'd; they punish a Failure in the tormentor who has suffer'd the Subject of his torture to Escape. In Hell all is Self Righteousness; there is no such thing there as Forgiveness of Sin; he who does Forgive Sin is Crucified as an Abettor of Criminals, & he who performs Works of Mercy in Any shape whatever is punish'd &, if possible, destroy'd, not thro' envy or Hatred or Malice, but thro' Self Righteousness that thinks it does God service, which God is Satan. They do not Envy one another: They contemn & despise one another: Forgiveness of Sin is only at the Judgment Seat of Jesus the Saviour, where the Accuser is cast out, not because he Sins, but because he torments the Just & makes them do what he condemns as Sin & what he knows is opposite to their own Identity.

It is not because Angels are Holier than Men or Devils that makes them Angels, but because they do not Expect Holiness from one another, but from God only.

The Player is a liar when he says: "Angels are happier than Men because they are better." Angels are happier than Men & Devils because they are not always Prying after Good & Evil in one another & eating the Tree of Knowledge for Satan's Gratification.

Thinking as I do that the Creator of this World is a very Cruel Being, & being a Worshipper of Christ, I cannot help saying: "the Son, O how unlike the Father!" First God Almighty comes with a Thump on the Head. Then Jesus Christ comes with a balm to heal it.

The Last Judgment is an Overwhelming of Bad Art & Science. Mental Things are alone Real; what is call'd Corporeal, Nobody Knows of its Dwelling Place: it is in Fallacy, & its Existence an Imposture. Where is the Existence Out of Mind or Thought? Where is it but in the Mind of a Fool? Some People flatter themselves that there will be No Last Judgment & that Bad Art will be adopted & mixed with Good Art, That Error or Experiment will make a Part of Truth, & they Boast that it is its Foundation; these People flatter themselves: I will not Flatter them. Error is Created. Truth is Eternal. Error, or Creation, will be Burned up, & then, & not till Then, Truth or Eternity will appear. It is Burnt up the Moment Men cease to behold it. I assert for My Self that I do not behold the outward Creation & that to me it is hindrance & not Action; it is as the dirt upon my feet, No part of Me. "What," it will be Question'd, "When the Sun rises, do you not see a round disk of fire somewhat like a Guinea?" O no, no, I see an Innumerable company of the Heavenly host crying, "Holy, Holy, Holy is the Lord God Almighty." I question not my Corporeal or Vegetative Eye any more than I would Question a Window concerning a Sight. I look thro' it & not with it.

Letters

Lambeth
6 *Decembr.* 1795

DEAR SIR,

I congratulate you, not on any atchievement, because I know that the Genius that produces the Designs can execute them in any manner, notwithstanding the pretended Philosophy which teaches that Execution is the power of One & Invention of Another—Locke says it is the same faculty that Invents Judges, & I say he who can Invent can Execute.

As to laying on the Wax, it is as follows:

Take a cake of Virgin's Wax (I don't know what animal produces it) & stroke it regularly over the surface of a warm plate (the Plate must be warm enough to melt the Wax as it passes over), then immediately draw a feather over it & you will get an even surface which, when cold, will receive any impression minutely.

NOTE: The danger is in not covering the plate *all over.*

Now you will, I hope, shew all the family of Antique Borers that Peace & Plenty & Domestic Happiness is the Source of Sublime Art, & prove to the Abstract Philosophers that Enjoyment & not Abstinence is the food of Intellect.

Yours sincerely,
WILL BLAKE.

Health to Mrs. Cumberland & family.

The pressure necessary to roll off the lines is the same as when you print, or not quite so great. I have not been able to send a proof of the bath tho' I have done the corrections, my paper not being in order.

TO THE REVD. DR. TRUSLER

13 Hercules Buildings,
Lambeth,
August 23, 1799.

REVD. SIR,

I really am sorry that you are fall'n out with the Spiritual World, Especially if I should have to answer for it. I feel very sorry that your Ideas & Mine on Moral Painting differ so much as to have made you angry with my method of study. If I am wrong, I am wrong in good company. I had hoped your plan comprehended All Species of this Art, & Especially that you would not regret that Species which gives Existence to Every other, namely, Visions of Eternity. You say that I want somebody to Elucidate my Ideas. But you ought to know that What is Grand is necessarily obscure to Weak men. That which can be made Explicit to the Idiot is not worth my care. The wisest of the Ancients consider'd what is not too Explicit as the fittest for Instruction, becauses it rouzes the faculties to act. I name Moses, Solomon, Esop, Homer, Plato.

But as you have favor'd me with your remarks on my Design, permit me in return to defend it against a mistaken one, which is, That I have supposed Malevolence without a Cause. Is not Merit in one a Cause of Envy in another, & Serenity & Happiness & Beauty a Cause of Malevolence? But Want of Money & the Distress of A Thief can never be alleged as the Cause of his Thieving, for many honest people endure greater hardships with Fortitude. We must therefore seek the Cause elsewhere than in want of Money, for that is the Miser's passion, not the Thief's.

I have therefore proved your Reasonings Ill proportion'd, which you can never prove my figures to be; they are those of Michael Angelo, Rafael & the Antique, & of the best living Models. I percieve that your Eye is perverted by Caricature Prints, which ought not to abound so much as they do. Fun I love, but too much Fun is of all things the most loathsom. Mirth is better than Fun, & Happiness is better than Mirth. I feel that a Man may be happy in This World. And I know that This World Is a World of Imagination & Vision. I see Every thing I paint In This World, but Every body does not see alike. To the Eyes of a Miser a Guinea is far more beautiful than the Sun, & a bag worn with the use of Money has more beautiful proportions than a Vine filled with Grapes. The tree which moves some to tears of joy is in the Eyes of others only a Green thing which stands in the way. Some see Nature all Ridicule & Deformity, & by these I shall not regulate my proportions; & some scarce see Nature at all. But to the Eyes of the Man of Imagination, Nature is Imagination itself. As a man is, so he sees. As the Eye is formed, such are its Powers. You certainly Mistake, when you say that the Visions of Fancy are not to be found in This World. To Me This World is all One continued Vision of Fancy or Imagination, & I feel Flatter'd when I am told so. What is it sets Homer, Virgil & Milton in so high a rank of Art? Why is the Bible more Entertaining & Instructive than any other book? Is it not because they are addressed to the Imagination, which is Spiritual Sensation, & but mediately to the Understanding or Reason? Such is True Painting, and such was alone valued by the Greeks & the best modern Artists. Consider what Lord Bacon says: "Sense sends over to Imagination before Reason have judged, & Reason sends over to Imagination before the Decree can be acted." See Advancemt. of Learning, Part 2 P. 47 of first Edition.

But I am happy to find a Great Majority of Fellow Mortals who can Elucidate My Visions, & Particularly they have been Elucidated by Children, who have taken a greater delight in contemplating my Pictures than I even hoped. Neither Youth nor Childhood is Folly or Incapacity. Some Children are Fools & so are some Old Men. But There is a vast Majority on the side of Imagination or Spiritual Sensation.

To Engrave after another Painter is infinitely more laborious than to Engrave one's own Inventions. And of the size you require my price has been Thirty Guineas, & I cannot afford to do it for less. I had Twelve for the Head I sent you as a specimen; but after my own designs I could do at least Six times the quantity of labour in the same time, which will account for the difference of price as also that Chalk Engraving is at least six times as laborious as Aqua tinta. I have no objection to Engraving after another Artist. Engraving is the profession I was apprenticed to, & should never have attempted to live by anything else, If orders had not come in for my Designs & Paintings, which I have the pleasure to tell you are Increasing Every Day. Thus If I am a Painter it is not to be attributed to seek-

ing after. But I am contented whether I live by Painting or Engraving.

I am, Revd. Sir, your very obedient servant,

WILLIAM BLAKE.

TO GEORGE CUMBERLAND

Hercules Buildings,
Lambeth,
Augst. 26, 1799.

DEAR CUMBERLAND,

I ought long ago to have written to you to thank you for
your kind recommendation to Dr. Trusler, which, tho' it has
fail'd of success, is not the less to be remember'd by me with
Gratitude.

I have made him a Drawing in my best manner; he has sent
it back with a Letter full of Criticisms, in which he says It accords not with his Intentions, which are to Reject all Fancy
from his Work. How far he Expects to please, I cannot tell. But
as I cannot paint Dirty rags & old shoes where I ought to
place Naked Beauty or simple ornament, I despair of Ever
pleasing one Class of Men. Unfortunately our authors of books
are among this Class; how soon we shall have a change for
the better I cannot Prophecy. Dr. Trusler says: *"Your Fancy,*
from what I have seen of it, & I have seen variety at Mr. Cumberland's, seems to be in the other world, or the World of Spirits, which accords not with my Intentions, which, whilst living
in This World, Wish to follow *the Nature of it."* I could not
help smiling at the difference between the doctrines of Dr.
Trusler & those of Christ. But, however, for his own sake I am
sorry that a Man should be so enamour'd of Rowlandson's caricatures as to call them copies from life & manners, or fit Things
for a Clergyman to write upon.

Pray let me intreat you to persevere in your Designing; it is
the only source of Pleasure. All your other pleasures depend
upon It. It is the Tree; your Pleasures are the Fruit. Your Inventions of Intellectual Visions are the Stamina of every thing
you value. Go on, if not for your own sake, yet for ours, who
love & admire your works; but, above all, For the Sake of the
Arts. Do not throw aside for any long time the honour in-

tended you by Nature to revive the Greek workmanship. I study your outlines as usual, just as if they were antiques.

As to Myself, about whom you are so kindly Interested, I live by Miracle. I am Painting small Pictures from the Bible. For as to Engraving, in which art I cannot reproach myself with any neglect, yet I am laid by in a corner as if I did not Exist, & since my Young's Night Thoughts have been publish'd, Even Johnson & Fuseli have discarded my Graver. But as I know that he who Works & has his health cannot starve, I laugh at Fortune & Go on & on. I think I foresee better Things than I have ever seen. My Work pleases my employer, & I have an order for Fifty small Pictures at one Guinea each, which is something better than mere copying after another artist. But above all, I feel myself happy & contented let what will come; having passed now near twenty years in ups & downs, I am used to them, & perhaps a little practise in them may turn out to benefit. It is now Exactly Twenty years since I was upon the ocean of business, & tho' [I] laugh at Fortune, I am perswaded that She Alone is the Governor of Worldly Riches, & when it is Fit she will call on me; till then I wait with Patience, in hopes that She is busied among my Friends.

With Mine & My Wife's best compliments to Mrs. Cumberland, I remain,

Yours sincerely,

WILLM. BLAKE.

TO WILLIAM HAYLEY

Lambeth,
May 6, 1800.

DEAR SIR,

I am very sorry for your immense loss, which is a repetition of what all feel in this valley of misery and happiness mixed. I send the shadow of the departed angel, and hope the likeness is improved. The lips I have again lessened as you advise, and done a good many other softenings to the whole. I know that our deceased friends are more really with us than when they were apparent to our mortal part. Thirteen years ago I lost a brother, and with his spirit I converse daily and hourly in the spirit, and see him in my remembrance, in the regions of my imagination. I hear his advice, and even now write from his dictate. Forgive me for expressing to you my enthusiasm, which I wish all to partake of, since it is to me a source of immortal joy, even in this world. By it I am the companion of angels. May you continue to be so more and more; and to be more and more persuaded that every mortal loss is an immortal gain. The ruins of Time build mansions in Eternity.

I have also sent a proof of Pericles for your remarks, thanking you for the kindness with which you express them, and feeling heartily your grief with a brother's sympathy.

I remain,
Dear Sir,
Your humble servant,
WILLIAM BLAKE.

TO JOHN FLAXMAN

[*September* 12, 1800.]

MY DEAREST FRIEND,

It is to you I owe All my present Happiness. It is to you I owe perhaps the Principal Happiness of my life. I have presum'd on your friendship in staying so long away & not calling to know of your welfare, but hope now every thing is nearly completed for our removal to Felpham, that I shall see you on Sunday, as we have appointed Sunday afternoon to call on Mrs. Flaxman at Hampstead. I send you a few lines, which I hope you will Excuse. And As the time is arriv'd when Men shall again converse in Heaven & walk with Angels, I know you will be pleased with the Intention, & hope you will forgive the Poetry.

To My Dearest Friend, John Flaxman, these lines:

I bless thee, O Father of Heaven & Earth, that ever I saw Flaxman's face.
Angels stand round my Spirit in Heaven, the blessed of Heaven are my friends upon Earth.
When Flaxman was taken to Italy, Fuseli was given to me for a season,
And now Flaxman hath given me Hayley his friend to be mine, such my lot upon Earth.

Now my lot in the Heavens is this, Milton lov'd me in childhood & shew'd me his face.

Ezra came with Isaiah the Prophet, but Shakespeare in riper
years gave me his hand;

Paracelsus & Behmen appear'd to me, terrors appear'd in the
Heavens above

And in Hell beneath, & a mighty & awful change threatened
the Earth.

The American War began. All its dark horrors passed before
my face

Across the Atlantic to France. Then the French Revolution
commenc'd in thick clouds,

And My Angels have told me that seeing such visions I could
not subsist on the Earth,

But by my conjunction with Flaxman, who knows to forgive
Nervous Fear.

    I remain, for Ever Yours,   WILLIAM BLAKE.

Be so kind as to Read & then seal the Inclosed & send it on
its much beloved Mission.

TO JOHN FLAXMAN

Felpham,
Septr. 21, 1800, *Sunday Morning.*

DEAR SCULPTOR OF ETERNITY,

    We are safe arrived at our Cottage, which is more beautiful
than I thought it, & more convenient. It is a perfect Model for
Cottages &, I think, for Palaces of Magnificence, only Enlarging, not altering its proportions, & adding ornaments & not
principals. Nothing can be more Grand than its Simplicity &
Usefulness. Simple without Intricacy, it seems to be the Spontaneous Effusion of Humanity, congenial to the wants of Man.
No other formed House can ever please me so well; nor shall I
ever be perswaded, I believe, that it can be improved either in
Beauty or Use.

    Mr. Hayley recieved us with his usual brotherly affection. I
have begun to work. Felpham is a sweet place for Study, because it is more Spiritual than London. Heaven opens here on
all sides her golden Gates; her windows are not obstructed by

vapours, voices of Celestial inhabitants are more distinctly heard, & their forms more distinctly seen; & my Cottage is also a Shadow of their houses. My Wife & Sister are both well, courting Neptune for an embrace.

Our Journey was very pleasant; & tho' we had a great deal of Luggage, No Grumbling; All was Chearfulness & Good Humour on the Road, & yet we could not arrive at our Cottage before half past Eleven at night, owing to the necessary shifting of our Luggage from one Chaise to another; for we had Seven Different Chaises, & as many different drivers. We set out between Six & Seven in the Morning of Thursday, with Sixteen heavy boxes & portfolios full of prints. And Now Begins a New life, because another covering of Earth is shaken off. I am more famed in Heaven for my works than I could well concieve. In my Brain are studies & Chambers filled with books & pictures of old, which I wrote & painted in ages of Eternity before my mortal life; & those works are the delight & Study of Archangels. Why, then, should I be anxious about the riches or fame of mortality? The Lord our father will do for us & with us according to his divine will for our Good.

You, O dear Flaxman, are a Sublime Archangel, My Friend & Companion from Eternity; in the Divine bosom is our dwelling place. I look back into the regions of Reminiscence & behold our ancient days before this Earth appear'd in its vegetated mortality to my mortal vegetated Eyes. I see our houses of Eternity, which can never be separated, tho' our Mortal vehicles should stand at the remotest corners of heaven from each other.

Farewell, My Best Friend! Remember Me & My Wife in Love & Friendship to our Dear Mrs. Flaxman, whom we ardently desire to Entertain beneath our thatched roof of rusted gold, & believe me for ever to remain

Your Grateful & Affectionate,

WILLIAM BLAKE.

TO THOMAS BUTTS

Felpham, *Octr.* 2d 1800.

FRIEND OF RELIGION & ORDER,

I thank you for your very beautiful & encouraging Verses, which I account a Crown of Laurels, & I also thank you for your reprehension of follies by me foster'd. Your prediction will, I hope, be fulfilled in me, & in future I am the determined advocate of Religion & Humility, the two bands of Society. Having been so full of the Business of Settling the sticks & feathers of my nest, I have not got any forwarder with "the three Marys" or with any other of your commissions; but hope, now I have commenced a new life of industry, to do credit to that new life by Improved Works. Recieve from me a return of verses, such as Felpham produces by me, tho' not such as she produces by her Eldest Son; however, such as they are, I cannot resist the temptation to send them to you.

> To my Friend Butts I write
> My first Vision of Light,
> On the yellow sands sitting.
> The Sun was Emitting
> His Glorious beams
> From Heaven's high Streams.
> Over Sea, over Land
> My Eyes did Expand
> Into regions of air
> Away from all Care,
> Into regions of fire
> Remote from Desire;
> The Light of the Morning
> Heaven's Mountains adorning:
> In particles bright
> The jewels of Light
> Distinct shone & clear.
> Amaz'd & in fear
> I each particle gazed,
> Astonish'd, Amazed;
> For each was a Man
> Human-form'd. Swift I ran,
> For they beckon'd to me
> Remote by the Sea,
> Saying: "Each grain of Sand,
> Every Stone on the Land,
> Each rock & each hill,
> Each fountain & rill,
> Each herb & each tree,
> Mountain, hill, earth & sea,

Cloud, Meteor & Star,
Are Men seen Afar."
I stood in the Streams
Of Heaven's bright beams,
And Saw Felpham sweet
Beneath my bright feet
In soft Female charms;
And in her fair arms
My Shadow I knew
And my wife's shadow too,
And My Sister & Friend.
We like Infants descend
In our Shadows on Earth,
Like a weak mortal birth.
My Eyes more and more
Like a Sea without shore
Continue Expanding,
The Heavens commanding,
Till the Jewels of Light,
Heavenly Men beaming bright,
Appear'd as One Man,
Who complacent began
My limbs to infold
In his beams of bright gold;
Like dross purg'd away
All my mire & my clay.
Soft consum'd in delight
In his bosom Sun bright
I remain'd. Soft he smil'd,
And I heard his voice Mild
Saying: "This is My Fold,
O thou Ram horn'd with gold,
Who awakest from Sleep
On the Sides of the Deep.
On the Mountains around
The roarings resound
Of the lion & wolf,
The loud Sea & deep gulf.
These are guards of My Fold,
O thou Ram horn'd with gold!"
And the voice faded mild.
I remain'd as a Child;

All I ever had known
Before me bright Shone.
I saw you & your wife
By the fountains of Life.
Such the Vision to me
Appear'd on the sea.

Mrs. Butts will, I hope, Excuse my not having finish'd the Portrait. I wait for less hurried moments. Our Cottage looks more & more beautiful. And tho' the weather is wet, the Air is very Mild, much Milder than it was in London when we came away. Chichester is a very handsome City, Seven miles from us; we can get most Conveniences there. The Country is not so destitute of accomodations to our wants as I expected it would be. We have had but little time for viewing the Country, but what we have seen is Most Beautiful, & the People are Genuine Saxons, handsomer than the people about London. Mrs. Butts will Excuse the following lines:

To Mrs. Butts.

Wife of the Friend of those I most revere,
Recieve this tribute from a Harp sincere;
Go on in Virtuous Seed sowing on Mold
Of Human Vegetation, & Behold
Your Harvest Springing to Eternal Life,
Parent of Youthful Minds, & happy Wife!

W.B.

I am for Ever Yours,
WILLIAM BLAKE.

TO THOMAS BUTTS

Felpham,
Jany. 10, 1802.

DEAR SIR,
Your very kind & affectionate Letter & the many kind things you have said in it, call'd upon me for an immediate answer; but it found My Wife & Myself so Ill, & My wife so very ill, that till now I have not been able to do this duty. The Ague & Rheumatism have been almost her constant Enemies, which she has

combated in vain ever since we have been here; & her sickness is always my sorrow, of course. But what you tell me about your sight afflicted me not a little, & that about your health, in another part of your letter, makes me intreat you to take due care of both; it is a part of our duty to God & man to take due care of his Gifts; & tho' we ought not [to] think *more* highly of ourselves, yet we ought to think *As* highly of ourselves as immortals ought to think.

When I came down here, I was more sanguine than I am at present; but it was because I was ignorant of many things which have since occurred, & chiefly the unhealthiness of the place. Yet I do not repent of coming on a thousand accounts; & Mr. H., I doubt not, will do ultimately all that both he & I wish—that is, to lift me out of difficulty; but this is no easy matter to a man who, having Spiritual Enemies of such formidable magnitude, cannot expect to want natural hidden ones.

Your approbation of my pictures is a Multitude to Me, & I doubt not that all your kind wishes in my behalf shall in due time be fulfilled. Your kind offer of pecuniary assistance I can only thank you for at present, because I have enough to serve my present purpose here; our expenses are small, & our income, from our incessant labour, fully adequate to them at present. I am now engaged in Engraving 6 small plates for a New Edition of Mr. Hayley's Triumphs of Temper, from drawings by Maria Flaxman, sister to my friend the Sculptor, and it seems that other things will follow in course, if I do but Copy these well; but Patience! if Great things do not turn out, it is because such things depend on the Spiritual & not on the Natural World; & if it was fit for me, I doubt not that I should be Employ'd in Greater things; & when it is proper, my Talents shall be properly exercised in Public, as I hope they are now in private; for, till then, I leave no stone unturn'd & no path unexplor'd that lends to improvement in my beloved Arts. One thing of real consequence I have accomplish'd by coming into the country, which is to me consolation enough: namely, I have recollected all my scatter'd thoughts on Art & resumed my primitive & original ways of Execution in both painting & engraving, which in the confusion of London I had very much lost & obliterated from my mind. But whatever becomes of my labours, I would rather that they should be preserv'd in your Green House (not, as you mistakenly call it, dunghill) than in the cold gallery of fashion.—The Sun may yet shine, & then they will be brought into open air.

But you have so generously & openly desired that I will divide my griefs with you, that I cannot hide what it is now become my duty to explain.—My unhappiness has arisen from a source which, if explor'd too narrowly, might hurt my pecuniary circumstances, As my dependence is on Engraving at present, & particularly on the Engravings I have in hand for Mr. H.: & I find on all hands great objections to my doing anything but the meer drudgery of business, & intimations that if I do not confine myself to this, I shall not live; this has always pursu'd me. You will understand by this the source of all my uneasiness. This from Johnson & Fuseli brought me down here, & this from Mr. H. will bring me back again; for that I cannot live without doing my duty to lay up treasures in heaven is Certain & Determined, & to this I have long made up my mind, & why this should be made an objection to Me, while Drunkenness, Lewdness, Gluttony & even Idleness itself, does not hurt other men, let Satan himself Explain. The Thing I have most at Heart—more than life, or all that seems to make life comfortable without—Is the Interest of True Religion & Science, & whenever any thing appears to affect that Interest (Especially if I myself omit any duty to my Station as a Soldier of Christ), It gives me the greatest of torments. I am not ashamed, afraid, or averse to tell you what Ought to be Told: That I am under the direction of Messengers from Heaven, Daily & Nightly; but the nature of such things is not, as some suppose, without trouble or care. Temptations are on the right hand & left; behind, the sea of time & space roars & follows swiftly; he who keeps not right onward is lost, & if our footsteps slide in clay, how can we do otherwise than fear & tremble? but I should not have troubled You with this account of my spiritual state, unless it had been necessary in explaining the actual cause of my uneasiness, into which you are so kind as to Enquire; for I never obtrude such things on others unless question'd, & then I never disguise the truth.—But if we fear to do the dictates of our Angels, & tremble at the Tasks set before us; if we refuse to do Spiritual Acts because of Natural Fears or Natural Desires! Who can describe the dismal torments of such a state!— I too well remember the Threats I heard!—"If you, who are organised by Divine Providence for spiritual communion, Refuse, & bury your Talent in the Earth, even tho' you should want Natural Bread, Sorrow & Desperation pursues you thro' life, & after death shame & confusion of face to eternity. Every one in Eternity will leave you, aghast at the Man who was crown'd with glory & honour by his brethren, & betray'd their cause to their enemies. You will be call'd the base Judas who betray'd his Friend!"—Such words would make any stout man tremble, & how then could I be at ease? But I am now no longer in That State, & now go on again with my Task, Fearless, and tho' my path is difficult, I have no fear of stumbling while I keep it.

My wife desires her kindest Love to Mrs. Butts, & I have permitted her to send it to you also; we often wish that we could unite again in Society, & hope that the time is not distant when we shall do so, being determin'd not to remain another winter here, but to return to London.

"I hear a voice you cannot hear, that says I must not stay,
I see a hand you cannot see, that beckons me away."

Naked we came here, naked of Natural things, & naked we shall return; but while cloth'd with the Divine Mercy, we are richly cloth'd in Spiritual & suffer all the rest gladly. Pray give my Love to Mrs. Butts & your family. I am, Yours Sincerely,

WILLIAM BLAKE.

P.S. Your Obliging proposal of Exhibiting my two Pictures likewise calls for my thanks; I will finish the other, & then we shall judge of the matter with certainty.

TO THOMAS BUTTS

Felpham, *Novr.* 22, 1802.

DEAR SIR,

My Brother tells me that he fears you are offended with me. I fear so too, because there appears some reason why you might be so. But when you have heard me out, you will not be so.

I have now given two years to the intense study of those parts of the art which relate to light & shade & colour, & am

Convinc'd that either my understanding is incapable of comprehending the beauties of Colouring, or the Pictures which I painted for you Are Equal in Every part of the Art, & superior in One, to any thing that has been done since the age of Rafael.—All Sr. J. Reynolds's discourses to the Royal Academy will shew that the Venetian finesse in Art can never be united with the Majesty of Colouring necessary to Historical beauty; & in a letter to the Revd. Mr. Gilpin, author of a work on Picturesque Scenery, he says Thus: "It may be worth consideration whether the epithet Picturesque is not applicable to the excellencies of the inferior Schools rather than to the higher. The works of Michael Angelo, Rafael, &c., appear to me to have nothing of it: whereas Rubens & the Venetian Painters may almost be said to have Nothing Else.—Perhaps Picturesque is somewhat synonymous to the word Taste, which we should think improperly applied to Homer or Milton, but very well to Prior or Pope. I suspect that the application of these words are to Excellencies of an inferior order, & which are incompatible with the Grand Style. You are certainly right in saying that variety of Tints & Forms is Picturesque; but it must be remember'd, on the other hand, that the reverse of this (*uniformity of Colour* & a *long continuation of lines*) produces Grandeur."—So says Sir Joshua, and so say I; for I have now proved that the parts of the art which I neglected to display in those little pictures & drawings which I had the pleasure & profit to do for you, are incompatible with the designs.— There is nothing in the Art which our Painters do that I can confess myself ignorant of. I also Know & Understand & can assuredly affirm, that the works I have done for you are Equal to Carrache or Rafael (and I am now seven years older than Rafael was when he died), I say they are Equal to Carrache or Rafael, or Else I am Blind, Stupid, Ignorant and Incapable in two years' Study to understand those things which a Boarding school Miss can comprehend in a fortnight. Be assured, My dear Friend, that there is not one touch in those Drawings & Pictures but what came from my Head & my Heart in Unison; That I am Proud of being their Author and Grateful to you my Employer; & that I look upon you as the Chief of my Friends, whom I would endeavour to please, because you, among all men, have enabled me to produce these things. I would not send you a Drawing or a Picture till I had again reconsider'd my notions of Art, & had put myself back as if I was a learner. I have proved that I am Right, & shall now Go on with the Vigour I was in my Childhood famous for.

But I do not pretend to be Perfect: but, if my Works have faults, Carrache, Corregio, & Rafael's have faults also; let me observe that the yellow leather flesh of old men, the ill drawn & ugly young women, &, above all, the dawbed black & yellow shadows that are found in most fine, ay, & the finest pictures, I altogether reject as ruinous to Effect, tho' Connoisseurs may think otherwise.

Let me also notice that Carrache's Pictures are not like Correggio's, nor Correggio's like Rafael's; &, if neither of them was to be encouraged till he did like any of the others, he must die without Encouragement. My Pictures are unlike any of these Painters, & I would have them to be so. I think the manner I adopt More Perfect than any other; no doubt They thought the same of theirs.

You will be tempted to think that, as I improve, The Pictures, &c., that I did for you are not what I would now wish them to be. On this I beg to say That they are what I intended them, & that I know I never shall do better; for, if I were to do them over again, they would lose as much as they gain'd, because they were done in the heat of my Spirits.

But you will justly enquire why I have not written all this time to you? I answer I have been very Unhappy, & could not think of troubling you about it, or any of my real Friends. (I have written many letters to you which I burn'd & did not send) & why I have not before now finish'd the Miniature I promiss'd to Mrs. Butts? I answer I have not, till now, in any degree pleased myself, & now I must intreat you to Excuse faults, for Portrait Painting is the direct contrary to Designing & Historical Painting, in every respect. If you have not Nature before you for Every Touch, you cannot Paint Portrait; & if you have Nature before you at all, you cannot Paint History; it was Michael Angelo's opinion & is Mine. Pray Give My Wife's love with mine to Mrs. Butts; assure her that it cannot be long before I have the pleasure of Painting from you in Person, & then that she may Expect a likeness, but now I have done All I could, & know she will forgive any failure in consideration of the Endeavour.

And now let me finish with assuring you that, Tho' I have been very unhappy, I am so no longer. I am again Emerged into the light of day; I still & shall to Eternity Embrace Christianity and Adore him who is the Express image of God; but I have travel'd thro' Perils & Darkness not unlike a Champion. I have Conquer'd, and shall Go on Conquering. Nothing can withstand the fury of my Course among the Stars of God & in the Abysses of the Accuser. My Enthusiasm is still what it was, only Enlarged and confirm'd.

I now Send Two Pictures & hope you will approve of them. I have inclosed the Account of Money receiv'd & Work done, which I ought long ago to have sent you; pray forgive Errors in omissions of this kind. I am incapable of many attentions which it is my Duty to observe towards you, thro' multitude of employment & thro' hope of soon seeing you again. I often omit to Enquire of you. But pray let me now hear how you do & of the welfare of your family.

Accept my Sincere love & respect.

I remain Yours Sincerely,

WILLM. BLAKE.

A Piece of Sea Weed serves for a Barometer; it gets wet & dry as the weather gets so.

TO THOMAS BUTTS

[November 22, 1802.]

DEAR SIR,

After I had finish'd my Letter, I found that I had not said half what I intended to say, & in particular I wish to ask you what subject you choose to be painted on the remaining Canvas which I brought down with me (for there were three), and to tell you that several of the Drawings were in great forwardness; you will see by the Inclosed Account that the remaining Number of Drawings which you gave me orders for is Eighteen. I will finish these with all possible Expedition, if indeed I have not tired you, or, as it is politely call'd, Bored you too much already; or, if you would rather cry out "Enough, Off, Off!", tell me in a Letter of forgiveness if you were offended, & of accustom'd friendship if you were not. But I will bore you more with some Verses which My Wife desires me to Copy out & send you with her kind love & Respect; they were Composed above a twelvemonth ago, while walking from Felpham to Lavant to meet my Sister:

With happiness stretch'd across the hills
In a cloud that dewy sweetness distills,
With a blue sky spread over with wings
And a mild sun that mounts & sings,
With trees & fields full of Fairy elves
And little devils who fight for themselves—
Rememb'ring the Verses that Hayley sung
When my heart knock'd against the root of my tongue—
With Angels planted in Hawthorn bowers
And God himself in the passing hours,
With Silver Angels across my way
And Golden Demons that none can stay,
With my Father hovering upon the wind
And my Brother Robert just behind
And my Brother John, the evil one,
In a black cloud making his mone;
Tho' dead, they appear upon my path,
Notwithstanding my terrible wrath:
They beg, they intreat, they drop their tears,
Fill'd full of hopes, fill'd full of fears—
With a thousand Angels upon the Wind
Pouring disconsolate from behind
To drive them off, & before my way
A frowning Thistle implores my stay.
What to others a trifle appears
Fills me full of smiles or tears;
For double the vision my Eyes do see,
And a double vision is always with me.
With my inward Eye 'tis an old Man grey;
With my outward, a Thistle across my way.
"If thou goest back," the thistle said,
"Thou art to endless woe betray'd;
For here does Theotormon lower
And here is Enitharmon's bower
And Los the terrible thus hath sworn,
Because thou backward dost return,
Poverty, Envy, old age & fear
Shall bring thy Wife upon a bier;
And Butts shall give what Fuseli gave,
A dark black Rock & a gloomy Cave."

I struck the Thistle with my foot,
And broke him up from his delving root:
"Must the duties of life each other cross?
Must every joy be dung & dross?
Must my dear Butts feel cold neglect
Because I give Hayley his due respect?
Must Flaxman look upon me as wild,
And all my friends be with doubts beguil'd?
Must my Wife live in my Sister's bane,
Or my Sister survive on my Love's pain?
The curses of Los, the terrible shade,
And his dismal terrors make me afraid."

So I spoke & struck in my wrath
The old man weltering upon my path.
Then Los appear'd in all his power:
In the Sun he appear'd, descending before
My face in fierce flames; in my double sight
'Twas outward a Sun, inward Los in his might.

"My hands are labour'd day & night,
And Ease comes never in my sight.
My Wife has no indulgence given
Except what comes to her from heaven.
We eat little, we drink less;
This Earth breeds not our happiness.
Another Sun feeds our life's streams,
We are not warmed with thy beams;
Thou measurest not the Time to me,
Nor yet the Space that I do see;
My Mind is not with thy light array'd,
Thy terrors shall not make me afraid."

When I had my Defiance given,
The Sun stood trembling in heaven;
The Moon that glow'd remote below,
Became leprous & white as snow;
And every soul of men on the Earth
Felt affliction & sorrow & sickness & dearth.
Los flam'd in my path, & the Sun was hot
With the bows of my Mind & the Arrows of Thought—
My bowstring fierce with Ardour breathes,

My arrows glow in their golden sheaves;
My brother & father march before;
The heavens drop with human gore.

Now I a fourfold vision see,
And a fourfold vision is given to me;
'Tis fourfold in my supreme delight
And threefold in soft Beulah's night
And twofold Always. May God us keep
From Single vision & Newton's sleep!

I also inclose you some Ballads by Mr. Hayley, with prints to them by your Hble. Servt. I should have sent them before now, but could not get any thing done for you to please myself; for I do assure you that I have truly studied the two little pictures I now send, & do not repent of the time I have spent upon them.

    God bless you.   Yours,

                                              W.B.

P.S. I have taken the liberty to trouble you with a letter to my Brother, which you will be so kind as to send or give him, & oblige yours,

                                              W.B.

TO THOMAS BUTTS

Felpham,
April 25, 1803.

MY DEAR SIR,

I write in haste, having reciev'd a pressing Letter from my Brother. I intended to have sent the Picture of the Riposo, which is nearly finish'd much to my satisfaction, but not quite; you shall have it soon. I now send the 4 Numbers for Mr. Birch, with best Respects to him. The Reason the Ballads have been suspended is the pressure of other business, but they will go on again soon.

    Accept of my thanks for your kind & heartening Letter. You have Faith in the Endeavours of Me, your weak brother and fellow Disciple; how great must be your faith in our Divine Master! You are to me a Lesson of Humility, while you Exalt me by such distinguishing commendations. I know that you see certain merits in me, which, by God's Grace, shall be made fully apparent & perfect in Eternity; in the mean time I must not bury the Talents in the Earth, but do my endeavour to live to the Glory of our Lord & Saviour; & I am also grateful to the kind hand that endeavours to lift me out of despondency, even if it lifts me too high.

And now, My Dear Sir, Congratulate me on my return to London, with the full approbation of Mr. Hayley & with Promise—But, Alas!

Now I may say to you, what perhaps I should not dare to say to anyone else: That I can alone carry on my visionary studies in London unannoy'd, & that I may converse with my friends in Eternity, See Visions, Dream Dreams & prophecy & speak Parables unobserv'd & at liberty from the Doubts of other Mortals; perhaps Doubts proceeding from Kindness, but Doubts are always pernicious, Especially when we Doubt our Friends. Christ is very decided on this Point: "He who is Not With Me is Against Me." There is no Medium or Middle state; & if a Man is the Enemy of my Spiritual Life while he pretends to be the Friend of my Corporeal, he is a Real Enemy—but the Man may be the friend of my Spiritual Life while he seems the Enemy of my Corporeal, but Not Vice Versa.

What is very pleasant, Every one who hears of my going to London again Applauds it as the only course for the interest of all concern'd in My Works, Observing that I ought not to be away from the opportunities London affords of seeing fine Pictures, and the various improvements in Works of Art going on in London.

But none can know the Spiritual Acts of my three years' Slumber on the banks of the Ocean, unless he has seen them in the Spirit, or unless he should read My long Poem descriptive of those Acts; for I have in these three years composed an immense number of verses on One Grand Theme, Similar to Homer's Iliad or Milton's Paradise Lost, the Persons & Machinery intirely new to the Inhabitants of Earth (some of the Persons Excepted). I have written this Poem from immediate Dictation, twelve or sometimes twenty or thirty lines at a time without Premeditation & even against my Will; the Time it has taken in writing was thus render'd Non Existent, & an immense Poem Exists which seems to be the Labour of a long

Life, all produc'd without Labour or Study. I mention this to
shew you what I think the Grand Reason of my being brought
down here.

I have a thousand & ten thousand things to say to you. My
heart is full of futurity. I percieve that the sore travel which
has been given me these three years leads to Glory & Honour. I
rejoice & I tremble: "I am fearfully & wonderfully made." I had
been reading the cxxxix Psalm a little before your Letter ar-
rived. I take your advice. I see the face of my Heavenly Father;
he lays his Hand upon my Head & gives a blessing to all my
works; why should I be troubled? why should my heart & flesh
cry out? I will go on in the Strength of the Lord; through Hell
will I sing forth his Praises, that the Dragons of the Deep may
praise him, & that those who dwell in darkness & in the Sea
coasts may be gather'd into his Kingdom. Excuse my, perhaps,
too great Enthusiasm. Please to accept of & give our Loves to
Mrs. Butts & your amiable Family, & believe me to be,

Ever Yours Affectionately,

WILL BLAKE.

TO THOMAS BUTTS

Felpham,
July 6, 1803.

DEAR SIR,

I send you the Riposo, which I hope you will think my best
Picture in many respects. It represents the Holy Family in
Egypt, Guarded in their Repose from those Fiends, the Egyptian Gods, and tho' not directly taken from a Poem of Milton's
(for till I had design'd it Milton's Poem did not come into my
Thoughts), Yet it is very similar to his Hymn on the Nativity,
which you will find among his smaller Poems, & will read with
great delight. I have given, in the background, a building,
which may be supposed the ruin of a Part of Nimrod's tower,
which I conjecture to have spread over many Countries; for he
ought to be reckon'd of the Giant brood.

I have now on the Stocks the following drawings for you:
1. Jephthah sacrificing his Daughter; 2. Ruth & her mother in
Law & Sister; 3. The three Maries at the Sepulcher; 4. The
Death of Joseph; 5. The Death of the Virgin Mary; 6. St. Paul
Preaching; & 7. The Angel of the Divine Presence clothing
Adam & Eve with Coats of Skins.

These are all in great forwardness, & I am satisfied that I improve very much & shall continue to do so while I live, which is a blessing I can never be too thankful for both to God & Man.

We look forward every day with pleasure toward our meeting again in London with those whom we have learn'd to value by absence no less perhaps than we did by presence; for recollection often surpasses every thing, indeed, the prospect of returning to our friends is supremely delightful—Then, I am determined that Mrs. Butts shall have a good likeness of You, if I have hands & eyes left; for I am become a likeness taker & succeed admirably well; but this is not to be atchiev'd without the original sitting before you for Every touch, all likenesses from memory being necessarily very, very defective; But Nature & Fancy are Two Things & can Never be join'd; neither ought any one to attempt it, for it is Idolatry & destroys the Soul.

I ought to tell you that Mr. H. is quite agreeable to our return, & that there is all the appearance in the world of our being fully employ'd in Engraving for his projected Works, Particularly Cowper's Milton, a Work now on foot by Subscription, & I understand that the Subscription goes on briskly. This work is to be a very Elegant one & to consist of All Milton's Poems, with Cowper's Notes and translations by Cowper from Milton's Latin & Italian Poems. These works will be ornamented with Engravings from Designs from Romney, Flaxman & Yr. hble Servt., & to be Engrav'd also by the last mention'd. The Profits of the work are intended to be appropriated to Erect a Monument to the Memory of Cowper in St. Paul's or Westminster Abbey. Such is the Project—& Mr. Addington & Mr. Pitt are both among the Subscribers, which are already numerous & of the first rank; the price of the Work is Six Guineas—Thus I hope that all our three years' trouble Ends in Good Luck at last & shall be forgot by my affections & only remember'd by my Understanding; to be a Memento in time to come, & to speak to future generations by a Sublime Allegory, which is now perfectly completed into a Grand Poem. I may praise it, since I dare not pretend to be any other than the Secretary; the Authors are in Eternity. I consider it as the Grandest Poem that this World Contains. Allegory addressed to the Intellectual powers, while it is altogether hidden from the Corporeal Understanding, is My Definition of the Most

Sublime Poetry; it is also somewhat in the same manner defin'd by Plato. This Poem shall, by Divine Assistance, be progressively Printed & Ornamented with Prints & given to the Public. But of this work I take care to say little to Mr. H., since he is as much averse to my poetry as he is to a Chapter in the Bible. He knows that I have writ it, for I have shewn it to him, & he has read Part by his own desire & has looked with sufficient contempt to enhance my opinion of it. But I do not wish to irritate by seeming too obstinate in Poetic pursuits. But if all the World should set their faces against This, I have Orders to set my face like a flint (Ezekiel iiiC, 9v) against their faces, & my forehead against their foreheads.

As to Mr. H., I feel myself at liberty to say as follows upon this ticklish subject: I regard Fashion in Poetry as little as I do in Painting; so, if both Poets & Painters should alternately dislike (but I know the majority of them will not), I am not to regard it at all, but Mr. H. approves of My Designs as little as he does of my Poems, and I have been forced to insist on his leaving me in both to my own Self Will; for I am determin'd to be no longer Pester'd with his Genteel Ignorance & Polite Disapprobation. I know myself both Poet & Painter, & it is not his affected Contempt that can move me to any thing but a more assiduous pursuit of both Arts. Indeed, by my late Firmness I have brought down his affected Loftiness, & he begins to think I have some Genius: as if Genius & Assurance were the same thing! but his imbecile attempts to depress Me only deserve laughter. I say thus much to you, knowing that you will not make a bad use of it. But it is a Fact too true That, if I had only depended on Mortal Things, both myself & my wife must have been Lost. I shall leave every one in This Country astonish'd at my Patience & Forbearance of Injuries upon Injuries; & I do assure you that, if I could have return'd to London a Month after my arrival here, I should have done so, but I was commanded by my Spiritual friends to bear all, to be silent, & to go thro' all without murmuring, &, in fine, hope, till my three years should be almost accomplish'd; at which time I was set at liberty to remonstrate against former conduct & to demand Justice & Truth; which I have done in so effectual a manner that my antagonist is silenc'd completely, & I have compell'd what should have been of freedom—My Just Right as an Artist & as a Man; & if any attempt should be made to refuse me this, I am inflexible & will relinquish any engagement of Designing at all, unless altogether left to my own Judgment, As you, My dear Friend, have always left me; for which I shall never cease to honour & respect you.

When we meet, I will perfectly describe to you my Conduct & the Conduct of others toward me, & you will see that I have labour'd hard indeed, & have been borne on angel's wings. Till we meet I beg of God our Saviour to be with you & me, & yours & mine. Pray give my & my wife's love to Mrs. Butts & Family, & believe me to remain,

Yours in truth & sincerity,
WILL BLAKE.

TO THOMAS BUTTS

Felpham,
August 16, 1803.

DEAR SIR,

I send 7 Drawings, which I hope will please you; this, I believe, about balances our account. Our return to London draws on apace; our Expectation of meeting again with you is one of our greatest pleasures. Pray tell me how your Eyes do. I never sit down to work but I think of you, & feel anxious for the sight of that friend whose Eyes have done me so much good. I omitted (very unaccountably) to copy out in my last Letter that passage in my rough sketch which related to your kindness in offering to Exhibit my 2 last Pictures in the Gallery in Berners Street; it was in these Words: "I sincerely thank you for your kind offer of Exhibiting my 2 Pictures; the trouble you take on my account, I trust, will be recompensed to you by him who seeth in secret; if you should find it convenient to do so, it will be gratefully remember'd by me among the other numerous kindnesses I have received from you."

I go on with the remaining Subjects which you gave me commission to Execute for you, but shall not be able to send any more before my return, tho' perhaps I may bring some with me finish'd. I am at Present in a Bustle to defend myself against a very unwarrantable warrant from a Justice of Peace in Chichester, which was taken out against me by a Private in Captn. Leathes's troop of 1st or Royal Dragoons, for an assault & seditious words. The wretched Man has terribly Perjur'd himself, as has his Comrade; for, as to Sedition, not one Word relating to the King or Government was spoken by either him or me. His Enmity arises from my having turned him out of my Garden, into which he was invited as an assistant by a Gardener at work therein, without my knowledge that he was so invited. I desired him, as politely as was possible, to go out of the Garden; he made me an impertinent answer. I insisted on his leaving the Garden; he refused. I still persisted in desiring his departure; he then threaten'd to knock out my Eyes, with many abominable imprecations & with some contempt for my Person; it affronted my foolish Pride. I therefore took him by the Elbows & pushed him before me till I had got him out; there I intended to have left him, but he, turning about, put himself into a Posture of Defiance, threatening & swearing at me. I, perhaps foolishly & perhaps not, stepped out at the Gate, &, putting aside his blows, took him again by the Elbows, & keeping his back to me, pushed him forwards down the road about fifty yards—he all the while endeavouring to turn round & strike me, & raging & cursing, which drew out several neighbours; at length, when I had got him to where he was Quarter'd, which was very quickly done, we were met at the Gate by the Master of the house, The Fox Inn (who is the proprietor of my Cottage), & his wife & Daughter & the Man's Comrade & several other people. My Landlord compell'd the Soldiers to go in doors, after many abusive threats against me & my wife from the two Soldiers; but not one word of threat on account of Sedition was utter'd at that time. This method of Revenge was Plann'd between them after they had got together into the stable. This is the whole outline. I have for witnesses: The Gardener, who is Hostler at the Fox & who Evidences that, to his knowledge, no word of the remotest tendency to Government or Sedition was utter'd: Our next door Neighbour, a Miller's wife, who saw me turn him before me down the road, & saw & heard all that happen'd at the Gate of the Inn, who Evidences that no Expression of threatening on account of Sedition was utter'd in the heat of their fury by either of the Dragoons; this was the woman's own remark, & does high honour to her good sense, as she observes that, whenever a quarrel happens, the offence is always repeated. The Landlord of the Inn & his Wife & daughter will Evidence the same, & will evidently prove the Comrade perjur'd, who swore that he heard me, while at the Gate, utter Seditious words & D— the K—, without which perjury I could not have been committed; & I had no witness with me before the Justices who could combat his assertion, as the Gardener remain'd in my Garden all the while, & he was the only person I thought necessary to take with me. I have been before a Bench of Justices at Chichester this morning; but they, as the Lawyer who wrote down the Accusation told me in private, are compell'd by the Military to suffer a prosecution to be enter'd into: altho' they must know, & it is manifest, that the whole is a Fabricated Perjury. I have been forced to find Bail. Mr. Hayley was kind enough to come forwards, & Mr. Seagrave, printer at Chichester; Mr. H. in £100, & Mr. S. in £50; & myself am bound in £100 for my appearance at the Quarter Sessions, which is after Michaelmas. So I shall have the satisfaction to see my friends in Town before this Contemptible business comes on. I say Contemptible, for it must be manifest to every one that the whole accusation is a wilful Perjury. Thus, you see, my dear Friend, that I cannot leave this place without some adventure; it has struck a consternation thro' all the Villages round. Every Man is now afraid of speaking to, or looking at, a Soldier; for the peaceable Villagers have always been forward in expressing their kindness for us, & they express their sorrow at our departure as soon as they hear of it. Every one here is my Evidence for Peace & Good Neighbourhood; & yet, such is the present state of things, this foolish accusation must be tried in Public. Well, I am content, I murmur not & doubt not that I shall recieve Justice, & am only sorry for the trouble & expense. I have heard that my Accuser is a disgraced Sergeant; his name is John Scholfield; perhaps it will be in your power to learn somewhat about the Man. I am very ignorant of what I am requesting of you; I only suggest what I know you will be kind enough to Excuse if you can learn nothing about him, & what, I as well know, if it is possible, you will be kind enough to do in this matter.

Dear Sir, This perhaps was suffer'd to Clear up some doubts, & to give opportunity to those whom I doubted to clear themselves of all imputation. If a Man offends me ignorantly & not designedly, surely I ought to consider him with favour & affection. Perhaps the simplicity of myself is the origin of all offences committed against me. If I have found this, I shall have learned a most valuable thing, well worth three years' perseverance. I have found it. It is certain that a too passive manner, inconsistent with my active physiognomy, had done me much mischief. I must now express to you my conviction that all is come from the spiritual World for Good, & not for Evil.

Give me your advice in my perilous adventure; burn what
I have peevishly written about any friend. I have been very
much degraded & injuriously treated; but if it all arise from my
own fault, I ought to blame myself.

> O why was I born with a different face?
> Why was I not born like the rest of my race?
> When I look, each one starts! when I speak, I offend;
> Then I'm silent & passive & lose every Friend.
>
> Then my verse I dishonour, My pictures despise,
> My person degrade & my temper chastise;
> And the pen is my terror, the pencil my shame;
> All my Talents I bury, and dead is my Fame.
>
> I am either too low or too highly priz'd;
> When Elate I am Envy'd, When Meek I'm despis'd.

This is but too just a Picture of my Present state. I pray God
to keep you & all men from it, & to deliver me in his own good
time. Pray write to me, & tell me how you & your family enjoy
health. My much terrified Wife joins me in love to you & Mrs.
Butts & all your family. I again take the liberty to beg of you to
cause the Enclos'd Letter to be deliver'd to my Brother, & remain Sincerely & Affectionately Yours,

                                        WILLIAM BLAKE.

TO WILLIAM HAYLEY

London,
7 *October*, 1803.

DEAR SIR,
   Your generous & tender solicitude about your devoted rebel
makes it absolutely necessary that he should trouble you with
an account of his safe arrival, which will excuse his begging
the favor of a few lines to inform him how you escaped the
contagion of the Court of Justice—I fear that you have & must
suffer more on my account than I shall ever be worth—Ar-
rived safe in London, my wife in very poor health, still I resolve
not to lose hope of seeing better days.
   Art in London flourishes. Engravers in particular are wanted.

Every Engraver turns away work that he cannot execute from his superabundant Employment. Yet no one brings work to me. I am content that it shall be so as long as God pleases. I know that many works of a lucrative nature are in want of hands; other Engravers are courted. I suppose that I must go a Courting, which I shall do awkwardly; in the meantime I lose no moment to complete Romney to satisfaction.

How is it possible that a Man almost 50 years of Age, who has not lost any of his life since he was five years old without incessant labour & study, how is it possible that such a one with ordinary common sense can be inferior to a boy of twenty, who scarcely has taken or deigns to take pencil in hand, but who rides about the Parks or saunters about the Playhouses, who Eats & drinks for business not for need, how is it possible that such a fop can be superior to the studious lover of Art can scarcely be imagin'd. Yet such is somewhat like my fate & such it is likely to remain. Yet I laugh & sing, for if on Earth neglected I am in heaven a Prince among Princes, & even on Earth beloved by the Good as a Good Man; this I should be perfectly contented with, but at certain periods a blaze of reputation arises round me in which I am consider'd as one distinguish'd by some mental perfection, but the flame soon dies again & I am left stupified and astonish'd. O that I could live as others do in a regular succession of Employment, this wish I fear is not to be accomplish'd to me—Forgive this Dirge-like lamentation over a dead horse, & now I have lamented over the dead horse let me laugh & be merry with my friends till Christmas, for as Man liveth not by bread alone, I shall live altho I should want bread—nothing is necessary to me but to do my Duty & to rejoice in the exceeding joy that is always poured out on my Spirit, to pray that my friends & you above the rest may be made partakers of the joy that the world cannot concieve, that you may still be replenish'd with the same & be as you always have been, a glorious & triumphant Dweller in immortality. Please to pay for me my best thanks to Miss Poole: tell her that I wish her a continued Excess of Happiness —some say that Happiness is not Good for Mortals, & they ought to be answer'd that Sorrow is not fit for Immortals & is utterly useless to any one; a blight never does good to a tree, & if a blight kill not a tree but it still bear fruit, let none say that the fruit was in consequence of the blight. When this Soldier-like danger is over I will do double the work I do now, for it will hang heavy on my Devil who terribly resents it; but I soothe him to peace, & indeed he is a good natur'd Devil after all & certainly does not lead me into scrapes—he is not in the least to be blamed for the present scrape, as he was out of the way all the time on other employment seeking amusement in making Verses, to which he constantly leads me very much to my hurt & sometimes to the annoyance of my friends; as I percieve he is now doing the same work by my letter, I will finish it, wishing you health & joy in God our Saviour.

To Eternity yours,
WILLM. BLAKE.

TO WILLIAM HAYLEY

23 October, 1804.

DEAR SIR,

I received your kind letter with the note to Mr. Payne, and have had the cash from him. I should have returned my thanks immediately on receipt of it, but hoped to be able to send, before now, proofs of the two plates, the Head of R[omney] and The Shipwreck, which you shall soon see in a much more perfect state. I write immediately because you wish I should do so, to satisfy you that I have received your kind favour.

I take the extreme pleasure of expressing my joy at our good Lady of Lavant's continued recovery: but with a mixture of sincere sorrow on account of the beloved Counsellor. My wife returns her heartfelt thanks for your kind inquiry concerning her health. She is surprisingly recovered. Electricity is the wonderful cause; the swelling of her legs and knees is entirely reduced. She is very near as free from rheumatism as she was five years ago, and we have the greatest confidence in her perfect recovery.

The pleasure of seeing another poem from your hands has truly set me longing (my wife says I ought to have said us) with desire and curiosity; but, however, "Christmas is a-coming."

Our good and kind friend Hawkins is not yet in town—hope soon to have the pleasure of seeing him, with the courage of conscious industry, worthy of his former kindness to me. For now! O Glory! and O Delight! I have entirely reduced that spectrous fiend to his station, whose annoyance has been the ruin of my labours for the last passed twenty years of my life. He is the enemy of conjugal love and is the Jupiter of the Greeks, an ironhearted tyrant, the ruiner of ancient Greece. I speak with perfect confidence and certainty of the fact which has passed upon me. Nebuchadnezzar had seven times passed over him; I have had twenty; thank God I was not altogether a beast as he was; but I was a slave bound in a mill among beasts and devils; these beasts and these devils are now, together with myself, become children of light and liberty, and my feet and my wife's feet are free from fetters. O lovely Felpham, parent of Immortal Friendship, to thee I am eternally indebted for my three years' rest from perturbation and the strength I now enjoy. Suddenly, on the day after visiting the Truchsessian Gallery of pictures, I was again enlightened with the light I enjoyed in my youth, and which has for exactly twenty years been closed from me as by a door and by window-shutters. Consequently I can, with confidence, promise you ocular demonstration of my altered state on the plates I am now engraving after Romney, whose spiritual aid has not a little conduced to my restoration to the light of Art. O the distress I have undergone, and my poor wife with me: incessantly labouring and incessantly spoiling what I had done well. Every one of my friends was astonished at my faults, and could not assign a reason; they knew my industry and abstinence from every pleasure for the sake of study, and yet—and yet—and yet there wanted the proofs of industry in my works. I thank God with entire confidence that it shall be so no longer—he is become my servant who domineered over me, he is even as a brother who was my enemy. Dear Sir, excuse my enthusiasm or rather madness, for I am really drunk with intellectual vision whenever I take a pencil or graver into my hand, even as I used to be in my youth, and as I have not been for twenty dark, but very profitable, years. I thank God that I courageously pursued my course through darkness. In a short time I shall make my assertion good that I am become suddenly as I was at first, by producing the Head of Romney and The Shipwreck quite another thing from what you or I ever expected them to be. In short, I am now satisfied and proud of my work, which I have not been for the above long period.

If our excellent and manly friend Meyer is yet with you, please to make my wife's and my own most respectful and

affectionate compliments to him, also to our kind friend at
Lavant.

I remain, with my wife's joint affection,

Your sincere and obliged servant,

WILL BLAKE.

TO WILLIAM HAYLEY

Sth. Molton Street,
11 *December,* 1805.

DEAR SIR,

I cannot omit to Return you my sincere & Grateful Acknowl-
edgments for the kind Reception you have given my New
Projected Work. It bids fair to set me above the difficulties I
have hitherto encountered. But my Fate has been so uncom-
mon that I expect Nothing. I was alive and in health and with
the same Talents I now have all the time of Boydell's, Machlin's,
Bowyer's, & other great works. I was known to them and was
look'd upon by them as Incapable of Employment in those
Works; it may turn out so again, notwithstanding appearances.
I am prepared for it, but at the same time sincerely Grateful
to Those whose Kindness & Good opinion has supported me
thro' all hitherto. You, Dear Sir, are one who has my Particular Gratitude, having conducted me thro' Three that would
have been the Darkest Years that ever Mortal Suffer'd, which
were render'd thro' your means a Mild and Pleasant Slumber.
I speak of Spiritual Things, Not of Natural; of Things known
only to Myself and to the Spirits Good and Evil, but Not known
to Men on Earth. It is the passage thro' these Three Years that
has brought me into my Present State, and I *know* that if I
had not been with You I must have Perish'd. Those Dangers
are now passed and I can see them beneath my feet. It will not
be long before I shall be able to present the full history of my
Spiritual Sufferings to the dwellers upon Earth and of the
Spiritual Victories obtained for me by my Friends. Excuse
this Effusion of the Spirit from One who cares little for
this World, which passes away, for suffering till the time of
complete deliverance. In the meanwhile I am kept Happy, as
I used to be, because I throw Myself and all that I have on
our Saviour's Divine Providence. O what wonders are the Children of Men! Would to God that they would consider it,—

that they would consider their Spiritual Life, regardless of that
faint Shadow called Natural Life, and that they would Pro-
mote Each other's Spiritual labours, each according to its Rank,
& that they would know that Receiving a Prophet as a Prophet
is a Duty which If omitted is more Severely Avenged than
Every Sin and Wickedness beside. It is the Greatest of Crimes
to Depress True Art and Science. I know that those who are
dead from the Earth, & who mocked and Despised the Meekness of True Art (and such, I find, have been the situation of
our Beautiful, Affectionate Ballads), I know that such Mock-
ers are Most Severely Punished in Eternity. I know it, for I
see it & dare not help. The Mocker of Art is the Mocker of
Jesus. Let us go on, Dear Sir, following his Cross: let us take
it up daily, Persisting in Spiritual Labours & the Use of that
Talent which it is Death to Bury, and of that Spirit to which
we are called.

Pray Present My Sincerest Thanks to our Good Paulina,
whose kindness to Me shall receive recompense in the Presence
of Jesus. Present also my Thanks to the generous Seagrave, In
whose debt I have been too long, but perceive that I shall be
able to settle with him soon what is between us. I have delivered to Mr. Sanders the 3 works of Romney, as Mrs. Lambert
told me you wished to have them. A very few touches will
finish the Shipwreck; those few I have added upon a Proof before I parted with the Picture. It is a Print that I feel proud of,
on a New inspection. Wishing you and All Friends in Sussex
Merry & Happy Christmas,

I remain, Ever Your Affectionate,

WILL BLAKE and his Wife CATHERINE BLAKE.

TO JOHN LINNELL

Feby. 1, 1826.

DEAR SIR,

I am forced to write, because I cannot come to you, & this
on two accounts. First, I omitted to desire you would come &
take a Mutton chop with us the day you go to Cheltenham,
& I will go with you to the Coach; also, I will go to Hampstead
to see Mrs. Linnell on Sunday, but will return before dinner
(I mean if you set off before that), & Second, I wish to have
a Copy of Job to shew to Mr. Chantry.

For I am again laid up by a cold in my stomach; the Hampstead Air, as it always did, so I fear it always will do this, Except it be the Morning air; & That, in my Cousin's time, I found I could bear with safety & perhaps benefit. I believe my Constitution to be a good one, but it has many peculiarities that no one but myself can know. When I was young, Hampstead, Highgate, Hornsea, Muswell Hill, & even Islington & all places North of London, always laid me up the day after, & sometimes two or three days, with precisely the same Complaint & the same torment of the Stomach, Easily removed, but excruciating while it lasts & enfeebling for some time after. Sr. Francis Bacon would say, it is want of discipline in Mountainous Places. Sr. Francis Bacon is a Liar. No discipline will turn one Man into another, even in the least particle, & such discipline I call Presumption & Folly. I have tried it too much not to know this, & am very sorry for all such who may be led to such ostentatious Exertion against their Eternal Existence itself, because it is Mental Rebellion against the Holy Spirit, & fit only for a Soldier of Satan to perform.

Though I hope in a morning or two to call on you in Cirencester Place, I feared you might be gone, or I might be too ill to let you know how I am, & what I wish.

> I am, dear Sir,
> Yours sincerely,
> WILLIAM BLAKE.

TO JOHN LINNELL

February, 1827.

DEAR SIR,

I thank you for the five pounds received to-day. Am getting better every morning, but slowly, as I am still feeble and tottering, though all the symptoms of my complaint seem almost gone. The fine weather is very beneficial and comfortable to me. I go on, as I think, improving my engravings of Dante more and more, and shall soon get proofs of these four which I have, and beg the favour of you to send me the two plates of Dante which you have, that I may finish them sufficiently to make show of colour and strength.

I have thought and thought of the removal. I cannot get my mind out of a state of terrible fear at such a step. The more I think, the more I feel terror at what I wished at first and thought a thing of benefit and good hope. You will attribute it to its right cause—intellectual peculiarity, that must be my-self alone shut up in myself, or reduced to nothing. I could tell you of visions and dreams upon the subject. I have asked and entreated Divine help, but fear continues upon me, and I must relinquish the step that I had wished to take, and still wish, but in vain.

Your success in your profession is, above all things to me, most gratifying. May it go on to the perfection you wish, and more. So wishes also

Yours sincerely,
WILLIAM BLAKE.

TO GEORGE CUMBERLAND

N 3, FOUNTAIN COURT, STRAND.
12 *April,* 1827.

I HAVE been very near the gates of death, and have returned very weak and an old man, feeble and tottering, but not in spirit and life, not in the real man, the imagination, which liveth for ever. In that I am stronger and stronger, as this fool-ish body decays. I thank you for the pains you have taken with poor Job. I know too well that the great majority of Eng-lishmen are fond of the indefinite, which they measure by Newton's doctrine of the fluxions of an atom, a thing which does not exist. These are politicians, and think that Republican art is inimical to their atom, for a line or a lineament is not formed by chance. A line is a line in its minutest subdivisions, straight or crooked. It is itself, not intermeasurable by anything else. Such is Job. But since the French Revolution Englishmen are all intermeasurable by one another: certainly a happy state of agreement, in which I for one do not agree. God keep you and me from the divinity of yes and no too—the yea, nay, creeping Jesus—from supposing up and down to be the same thing, as all experimentalists must suppose.

You are desirous, I know, to dispose of some of my works, but having none remaining of all I have printed, I cannot print more except at a great loss. I am now painting a set of the Songs of Innocence and Experience for a friend at ten guineas. The last work I produced is a poem entitled Jerusalem, the Emanation of the Giant Albion, but find that to print it will cost my time the amount of Twenty Guineas. One I have Finish'd. It contains 100 Plates, but it is not likely I shall get a Customer for it.

As you wish me to send you a list with the Prices of these things, they are as follows:

	£	s.	d.
America	6	6	0
Europe	6	6	0
Visions, &c.	5	5	0
Thel	3	3	0
Songs of Inn. & Exp.	10	10	0
Urizen	6	6	0

The Little Card I will do as soon as Possible, but when you Consider that I have been reduced to a Skeleton, from which I am slowly recovering, you will, I hope, have Patience with me.

Flaxman is Gone, & we must All soon follow, every one to his Own Eternal House, Leaving the delusive Goddess Nature & her Laws, to get into Freedom from all Law of the Members, into The Mind, in which every one is King & Priest in his own House. God send it so on Earth, as it is in Heaven.

I am, dear Sir, Yours affectionately,

WILLIAM BLAKE.

MARGINALIA[1]

Marginalia to Lavater's APHORISMS ON MAN

244.

Who writes what he should tell, and dares not tell what he
writes, is either like a wolf in sheep's clothing, or like a sheep
in a wolf's skin.

Some cannot tell what they can write, tho' they dare.

301.

He has not a little of the devil in him who prays and bites.

There is no other devil; he who bites without praying is only
a beast.

309.

He who, at a table of forty covers, thirty-nine of which are
exquisite, and one indifferent, lays hold of that, and with a
"damn your dinner" dashes it in the landlord's face, should be
sent to Bethlem or to Bridewell—and whither he, who blas-
phemes a book, a work of art, or perhaps a man of nine-and-
thirty good and but one bad quality, and calls those fools or
flatterers who, engrossed by the superior number of good
qualities, would fain forget the bad one.

To hell till he behaves better! mark that I do not believe there
is such a thing literally, but hell is the being shut up in the
possession of corporeal desires which shortly weary the man,
for ALL LIFE IS HOLY.

[1] In this section, Blake's comments are in larger type after each
selection.

407.

Whatever is visible is the vessel or veil of the invisible past,
present, future—as man penetrates to this more, or perceives it
less, he raises or depresses his dignity of being.

A vision of the Eternal Now.

409.

He alone is good, who, though possessed of energy, prefers
virtue, *with the appearance of weakness, to the invitation of
acting brilliantly ill.*

Noble! But Mark! Active Evil is better than Passive Good.

489.

An entirely honest man, in the severe sense of the word, exists
no more than an entirely dishonest knave: the best and the
worst are only approximations of those qualities. Who are those
that never contradict themselves? yet honesty never contradicts
itself: who are those that always contradict themselves? yet
knavery is mere self-contradiction. Thus the knowledge of man
determines not the things themselves, but their proportions, the
quantum of congruities and incongruities.

Man is a twofold being, one part capable of evil & the other
capable of good; that which is capable of good is not also
capable of evil, but that which is capable of evil is also capable
of good. This aphorism seems to consider man as simple & yet
capable of evil: now both evil & good cannot exist in a simple
being, for thus 2 contraries would spring from one essence,
which is impossible; but if man is consider'd as only evil &
god only good, how then is regeneration effected which turns
the evil to good? by casting out the evil by the good? See
Matthew xii Ch., 26, 27, 28, 29v.

605.

He who pursues the glimmering steps of hope, with stedfast,
not presumptuous, eye, may pass the gloomy rock, on either side
of which superstition [*altered by Blake to* hypocrisy] and in-
credulity their dark abysses spread.

Superstition has been long a bugbear by reason of its being united with hypocrisy; but let them be fairly seperated & then superstition will be honest feeling, & God, who loves all honest men, will lead the poor enthusiast in the paths of holiness.

612.

Men carry their character not seldom in their pockets: you might decide on more than half of your acquaintance, had you will or right to turn their pockets inside out.

I seldom carry money in my pockets; they are generally full of paper.

630.

A GOD, an ANIMAL, a PLANT, are not companions of man; nor is the FAULTLESS—then judge with lenity of all; the coolest, wisest, best, all without exception, have their points, their moments of enthusiasm, fanaticism, absence of mind, faint-heartedness, stupidity—if you allow not for these, your criticisms on man will be a mass of accusations or caricatures.

It is the God in *all* that is our companion & friend, for our God himself says: "you are my brother, my sister & my mother," & St. John: "whoso dwelleth in love dwelleth in God & God in him," & such an one cannot judge of any but in love, & his feelings will be attractions or repulses. See Aphorisms 549, 554. God is in the lowest effects as well as in the highest causes; for he is become a worm that he may nourish the weak. For let it be remember'd that creation is God descending according to the weakness of man, for our Lord is the word of God & every thing on earth is the word of God & in its essence is God.

.   .   .

Man is bad or good as he unites himself with bad or good spirits: tell me with whom you go & I'll tell you what you do.

As we cannot experience pleasure but by means of others, who experience either pleasure or pain thro' us, And as all of us on earth are united in thought, for it is impossible to think without images of somewhat on earth—So it is impossible to know God or heavenly things without conjunction with those who know God & heavenly things; therefore all who converse in the spirit, converse with spirits.

For these reasons I say that this Book is written by consultation with Good Spirits, because it is Good, & that the name Lavater is the amulet of those who purify the heart of man.

There is a strong objection to Lavater's principles (as I understand them) & that is He makes every thing originate in its accident; he makes the vicious propensity not only a leading feature of the man, but the stamina on which all his virtues grow. But as I understand Vice it is a Negative. It does not signify what the laws of Kings & Priests have call'd Vice; we who are philosophers ought not to call the Staminal Virtues of Humanity by the same name that we call the omissions of intellect springing from poverty.

Every man's leading propensity ought to be call'd his leading Virtue & his good Angel. But the Philosophy of Causes & Consequences misled Lavater as it has all his Contemporaries. Each thing is its own cause & its own effect. Accident is the omission of act in self & the hindering of act in another; This is Vice, but all Act is Virtue. To hinder another is not an act; it is the contrary; it is a restraint on action both in ourselves & in the person hinder'd, for he who hinders another omits his own duty at the same time.

Murder is Hindering Another.

Theft is Hindering Another.

Backbiting, Undermining, Circumventing, & whatever is Negative is Vice. But the origin of this mistake in Lavater & his contemporaries is, They suppose that Woman's Love is Sin; in consequence all the Loves & Graces with them are Sins.

Marginalia from Swedenborg's
DIVINE LOVE AND WISDOM

Page 10.

It hath been said, that in the spiritual World Spaces appear
equally as in the natural World. . . . Hence it is that the Lord,
although he is in the Heavens with the Angels everywhere,
nevertheless appears high above them as a Sun: And whereas
the Reception of Love and Wisdom constitute Affinity with
him, therefore those Heavens appear nearer to him where the
Angels are in a nearer Affinity from Reception, than where they
are in a more remote Affinity.

He who Loves feels love descend into him & if he has wisdom
may perceive it is from the Poetic Genius, which is the Lord.

Page 11.

In all the Heavens there is no other Idea of God than that of a
Man.

Man can have no idea of any thing greater than Man, as a
cup cannot contain more than its capaciousness. But God is a
man, not because he is so perceiv'd by man, but because he is
the creator of man.

Page 12.

"The Gentiles, particularly the Africans . . . entertain an Idea
of God as of a Man, and say that no one can have any other
Idea of God: When they hear that many form an Idea of God
as existing in the Midst of a Cloud, they ask where such
are. . . ."

Think of a white cloud as being holy, you cannot love it;
but think of a holy man within the cloud, love springs up in
your thoughts, for to think of holiness distinct from man is
impossible to the affections. Thought alone can make monsters, but the affections cannot.

Page 24.

What Person of Sound Reason doth not perceive, that the
Divine is not divisible. . . . If another, who hath no Reason,
should say that it is possible there may be several Infinities,
Uncreates, Omnipotents and Gods, provided they have the same
Essence, and that thereby there is one Infinite, Uncreate, Omnipotent and God—is not one and the same Essence one and the
same Identity?

Answer: Essence is not Identity, but from Essence proceeds
Identity & from one Essence may proceed many Identities,
as from one Affection may proceed many thoughts. Surely
this is an oversight.

That there is but one Omnipotent, Uncreate & God I agree,
but that there is but one Infinite I do not; for if all but God
is not Infinite, they shall come to an End, which God forbid.

If the Essence was the same as the Identity, there could be
but one Identity, which is false. Heaven would upon this
plan be but a Clock; but one & the same Essence is therefore
Essence & not Identity.

Pages 195-6.

These three Degrees of Altitude are named Natural, Spiritual
and Celestial. . . . Man, at his Birth, first comes into the
natural Degree, and this increases in him by Continuity according to the Sciences, and according to the Understanding acquired
by them, to the Summit of Understanding which is called
Rational.

Study Sciences till you are blind, Study intellectuals till you
are cold, Yet science cannot teach intellect. Much less can
intellect teach Affection. How foolish then is it to assert
that Man is born in only one degree, when that one degree
is reception of the 3 degrees, two of which he must destroy
or close up or they will descend; if he closes up the two
superior, then he is not truly in the 3d, but descends out of it
into meer Nature or Hell. Is it not also evident that one degree
will not open the other, & that science will not open intellect, but that they are discrete & not continuous so as to
explain each other except by correspondence, which has
nothing to do with demonstration; for you cannot demonstrate

one degree by the other; for how can science be brought to demonstrate intellect without making them continuous & not discrete?

Marginalia from Bishop Watson's APOLOGY FOR THE BIBLE . . . ADDRESSED TO THOMAS PAINE

To me, who believe the Bible & profess myself a Christian, a defence of the Wickedness of the Israelites in murdering so many thousands under pretence of a command from God is altogether Abominable & Blasphemous. Why did Christ come? Was it not to abolish the Jewish imposture? Was not Christ marter'd because he taught that God loved all Men & was their father & forbad all contention for Worldly prosperity in opposition to the Jewish Scriptures, which are only an Example of the wickedness & deceit of the Jews & were written as an Example of the possibility of Human Beastliness in all its branches? Christ died as an Unbeliever & if the Bishops had their will so would Paine: see page 1: but he who speaks a word against the Son of man shall be forgiven. Let the Bishop prove that he has not spoken against the Holy Ghost, who in Paine strives with Christendom as in Christ he strove with the Jews.

.   .   .

If Paine means that a history, tho' true in itself, is false when it is attributed to a wrong author, he's a fool. But he says that Moses, being proved not the author of that history which is written in his name & in which he says I did so & so, Undermines the veracity intirely. The writer says he is Moses; if this is proved false, the history is false (Deut. xxxi, v. 24). But perhaps Moses is not the author & then the Bishop loses his Author.

Jesus could not do miracles where unbelief hindered, hence we must conclude that the man who holds miracles to be ceased puts it out of his own power to ever witness one. The manner of a miracle being performed is in modern times considered as an arbitrary command of the agent upon the patient, but this is an impossibility, not a miracle, neither did Jesus ever do such a miracle. Is it a greater miracle to feed five thousand men with five loaves than to overthrow all the armies of Europe with a small pamphlet? Look over the events of your own life & if you do not find that you have both done such miracles & lived by such you do not see as I do. True, I cannot do a miracle thro' experiment & to domineer over & prove to others my superior power, as neither could Christ. But I can & do work such as both astonish & comfort me & mine. How can Paine, the worker of miracles, ever doubt Christ's in the above sense of the word miracle? But how can Watson ever believe the above sense of a miracle, who considers it as an arbitrary act of the agent upon an unbelieving patient, whereas the Gospel says that Christ could not do a miracle because of Unbelief?

If Christ could not do miracles because of Unbelief, the reason alledged by Priests for miracles is false; for those who believe want not to be confounded by miracles. Christ & his Prophets & Apostles were not Ambitious miracle mongers.

· · ·

Prophets, in the modern sense of the word, have never existed. Jonah was no prophet in the modern sense, for his prophecy of Nineveh failed. Every honest man is a Prophet; he utters his opinion both of private & public matters. Thus: if you go on So, the result is So. He never says, such a thing shall happen let you do what you will. A Prophet is a Seer, not an Arbitrary Dictator. It is man's fault if God is not able to do him good, for he gives to the just & to the unjust, but the unjust reject his gift.

· · ·

Nothing can be more contemptible than to suppose Public RECORDS to be True. Read, then, & Judge, if you are not a Fool.

Of what consequence is it whether Moses wrote the Pentateuch or no? If Paine trifles in some of his objections it is folly to confute him so seriously in them & leave his more material ones unanswered. Public Records! As if Public Records were True! Impossible; for the facts are such as none but the actor could tell. If it is True, Moses & none but he could write it, unless we allow it to be Poetry & that poetry inspired.

If historical facts can be written by inspiration, Milton's Paradise Lost is as true as Genesis or Exodus; but the Evidence is nothing, for how can he who writes what he has neither seen nor heard of be an Evidence of The Truth of his history.

I cannot conceive the Divinity of the books in the Bible to consist either in who they were written by, or at what time, or in the historical evidence which may be all false in the eyes of one man & true in the eyes of another, but in the Sentiments & Examples, which, whether true or Parabolic, are Equally useful as Examples given to us of the perverseness of some & its consequent evil & the honesty of others & its consequent good. This sense of the Bible is equally true to all & equally plain to all. None can doubt the impression which he receives from a book of Examples. If he is good he will abhor wickedness in David or Abraham; if he is wicked he will make their wickedness an excuse for his & so he would do by any other book.

. . .

All Penal Laws court Transgression & therefore are cruelty & Murder. The laws of the Jews were (both ceremonial & real) the basest & most oppressive of human codes, & being like all other codes given under pretence of divine command were what Christ pronounced them, The Abomination that maketh desolate, *i.e.* State Religion, which is the source of all Cruelty.

. . .

It appears to me Now that Tom Paine is a better Christian than the Bishop.

I have read this Book with attention & find that the Bishop has only hurt Paine's heel while Paine has broken his head. The Bishop has not answer'd one of Paine's grand objections.

Marginalia from Bacon's ESSAYS

GOOD advice for Satan's Kingdom.

Is it true or is it false that the wisdom of the world is foolishness with God? This is certain: if what Bacon says is true, what Christ says is false. If Caesar is right, Christ is wrong, both in politics and religion, since they will divide themselves in two.

Everybody knows that this is epicurism and libertinism, and yet everybody says that it is Christian philosophy. How is this possible? Everybody must be a liar and deceiver? No! "Everybody" does not do this; but the hirelings of Kings and Courts, who made themselves "everybody", and knowingly propagate falsehood. It was a common opinion in the Court of Queen Elizabeth that knavery is wisdom. Cunning plotters were considered as wise Machiavels.

Of Unity in Religion.

It was great Blasphemy, when the Devil said, "I will ascend, and be like the Highest"; but it is greater blasphemy to personate God, and bring him in saying, "I will descend, and be like the Prince of Darkness."

Did not Jesus descend and become a servant? The Prince of Darkness is a gentleman and not a man: he is a Lord Chancellor.

Marginalia from Reynolds's DISCOURSES

THIS Man was Hired to Depress Art.

This is the Opinion of Will Blake: my Proofs of this Opinion are given in the following Notes.

Advice of the Popes who succeeded the age of Rafael
Degrade first the Arts if you'd Mankind Degrade.
Hire Idiots to Paint with cold light & hot shade:
Give high Price for the worst, leave the best in disgrace,
And with Labours of Ignorance fill every place.

Having spent the Vigour of my Youth & Genius under the Opression of Sr Joshua & his Gang of Cunning Hired Knaves Without Employment & as much as could possibly be Without Bread, The Reader must Expect to Read in all my Remarks on these Books Nothing but Indignation & Resentment. While Sr Joshua was rolling in Riches, Barry was Poor & Unemploy'd except by his own Energy; Mortimer was call'd a Madman, & only Portrait Painting applauded & rewarded by the Rich & Great. Reynolds & Gainsborough Blotted & Blurred one against the other & Divided all the English World between them. Fuseli, Indignant, almost hid himself. I am hid.

The Arts & Sciences are the Destruction of Tyrannies or Bad Governments. Why should A Good Government endeavour to Depress what is its Chief & only Support?

The Foundation of Empire is Art & Science. Remove them or Degrade them, & the Empire is No More. Empire follows Art & Not Vice Versa as Englishmen suppose.

Page i.

TO THE KING

The regular progress of cultivated life is from necessaries to accommodations, from accommodations to ornaments.

The Bible says That Cultivated Life Existed First. Uncultivated Life comes afterwards from Satan's Hirelings. Necessaries, Accomodations & Ornaments are the whole of Life. Satan took away Ornament First. Next he took away Accomodations, & then he became Lord & Master of Necessaries.

Page ii.

[*Dedication, continued*]

To give advice to those who are contending for royal liberality, has been for some years the duty of my station in the Academy.

Liberality! we want not Liberality. We want a Fair Price & Proportionate Value & a General Demand for Art.

Let not that Nation where Less than Nobility is the Reward, Pretend that Art is Encouraged by that Nation. Art is First in Intellectuals & Ought to be First in Nations.

Page iii.

Invention depends Altogether upon Execution or Organization; as that is right or wrong so is the Invention perfect or imperfect. Whoever is set to Undermine the Execution of Art is set to destroy Art. Michael Angelo's Art depends on Michael Angelo's Execution Altogether.

Page xlvii.

[*To a footnote on George Michael Moser, Keeper of the Royal Academy.*]

I was once looking over the Prints from Rafael & Michael Angelo in the Library of the Royal Academy. Moser came to me & said: "You should not Study these old Hard, Stiff & Dry, Unfinish'd Works of Art—Stay a little & I will shew you what you should Study." He then went & took down Le Brun's & Rubens's Galleries. How I did secretly Rage! I also spoke my Mind. . . .

I said to Moser, "These things that you call Finish'd are not Even Begun; how can they then be Finish'd? The Man who does not know The Beginning never can know the End of Art."

Page xcviii.

He was a great generalizer. . . . But this disposition to abstractions, to generalizing and classification, is the great glory of the human mind. . . .

To Generalize is to be an Idiot. To Particularize is the Alone Distinction of Merit. General Knowledges are those Knowledges that Idiots possess.

Page cix.

[*To the account of Reynolds's death in* 1792.]

When Sr Joshua Reynolds died
All Nature was degraded;

> The King drop'd a tear into the Queen's Ear
> And all his Pictures Faded.

DISCOURSE I

Page 2.

I consider Reynolds's Discourses to the Royal Academy as the Simulations of the Hypocrite who smiles particularly where he means to Betray. His Praise of Rafael is like the Hysteric Smile of Revenge. His Softness & Candour, the hidden trap & the poisoned feast. He praises Michel Angelo for Qualities which Michel Angelo abhorr'd, & He blames Rafael for the only Qualities which Rafael Valued. Whether Reynolds knew what he was doing is nothing to me: the Mischief is just the same whether a Man does it Ignorantly or Knowingly. I always consider'd True Art & True Artists to be particularly Insulted & Degraded by the Reputation of these Discourses, As much as they were Degraded by the Reputation of Reynolds's Paintings, & that Such Artists as Reynolds are at all times Hired by the Satans for the Depression of Art—A Pretence of Art, To destroy Art.

Page 4.

The Rich Men of England form themselves into a Society to Sell & Not to Buy Pictures. The Artist who does not throw his Contempt on such Trading Exhibitions, does not know either his own Interest or his Duty.

> When Nations grow Old, The Arts grow Cold
> And Commerce settles on every Tree,
> And the Poor & the Old can live upon Gold,
> For all are Born Poor, Aged Sixty three.

Page 5.

Reynolds's Opinion was that Genius May be Taught & that all Pretence to Inspiration is a Lie & a Deceit, to say the least of it. For if it is a Deceit, the whole Bible is Madness. This Opinion originates in the Greeks' calling the Muses Daughters of Memory.

The Enquiry in England is not whether a Man has Talents & Genius, But whether he is Passive & Polite & a Virtuous Ass & obedient to Noblemen's Opinions in Art & Science. If he is, he is a Good Man. If Not, he must be Starved.

Page 15.

They wish to find some shorter path to excellence, . . . They must therefore be told again and again, that labour is the only price of solid fame, . . .

This is All Self-Contradictory, Truth & Falsehood Jumbled Together.

When we read the lives of the most eminent Painters, every page informs us that no part of their time was spent in dissipation . . . They pursued their studies . . .

The Lives of Painters say that Rafael Died of Dissipation. Idleness is one Thing & Dissipation Another. He who has Nothing to Dissipate Cannot Dissipate; the Weak Man may be Virtuous Enough, but will Never be an Artist.

Painters are noted for being Dissipated & Wild.

DISCOURSE II

Page 32.

How incapable those are of producing anything of their own, who have spent much of their time in making finished copies, is well known to all who are conversant with our art.

This is most False, for no one can ever Design till he has learn'd the Language of Art by making many Finish'd Copies both of Nature & Art & of whatever comes in his way from Earliest Childhood. The difference between a bad Artist & a Good One Is: the Bad Artist Seems to copy a Great deal. The Good one Really does Copy a Great deal.

Page 42.

The Venetian and Flemish schools, which owe much of their fame to colouring, have enriched the cabinets of the collectors of drawings with very few examples.

—because they could not draw.

Pages 46, 48.

He regards all Nature with a view to his profession; and com-
bines her beauties, or corrects her defects. . . .
    The well-grounded painter . . . is contented that all shall be
as great as himself, who have undergone the same fatigue . . .

The Man who asserts that there is no such Thing as Softness
in Art, & that every thing in Art is Definite & Determinate,
has not been told this by Practise, but by Inspiration & Vision,
because Vision is Determinate & Perfect, & he Copies That
without Fatigue, Every thing being Definite & determinate.
Softness is Produced alone by Comparative Strength & Weakness in the Marking out of the Forms. I say These Principles
could never be found out by the Study of Nature with Con—,
or Innate, Science.

DISCOURSE III

Page 50.

A work of Genius is a Work "Not to be obtain'd by the Invo-
cation of Memory & her Syren Daughters, but by Devout
prayer to that Eternal Spirit, who can enrich with all utter-
ance & knowledge & sends out his Seraphim with the hallowed
fire of his Altar to touch & purify the lips of whom he
pleases." MILTON.
    The following Discourse is particularly Interesting to Block
heads, as it endeavours to prove That there is No such thing
as Inspiration & that any Man of a plain Understanding may
by Thieving from Others become a Mich. Angelo.

Page 52.

The wish of the genuine painter must be more extensive: instead
of endeavouring to amuse mankind with the minute neatness of
his imitations, he must endeavour to improve them by the
grandeur of his ideas.

Without Minute Neatness of Execution The Sublime cannot
Exist! Grandeur of Ideas is founded on Precision of Ideas.

Page 60.

Thus it is from a reiterated experience and a close comparison
of the objects in nature, that an artist becomes possessed of the
idea of that central form . . . from which every deviation is
deformity.

One Central Form composed of all other Forms being
Granted, it does not therefore follow that all other Forms
are Deformity.

All Forms are Perfect in the Poet's Mind, but these are not
Abstracted nor compounded from Nature, but are from
Imagination.

DISCOURSE IV

Page 99.

If the Venetian's Outline was Right, his Shadows would
destroy it & deform its appearance.

> A Pair of Stays to mend the Shape
> Of crooked, Humpy Woman
> Put on, O Venus! now thou art
> Quite a Venetian Roman.

Page 111.

The errors of genius . . . are pardonable . . .

Genius has no Error; it is Ignorance that is Error.

DISCOURSE V

Page 114.

Gainsborough told a Gentleman of Rank & Fortune that the
Worst Painters always chose the Grandest Subjects. I desired
the Gentleman to Set Gainsborough about one of Rafael's
Grandest Subjects, Namely Christ delivering the Keys to St.
Peter, & he would find that in Gainsborough's hands it would
be a Vulgar Subject of Poor Fishermen & a Journeyman
Carpenter.

The following Discourse is written with the same End in

View that Gainsborough had in making the Above assertion, Namely To Represent Vulgar Artists as the Models of Executive Merit.

DISCOURSE VI

Page 154.

> He who first made any of these observations . . . had that merit, but probably no one went very far at once . . . others worked more and improved further . . .

If Art was Progressive We should have had Mich. Angelos & Rafaels to Succeed & to Improve upon each other. But it is not so. Genius dies with its Possessor & comes not again till Another is Born with It.

Page 157.

> . . . our minds should be habituated to the contemplation of excellence . . . we should to the last moment of our lives continue a settled intercourse with all the true examples of grandeur. Their inventions are not only the food of our infancy, but the substance which supplies the fullest maturity of our vigour.

Reynolds Thinks that Man Learns all that he knows. I say on the Contrary that Man Brings All that he has or can have Into the World with him. Man is Born Like a Garden ready Planted & Sown. This World is too poor to produce one Seed.

> The mind is but a barren soil; a soil which is soon exhausted, and will produce no crop, . . .

The mind that could have produced this Sentence must have been a Pitiful, a Pitiable Imbecillity. I always thought that the Human Mind was the most Prolific of All Things & Inexhaustible. I certainly do Thank God that I am not like Reynolds.

DISCOURSE VII

Page 188.

The Purpose of the following discourse is to Prove That Taste & Genius are not of Heavenly Origin & that all who have supposed that they Are so, are to be Consider'd as Weak headed Fanatics.

The Obligations Reynolds has laid on Bad Artists of all Classes will at all times make them his Admirers, but most especially for this discourse, in which it is proved that the Stupid are born with Faculties Equal to other Men, Only they have not Cultivated them because they thought it not worth the trouble.

Page 200.

It is the very same taste which relishes a demonstration in geometry, that is pleased with the resemblance of a picture to an original, and touched with the harmony of musick.

Demonstration, Similitude & Harmony are Objects of Reasoning. Invention, Identity & Melody are Objects of Intuition.

DISCOURSE VIII

Page 244.

Burke's Treatise on the Sublime & Beautiful is founded on the Opinions of Newton & Locke; on this Treatise Reynolds has grounded many of his assertions in all his Discourses. I read Burke's Treatise when very Young; at the same time I read Locke on Human Understanding & Bacon's Advancement of Learning; on Every one of these Books I wrote my Opinions, & on looking them over find that my Notes on Reynolds in this Book are exactly Similar. I felt the Same Contempt & Abhorrence then that I do now. They mock Inspiration & Vision. Inspiration & Vision was then, & now is, & I hope will always Remain, my Element, my Eternal Dwelling place; how can I then hear it Contemned without returning Scorn for Scorn?

Page 274.

The conduct of Titian in the picture of Bacchus and Ariadne, has been much celebrated, and justly, for the harmony of colouring.

Such Harmony of Colouring is destructive of Art. One species of General Hue over all is the Cursed Thing call'd Harmony; it is like the Smile of a Fool.

Marginalia from Wordsworth's POEMS

Page viii.

The powers requisite for the production of poetry are, first,
those of observation and description . . . 2dly, Sensibility.

One Power alone makes a Poet: Imagination, The Divine
Vision.

Page 1.

"Poems Referring to the Period of Childhood."

I see in Wordsworth the Natural Man rising up against the
Spiritual Man Continually, & then he is No Poet but a
Heathen Philosopher at Enmity against all true Poetry or
Inspiration.

Page 3.

> And I could wish my days to be
> Bound each to each by natural piety.

There is no such Thing as Natural Piety Because The Natural
Man is at Enmity with God.

Page 43.

"To H.C. Six Years Old."

This is all in the highest degree Imaginative & equal to any
Poet, but not Superior. I cannot think that Real Poets have
any competition. None are greatest in the Kingdom of
Heaven; it is so in Poetry.

Page 44.

"Influence of Natural Objects
In calling forth and strengthening the Imagination
in Boyhood and early Youth."

Natural Objects always did & now do weaken, deaden &
obliterate Imagination in Me. Wordsworth must know that

what he Writes Valuable is Not to be found in Nature. Read
Michael Angelo's Sonnet, vol. 2, p. 179.*

Page 341.

"Essay, Supplementary to the Preface."

I do not know who wrote these Prefaces: they are very mis-
chievous & direct contrary to Wordsworth's own Practise.

Pages 364-5.

In Macpherson's work it is exactly the reverse; every thing (that
is not stolen) is in this manner defined, insulated, dislocated,
deadened,—yet nothing distinct . . . Yet, much as these pretended treasures of antiquity have been admired, they have
been wholly uninfluential upon the literature of the country . . .
no Author in the least distinguished, has ventured formally to
imitate them—except the Boy, Chatterton, on their first appearance.

I Believe both Macpherson & Chatterton, that what they say
is Ancient Is so.

I own myself an admirer of Ossian equally with any other
Poet whatever, Rowley & Chatterton also.

Pages 374-5.

Is it the result of the whole that, in the opinion of the Writer,
the judgment of the People is not to be respected? The thought
is most injurious; . . . to the People . . . his devout respect, his
reverence, is due. He . . . takes leave of his Readers by assuring them—that if he were not persuaded that the Contents of
these Volumes, and the Work to which they are subsidiary,
evinced something of the "Vision and the Faculty divine", . . .
he would not, if a wish could do it, save them from immediate
destruction.

It appears to me as if the last Paragraph beginning with "Is it
the result" Was writ by another hand & mind from the rest of
these Prefaces. Perhaps they are the opinions of a Portrait or

* Heaven-born, the Soul a heaven-ward course must hold;
  Beyond the visible world She soars to seek,
  (For what delights the sense is false and weak)
  Ideal Form, the universal mould.

Landscape painter. Imagination is the Divine Vision not of
The World, or of Man, nor from Man as he is a Natural Man,
but only as he is a Spiritual Man. Imagination has nothing
to do with Memory.

Marginalia from Thornton's NEW TRANSLATION OF THE LORD'S PRAYER

THE LORD'S PRAYER

Translated from the Greek, by Dr. Thornton.

Come let us worship, and bow down, and kneel, before the
Lord, our Maker. Psalm xcv.

O Father of Mankind, Thou, who dwellest in the highest of
the Heavens, Reverenc'd be Thy Name.

May Thy Reign be, every where, proclaim'd so that Thy Will
may be done upon the Earth, as it is in the Mansions of
Heaven:

Grant unto me, and the whole world, day by day, an abun-
dant supply of spiritual and corporeal Food:

Forgive us our transgressions against Thee, as we extend our
Kindness, and Forgiveness, to all:

O God! abandon us not, when surrounded, by trials;

But preserve us from the Dominion of Satan: For Thine only,
is the Sovereignty, the power, and the glory, throughout Eternity!!!

Amen.

Fly-leaf.

This is Saying the Lord's Prayer Backwards, which they say
Raises the devil.

Doctor Thornton's Tory Translation, Translated out of its
disguise in the Classical & Scotch languages into the vulgar
English.

Our Father Augustus Ceasar, who art in these thy Substantial Astronomical Telescopic Heavens, Holiness to thy Name

or Title, & reverence to thy Shadow. Thy Kingship come
upon Earth first & then in Heaven. Give us day by day our
Real Taxed Substantial Money bought Bread; deliver from
the Holy Ghost whatever cannot be Taxed; for all is debts &
Taxes between Caesar & us & one another; lead us not to
read the Bible, but let our Bible be Virgil & Shakespeare; &
deliver us from Poverty in Jesus, that Evil One. For thine is
the Kingship, [or] Allegoric Godship, & the Power, or War,
& the Glory, or Law, Ages after Ages in thy descendants;
for God is only an Allegory of Kings & nothing Else.

                                                            Amen.

NOTES

Page 3. *Poetical Sketches* has been fully studied by Margaret
Lowery in *Windows of the Morning* (New Haven, 1940).
The volume contains also some interesting experiments
in rhetorical prose, not given here, which are obviously
the first attempts at the form of the "Prophecy."

Page 22. The *Songs of Innocence* were first engraved in 1789:
note that some of them appear in *An Island in the Moon*
(c. 1787): see pp. 354-55. The *Songs of Experience* were
first engraved in 1794, "To Tirzah" being added later
and "A Divine Image" kept separate from the series.
After completing the *Songs of Experience*, Blake engraved the two sets together, with the subtitle given on
p. 22. A general scheme of correspondence runs through,
indicated by the poems with identical titles ("Holy
Thursday," "Nurse's Song") and contrasting ones (cf.
"The Lamb" and "The Tyger," "The Divine Image" and
"The Human Abstract," etc.). The original title of "A
Poison Tree" (p. 48) was "Christian Forbearance."

Page 53. The Rossetti MS (it was owned and edited by the
poet Dante Gabriel Rossetti) is a notebook of fifty-eight
leaves, originally belonging to Blake's younger brother
Robert, which Blake kept by him for over thirty years
and used for a great variety of purposes. It has been
reproduced in facsimile by Geoffrey Keynes, *The Note-
Book of William Blake* (London, 1935), but some of its
scribbles are not yet fully deciphered. It contains early
drafts of the *Songs of Experience*, the designs for *The
Gates of Paradise* (not given here) and a great variety
of fragmentary poems, sketches and prose essays. (Mr.
Keynes explains in his introduction to *The Poetry and*

459

Prose of William Blake that a few of the poems are, as
given here, in a consecutive form which to some extent
is his reconstruction.) Sometimes an accompanying
sketch throws a different light on a poem: thus "When
a Man has Married a Wife," p. 70, is the caption of a
sketch showing Mrs. Blake (presumably) sitting on the
edge of a bed getting dressed and her husband watching
her from the bed. The poems from pp. 53 to 66 are
usually dated around 1793; the poems from "When
Klopstock England defied" to "The Birds" probably belong to the Felpham period (1800-03), and the poems
from "The Angel that Presided" to the end of the section
belong to the period 1808-11.

Page 71. "To the Queen" is not from the Rossetti MS: it is
Blake's dedication of his illustrated edition of *The Grave*,
by Robert Blair, published in 1808, and one of his most
successful illustrating enterprises.

Page 73. Blake's painting of the Last Judgment for the Countess of Egremont is reproduced in Darrell Figgis, *The
Paintings of William Blake*, Plate 7, and described by
Blake in a letter to Ozias Humphrey dated January
18, 1808.

Page 81. The Pickering MS (it was bought by a Mr. B. M.
Pickering in 1866) is a carefully written MS of eleven
sheets, in which the poems given here are transcribed in
what was evidently intended to be their final form. It
belongs to the period 1800-03.

Page 99. In these three sets the aphorisms were engraved sepa-
rately on tiny little plates, the first attempts at the new
engraving process. They belong to the year 1788. Many
of the originals have disappeared, one of them completely: others are known only by facsimile reproductions.

Page 101. *The Book of Thel*, in eight plates, was first engraved
in 1789.

Page 106. The first book of *The French Revolution* (1791)
survives only in one set of page proofs: there is no evi-

dence that Blake intended to provide designs for it. The publisher was Joseph Johnson. The introduction states that the other six books "are finished, and will be published in their Order," but no trace of them remains, and it is probable that Blake, like Coleridge, was inclined to anticipate his achievements.

Page 122. *The Marriage of Heaven and Hell,* in twenty-seven plates, was probably written in 1790, as "thirty-three years" (p. 123) refers to Swedenborg's statement that the Last Judgment occurred in the spiritual world in 1757 (the year of Blake's birth).

Page 136. *Visions of the Daughters of Albion,* in eleven plates, is dated 1793.

Page 144. *America: A Prophecy,* in eighteen plates, is dated 1793, and the cancelled plates, which have a different interpretation of the effect of the American Revolution on English politics, must have been made at the same time.

Page 155. *Europe: A Prophecy,* in eighteen plates, was engraved in 1794. The allegory refers in passing to the collapse of Thurlow's ministry in 1792. The "Introduction" is found in only two of the nine surviving copies; the Frontispiece is the famous "Ancient of Days."

Page 163. *The First Book of Urizen,* in twenty-eight plates, was engraved in 1794. Pictorially, it is one of Blake's most splendid efforts, and there are ten full-page plates without text. Blake may have planned a series of poems to re-interpret the Bible in his own symbolism, thus providing the "Bible of Hell" referred to at the end of *The Marriage of Heaven and Hell.* The present book is to some extent Blake's interpretation of Genesis, but Blake clearly soon abandoned the idea of a series of books under the same name, and deleted the word "First" in one copy.

Page 179. *The Book of Ahania,* in five plates, was engraved in 1795, and is a sequel to *Urizen,* covering the events of the Book of Exodus. Only one copy exists.

Page 186. *The Song of Los,* in eight plates, was engraved in
1795, and completes a group of "continent" poems, the
other two being *America* and *Europe.* The last line of
"Africa" is identical with the opening line of *America.*

Page 193. *The Four Zoas* is dated 1797, but may have been begun as early as 1795, and was probably not abandoned
until at least 1804. Its first title was "Vala, or The Death
and Judgement of the Ancient Man: a Dream of Nine
Nights." The second title was "The Four Zoas: The
Torments of Love & Jealousy in the Death and Judgement of Albion the Ancient Man." A separate title,
"The Bible of Hell, in Nocturnal Visions collected,"
may belong to this poem also. It has at the beginning
the motto "Rest before Labour" and the quotation in
Greek of Ephesians 6:12. For the relation of the nine
nights to Young's *Night Thoughts* see the introduction.
A few of the sketches accompanying the manuscript
are reproduced in the Ellis and Yeats edition. Two
versions of "Night the Seventh" survive; most of what
Blake wanted to keep from the earlier version was trans-
ferred to *Jerusalem.* The main influences on the poem,
apart from Young, are the Icelandic Eddas and the Bible.
The name "Vala" comes from the former and the "Four
Zoas" from the Greek text of Rev. 4:6.

Page 202. The "he" in the first line of the extract from
Night the Fifth is Los.

Page 203. The "His" in the first line of the second extract refers to Orc, who is also the "terrible child" of the
previous extract.

Page 244. *Milton* is now in two books, though Blake may have
intended at one time to write twelve. It was written and
engraved between 1804 and 1808, but the four surviving
copies indicate some uncertainty about the status of the
first half-dozen plates. The Preface is missing in two of
them.

Page 264. *Jerusalem* is dated 1804, but can at most only have
been begun in that year. None of the six surviving copies
is earlier than 1818.

Page 264. Part One is addressed "To the Public."

Page 305. The extract following the lyric is part of a lamentation spoken by Jerusalem.

Page 317. *The Everlasting Gospel* was written about 1818 in the Rossetti MS, and no final continuous form was given it by Blake. For the title see Rev. 14:6.

Page 328. These aphorisms are written around a single line engraving of the Laocoon, which Blake regarded as originally a representation of Jehovah and his two "sons" Satan and Adam strangled by the serpents of morality, copied by Rhodian sculptors from Solomon's Temple and adapted to Classical mythology. The view that Classical art is plagiarized from Asiatic art is frequently expressed by Blake.

Page 331. The aphorisms on Homer and Virgil form a single plate engraved about 1820.

Page 332. *The Ghost of Abel* is dated 1822: the meaning of the phrase "original stereotype" in the colophon (p. 334) appears to be "first use of the engraving process employed here." As we have it the poem cannot be earlier than the publication of Byron's *Cain* in December, 1821.

Page 337. *An Island in the Moon* is in manuscript, and was probably written about 1787. The title is not Blake's: it is derived from the opening words. It has been suggested that the word "moon" alludes to a scientific club in Birmingham known as the Lunar Society. Joseph Priestley, Thomas Taylor, Flaxman, Wedgwood, Erasmus Darwin and Charlotte Lennox are among those proposed as originals for the characters.

Page 358. The circumstances surrounding the printing of the *Descriptive Catalogue* which accompanied Blake's exhibition of 1809 have been outlined in the introduction.

Page 386. *A Vision of the Last Judgment* is a detailed description of an immense fresco, seven by five feet, and containing about a thousand figures, which was in existence in the time of Gilchrist, but is now gone, probably destroyed. The text comes from the Rossetti MS, to which the page numbers refer.

Page 401. George Cumberland, the author of *Thoughts on Outline,* was a friend of Blake's also interested, as this letter shows, in developing an engraving process.

Page 402. The Rev. Dr. Trusler was the author of *Hogarth Moralized* (hence Blake's reference to his eye being perverted by caricature prints). For the circumstances see the next letter. Trusler endorsed Blake's letter with the words "Blake, dim'd with superstition."

Page 405. Hayley's loss was the death of his illegitimate son Thomas. Blake said that the idea for his engraving process was given him in a dream by his brother Robert soon after the latter's death in 1787.

Page 414. The brother referred to in the Butts letters is an elder brother, James Blake, at whose shop Blake held his exhibition.

Page 430. The references at the beginning of the second paragraph are to two of Hayley's friends, Harriet Poole and Samuel Rose, Blake's counsel in the Schofield trial. For the significance of the period of twenty years referred to below, see "William Blake's Exactness in Dates," by David Erdman, *Philological Quarterly,* Oct. 1949.

Page 436. The "Little Card," Cumberland's message card, was Blake's last engraving.

Page 437. Lavater's *Aphorisms on Man* was published in London in 1788, the translator being Fuseli.

Page 441. The edition of Swedenborg's *Divine Love and Wisdom* Blake used was published in London in 1788, and Blake's annotations were probably made in 1789, the year in which Blake and his wife were attached to a Swedenborgian society.

Page 443. Bishop Watson's *Apology for the Bible* was published in 1796, and Blake's comments on it are dated 1798. For Bishop Watson see a lively digression in De Quincey's account of Wordsworth in his *Recollections of the Lake Poets.*

Page 446. The annotations to Bacon's *Essays* were made to an edition published in 1798. Blake's copy has not survived, but was available to Gilchrist, who transcribed Blake's notes.

Page 446. The annotations to Reynolds's *Discourses* were made about 1808, and as they assume a reader, they may have been intended for some sort of publication. The edition Blake used was in three volumes, but the annotations cover only the first.

Page 455. The annotations to Wordsworth's *Poems* were written in 1826. They are known to us largely through Crabb Robinson's *Diary* and *Reminiscences.* The passage from the translation by Wordsworth of the Michelangelo Sonnet referred to on p. 456 was copied by Blake into a friend's autograph album in the same year.

Page 457. Thornton's translation of the Lord's Prayer was made in 1827, and was annotated by Blake in the same year. It was for Thornton's edition of Virgil's *Eclogues* that Blake had made a delightful series of woodcut illustrations.

INDEX OF TITLES AND FIRST LINES